Elements of Object-Oriented COBOL

Second Edition

Wilson Price
Object-Z Systems, Inc
Danville, CA

Object-Z Publishing
Danville, California

Object-Z Publishing
Danville, California

Object-Z Publishing
Danville, California

Elements of Object-Oriented Cobol, Second Edition

Copyright 2001 by Wilson Price All rights reserved. Printed in the United States of America. Except as permitted under the United States Copyright Act of 1976, no part of this publication may be reproduced or distributed in any form or by any means, or stored in a database or retrieval system, without the prior written permission of the publisher.

Disclaimer: This book and the accompanying magnetic disk are designed to help you improve your computer use. However, the author and publisher assume no responsibility whatsover for the uses made of this material or for decisions based on their use, and make no warranties, either expressed or implied, regarding the contents of this book or any accompanying magnetic disk, its merchantability, or its fitness for any particular purpose.
Neither the publisher nor anyone else who has been involved in the creation, production, or delivery of this product shall be liable for any direct, incidental, or consequential damages resulting from its use or from any breach of any warranty. No dealer, company, or person is authorized to alter this disclaimer

Cover design by Kevin Mykal Long

Production/printing by Norcal Printing, San Francisico

98765432

Email author at: wprice@objectz.com

For information about other Object-Z publications: www.objectz.com

Order Information:
Elements of Object-Oriented Cobol, Second Edition
ISBN 0-9655945-6-4 (without Net Express, University Edition)
ISBN 0-9655945-7-2 (with Net Express, University Edition)
Object-Z Publishing
808 Glen Road
Danville, CA 94526
925-362-0609
925-362-0779 (fax)

To My Grandchildren

Christie

Christopher (in memory of)

Dana

Emmi

Erica

Katie

Pamela

Contents Summary

Chapter

1. Where We Are
2. Where We are Going
3. Introduction to Classes and Objects
4. Using a Database Interface Class
5. Full Object-Orientation of the Room Example
6. Object-Oriented Design
7. Processing Indexed Files
8. Inheritance
9. Aggregate Structures in OOCobol
10. Other OO Cobol Goodies
11. Collection Classes

Appendixes

A. The Examples CD
B. Getting Started: Net Express
C. Getting Started: Personal COBOL
D. File Listings

Detailed Contents

Chapter 1 Where We Are

Structured! Programming, Analysis, Design 4
    What is Structured Programming? 4
    Meaning of Abstraction 4
    Meaning of Systematic 5
    Functional Components 5
    Methods of Documentation 6
Focus on the Waterfall 6
    Structured Analysis 6
    Structured Design 6
    Structured Programming 8
Structured! 9
    What is Structured Methodology? 9
Characteristics of Structured Programs 10
    Coupling 10
    Cohesion 11
Shortcomings of the Structured Methodology 11
    An Unnatural View of the World 11
    Communication Between the Systems Analyst
        and the Programmer 12
    Program Modules Not Truly Independent 12
An Example Application 13
A Simple Query Program 13
    Data Division Entries 14
    Procedure Division 15
Using a Subprogram 15
    About Subprograms 15
    Local and Global Data 16
    A Program Calling a Subprogram 17
The Subprogram 18
    Subprogram Linkage 18
    Overall Program/Subprogram Execution 19
    More About Subprogram Data Definitions 19
    Other Inter-Program Communication Features 20
    Program Execution 20
Some Programming Style Standards 21
    Free Format and Inline Comments 21
    Compiler Directives 23
    Recommended Standard Forms 23
Summing Up 24
    Project Summary 24
    General Summary 24
Coming Up 25
Assignment 25

Chapter 2 Where We are Going

What is Object Orientation? 28
    Our View of the World 28
    About Designing and Building Machines 28
    About Designing and Building Programs 28
    Some Basic Object-MethodologyTerminology .. 29
    Creating Instances of a Rectangle 30
Abstract Data Types—A Cornerstone of
        Object-Oriented Programming Languages 32
    What is an Abstract Data Type? 32
    Cobol Data Types 32
    Let's Be Original—Data Definition 33
Operations for the Data Type 33
Classes and Abstract Data
    Types in OOCobol 34
    Using Class Definitions 35
About Object Orientation 36
    Describing a Game from an
        Object Viewpoint 36
    Advantages of the Object-Oriented Approach ... 37
Summing Up 39
Coming Up 39

Chapter 3 Introduction to Classes and Objects

First Look 42
    Road Map to the Room Application 42
    Class Users and Class Builders 42
    Features of the Room Class 43
    The Dialect Directive 44
    Selecting Program Names 44
The Driver Program 45
    Identification Division 45
    Environment Division Entries 45
    The Invoke Statement 47
    Invoking the Method 48
The Class Definition 48
    Structure of a Class Program 48
    Basic Elements 50
    The Identification and Environment Divisions ... 51
The Factory Object Definition 51
Defining the Factory Object 51
    Methods 52
    End Markers 53
    Special ISO2000 Requirement 53
Multiple Methods in a Class 53
    Expanding the Basic Room Class 53
    Modifications to the Program Driver 55
    Additions to the Class Definition 56
Formalizing Some Principles 57
    Terminology 57
    Recommended Styles 57
    Micro Focus and ISO2000 Differences 59
Summing Up 60
Coming Up 60
Assignments 61

Chapter 4 Using a Database Interface Class

Processing With an Instance Object 66
   Some Basics 66
   The Driver Program—r05-drvr 68
   The Object Handle 69
   Invoking a Method of the
      Newly Created Object 70
   The Class Program—R05-room 70
About Object Data 70
   Reviewing Room05 70
   Populating an Object 72
Using a Database Interface Class 73
   Expanding Room05 73
   DBI Class Description—R06-dbi 75
   The DBI Class Definition 75
The Room Class—R06-room 77
The Driver Program—R06-drvr 79
Final Comment on Room06 79
Commentary on Data Types 80
Creating Multiple Instances 81
   Two Instances of the Room Class 81
   Subscripting Object Handles 83
Providing for Repetition 84
   The Driver Program Room07dr 84
   Multiple Instantiations of a Class 84
Summing Up 87
   Project Summary 87
   General Summary 87
Coming Up 87
Assignments 88

Chapter 5 Full Object Orientation of the Room Example

Creating a User Interface Class 92
   Reviewing the Driver R07-drvr 92
   A User Interface Class 94
   The Class User Perspective of the
      User Interface Class 96
   The Driver Program 96
   Component Reusability 98
Final Conversion of Room System
   to Object Orientation 98
   A Room Manager Class 98
   The Driver and Room Manager—Room09 98
   The Notion of Public and Private Methods 100
Creating All Classes with Instance
   Object Definitions 100
   About this Example 100
   Instantiating all Objects in Driver 102
   Instantiating the Classes in
      Room Manager's Factory 106
Summing Up 108
   Project Summary 108
   General Summary 108
Coming Up 109
Assignment 109

Chapter 6 Object-Oriented Analysis & Design

Some Basic Concepts 112
   Analysis and Design 112
   Categories of Classes 113
Object-Oriented Design Tools 113
   Object Think 114
   Use-Case Scenarios 114
   Identifying Classes from a
      Problem Statement 115
   Responsibility-driven design 115
   CRC Cards
      (Class-Responsibility-Collaborator) 117
   Class Diagrams 118
Phase I: Analysis and Modeling 119
   Finding Candidate Classes 119
   Use-Case Scenarios 119
Problem Statement Analysis 121
CRC Cards 122
Phase II—High-Level Design 122
   Activities of Phase II 122
   More on Classes and Class Diagrams 123
Phase III—Low-Level Design 124
   About Modeling and Documentation 124
About Documentation 125
   An Example Documentation Form 125
   A Documentation Template 128
   Setting Up and Using the Template 131
Summing Up 132
Coming Up 132
Design Assignments 133

Chapter 7 Processing Indexed Files

Using a File-Processing Class 138
    The Basic Concept 138
    The Room11 Project 140
    Room Manager—R11-mgr 140
    The Database Interface 142
    The Room File Processor—r11-r-fp 143
Updating Records of a File 146
    Some Program Design Considerations 146
    Additions to Room and
       Room Manager—Room12 148
    The Room Class—R12-room 150
Room Manager—R12-mgr 150
    The Room File Processor—R12-r-fp 154
    The DBI—R12-dbi 154

Accessing Data From a
    Subordinate File—Project 13 155
    Problem Definition 155
    The Room Class—R13-room 155
    The DBI—R13-dbi 156
    The File Processors: R13-r-fp and R13-t-fp 158
Room Manager—R13-mgr 158
Summing Up 158
    Project Summary 158
    General Summary 160
Coming Up 160
Assignments 160

Chapter 8 Inheritance

Two Room Classes—Room14 164
    Problem Definition 164
    The Room Data File 164
    Project Documentation 166
    The Room Classes 166
    The DBI 168
    Room Manager 169
    Overall View of Room14 169
    Redundancy in Room12 169
Classification Structures 171
    Selecting a Pet 171
    Classifying Computers 173
A Simple Example of Inheritance—Room15 173
    Room Classes 173

    A Class and Subclasses 174
    Room Class Documentation 175
    The Room Class Definitions 177
A Variation of the Room Example—Room16 178
    A Sample Dialogue 178
    The Class and Subclasses 180
More About Inheritance 183
    Different Inheritance Scenarios 183
    Inheritance and the Factory Object 185
Summing Up 185
    Project Summary 185
    General Summary 186
Coming Up 186
Assignments 186

Chapter 9 Aggregate Structures in Object-Oriented Cobol

The Aggregation Structure 192
    Reviewing the Classification Hierarchy 192
    Simple Examples of
       Aggregation Structures 192
    A Combination Structure 193
    About Inheritance 193
    A Road Map to this
       Chapter's Examples 193
    The Client Manager Class 195
Room17's Aggregate Structure 196
    Documentation 196
    Instantiating a Class from the
       Class's Factory 198
    The Client Class 198
Features of the Database Interface 201
    Input Data Files 201
    Database Interface Documentation 201
    The Company File Processor 204

Adding a Calendar Class to the
    Aggregate Structure 207
About Room18 207
Company 207
The Case for a Calendar Class 208
The Client Manager Class 209
The Calendar Class—Room18 212
    Data Definition 212
    Searching the Calendar Table 212
Other Components of Room18 214
    The Client Class 214
    The Calendar File 216
Calendar Database Access 216
Summing Up 218
    Project Summary 218
    General Summary 218
Coming Up 218
Assignments 219

Chapter 10 Other OO Cobol Goodies

ISO2000 Features 224
Interface Definitions 225
   Restricting Access to Methods of a Class 225
   Interface Definition General Form 226
   An Interface Example—Documentation 226
   The Client Interface 227
   Room Manager 229
Inline Invoke 229
Property Clause 232
   Data Name Qualification 232
   Qualification to an Object 232
   Get and Set Methods and the
      Property Clause 234
   The RDF File 235
Summing Up 236
   Project Summary 236
   General Summary 236
Coming Up 236

Chapter 11 Collection Classes

The Concept of the Collection Class 240
   The Table as a Container 240
   Simplifying Examples 241
Micro Focus Collection Classes 242
   About Collection Classes 242
   Collection Class Types 242
   Method Name Conventions 244
   Collection Class Constructor Methods 244
   Collection Class Instance Methods 245
   About Parameters 245
The Bag Collection Class 246
   About Bags 246
   About Room21 246
   The Room Class—r21-room 248
   Creating and Using a Bag—r21-drvr 248
Using an Iterator on a Bag 251
   Principles of the Callback 251
   Iterating the Callback Method 252
The Select Iterator—Room22 252
   Sample Display 252
   Room's Select Callback Method 253
   Invoking the Select Method—r22-drvr 253
Returning Results From an Iterator 254
   Creating an Intrinsic Data Class 254
   Callback with Optional Parameters 256
   About Room23 257
   Using an Optional Parameter in
      the Callback—r23-drvr 258
   The Callback Method compute-capacity
      from r23-tran 259
Preview of Next Three Examples 260
Using the Array Collection Class—Room24 260
   About Room24 260
   Driver—Room24 261
Searching an Array for a Desired
   Block—Room25 263
   About Room25 263
   The Calendar Class 264
Using a Dictionary—Room26 266
   About Cobol Tables 266
   About the Dictionary Collection Class 267
   Multiple Room Calendars—Room26 267
   Creating a Dictionary 268
   Loading the Dictionary 270
   Accessing a Dictionary 271
   Room Manager—r26-mgr 272
More About Collection Classes 272
   Features of the Micro Focus
      Collection Classes 272
   Some Other Typical Collection
      Class Instance Methods 274
Summing Up 275
   Project Summary 275
   General Summary 276
Assignments 276

Appendix A The Examples CD

Loading the Examples CD 280
   Folder (Subdirectory) Contents 280
   Loading Files From the Examples CD 280
   Alternate Loading of CD 281
Conventions Used in this Book 281
   Example Applications Arranged by Project 281
   Folders for Examples and Assignments 281
   Program Naming Conventions 282

Appendix B Getting Started: Net Express

The Interactive Development Environment:
    First Look 286
Net Express Projects 286
A Sample Project 286
Creating a New Project 286
The Project Window 290
The NetExpress Toolbar 290
Compiling Programs of a Project 291
The Animator—Running a Program 291
Stopping the Animator 292

Handling Program Errors 292
    Correcting Compiler Errors 292
    Stepping Through a Program for Debugging .. 293
    Using Breakpoints for Debugging 295
Entering Programs 296
    Setting Edit Options 296
    Entering a New Program 296

Appendix C Getting Started: Personal COBOL for Windows

Using the Class Browser 300
    The Browser Environment 300
    Creating a Project 300
Error Correction 303

Entering Programs 304
Animator 304
Breakpoints 306
Two Commonly Encountered Execution Errors ... 307

Appendix D File Listings

Files in the Eooc2 Folder 312
Assignment DBI Class Definitions 312
    Event DBI (Net Express) 312
    Dessert DBI (Net Express) 313
    Event DBI (Personal COBOL) 314
    Dessert DBI (Personal COBOL) 315
Data File Listings 316
    Data Files for Assignments 316
        Event record description 316
        Event file listing 316
        Dessert record description 316
        Dessert file listing 317
        Site record description 317
        Site file listing 317
        Box record description 317
        Box file listing 317

Data Files for Examples 318
    Calendar record description 318
    Calendar file listing 318
    Company record description 318
    Company file listing 319
    Representative (Rep) description 319
Representative (Rep) file listing 319
    Room record description 319
Room file listing 319
    Tax record description 319
Tax file listing 319

Preface

Introduction

With the introduction of structured methodology to the Cobol world over 30 years ago, we witnessed a revolution in carefully designed, well documented business-programming applications. However, as the size and complexity of programs has increased, structured Cobol has begun to show frayed edges. The development of object-oriented methodology in recent years has shown the promise of a greatly improved tool for the business world. Until recently, our alternatives have been C++, Java, and Visual Basic, not very appealing considering our investment in Cobol. The new standard, with its superb object technology features, changes the landscape. We now have the tool to take advantage of this powerful methodology. This second edition of this book is dedicated to showing the way with Object-Oriented Cobol.

Intended Audience

This book is designed as a transitional book from procedural Cobol to Object-Oriented Cobol (OOCobol). Prerequisites for its use are (1) a first Cobol course, or (2) Cobol programming experience.

A Consistent Example

A room rental application is introduced in Chapter 1 to illustrate principles of using subprograms, techniques that are critical to OOCobol. This application is expanded in later chapters being used as a consistent basis for introducing new concepts.

Features of the Second Edition

Needless to say, every effort has been made in this second edition to include and expand upon the strong points of the first edition and to eliminate or replace those portions that were weak and/or have become outdated. Improvements over the first edition include the following.

- A description of abstract data types to set the stage for the notion of classes and objects.
- Extensive use of the Factory in classes for which there will never be more than one instance (for example, a database interface class). This considerably simplifies the reader's first introduction to object-oriented Cobol.
- A standardized class documentation device in the form of a Word template stored on the CD accompanying this book.
- Placement of each example application in a separate project folder.
- A standardized two-level approach to handling indexed files. Data access is via a "front-end" database processor (unique to the application) communicating with one or more "back-end" file processors (each unique to a specific file).
- An expanded, more rigorous chapter on aggregate structures.

- A restructuring of the chapter on collection classes to make this complex subject more understandable.

The Examples CD

The Examples CD included with this book contains:

- 100 programs comprising the 27 projects used to introduce new topics.
- Data files for examples.
- Data files for assignments.

Loading and using this CD is described in Appendix A.

The COBOL Standard

This book closely adheres to syntax as defined in draft edition of the Cobol Standard available as of the publication date of this book. The book includes only two relatively minor deviations from the Standard: the result of the current Micro Focus implementation. They are described in the text.

Software from Micro Focus

This is a hands-on book. As such, you need an OOCobol compiler. To this end, Micro Focus markets two Cobol software systems for use on the personal computer: Net Express and Personal COBOL for Windows. In addition to their full Net Express product, Merant/Micro Focus markets Net Express, University Edition, a powerful version, specifically designed for learning, that you can run on your personal computer. If your copy of this book does not included Net Express you can order it (or Personal COBOL) from Merant (701 East Middlefield Road, Mountain View, CA 94043) phone 800-551-5269.

Let's Make COBOL Proper

We all know that COBOL is an acronym for COmmon Business Oriented Language. Consequently, we use uppercase for all letters. But isn't it time we consider it a word in its own right? If we treat it as a proper noun (as we should), then we have Cobol. So let's give the name of our language the honor it deserves and refer to it as Cobol. Let's make Cobol proper. To that end, you will see Cobol, not COBOL, throughout this book. The only exceptions are in referring to published titles such as Personal COBOL for Windows, or COBOL 85.

Cobol Program Listings

Programming books in which example programs span several pages have always been one of my pet peeves. To that end I have (1) kept lines of code short so that code can be listed in two columns within a page (2) minimized the number of comment lines, and (3) omitted sections of program code that are not relevant to the topic being discussed. As a consequence, no program listings in this book span two or more pages. Do *not* follow my "narrow-line" nor "minimum comment line" techniques—use the full page width and generous comments to help make your programs easily read and understood.

Project Markers

For your convenience, each example project described in this book is marked with an identifying icon in the outside margin of the page (marking the beginning of the discussion on the project). For instance, the application Room06 stored in the folder Proj0402 would be indicated by the marker to the left.

Acknowledgements

A textbook is never the product of a single person's thoughts and ideas. We all learn and build from others. I'm no exception. During nearly four decades of writing, I have many to thank for their input. This project has been especially rewarding in that so many have contributed their ideas and helped me refine mine. I can't say enough about the extent to which I've benefited from input of my colleagues and students. The wisdom I've gained from participants in 14 workshops for college faculty I've conducted (under the sponsorship of Merant Micro Focus) is reflected throughout this second edition.

My students at California State University, Hayward, over 200 participants in workshops, colleagues, and readers of the first edition contributed immensely to the finished product. Michael Turk (University of Western Sidney) provided numerous good ideas for the analysis and design chapter. Gene Webb, a participant in one of my early workshops, was a vital resource numerous times when I found myself perplexed. Paul Halpern of Merant Micro Focus has been outstanding in his support of this book, the workshops, and numerous other projects. All of you have my sincerest thanks for your invaluable contributions.

Where We Are

Chapter Contents

Structured! Programming, Analysis, Design 4
    What is Structured Programming? 4
    Meaning of Abstraction 4
    Meaning of Systematic 5
    Functional Components 5
    Methods of Documentation 6
Focus on the Waterfall 6
    Structured Analysis 6
    Structured Design 6
    Structured Programming 8
Structured! 9
    What is Structured Methodology? 9
Characteristics of Structured Programs 10
    Coupling 10
    Cohesion 11
Shortcomings of the Structured Methodology 11
    An Unnatural View of the World 11
    Communication Between the Systems Analyst and the Programmer 12
    Program Modules Not Truly Independent 12
An Example Application 13
    A Simple Query Program 13
    Data Division Entries 14
    Procedure Division 15
Using a Subprogram 15
    About Subprograms 15
    Local and Global Data 16
    A Program Calling a Subprogram 17
The Subprogram 18
    Subprogram Linkage 18
    Overall Program/Subprogram Execution 19
    More About Subprogram Data Definitions 19
    Other Inter-Program Communication Features 20
    Program Execution 20
Some Programming Style Standards 21
    Free Format and Inline Comments 21
    Compiler Directives 23
    Recommended Standard Forms 23
Summing Up 24
    Project Summary 24
    General Summary 24
Coming Up 25
Assignment 25

Chapter 1

Chapter Introduction

This book is about Object-Oriented Cobol programming. In all likelihood, the reason you are reading this is to assist you in making the transition from structured programming methodology, the "old" way, to object orientation, the "new" way. This chapter covers the following conventional topics in reviewing features of structured methodology and of subprograms.

- Structured analysis/design methodology and tools.
- The nature of the subprogram and subprogram linkage using a room-rental example application. This application forms the basis for object-oriented examples in chapters that follow.
- Interprogram communication.
- Local and global data.

Structured! Programming, Analysis, Design

What is Structured Programming?

The emergence of high-level programming languages in the late 1950s and early 1960s is one of several milestones in the history of computing. With high-level languages, the programmer was freed from excruciating details of machine code, assigning memory for data, and numerous other fine points. To a large extent, programmers "went forth and programmed," often with little attention to technique. As applications increased in size and complexity, programs became nearly unfathomable mazes: difficult to debug and terrible to maintain. Two computer scientists (Bohm and Jacopini) presented a paper in 1966 that laid the basis for a highly formalized structured approach. The structured methodolgy, with which we are familiar today, resulted from the work of Edsger Dijkstra during the late 1960s and early 1970s. Application of structured techniques during the 1970s resulted in remarkable improvement in both programmer productivity and program maintainability.

Exactly what is **structured programming**? Following is a brief, but adequate definition.

> *Structured programming* is the systematic use of abstraction to control a mass of detail in breaking an application down into its basic functional components using standardized methods of documentation.

At first glance, this may not appear to say much, but actually, there are four significant terms used in this definition.

1. Abstraction.
2. Systematic.
3. Functional components.
4. Methods of documentation.

Meaning of Abstraction

In the preceding definition of structured programming, **abstraction** refers to the act of separating the relevant from the irrelevant, or separating what is important to a given application from what is not important.

The application being developed determines what is important and what is not important. As an example, you might be interested in a investment system that calculates the best time to buy and sell particular stocks. After due study, you determine that the rate of inflation, the interest rate, a company's projected earnings, and other identified factors all bear relevancy and are significant to the application. On the other hand, the regional unemployment rate may be only marginally relevant so you choose to ignore it. You would likely consider other information coming across your desk, for instance, the winner of the Kentucky Derby, as totally irrelevant so you would ignore it.

> There are two approaches to solving problems. The first is the **algorithmic approach**: defining algorithms. **Algorithms** are precise, step-by-step, instructions that lead one to the correct or best solution for a given problem. For instance, to determine the area of a rectangle we use the algorithm length times width, or:
>
> $A = l * w$
>
> The second is the **heuristic approach**. The heuristic approach is much less precise than the algorithmic approach. It is one of probing and discovery and building on experience. The waterfall lifecycle is a heuristic approach for developing software. In a strange twist of fate, although programs are themselves algorithms, there is no general purpose algorithm for developing programs. We use algorithms when they are available, when they are not we resort to the heuristic approach.

Meaning of Systematic

In this definition of structured programming, **systematic** means *methodical*. Stated another way, systematic means following a plan. The plan we generally follow when developing structured applications is the waterfall lifecycle illustrated in Figure 1-1. Following this approach, we proceed from the analysis phase, to the design phase, to the programming phase, and so on. (Figure 1-1 is actually a simplification because most techniques involve a degree of feedback.)

Functional Components

Some of the components of an order processing system are calculating the total charges, printing an invoice, and updating the customer's record. They are termed a **functional components** because they are individual parts of the application based

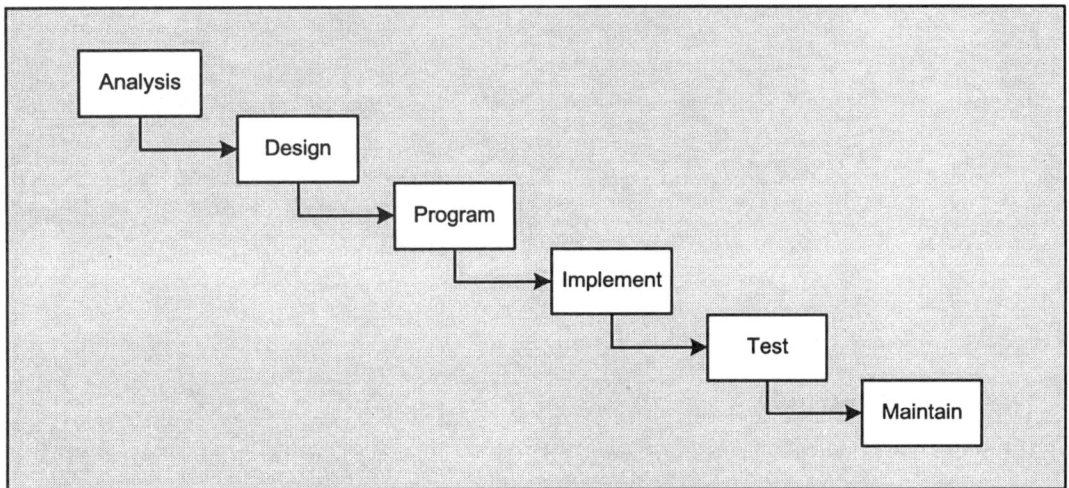

Figure 1-1. The waterfall program development cycle.

on a function (or activity) necessary in the processing cycle. The heart of structured programming is identifying basic functional components of an application.

Methods of Documentation

Our consideration here will be on the first three phases of the waterfall approach: analysis, design, and programming. Each phase has its special tool for documentation. For the analysis phase we commonly use the data flow diagram. For the design phase, we use the system flowchart and hierarchy chart. Finally, for the programming phase, we use the program flowchart and pseudocode.

Focus on the Waterfall

Let's focus more detailed attention on the first three phases of the waterfall methodology.

Structured Analysis

The goal of the analysis phase of creating a system is to define the flow of information within the system that best satisfies information needs of users. Doing so means defining the boundaries of the system. In addition, data sources are identified; inputs are traced through the system; operations on data are identified; and required reports are listed.

Some things that may have appeared, at first glance, to be irrelevant to an application may actually be very important. For example, if a portion of an investment system mentioned earlier is to focus on employment agencies, the unemployment rate would be viewed as a relevant factor. Even the apparent totally unrelated Kentucky Derby winner would become very relevant if a portion of the portfolio included companies involved in breeding race horses. Basically, the system analyst together with the end-users must determine these system boundaries: that is, "What is relevant to the system being developed?"

One of the tools of the system analyst in documenting gathered information is the **data flow diagram**. Figure 1-2 is a simplified data flow diagram for a tool rental business. Notice that this diagram depicts the nature of the application to be programmed; it shows how data flows throughout the system. It is a semi-technical document that has meaning to the both the technical and nontechnical members of the organization. Basically, the system analyst and the end user "understand the same language." The analyst can sit down with management and/or end users and review the data flow documentation to ensure that he/she has properly interpreted the organization's needs.

Structured Design

When the analysis phase is complete, design begins. At this stage, the focus becomes much more technical and detailed. The way in which functions and physical characteristics of the new system are implemented is defined. One commonly used

Where We Are

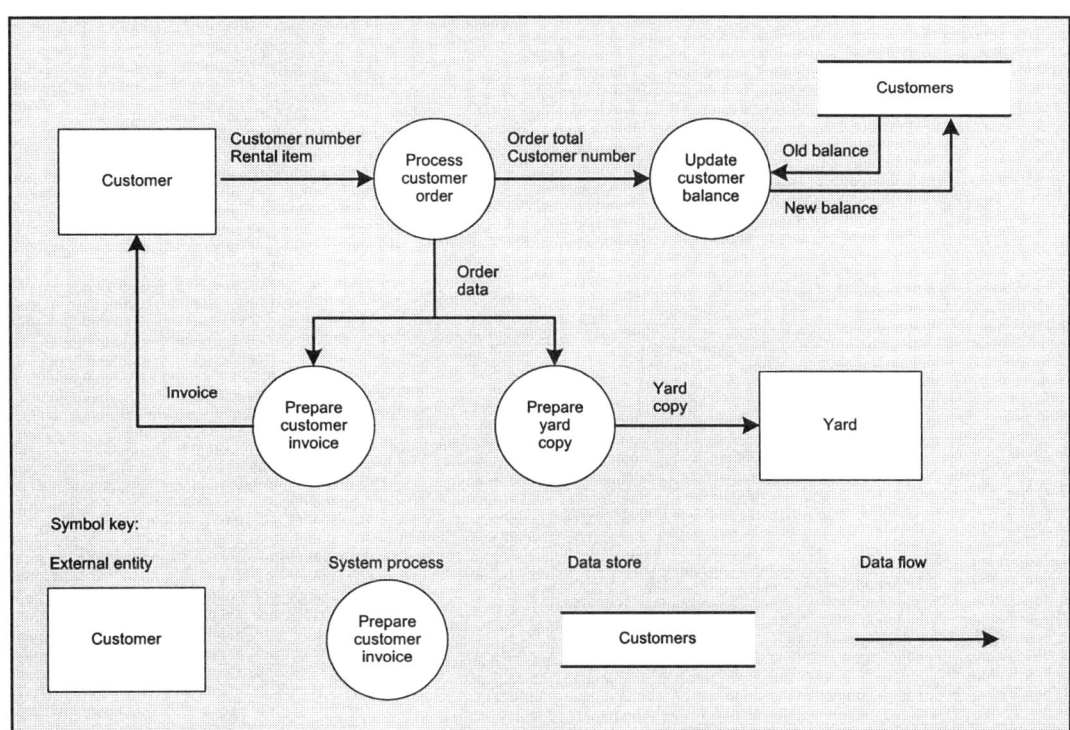

Figure 1-2. A typical flow diagram.

tool for this is the **system flowchart**, a tool to document an information system's hardware, software, and data files. Where flow diagrams use one set of conventions and symbols, system flowcharts use another. A simple version of the tool rental system's flowchart might appear as shown in Figure 1-3.

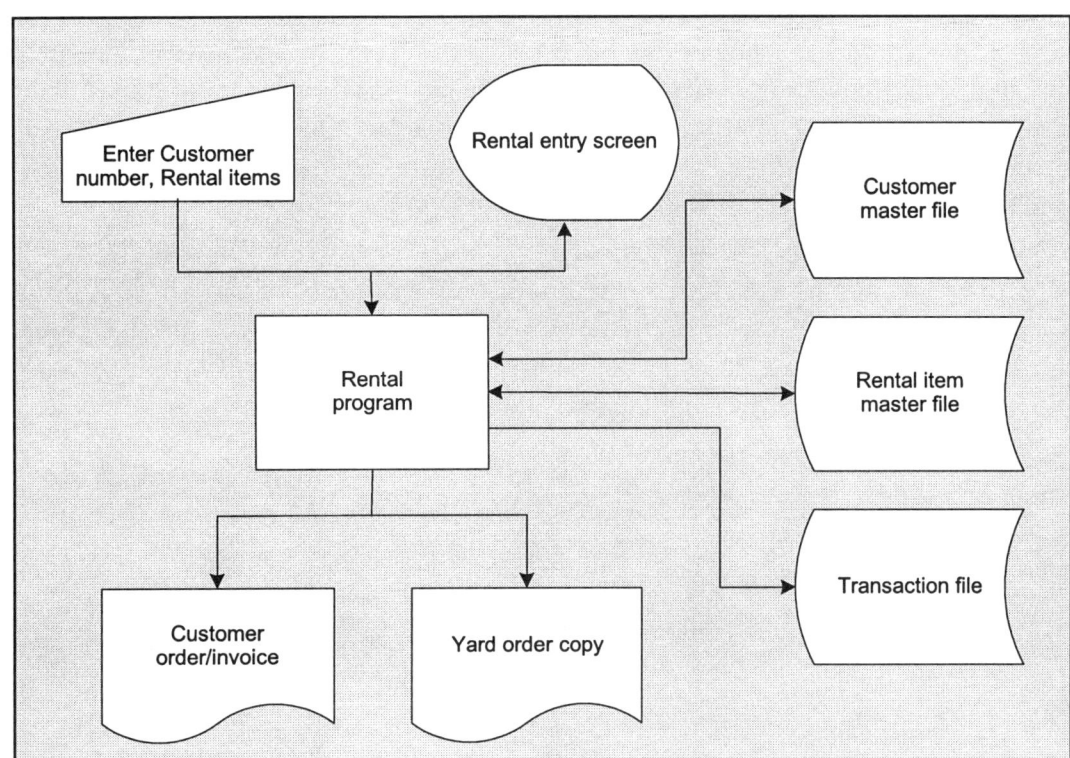

Figure 1-3. A typical system flowchart.

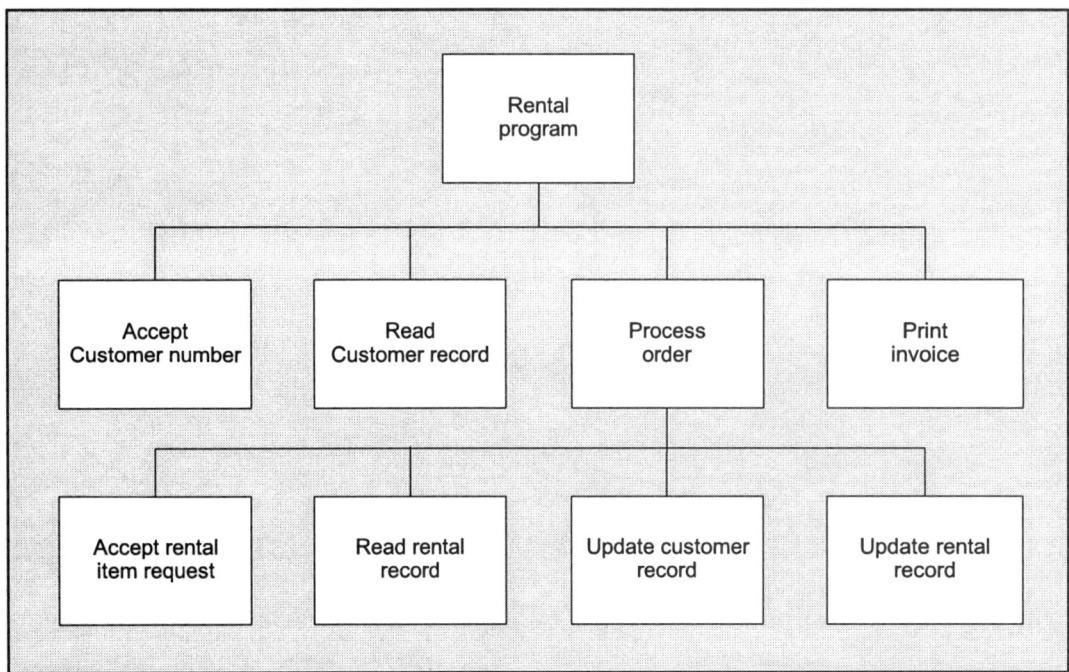

Figure 1-4. A typical hierarchy chart.

The **hierarchy** or **structure chart** is a tool shared by the system designer and the programmer. It provides a hierarchical view of individual program components in a system and is commonly called a **procedure call tree**. Figure 1-4 is a simplified hierarchy chart of the basic rental program. Breaking an application down into basic component parts is called **functional decomposition** and is the linchpin underlying the entire structured approach. You can think of functional decomposition as the "structured mindset." It is the grand strategy we employ to transform the whole into its constituent parts. Functional decomposition decomposes a system around its processes (functions) and its data.

Structured Programming

When the program design is complete, the task moves to the programming phase. The **program flowchart**, such as that in Figure 1-5, and pseudocode serve as the basic documentation and planning tools. The hierarchy chart documents "what" is to be done; the flowchart documents "how" it is to be done. Now, activities become highly technical and there is little apparent relationship between the data flow diagram of the analysis phase and the program flowchart of the programming phase.

Structured programming is a means to an end: it is the systematic approach we use to create structured programs. Structured programs have certain characteristics. We can look at a program and determine if it is "structured."

Structured!

What is Structured Methodology?

Early in this chapter, you read a brief, generalized definition of stuctured programming. Let's consider this methodology in more detail. One of the cornerstones of structured programming was set forth in a paper presented in 1966 by two computer

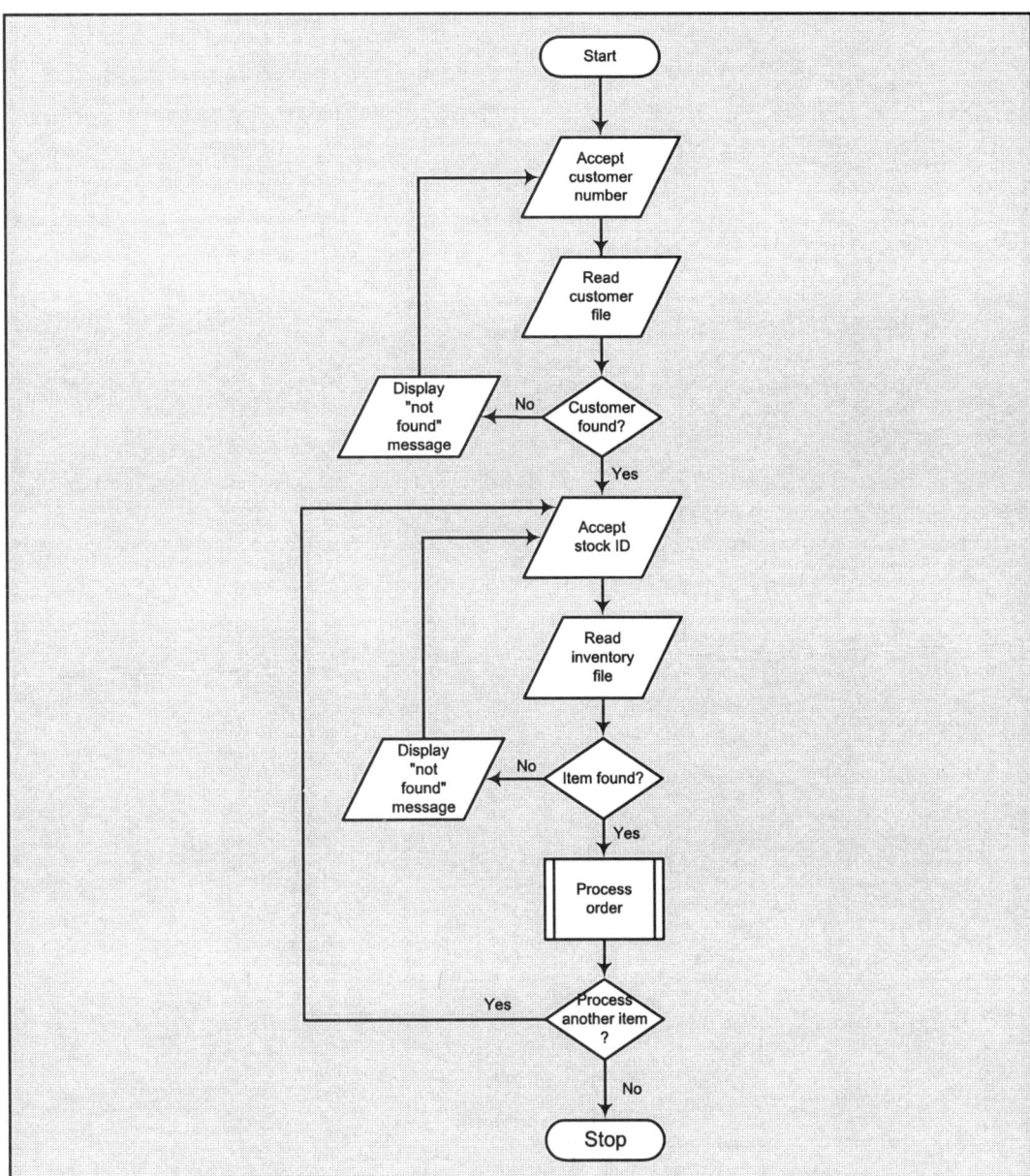

Figure 1-5. A typical program flowchart.

scientists (Bohm and Jacopini). In their paper they proved mathematically that any computer program can be represented in chart form using the three basic structured flowchart forms of Figure 1-6.

In considering the transition from "structured" to "objects" many practitioners of structured methodology view the constructs of Figure 1-6 as *the* basis for structured. You will commonly hear an argument that goes something like: "Even with object-oriented programming, we must still maintain structure." Anyone making that argument is absolutely correct. We must always build our program "modules" (whether structured or object-oriented) from the basic structures of Figure 1-6. The misleading element of this argument is the implication that structured programming is synonymous with Figure 1-6's constructs. In fact, the basis for structured methodology is the breaking down of an application according to processes (as described in the previous section entitled Structured Design).

For instance, look at the hierarchy chart of Figure 1-4. Each box represents an action. A complex application is broken down into simple, relatively independent modules, each intended to perform a single function. For instance, *Process order*, is made up of the lower level actions *Accept rental item request*, *Read rental record*, and other elements. The objective is to create a structure in which each module represents an independent activity, or function. As described earlier, this is called functional decomposition and forms the basis for the structured mindset.

Characteristics of Structured Programs

Coupling

Coupling relates to independence between modules of a program. Modules with functions that do not depend upon data from other modules are said to be "loosely coupled." Such data independence is highly desirable because it reduces program testing, debugging, and maintenance efforts.

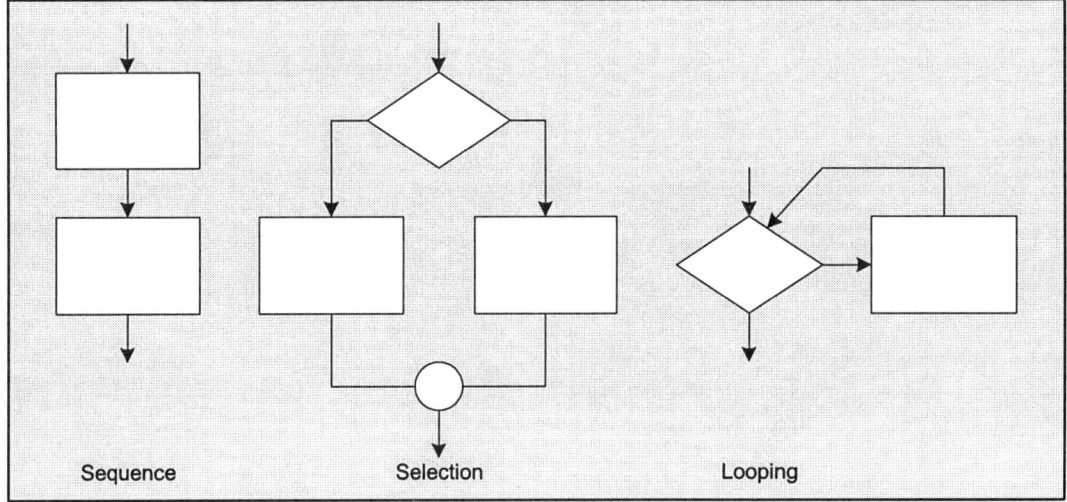

Figure 1-6. Structured programming constructs.

One characteristic of Cobol is that data defined in the Data Division of a program is "visible" to every program module. For instance, the code of a typical control break program will probably change the value of a line counter data item in several widely separated modules. As every experienced Cobol programmer knows, this global data availability can cause bugs that are extremely difficult to locate when programming the application. During later program modification, additional code that operates on data at one point in a program can have serious consequences elsewhere, thereby rendering a previously flawless program a nightmare.

Cobol subprograms and nested programs (the latter a feature of COBOL 85) provide a means for isolating data. In a letter entitled "Perform Considered Harmful" to the Communications of ACM, Richard Rhiele suggests that coupling can be minimized in Cobol programs by coding each module as a nested program rather than as a paragraph. There is much to say for this approach for structured Cobol programming. However, as you will learn, object-orientated features of Cobol's new standard provide a low coupling environment.

Cohesion

One objective of structured programming is that each program module perform one task. For instance, one module's sole purpose might be to calculate interest based on principle, interest rate, and elapsed time and another's to determine the date 90 days from the current date. These modules would be considered **functionally cohesive** because of their singleness of purpose. You would not likely put both functions in a single module.

Sometimes we violate functional cohesion from a practical point of view. For instance, an initialization module that initializes a broad range of variables is said exhibit **temporal cohesion** because, although unrelated, the actions are carried out at the same time. Although structured theory considers temporal cohesion undesirable, it commonly sneaks into our modules because of convenience. A danger the programmer must avoid is to combine too many unrelated tasks solely because they are executed at approximately the same time.

The worst case is to combine in a single module two or more tasks that have no relationship to one another. We even do that occasionally in the interest of avoiding numerous one-line modules. For example, in report generation from a sequential file, you commonly see a module that prepares and prints the output line then reads the next sequential record.

Shortcomings of the Structured Methodology

An Unnatural View of the World

As indicated in a preceding section, the cornerstone of structured methodology is breaking an application down according to processes: functional decomposition. Unfortunately, that is not the way in which we view the world. In attempting to understand a complex entity (whether a physical object or a process), our dissection process involves looking for "things." On a broad basis, as human beings we view the world as a collections of "things" or objects that are capable of actions For instance, there are transportation objects that move us from one place to another. We use these objects by putting gasoline (or money) into them (input) and being transported (output). We also classify them according to type: for instance, airplane objects, bus objects, automobile objects, and so on. So our view of the world is a vast collection of objects that do things, or have responsibilities. Note that we do not view the world as a collection of algorithms.

It is interesting to note that the first object-oriented language Smalltalk was devised at the Palo Alto Research Center of Xerox to teach small children how to program. In experiments, children were unable to comprehend the function (algorithmic) approach. Through studies, researchers discovered that children learn by perceiving the world as composed of "things." Working with Smalltalk, children had little difficulty in mastering programming concepts through the object perspective.

Communication Between the Systems Analyst and the Programmer

Consider the tools used in the first three steps of the program development cycle of Figure 1-1.

- The analyst uses the data flow diagram of Figure 1-2; it provides a vehicle of communication between the analyst and the user in a form meaningful and understandable to both.
- The designer uses the system flowchart of Figure 1-3 and the hierarchy chart of Figure 1-4. This begins the transition to computer-oriented representations that have limited meaning to the user thereby isolating the user from the system's workings and diminishing his/her input to the designer.
- The programmer uses the hierarchy chart and the program flowchart of Figure 1-5. Unfortunately these bear no resemblance to the real-world perspective from the user's eyes. The programmer and the user speak two completely different "languages" thereby seriously impairing interchange between them.

The bottom line with the structured approach is that the output of each waterfall phase does not map directly to the input of the next phase: considerable translation is required. With this "translation" process from analysis to design to programming, it is no wonder that many large, complex projects fail to meet requirements and, in some cases, fail completely.

Program Modules Not Truly Independent

If you inspect a typical hierarchy chart, you will see that most of the work is done in the leaf nodes: the boxes at the bottom that have no components. For instance, in a payroll application a "Calculate Deductions" box itself may not represent a module that does any calculations. They might be done by subordinate modules such as "Federal Withholding", "Union Dues", and so on. The purpose of performing any level of operations is only evident by inspecting higher levels of the chart. Components of the chart are highly coupled. To truly understand the significance of a given module or module level, you must understand the entire application. In practice, modules resulting from functional decomposition are not nearly as independent as we might like them to be.

An Example Application

The example application from which you will gain your first glimpse of object technology is built around Object Training Center, Inc. (OTC). One of OTC's ventures is the daily rental of its conference rooms to local businesses and training organizations. For the first example program, consider the following simplified case.

- OTC rents one room.
- The room is available in a "standard" configuration or a "special" configuration. Each of the two configurations has its own daily room rental fee.
- Qualifying groups and individuals receive a discount on the rental fee.

The first example program is as simple as possible. It allows a user to query for the full or discounted price of the room. It does not allow repetition. Furthermore, room data is declared with Value clauses in the Working-Storage Section (rather than a file) to avoid the code required for file processing. You will appreciate the simplicity when you begin your study of object-oriented concepts in Chapter 3.

A Simple Query Program

The source program for this example (r01-prog.cbl) is stored on the CD accompanying this book. You may want to execute it to gain a feel for how it works. A complete listing is shown in Figure 1-7. As with all programs of this book, source code lines are purposely kept short so that listings can be included in a single page using double columns.

Example programs in this book are grouped by project. The source file name identifies the project number and the type of program. For instance, parts of the name r01-prog.cbl tell you the following.

    r   This file is a component of the room rental application.
    01   Indicates example 1 of the room application.
    prog This file as the program component of this example.
    cbl   The extension indicates a Cobol source program (this is the default for both Net Express and Personal COBOL).

As you will see, the second example of this chapter involves two programs: a calling program and a subprogram. The source files are named r02-prog.cbl and r02-sub.cbl.

You probably notice that the source program uses both uppercase and lowercase letters. This is in contrast to most Cobol programs in which uppercase is used throughout. The reason for uppercase goes back to the time when the primary input medium for programs was the punched card. Punched card machines could record only uppercase. COBOL 85 permits any combination of uppercase and lowercase. As pro-

```
1  ****************************************************
2  * Room Rental System
3  * W. Price  03/22/00                    ROOM01PR.CBL
4  *
5  * This is a standard COBOL program that sets the
6  * basis for exploring principles of OO COBOL. It
7  * includes one record containing the following
8  * fields:
9  *     Room number
10 *     Room rental prices: Standard and
11 *                         Special Configurations
12 *     Room discount rate
13 *     Room capacity
14 * Through this program, you can display the full
15 * price or the discounted price.
16 ****************************************************
17
18  Identification Division.
19  Program-ID.  Room01Program.
20 *             R01-PROG.CBL
21
22  Data Division.
23  Working-Storage Section.
24
25  01  rd-room-data.
26      10  rd-room-number        pic 9(03)     value 100.
27      10  rd-std-config-price   pic 9(03)     value 225.
28      10  rd-spec-config-price  pic 9(03)     value 385.
29      10  rd-room-discount      pic v9(02)    value .05.
30      10  rd-room-capacity      pic 9(02)     value 38.
31
32  01  room-prices.
33      10  std-config-price      pic 9(03).
34      10  spec-config-price     pic 9(03).
35
36  01  apply-discount-sw         pic X(01).
37      88  apply-discount              value "Y" "y".
38  01  price-factor              pic 9(01)v9(03).

39
40  Procedure Division.
41
42  000-process-room-data.
43      Perform 200-get-user-request
44      Perform 250-get-room-prices
45      Perform 300-display-room-prices
46      Stop run
47      .
48  200-get-user-request.
49      Display " "
50      Display "Do you want discounted price <Y/N>? "
51                 with no advancing
52      Accept apply-discount-sw
53      .
54  250-get-room-prices.
55      Move rd-std-config-price to std-config-price
56      Move rd-spec-config-price to spec-config-price
57      If apply-discount
58          Subtract rd-room-discount from 1.0
59                          giving price-factor
60          Multiply price-factor by std-config-price
61          Multiply price-factor by spec-config-price
62      End-If
63      .
64  300-display-room-prices.
65      Display " "
66      Display "Standard configuration price: "
67                        std-config-price
68      Display "Special configuration price:  "
69                        spec-config-price
70      .
```

Figure 1-7. Room rental program—Room01.

grammers we should take advantage of this and use upper- and lowercase where it improves readability.

Data Division Entries

First, let's look at the room data a user will be accessing; it is defined under rd-room-data.

```
01  rd-room-data.
    10  rd-room-number        pic X(03)     value "100".
    10  rd-std-config-price   pic 9(03)     value 225.
    10  rd-spec-config-price  pic 9(03)     value 385.
    10  rd-room-discount      pic v9(02)    value .05.
    10  rd-room-capacity      pic 9(02)     value 38.
```

Here you see the assigned values designated with value clauses. Other data items used in the program are:

room-prices   Data is moved to these work items prior to applying the discount (if requested by the user). This avoids changing the original data defined with value clauses.

price-factor   Used to calculate a discounted price.

apply-discount-sw   Data name for the Accept statement that allows the user to designate whether or not the discount is to be applied.

Procedure Division

In the program of Figure 1-7 you see four modules. The main module 000 accesses the three subordinate modules. There is no repetition; the program executes a single pass.

The 200 module queries the user whether or not to apply the discount to the room prices. Notice that the program uses the data item `apply-discount-sw` to accept the user response (line 52).

The 250 module accesses the two prices from `rd-room-data`. The condition name (defined at line 37) determines whether or not to calculate discounted prices at lines 57-62.

The 300 module is straightforward; it displays the prices on the screen.

Using a Subprogram

About Subprograms

As a Cobol programmer, you know that one of the objectives of structured programming is modularization: the organization of components of a program into relatively independent modules that can be coded and tested independent of one another. For instance, r01-prog includes a controlling module and three subordinate modules. Execution of a module (paragraph) is illustrated in Figure 1-8(a) where you see control transferred to the designated module and then returned upon completion of the module.

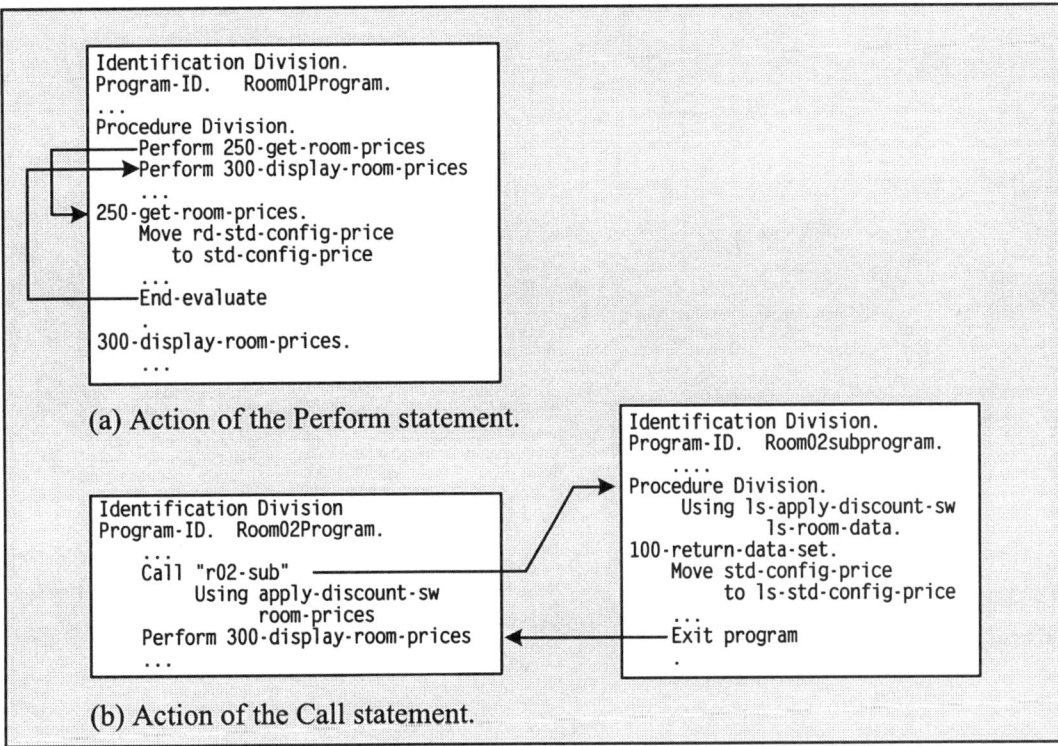

Figure 1-8. Executing out-of-line code.

If you have a module you plan to use in several programs, you may want to code and compile it separately as a **subprogram**. To illustrate principles of subprograms, consider the room pricing program as two components. One is a program that provides overall control and interfaces with the user; the other is a subprogram that contains the data and performs the basic data handling functions. This technique is illustrated in Figure 1-8(b) where you can see that the main program transfers control to the subprogram through use of the Call statement. When the subprogram finishes executing, it transfers control back to the main program. The action is similar to that of the Perform in Figure 1-8(a) except control is passed to a completely independent program.

Local and Global Data

One important difference between the two techniques concerns the visibility of data. For instance, in r01-prog data is said to be **global**. That is, the data is available to any portion of the program, whether the program is one page in length or one hundred. Look at the depiction of Figure 1-9 where temp-bal is defined on page 3 of the program and changed on pages 17, 22, and 26. If during program testing you find that the final value in temp-bal is incorrect, finding the error can be quite a chore. Furthermore, when modifying the program later, it is easy to make a change at one point without realizing an inadvertant effect at another point. For instance, you might accidentally execute the Move on page 17 thereby zeroing the data item.

On the other hand, data defined in one of the Figure 1-8(b) programs (main program or subprogram) is totally independent of that defined in the other program. That is, data defined in the main program is **local** to the main program; similarly, data defined in the subprogram is local to the subprogram. Remember, these pro-

```
Page 3
    ...
    10 temp-bal    pic 999V99.
    ...

Page 17
    ...
    Move 0 to temp-bal
    ...

Page 22
    ...
    Add charge to temp-bal
    ...

Page 26
    ...
    Add penalty to temp-bal
    ...
```

Figure 1-9. Global data.

grams are compiled separately. Consequently, a means is necessary for data to be passed back and forth between the two. When using a subprogram, you do *not* need to know anything about *how* the subprogram works. You only need to know what it does and how you use it. So, for now let's consider the room subprogram as a "black box" with the following characteristics.

1. It stores the room prices and discount rate. This data is available to the calling program through the procedure of the subprogram.
2. The subprogram can carry out two actions.
    a) Apply the discount calculation to the room prices if requested by the user.
    b) Return the two prices to the calling program.

From the preceding descriptions, you can see that the main program and the subprogram must communicate with each other. That is, the main program must tell the subprogram whether or not to apply the discount. Similarly, the subprogram must return requested data to the main program. The main program accesses a subprogram with the `Call` statement. This statement names the subprogram to be called and identifies data-items used by the subprogram. Let's look at the calling program shown on the left in Figure 1-10.

A Program Calling a Subprogram

In the main program (often referred to as the **calling program**) of Figure 1-10, you see the following `Call` statement at lines 32 and 33.

```
Call "r02-sub" Using apply-discount-sw
                     room-prices
```

Proj0102
Room02

Consider the following components of the `Call`.

1. Immediately following the verb `Call`, the file name of the called subprogram (`r02-sub`) is enclosed in quotes.
2. After the reserved word `Using` is a list of the data items used to communicate data between the two programs. These are commonly called **parameters**. The way in which this subprogram was written, the parameters must be:
    a) A one character elementary item (`apply-discount-sw` in this case) indicating whether or not to compute discounted room prices.
    b) A group item (`room-prices` in this case) composed of the data to be returned to the calling program.

If you compare this program to the that of Figure 1-7, you will see that the main processing modules (000) are almost identical. That is, the `Call` of r02-prog (line 32) replaces the Perform 250 of r01-prog (line 44).

```
 1  *****************************************************       1  *****************************************************
 2  * Room Rental System                                         2  * Room Rental System
 3  * W. Price  01/01/2000                    R02-PROG.CBL       3  * W. Price  01/01/2000                     R02-SUB.CBL
 4  *                                                            4  *
 5  * The program R01-PROG has been split into two               5  * This subprogram contains data for one room.
 6  * parts: this calling program & the accompanying             6  * Subprogram parameters are:
 7  * subprogram.  Actions of the program/subprogram             7  *    Input:  Discount switch
 8  * pair are identical to those of R01-PROG.  The              8  *    Output: Standard configuration price
 9  * room data is stored in the subprogram.  Access             9  *            Special configuration price
10  * to it is provided by the procedural statements            10  *****************************************************
11  * of the subprogram.                                        11
12  *****************************************************      12  Identification Division.
13                                                              13  Program-id.  Room02subprogram.
14  Identification Division.                                    14  *            R02-SUB.CBL
15  Program-ID.  Room02Program.                                 15
16  *            R02-PROG.CBL                                   16  Data Division.
17                                                              17
18  Data Division.                                              18  Working-Storage Section.
19  Working-Storage Section.                                    19  01  rr-room-data.
20                                                              20      10  rr-room-number        pic X(03) value "100".
21  01  room-prices.                                            21      10  rr-std-config-price   pic 9(03) value 225.
22      10  std-config-price         pic 9(03).                 22      10  rr-spec-config-price  pic 9(03) value 385.
23      10  spec-config-price        pic 9(03).                 23      10  rr-room-discount      pic v9(02) value .05.
24                                                              24      10  rr-room-capacity      pic 9(02) value 38.
25  01  apply-discount-sw            pic X(01).                 25
26      88  apply-discount                  value "Y" "y".      26  01  price-factor              pic 9(01)v9(02).
27                                                              27
28  Procedure Division.                                         28  Linkage Section.
29                                                              29  01  ls-apply-discount-sw      pic x(01).
30  000-process-room-data.                                      30      88  ls-apply-discount               value "Y" "y".
31      Perform 200-get-user-request                            31  01  ls-room-data.
32      Call "r02-sub" Using apply-discount-sw                  32      10  ls-std-config-price   pic 9(03).
33                           room-prices                       33      10  ls-spec-config-price  pic 9(03).
34      Perform 300-display-room-prices                         34
35      Stop run                                                35  Procedure Division  using ls-apply-discount-sw
36      .                                                       36                            ls-room-data.
37  200-get-user-request.                                       37  100-return-data-set.
38      Display " "                                             38      Move rr-std-config-price to ls-std-config-price
39      Display "Do you want discounted price <Y/N>? "          39      Move rr-spec-config-price to ls-spec-config-price
40                   with no advancing                          40      If ls-apply-discount
41      Accept apply-discount-sw                                41          Subtract rr-room-discount from 1.0
42      .                                                       42                          giving price-factor
43  300-display-room-prices.                                    43          Multiply price-factor
44      Display " "                                             44                          by ls-std-config-price
45      Display "Standard configuration price: "                45          Multiply price-factor
46                           std-config-price                   46                          by ls-spec-config-price
47      Display "Special configuration price: "                 47      End-If
48                           spec-config-price                  48      Exit program
49      .                                                       49      .
```

Figure 1-10. The room rental program and subprogram—Room02.

The Subprogram

Subprogram Linkage

Cobol requires that each subprogram (program to be called by another program) include special **subprogram linkage** entries. They alert the compiler to include inter-program communication components with the program. You see these in the subprogram r02-sub listed to the right in Figure 1-10.

1. The Data Division requires a Linkage Section that defines the parameters used to pass data back and forth between the two programs. In lines 29-33 you see that each of these data items includes the prefix `ls-` meaning `Linkage Section`. The sole purpose of "ls-" is for documentation.

2. The Procedure Division header must include a Using clause identifying parameters defined in the Linkage Section. Its form, from lines 35-36 is as follows.

```
Procedure Division using ls-apply-discount-sw
                         ls-room-data.
```

Notice that the listed parameters are identical in composition and order to those of the Call statement in the calling program.

Overall Program/Subprogram Execution

Let's now step through partial execution of the program/subprogram pair.

1. In the main program of Figure 1-10, the user is queried (200 module) regarding whether or not he/she wants discounted prices. The data item of the Accept statement of line 41 (apply-discount-sw) is the first parameter of the Call at line 32.
2. In the subprogram, the corresponding parameter is named ls-apply-discount-sw (defined at line 29). Its value is used in the If statement beginning line 40 to determine whether or not to apply the discount.
3. The Exit program statement of line 48 returns control to line 34 of the calling program. (Note: The Exit program statement is not required when the last physical statement of the subprogram is the last statement to be executed.)

The remainder of the program functions in exactly the same way as does r01-prog. From the end user perspective, the two programs are identical.

More About Subprogram Data Definitions

Perhaps you have noticed that data item names of the calling program are slightly different from their counterparts in the called program. Data items of the called program are associated with corresponding names of the calling program strictly by their relative positions in the corresponding Using statements. Remember, data names are local to individual programs.

In this implementation, room pricing data of the subprogram is protected from accidental corruption by the main program because it is local to the subprogram. As you see, *the only access to this data is through the procedure of the subprogram.* You will learn that this notion has significant implications in OOCobol.

Perhaps you noticed that the room data of this example application includes the room capacity which is not used in the application. If you wanted to display the capacity in the original program (Figure 1-7), you would simply insert the following statement after line 69.

```
Display "Room capacity: " rd-room-capacity
```

The capacity is readily accessible because all data of the program is global.

However, with the program/subprogram pair (Figure 1-10) the room capacity is local to the subprogram. Thus, additional coding would be needed in both program components to give the calling program access to this data. This also has important implications in OOCobol, as you will see in the next chapter.

Other Inter-Program Communication Features

Techniques used in this example illustrate some of the features of inter-program communication; other notable points are as follows.

- Coding a Linkage Section in a subprogram follows most of the same rules as coding a Working-Storage Section. However, the Value clause is not allowed except to define condition-names (88-level items). Also, a data-name used in the Using must not have been defined by a redefines clause.
- Cobol places no limit on the number of parameters that can be listed in the Call, but they must be 01 level or elementary items. They can be defined in either the File Section or the Working-Storage Section.
- The Procedure Division header of the called subprogram must contain a Using clause that corresponds to the Call statement Using clause of the calling program. Data items in the Using clauses of the calling and called programs must correspond in number, type, and size. The correspondence between data-items of the calling and called programs is positional and is independent of actual names used. That is, the first listed parameter in the calling program corresponds to the first listed parameter of the called program, and so on. Each entry in this header must be a record description (level 01). Lower level entries are not allowed.
- The data items comprising the Linkage Section of the called subprogram can be operated on in the called subprogram just as any other data items. However, a change in any of them will change the value of the corresponding data item of the calling program. (If you don't want this to occur, you can use the optional By value phrase to prohibit such a change.)

Program Execution

When you run the program of Figure 1-10, the following actions take place.

1. The compiled program and subprogram are loaded into memory as illustrated in Figure 1-11(a).
2. The loader "tells" the calling program where in memory the subprogram has been loaded.
3. Execution begins with the main program.
4. Upon encountering the Call statement, the main program calls the subprogram (transfers control to it).
5. Code of the subprogram is executed.
6. Upon reaching the Exit program statement (line 48), control is returned to the main program.

Where We Are

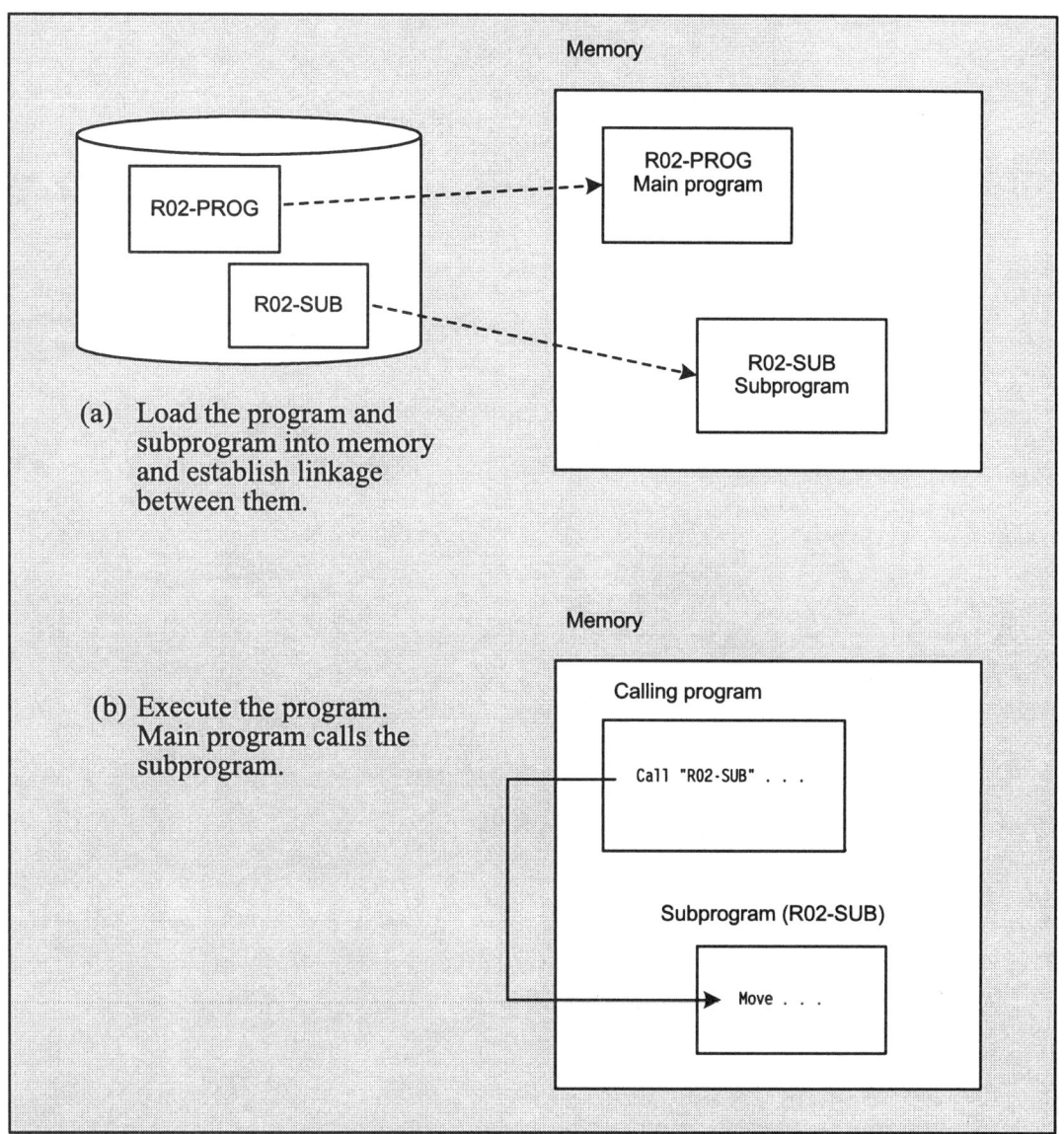

Figure 1-11. Loading and executing a program/subprogram pair.

Some Programming Style Standards

Free Format and Inline Comments

Before jumping into object-oriented features of the next Cobol standard, let's look at a feature that will bring joy to the hearts of most Cobol programmers: **free format**. You are no longer locked into the A- and B-margins and column 72. With free format, you position statements anywhere you want on the line. So you can use indenting to clarify structure without restriction. With free format you can no longer use the asterisk in column 7 to indicate a comment line. Instead, you use two consecutive characters: *>. To illustrate these principles, look at the free format version of r01-prog shown in Figure 1-12. Note: The line numbers are not part of the program; they are included only for reference.

Notice some features of this example.

1. Code begins in column 1.
2. If you count positions, you will see that the Display statement of line 35 extends to column 73.
3. The *> combination, entered at any position, indicates a comment. For instance, look at lines 1 and 5.
4. The *> combination also allows you to enter inline comments. If a statement is followed by this comment indicator, the remainder of the line is treated as a comment (ignored by the compiler). You see examples of inline comments in lines 10, 17, 41, and 45.

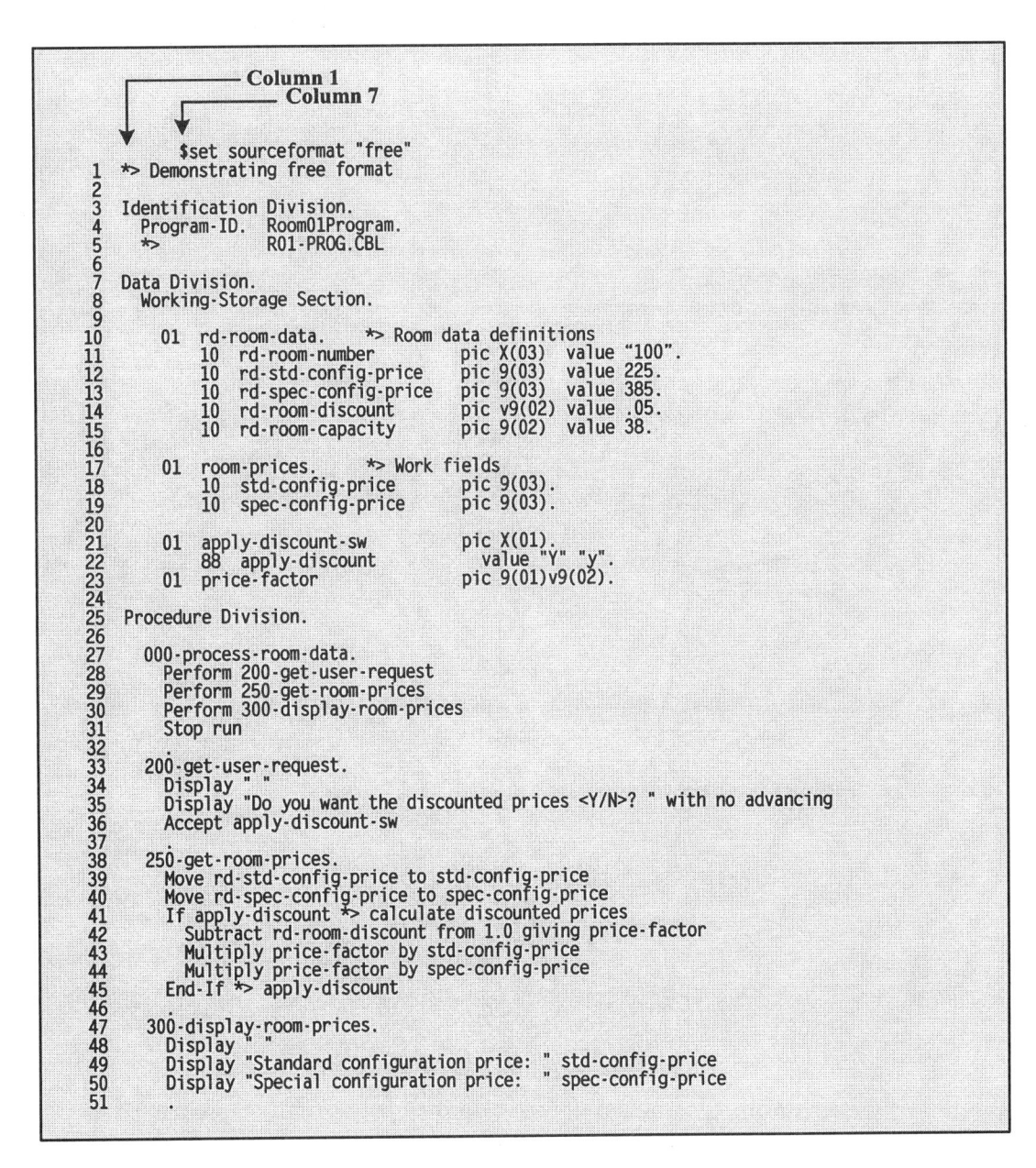

```
                  Column 1
                   Column 7
           $set sourceformat "free"
 1  *> Demonstrating free format
 2
 3  Identification Division.
 4    Program-ID.  Room01Program.
 5    *>           R01-PROG.CBL
 6
 7  Data Division.
 8    Working-Storage Section.
 9
10      01 rd-room-data.        *> Room data definitions
11         10  rd-room-number         pic X(03)   value "100".
12         10  rd-std-config-price    pic 9(03)   value 225.
13         10  rd-spec-config-price   pic 9(03)   value 385.
14         10  rd-room-discount       pic v9(02)  value .05.
15         10  rd-room-capacity       pic 9(02)   value 38.
16
17      01 room-prices.         *> Work fields
18         10  std-config-price       pic 9(03).
19         10  spec-config-price      pic 9(03).
20
21      01 apply-discount-sw           pic X(01).
22         88  apply-discount             value "Y" "y".
23      01 price-factor                pic 9(01)v9(02).
24
25  Procedure Division.
26
27  000-process-room-data.
28    Perform 200-get-user-request
29    Perform 250-get-room-prices
30    Perform 300-display-room-prices
31    Stop run
32
33  200-get-user-request.
34    Display " "
35    Display "Do you want the discounted prices <Y/N>? " with no advancing
36    Accept apply-discount-sw
37
38  250-get-room-prices.
39    Move rd-std-config-price to std-config-price
40    Move rd-spec-config-price to spec-config-price
41    If apply-discount *> calculate discounted prices
42      Subtract rd-room-discount from 1.0 giving price-factor
43      Multiply price-factor by std-config-price
44      Multiply price-factor by spec-config-price
45    End-If *> apply-discount
46
47  300-display-room-prices.
48    Display " "
49    Display "Standard configuration price: " std-config-price
50    Display "Special configuration price: " spec-config-price
51    .
```

Figure 1-12. Free format.

If you are wondering how long a source line can be with free format, hold your breath. The new standard allows for lines of up to 250 columns. (As indicated earlier, source code lines in example programs are kept short to facilitate double column listing in pages of this book.)

Compiler Directives

Because of the vast amount of fixed format code in existence, free format is not automatic. Thus you need the ability to provide instructions to the compiler indicating that all or part of the code in a program is free format. With both Net Express and Personal COBOL you use the $SET statement which contains **compiler directives**, special instructions to be applied when the program is compiled. For instance, the directive parameter sourceformat "free" is used in the following directive of Figure 1-13 and tells the compiler that following code is in free format.

```
$set sourceformat "free"
```

As fixed format is the default, the directive $SET must begin in column 7.

Within a program, you can switch between free and fixed format by using fixed in place of free in the above $set directive. Programs in this book use free format.

Recommended Standard Forms

Computer programs, like ordinary printed text, are easier to read if a standard form is adopted and used throughout. However, the rules of standardization should not be so complicated that it becomes clumsy for the programmer to follow them. With these thoughts in mind, the following standards are used throughout this book.

1. Free format is used.
2. Lowercase is predominant with uppercase on the first letter of the following:
   Division headers
   Section headers
   The letter X in pic X (to match the 9 size)
   The verb of each command (for instance, Perform)
   The word Using in a subprogram call
   Certain reserved words are all caps (for instance, TRUE)
3. The primary division headers of the program begin in column 1. For instance, refer to lines 3, 7, and 25 in Figure 1-12. In Chapter 3 you will see how object-oriented features allow for nesting of division components.
4. Each lower level is indented two positions (except for data definitions). For example, the Working-Storage Section header (line 8) begins in column 3 indicating at a glance that it is subordinate to the Data Division header.
5. Data definition entries are indented four positions—see lines 10-23.
6. In the Procedure Division, two-position indention is used to indicate components of conditionally executed statements—refer to lines 41-45.
7. As required by the ANSI Standard, each Procedure Division paragraph name is followed by a period. The last statement of the paragraph is terminated with a period on a separate line. No periods are used within the paragraph.

8. Scope terminators are used for all conditional statements.
9. The End-If is followed by an inline comment containing the If condition. (Do the same for Evaluate statements.) You see an example of this in line 45 of Figure 1-12. Following is another example.

   ```
   If menu-selection
   ...
   End-If *>menu-selection
   ```

   This form provides excellent documentation and helps clarify multiple levels of nesting.
10. Always precede Linkage Section data names with ls-.

Summing Up

Project Summary

Room01 (Proj0101) consisting of a single program introduces the room rental application—the example used throughout this book.

Room02 (Proj0102) breaks the program of Room01 into a calling program and a called subprogram to introduce the principles of independence of program modules and inter-program communication

General Summary

This chapter has introduced you to the room application; it will serve as the basis for your exploration of Object-Oriented Cobol. Following are significant points of the chapter.

- The basis for structured programming is functional decomposition: the process of breaking a complex problem into relatively independent modules based on functions performed.
- Data within a Cobol program is global throughout the program (except for a nested program).
- The subprogram is a vital tool for preparing program components as separate, independent entities.
- Communication between a program and a subprogram is via parameters listed in the Call statement of the calling program and the Procedure Division header of the called subprogram.
- Free format of the new standard frees the programmer from the traditional A- and B-areas of the source code form.

Coming Up

In Chapter 2 you will be introduced to basic principles of object methodology including some of the terminology that comprise the "language" of object methodology. The basic principles of classes and objects will be explored in detail.

Assignment

1-1

The subprogram of this chapter consists of one "procedure" that provides for the return of room prices. Assume that a different version of this subprogram is required containing two procedures. One is to calculate and make available the room price, coded as a separate paragraph—call it 300-get-price. The other is to calculate and return the room capacity; treat it as a separate paragraph named 325-get-capacity. Write skeleton code for both the calling program and the subprogram that allows for return of either the price or capacity as required by the user.

Comment: A Cobol subprogram has a single entry point. That is, you cannot specify a paragraph entry point in the Call; execution always begins at the first statement of the subprogram. Therefore, the call parameter list must include a switch to indicate the action. You'll learn in Chapter 2 that an OO class allows you to define numerous procedures (called methods) within a single class program.

Where We Are Going

Chapter Contents

What is Object Orientation? 28
    Our View of the World 28
    About Designing and Building Machines 28
    About Designing and Building Programs 28
    Some Basic Object-MethodologyTerminology 29
    Creating Instances of a Rectangle 30
Abstract Data Types—A Cornerstone of Object-Oriented Programming Languages.......32
    What is an Abstract Data Type? 32
    Cobol Data Types 32
    Let's Be Original—Data Definition 33
    Operations for the Data Type 33
    Classes and Abstract Data Types in OOCobol 34
    Using Class Definitions 35
About Object Orientation 36
    Describing a Game from an Object Viewpoint 36
    Advantages of the Object-Oriented Approach 37
Summing Up 39
Coming Up 39

Chapter 2

Chapter Introduction

The purpose of this chapter is to provide you a basic insight to the principles of object technology. From the chapter you will learn about the following.

- The way in which we, as human beings view the world: as a collection of "things" capable of actions.
- Basic terminology commonly encountered in the object world: abstraction, encapsulation, message communication, reuse, inheritance, polymorphism, class, object, and instance.
- The principles of the abstract data type as a definition of data and procedures associated with that data. This forms a basis for object methodology.
- The notion of a class definition in Cobol.
- Advantages of the object-oriented approach over the structured approach.

What is Object Orientation?

Our View of the World

As human beings, we view the world as a collections of "things" or objects capable of "actions." For instance, there are transportation objects that move us from one place to another. We use these objects by putting gasoline (or money) into them (input) and being transported (output). We also classify them according to type: for instance, airplane objects, bus objects, automobile objects, and so on. So our view of the world is a vast collection of objects that do things, or have responsibilities. Note that we do not view the world as a collection of algorithms.

About Designing and Building Machines

The design engineer, whether designing an automobile or a computer, also views the item to be designed as a collection of objects. Each object has its function to be performed: its **responsibilities**. Each object also works in conjunction with other objects to perform its functions: it **collaborates** with other objects. For instance, consider the carburetor of an automobile engine. It has the **responsibility** to deliver the proper air-fuel mixture to the engine. It **collaborates** with engine sensors to fulfill this responsibility.

Nowhere is the notion of objects more notable than in computer design. The computer engineer views a new computer design in terms of interacting components or objects. That is, the motherboard will contain a microprocessor chip, control chips, memory chips, and so on. Each chip will have its specific responsibilities and each will work in conjunction with other chips, that is, will have its collaborators.

It is significant to note that constructing a computer does not normally involve designing and building each component. For instance, the engineer will select an existing off-the-shelf memory chip and, working within its specifications, incorporate it into her/his design. In this context, you can think of the memory chip as a **reusable component**. It is a stock item: its functions are well defined and make it easy to incorporate into a variety of electronic devices. As a rule, the engineer does not know details of its internal components or exactly how it performs its actions. She/he only need know the input and output technical specifications.

If each single component of each computer model were designed and constructed from scratch, the computer capabilities we now enjoy would be in the realm of science fiction.

About Designing and Building Programs

Engineers design and build computers by bringing together reusable objects. To a limited extent, programmers mimic this by using subprograms and source code libraries. However, using structured techniques, programmers build almost every component of a program virtually from scratch, even though a given task may have been programmed many times before. Functional decomposition and the algorithmic methodology virtually dictate this. Basically, the programmer is continually reinventing the wheel.

Some Basic Object-Methodology Terminology

Let's take a look at some of the terminology you will encounter in reading about object technology. You are already familiar with some of the concepts (although perhaps not the specific terminology).

- Abstraction
- Encapsulation (information hiding)
- Message communication
- Reuse
- Inheritance
- Polymorphism
- Classes and objects
- Instance
- Instantiate

Abstraction. In Chapter 1 you read that to abstract refers to the act of separating the relevant from the irrelevant. (One definition of the noun "abstract" is "something that concentrates within itself the essential qualities of a larger thing.") From the structural perspective, abstraction is the principle that any operation that achieves a well-defined effect can be treated by its users as a single entity (even though that operation may involve a sequence of lower-level operations). With *structured methodology* we focus on the abstraction of *procedures*. Functional decomposition yields modules (that translate to paragraphs) each with a singleness of purpose. With object methodology, we take this one step further and work with **data abstraction**: The principle of defining a data type in terms of the operations that apply to occurrences of that type. This includes the restriction that occurrences of the type can be accessed only through those operations.

Encapsulation (Information hiding) is the principle that a software component should isolate (hide) a single design decision. As Cobol programmers, we work with procedural encapsulation all the time. We use subprograms and intrinsic functions without knowing their internal workings. We only need to know the interface. With object methodology we focus on the abstraction/encapsulation of data and its associated procedures.

Message communication is the means by which one program communicates with another. In conventional Cobol this boils down to subprogram and intrinsic function calls and their associated parameters. In object methodology, the definition is broadened to the means by which objects (the "containers" of encapsulated data and procedures) communicate with one another.

Polymorphism, by definition, means *many forms*. It is a critical feature of object-oriented languages; its presence (or absence) separates truly object-oriented languages from those that purport to be object oriented. In object methodology, it means that the same message to different receivers will produce different results.

Cobol actually exhibits a simple form of polymorphism. For instance, consider the output statement

```
Write out-record
```

If your program contains the following Select/FD sequence, the output record is written to a disk file.

```
File-Control.
    Select out-file assign to disk "this-file".
...
FD  out-file.
01  out-record ...
```

On the other hand, if your Select clause is at follows, quite a different action occurs: your output is directed to a printer.

```
Select out-file assign to printer.
```

Note that you need not make any special designation in the Write statement: the action is handled automatically by the system. In this sense, the Write statement is polymorphic.

Classes and objects are the basis for object methodology and have no equivalent in COBOL-85. A class definition is effectively a "template" describing a real-world thing: its data and its procedures. An object is an occurrence or an **instance** of a class. The next section of this chapter places the notion of a class and objects created from the class in the context of the familiar drawing toolbar of Windows.

Instantiate is the action of creating an instance of a class (an object). As you will learn, you can create and operate on one or more instances during a program run.

Creating Instances of a Rectangle

In the Microsoft drawing toolbar of Figure 2-1(a) you see a variety of shapes you can create. Each of these represents a *class* of shape from which you can create an *instance* (an *object*). For instance, consider the rectangle. Windows includes a soft-

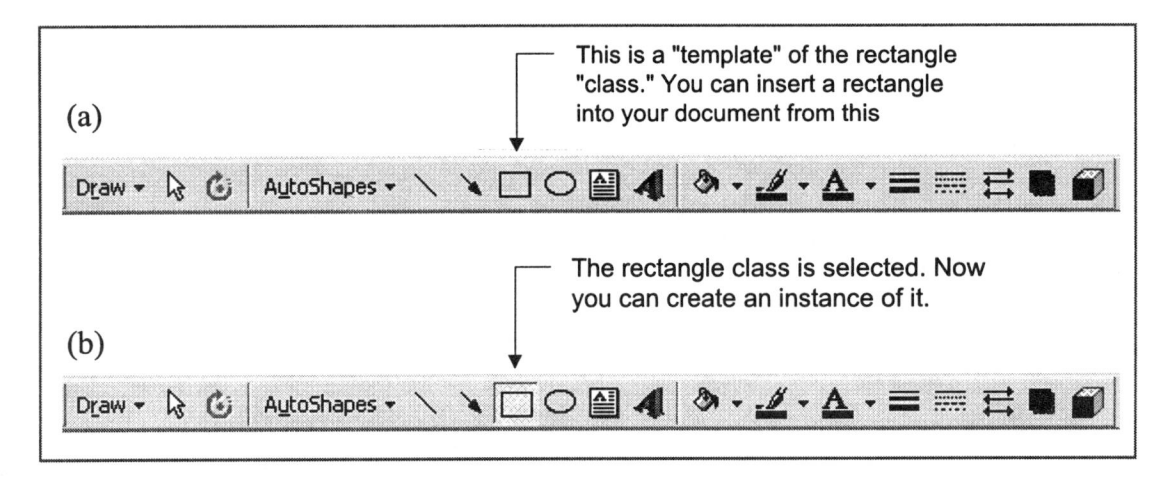

Figure 2-1. The Windows drawing toolbar.

Figure 2-2.
An instance of
the rectangle class.

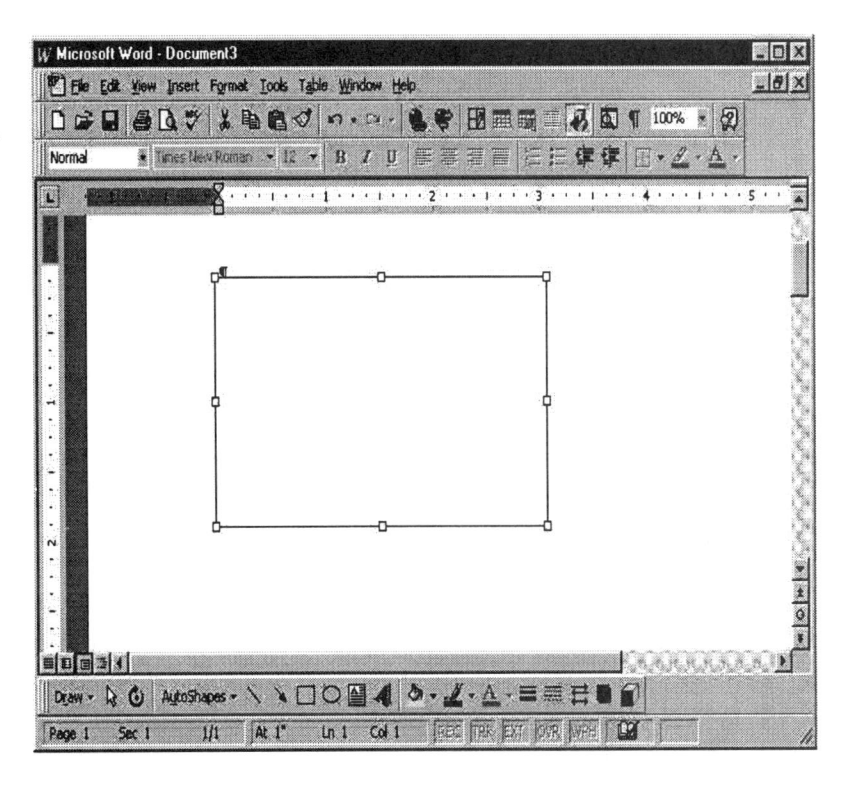

ware definition of the characteristics of a rectangle: four sides with included angles all right angles. By selecting the rectangle of the toolbar [as illustrated in Figure 2-1(b)], your cursor changes to a crosshair thereby allowing you to create an instance of the rectangle (a rectangle object) as shown in Figure 2-2. Through the selection handles on the object's sides and corners you can move it, change its dimensions, and rotate it as illustrated in Figure 2-3. If your application requires, you can create several such objects and manipulate each independent of the other.

The notion of a master definition and your ability to create instances of that master is precisely what you will be doing in programming with Cobol objects. However, as you will see in the next chapter, part of your programming task is creating the master (a class definition) as well as using it.

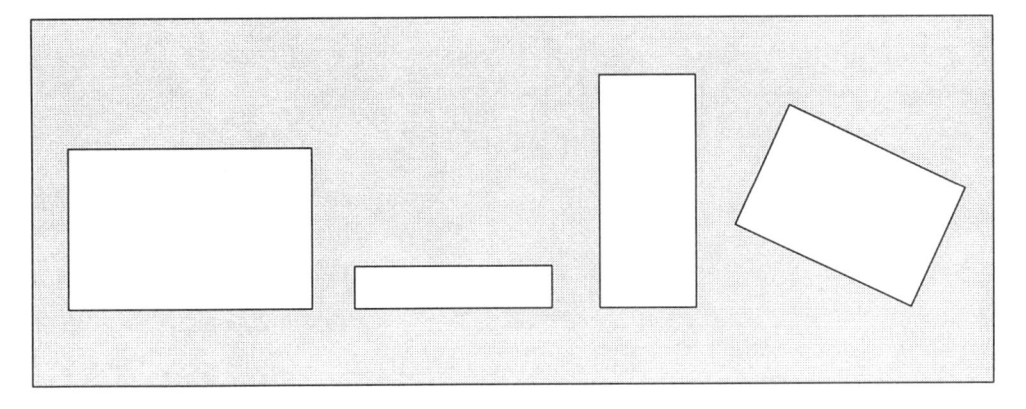

Figure 2-3. Manipulating the rectangle instance.

Abstract Data Types—A Cornerstone of Object-Oriented Programming Languages

What is an Abstract Data Type?

One of the key concepts of object-oriented programming languages is the *abstract data type*. If programming theory is not one of your strong points, you probably find the term a little intimidating (not uncommon, most of us do). Let's see if we can't examine the concept in terms of something familiar, then expand it to its full meaning in object methodology.

Forget about Cobol for the moment and consider the integers. We can view the integers as a *type of data*—the type includes only whole numbers, not fractional quantities. Can we reverse the order of the words *type of data* and say it is a *data type*? Well, let's not do that until we investigate further.

Although we don't give it much thought, the basic arithmetic operations we can perform on integers are an inseparable component of those things we call integers. In other words, when we talk about the integers, we implicitly include the basic operations addition, subtraction, multiplication, and division. Now we have everything necessary to use the words **abstract data type**: the combination of the integers and the permissible operations that can be performed on those integers.

Cobol Data Types

Consider the Picture clause, for example:

```
pic 99.
```

This "defines" a specific set of integers: 0 through 99; technically we would refer to it as a subset of the integers. In Cobol we recognize it as a numeric data type. But more specifically, we can narrow our description to a "two-digit integer data type." Are there operations associated with this specific data type? Of course there are; we can add, subtract, multiply, and divide quantities of this type. Admittedly when we stick to this single category (pic 99), arithmetic operations can produce incorrect results from overflow and loss of sign but that's beside the point. Therefore, the declaration pic 99 *and* the implicit operations associated with it define an abstract data type. Let's think of this as defining a *class* of data, or simply as a *class definition*.

Notice here that pic 99 defines what the data of this class looks like. It does not define data per se. For example, you do not add pic 99 to pic 99. You do add actual instances of data items declared with that picture. That is, within a program, you use this pic as a "template" and create specific data occurrences such as the following.

```
01  pic-99-occurences.
    10  first-num    pic 99.
    10  second-num   pic 99.
```

Now you can add first-num to second-num (or whatever). To be complete, you should recognize that this exercise involves a multi-step approach.

1. That is, we settled upon a class definition—the simple data type type pic 99.
2. Then we declared instances of that type (first-num and second-num).
3. During program execution, the program "populates" instances with data and operates on them. As you will see, this is roughly analogous to using classes in object-oriented Cobol.

Let's Be Original—Data Definition

Now let's diverge from Cobol again and invent a new language that provides for defining abstract data types. Two components required of our language are: a statement that allows you to describe the data type, and a statement that allows you to create instances of that data type as follows.

- The TYPE statement allows you to define a new type of data and identify its allowable elements. (We haven't needed this in Cobol because our data types are defined as part of the language—for example, numeric, alphanumeric, and so on.) The statement syntax is as follows.

    Type *data-type-name* (*data-value1, data-value2, ...*)

For instance, consider the following example

    Type week-days (MON, TUE, WED, THU, FRI, SAT, SUN)

This defines the data type week-days. This type will be a type in the same sense that comp, binary, and display are data types. It is a general category, not a specific value. The possible values of this data type are the three-letter day abbreviations:

    MON, TUE, WED, THU, FRI, SAT, SUN

- The DATA statement for creating variables of the new type. It is much like the entries we make in the Working-Storage Section of our Cobol programs using the Picture clause. The statement syntax is as follows.

    Data *data-type-name*: *data-item1, data-item2, ...*

To illustrate, assume your program requires the three data items work-day, some-day, and save-day each of type week-days. Then your program would include the following statement.

    Data week-days: work-day, some-day, save-day

Operations for the Data Type

Now let's describe the operations that can be performed on our new data type—then we will have completed the creation of an abstract data type. Assume that you have written three routines successor, predecessor, and difference. Successor allows you to change the value of a week-days type data item to its next value. For instance, if a data item contains WED, successor changes it to THU. Predecessor does the reverse. For instance, if a data item contains WED, predecessor changes it to TUE. Difference gives you the number of days between any two week-day data-items. For example, difference applied to TUE and FRI returns a value of 3. There are numerous other actions we could define but these three will do.

- Successor (+): Gives a successive day
    Syntax: *data-item1 = data-item2 + integer*
- Predecessor (-): Gives a previous day
    Syntax: *data-item1 = data-item2 – integer*
- Difference (|): Gives number of days between two days.
    Syntax: *integer-data-item = data-item1 | data-item2*

With this, a typical "procedure division" sequence of statements might look like the following:

```
work-day = WED              (places WED in work-day)
save-day = work-day + 1     (save-day will contain THU)
some-day = work-day - 2     (some-day will contain MON)
day-count = some-day | save-day   (day-count will contain 3)
```

We now have a structure that allows us to create abstract data types; it consists of the following components.

- The Type statement by which we define the values that data of this type can assume. It serves as the "template" for the data type—in that sense, it is similar to the rectangle icon on the drawing toolbar of the Microsoft Word illustration.
- The Data statement that allows us to create instances of the data type (instantiate this class of data).
- Procedures for operating on instances of this data type.

Now let's port this over to something that we Cobol programmers can sink our teeth into. Then you can take a glance at how all of this involves object-oriented Cobol.

Classes and Abstract Data Types in OOCobol

A lending library deals with books. At any given time an individual book can either be checked out or it can be on the shelf (checked in). For this discussion, let's focus on three attributes of the classification Book: ISBN, title, and book-status. With Data Division entries, we can declare the record book-info as follows.

```
01  book-info.
    10   ISBN            pic x(13).
    10   title           pic x(30).
    10   book-status     pic x(01).
         88   checked-out    value "O".
         88   checked-in     value "I".
```

As you know, this declaration does not specify a specific book. It is simply a "template" of what the book data will look like. (Of course, it will designate a particular book after the program moves data into it.)

There are numerous operations that you need to associate with this book "data class." You want to be able to populate it with selected book data from the book database; you want it to tell you whether or not the particular book is checked out, and so on. But for this example, let's focus on the simple actions of (1) checking a book out, and (2) checking a book in. These actions involve changing the book-status data item. For this, the data and the procedures will be wrapped up in an object Cobol **class definition**. Where a conventional program includes a Program-ID paragraph, a class definition includes a Class-ID paragraph. Figure 2-4 is a partial class definition for a class given the name BookClass.

The Working-Storage Section entries designate the object data associated with this class. Procedures that can operate on the object data of this class are defined as **methods**. You see the two needed methods.

Let's step back and consider what we have here. We have a class definition (BookClass) that includes a data "type" (book-info) and methods (procedures) that operate on that data. Is this an abstract data type? The answer is a resounding "YES!"

Using Class Definitions

How does a class definition such as this actually fit into the overall picture in the Cobol environment? The answer is that the class definition is loaded together with other program components of an application. During execution, code of your program will carry out the following actions when processing book data.

1. Create an instance of this book class (a book object)—that is, instantiate the class.

```
Identification Division.
Class-ID. BookClass.
   :
   Data Division.
      Working-Storage Section.
         01  Book-Info.
             10  SSBN          pic x(13).
             10  title         pic x(30).
             10  book-status   pic x(01).
                 88  checked-out   value "O".
                 88  checked-in    value "I".
   :
   Procedure Division.
      Method-ID. check-out.
         Procedure Division.
            Set checked-out to true
            .
         End Method check-out.

      Method-ID. check-in.
         Procedure Division.
            Set checked-in to true
            .
         End Method check-in.
```

Figure 2-4.
Class definition for BookClass.

2. Obtain book data to be operated on. It may be input from the keyboard or from a database.
3. Insert appropriate data for a particular book into the object's data items (ISBN, title, and book-status). The object's data is then available to your program via the methods of the class.
4. Process the instance data. For example, book-status could be changed from checked-in to checked-out.
5. If appropriate, write the instance data to a database.

If your application requires concurrent processing of two or more books, you would code your program to create a book class instance for each book to be processed.

About Object Orientation

Describing a Game from an Object Viewpoint

Assume you must explain the nature of a game—say ice hockey—to a friend who has never heard of the sport. (Or it could be soccer or water polo, as they are similar.) You would be very ineffective if you gave a running account of the game. But rather you would begin by identifying "objects" associated with the game. As a first cut, you might identify players, the goals, and the puck. After describing the physical layout of the playing surface and the objective of the game (place the puck in other teams goal), you might focus on individual positions. For instance, you might formalize two of the people "objects" as follows.

Goalie
    Description:
        The object (person) that stands in front of the goal.
    Responsibilities:
        Keep the puck out of the goal.
        Clear the puck to nearby defense players.
    Collaborators:
        Defense players.

Referee
    Description:
        One of the objects that judges the action.
    Responsibilities:
        Maintain order.
        Assess penalties.
    Collaborators:
        Line judge.

You might even consider the goal in the same context and think of it as having "human" qualities, for instance:

Goal
    Description:
        The area where the opposing teams attempts to place the puck.
    Responsibility:
        Know whether or not the puck has entered its area.

This is the essence of object technology: identifying objects of an application then determining the responsibilities and collaborators of each. The object-oriented methodology takes a different view of the world than the structured methodology. It is a change in perspective and it requires a change in our perspective to begin using it effectively.

Advantages of the Object-Oriented Approach

We can view the advantages of object orientation from two perspectives: the overall system and the actual programming. From the system perspective, the system analyst, the system designer, the programmer, and even the end user all use the same language: *objects*. The analyst and designer identify objects of an application then determine responsibilities and collaborators. This information is passed to the programmer who codes in terms of the objects, their responsibilities and collaborators. All can maintain continuous dialogue with the end user. Everyone speaks the same "language"—one that is understandable not only to the technical staff but equally to the end user. Although the end user may not understand code syntax, she/he understands the nature and purpose of each coded object. So rather than the discontinuities of the traditional structured waterfall of Figure 1-1, you have a seamless flow of Figure 2-5. Actually, this spiral representation does not do the object-oriented method justice. The sequence analysis/design/programming are really much more of a discovery process where discoveries of the design phase lead back to analysis phase

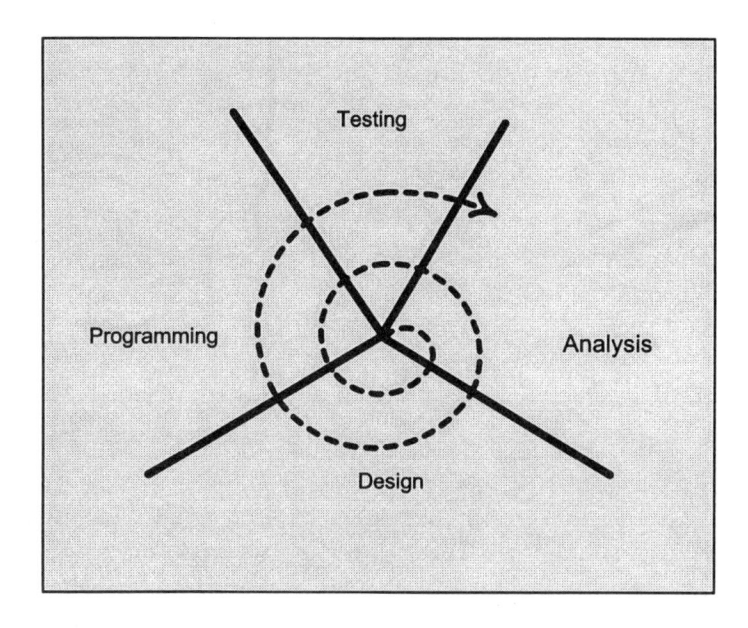

Figure 2-5.
The spiral model.

modifications. Similarly, discoveries of the programming phase can reflect back to modifications of the design phase.

Another point that is often overlooked is that structured decomposition is somewhat arbitrary; the end result of one designer might be significantly different from that of another. On the other hand, object-oriented methods, because they are anchored in the problem domain, have a tendency to generate the same objects when analyzed by different developers.

From the programmer perspective, the structured programmer sees his/her program as a massive collection of code. Code in which understanding the state (the value of all the data variables at any given time) is awkward, at best, and impossible at worst. With the global nature of data, side-effects (variables that are unwittingly changed) are the source of numerous errors and endless debugging.

With object orientation, the programmer no longer sees the program as a single mass; it is a collection of independent objects working together. Each object "owns" its data and includes all necessary procedures to operate on that data independent of other objects. Objects comprising a program are loosely coupled in that they are highly independent of one another. In a good design, they are also highly cohesive in that the purpose of a class's methods is to manage the data of that object.

Practically every programmer knows about subprograms: code stored in a library that can be used in any application to perform a particular task. For instance, prior to the introduction of the date functions in the 1989 Cobol supplement, many installations used subprograms to perform common date functions (for instance, determine the date 45 days from the current date). We think of this as **reusable code**: code that is written general in nature so that it can be imported into any application. As you will learn from chapters that follow, reusability is a significant feature of object technology.

Summing Up

This chapter has introduced you to the following basic principles of object orientation.

- Some of the basic terms of object methodology are:
  - Abstraction: The separation of the irrelevant from the relevant
  - Encapsulation: The principle that a software component should hide a single design decision.
  - Message communication: Transmission of information between program modules.
  - Polymorphism: The principle that the same message to different receivers will produce different results.
  - Class: A definition describing the data and procedures of a real-world entity.
  - Object: An instance of a class.
  - Instantiate: The action of creating an instance of a class from the class's definition.
- An abstract data type is a combination of data definitions and actions that can be performed on elements of the data type.
- Cobol's object capabilities allow you to write class definitions (program modules) from which you can create instances
- As programmers, we view class programs from two different perspectives: (a) class users without the need for knowledge of the internal details of the class definition, and (2) class writers with the responsibility for writing and maintaining class programs.

Coming Up

In Chapter 3 you will see the program/subprogram pair of Chapter 1 converted to an object-oriented form using the object-oriented features of Cobol. The chapter illustrates the notions of classes and objects and demonstrates the structure of a class program.

Introduction to Classes and Objects

Chapter Contents

First Look 42
   Road Map to the Room Application 42
   Class Users and Class Builders 42
   Features of the Room Class 43
   The Dialect Directive 44
   Selecting Program Names 44
The Driver Program 45
   Identification Division 45
   Environment Division Entries 45
   The Invoke Statement 47
   Invoking the Method 48
The Class Definition 48
   Structure of a Class Program 48
   Basic Elements 50
   The Identification and Environment Divisions 51
The Factory Object Definition 51
Defining the Factory Object 51
   Methods 52
   End Markers 53
   Special ISO2000 Requirement 53
Multiple Methods in a Class 53
   Expanding the Basic Room Class 53
   Modifications to the Program Driver 55
   Additions to the Class Definition 56
Formalizing Some Principles 57
   Terminology 57
   Recommended Styles 57
   Micro Focus and ISO2000 Differences 59
Summing Up 60
Coming Up 60
Assignments 61

Chapter

3

Chapter Introduction

In this chapter's first example, you will see the program/subprogram pair of Chapter 1 rewritten as a *driver* program and a *class definition program*. Although the class definition in this chapter looks much like the subprogram of Chapter 1, the class definition is much more. As you learned from Chapter 2, a class definition is basically a "template" for *creating* an object. This chapter introduces you to object-oriented Cobol classes and objects. From it you will learn the following.

- The distinction between a class and an object.
- The structure of a class program.
- The mechanism for accessing to an object
- Multiple procedures (called methods) in a class definition.

First Look

Road Map to the Room Application

As indicated in Chapter 1, concepts of this book revolve around a room rental system. In this chapter you will see basic object concepts introduced through an example in which the calling program and the subprogram of Chapter 1 are replaced by a driver program (Driver) and a class program (Room) as illustrated in Figure 3-1. As does the subprogram, Room (the class program) contains Value clauses defining the data. Although contrived, this serves to provide your first insight to writing and using class programs without the complexity of data access.

Chapter 4 removes Value clauses from the room class in favor of a second class program that accesses data from a data base as illustrated in Figure 3-2. Driver includes provisions for repetition whereby the user can enter a room number, designate the information to be accessed, and view the result.

As you will see, the example of Chapter 4 only partially embraces object methodology as Driver contains much of the processing code (in a structured form). The ultimate goal in Chapter 5 is to remove all processing activities from Driver by incorporating them into appropriate class programs. Figure 3-3 is a class diagram illustrating this concept. As you will learn, the sole function of Driver is to begin the process, then turn control over to Room Manager.

Class Users and Class Builders

As programmers, we have two perspectives of classes: as class *users* and as class *builders*. Actually, we function that way in all aspects of life. For example, consider the word processor. If you have used it extensively, you probably know most of its features. But what do you know about its internal code and how it carries out those tasks to which you are accustomed? The answer is, you don't; and furthermore, you don't care. You simply know the rules for using the software. On the other hand, if you are a software engineer writing word processors, you would be keenly aware of the internal workings of the software.

Object Cobol programmers function as both class users and class builders. For instance, in a typical installation an object-oriented programming project will involve writing new code that incorporates prewritten classes. They may be classes written by other programmers in the organization, or they may come from class libraries the organization has purchased. As a rule, you will know how to use these

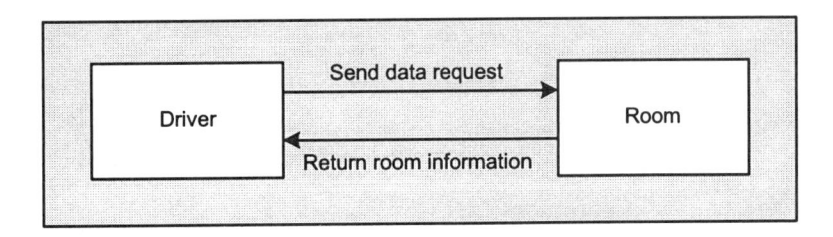

Figure 3-1. The basic Driver/Room class relationship.

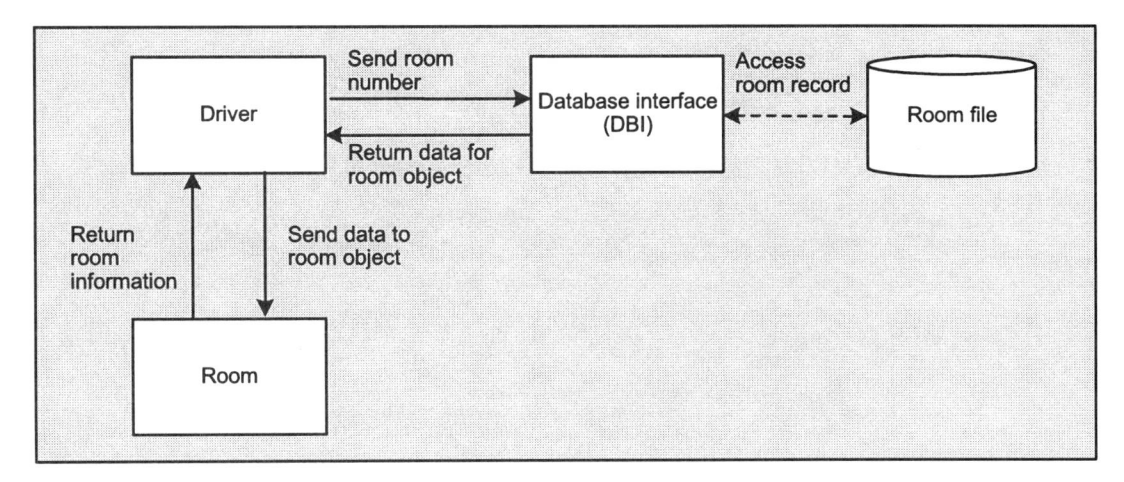

Figure 3-2. Introducing a database interface.

prewritten classes but you will not know (nor will you care) how they accomplish their tasks.

In examples of this book, you will see each class definition from both the class user perspective and the class builder perspective. This is part of the learning process.

Features of the Room Class

Obviously, you need to know how to use the room class before you can incorporate it into a driver program. In that respect, the room class has the following features.

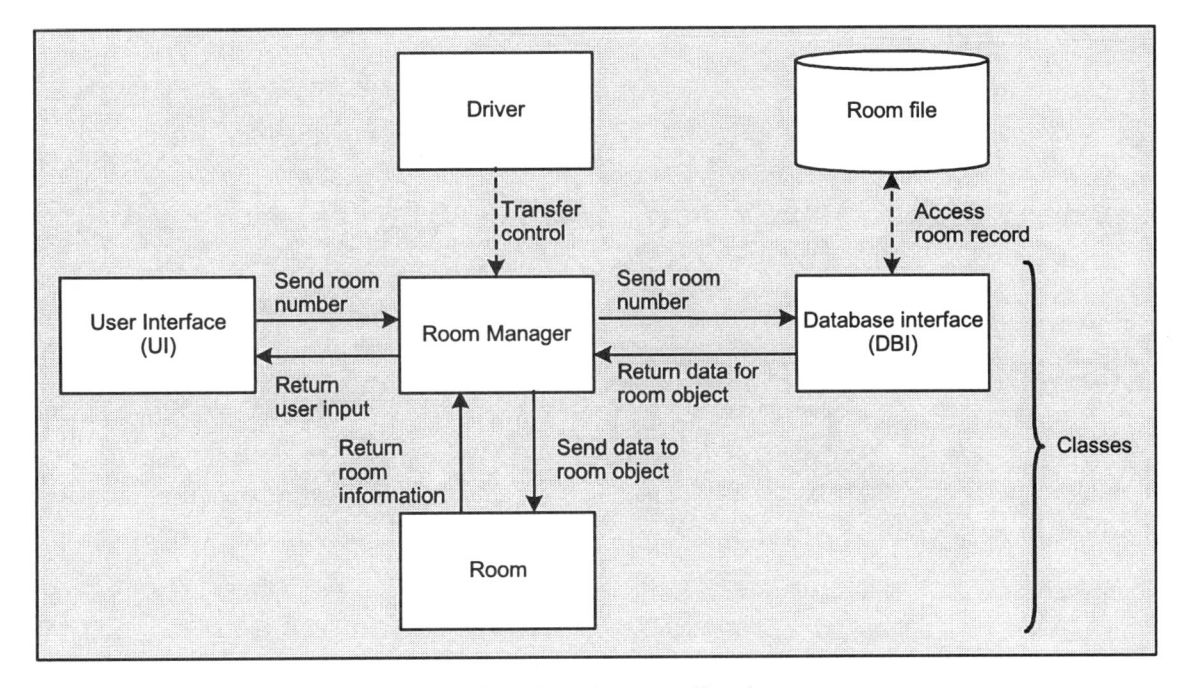

Figure 3-3. Class relationships—the complete application.

Class Name (file name)   r03-room.cbl

Description   This class contains and manages room data.

Class method
   get-room-prices.
      Input:
         Discount switch   pic X(01)
            value "Y" designates discounted prices
      Output:
         A record containing
            Standard room price   pic 9(03)
            Special room price   pic 9(03)

The Dialect Directive

Although Cobol is standardized, most vendors include non-standard enhancements to improve the functionality of their compiler. Micro Focus software systems allow you to work with them through the use of language "dialect" directive entries. (You are already familiar with the concept of the compiler directive from the discussion in Chapter 1 of the sourceformat directive.) With Net Express the dialect directive allows you to designate the Cobol language dialect you are using as follows.

- `Dialect (MF)` Designates that the containing source program uses the Micro Focus extensions to the language. It is the default value.
- `Dialect (ANS85)` Designates that the containing source program conforms to the 1985 Standard.
- `Dialect (ISO2000)` Designates that the containing source program conforms to the new Cobol Standard.

When I first began this revision of the book I had intended to use the ISO2000 dialect. However, at that time, Merant had not yet fully implemented the feature so I stayed with the MF dialect (as in the First Edition of this book). On the other hand, for topics covered in this book, the differences between the two are relatively minor and are pointed out with the individual topic.

Selecting Program Names

Unfortunately, file names under Personal COBOL are limited to eight characters (plus the three-character .cbl extension). Correspondingly, all program names in this book adhere to the restriction, even though Net Express is not so constrained. For the sake of documentation, I've selected the following file naming format (as described in Chapter 1).

   Examples: r03-room.cbl
                 r03-mgr.cbl

   Where: r indicates the Room application
                03 identifies the project (example) number
                room (or mgr) identifies the particular class program.

Introduction to Classes and Objects

You should use lower-case for class program names (discussed later in this chapter).

If you are using Net Express, I suggest you use this naming convention but do not limit yourself to eight characters. For instance, you might use room03-manager rather than r03-mgr.

The Driver Program

Figure 3-4 lists two versions of the Driver program (refer to it simply as "Driver"): `Proj0301 Room03`

- The 3-4(a) version uses the Micro Focus dialect (the default) and can be used with both Net Express Personal COBOL.
- The 3-4(b) version conforms to ISO2000 (the new Cobol standard). This example can be compiled and run with Net Express. Notice the ISO2000 dialect directive on the first line.

Scan these programs and you will see that they are not much different from r02-prog (the subprogram-calling program) of Chapter 1.

Identification Division

As with 1985 Cobol, the only required entry in the Identification Division is the Program-ID containing the program. In Figure 3-4(b), the "as" phrase

    as "r03-drvr"

(a feature of the new standard) allows you to specify the name Net Express will use for the resulting executable code resulting from the compile. Technically, this is referred by the Standard as an externalized name (it is external to the program). If you elect to try the ISO2000 dialect, I suggest the following two rules regarding the name designated in the as phrase (to avoid baffling errors).

1. It must be the same as the name of the source file (except omit the extension). For instance, the driver of Figure 3-4(a) has the file name is r03-drvr.cbl; line 15 designates r03-drvr. When you compile, you will see two or more files with other extensions, for instance, the executable will be r03-drvr.obj.
2. It must be in lower-case. Although case (lower versus upper) is not as significant for program names, at the time of the publication of this book, it was critical for ISO2000 dialect class names (as you will learn later in this chapter). So get in the habit of always using lower-case for these externalized names.

Environment Division Entries

Before looking at this program's Environment Division, consider the entries you must make in a program that processes a file. For example, if you are writing a program that uses the file SOFTWARE.DI, you must include entries such as the following in your program.

```
Environment Division.
Input-Output Section.
File-Control.
    Select SoftwareFile assign to disk "SOFTWARE.DI".
```

The Select clause relates the external file name SOFTWARE.DI to the internal name SoftwareFile that you will use within your program (for instance, in the Open and Read statements).

```
                $set sourceformat "free"
 1 *>*****************************************
 2 *> Room Rental System
 3 *> W. Price  31 August, 1999        R03-DRVR.CBL
 4 *> Personal Cobol example
 5 *> This program and its invoked class program
 6 *> correspond to the ROOM02 program and subprogram.
 7 *> This driver program does the following.
 8 *>   Queries the user about discounting
 9 *>   Invokes a room class method to return data
10 *>   Displays the room rental prices
11 *>*****************************************
12
13 Identification Division.
14     Program-ID.  Room03Driver.
15
16
17 Environment Division.
18     Object Section.
19        Class-Control.
20          RoomClass is class "r03-room"
21          .
22 Data Division.
23
24   Working-Storage Section.
25
26    01  room-prices.
27        10  std-config-price      pic 9(03).
28        10  spec-config-price     pic 9(03).
29
30    01  apply-discount-sw         pic X(01).
31        88  apply-discount        value "Y" "y".
32
33 Procedure Division.
34
35   000-process-room-prices.
36     Perform 200-get-user-request
37    *>Access object data through the class's method
38     Invoke RoomClass "get-room-prices"
39                Using apply-discount-sw
40                Returning room-prices
41     Perform 300-display-room-data
42     Stop run
43     .
44   200-get-user-request.
45     Display " "
46     Display "Do you want discounted prices <Y/N>? "
47              with no advancing
48     Accept apply-discount-sw
49     .
50   300-display-room-data.
51     Display " "
52     Display "Standard configuration price: "
53                               std-config-price
54     Display "Special configuration price: "
55                               spec-config-price
56     .

        (a) Micro Focus dialect.
```

```
                $set dialect(iso2000)
                $set sourceformat "free"
 1 *>*****************************************
 2 *> Room Rental System
 3 *> W. Price  30 August 1999         R03-DRVR.CBL
 4 *> Net Express example
 5 *> This program and its invoked class program
 6 *> correspond to the ROOM02 program and subprogram.
 7 *> This driver program does the following.
 8 *>   Queries the user about discounting
 9 *>   Invokes a room class method to return data
10 *>   Displays the room rental prices
11 *>*****************************************
12
13 Identification Division.
14     Program-ID.  Room03Driver
15                  as "r03-drvr"
16                  .
17 Environment Division.
18     Configuration Section.
19        Repository.
20          Class RoomClass as "r03-room"
21          .
22 Data Division.
23
24   Working-Storage Section.
25
26    01  room-prices.
27        10  std-config-price      pic 9(03).
28        10  spec-config-price     pic 9(03).
29
30    01  apply-discount-sw         pic X(01).
31        88  apply-discount        value "Y" "y".
32
33 Procedure Division.
34
35   000-process-room-prices.
36     Perform 200-get-user-request
37    *>Access object data through the class's method
38     Invoke RoomClass "get-room-prices"
39                Using apply-discount-sw
40                Returning room-prices
41     Perform 300-display-room-data
42     Stop run
43     .
44   200-get-user-request.
45     Display " "
46     Display "Do you want discounted prices <Y/N>? "
47              with no advancing
48     Accept apply-discount-sw
49     .
50   300-display-room-data.
51     Display " "
52     Display "Standard configuration price: "
53                               std-config-price
54     Display "Special configuration price: "
55                               spec-config-price
56     .

        (b) ISO2000 dialect.
```

Figure 3-4. The r03-drvr driver program.

Similarly, Cobol requires that you identify class programs that you will use in a program in much the same way you identify files. For instance, at lines 17-20 of Figure 3-4(a) you see the following code.

```
Environment Division.
    Object Section.
        Class-Control.
            RoomClass is class "r03-room"
```

These entries designate that the program uses a class. Within the program, you use the programmer-defined name RoomClass. This is equated to the externalized class name r03-room, the name you will designate when you create the class program. Reference to this class program from within Driver will be via this name.

The ISO2000 dialect uses the following form to define classes (this is consistent with provisions of the standard).

```
Environment Division.
    Configuration Section.
        Repository.
            Class RoomClass is "r03-room"
```

The Invoke Statement

Let's review Chapter 1's example of the the subprogram Call statement.

```
Call "r02-sub" Using apply-discount-sw, room-prices
```

Components of the Call are:

1. The keyword Call.
2. Identification of the external module r02-sub.
3. A Using phrase that lists the parameters. In this example, the first parameter designates data passed to the called subprogram. The second parameter designates the data item into which the subprogram places data to be returned to the calling program.

The new Standard still uses the Call verb for subprograms but includes a new verb, Invoke, for use with classes and class instances. Following is an abbreviated version of the Invoke's general form.

$$\underline{\text{INVOKE}}\ \text{identifier-1}\ \left\{ \begin{array}{l} \text{identifier-2} \\ \text{literal-1} \end{array} \right\}\ [\underline{\text{USING}}\ \text{identifier-3}\ ...]$$
$$[\underline{\text{RETURNING}}\ \text{identifier-4}]$$

Here you see the following components.

1. The keyword Invoke.
2. Identifier-1 is an identifier defined as either a class name or as an object reference. For examples of this chapter, it is the name of the class program that is to be invoked. This is the class name identified in the Environment Division. As you will learn in the next chapter, it can also be a reference to an object that you create.
3. A class program can contain one or more sets of procedural code called

methods. The name of the class's method to be invoked must be designated either as a literal (literal-1) or must be contained in a data item (identifier-2). There is no equivalent to this in the Standard Cobol subprogram Call.
4. Optionally, depending upon the nature of the class's method, a Using phrase to designate the parameter(s)—(identifier-3 ...)—of this Invoke. As with the Call, these data items can serve as input to or output from the class program (or as both). Also, like the Call, the Invoke can include the by Reference, by Content, and by Value phrases.
5. Optionally, depending upon the nature of the class's method, a Returning phrase to designate *a single* output item from the class. Although limited to a single parameter, identifier-4 can be a group data item.

Invoking the Method

Remember from the earlier description of the room class that it includes one method: get-room-prices. It requires both input and output parameters. With this, the Invoke of lines 38-40 (repeated here from Figure 3-4) should be reasonably straightforward.

```
Invoke RoomClass "get-room-prices"
        Using apply-discount-sw
        Returning room-prices
```

1. The class name follows the keyword Invoke.
2. Input to the method is designated by the Using; you see its data item defined in line 30.
3. Output is designated by the Returning; you see its data item defined in lines 26-28.

The Class Definition

Structure of a Class Program

As Cobol programmers most of us see a Cobol program as containing the following four division.

```
IDENTIFICATION DIVISION.
  PROGRAM-ID. program-name ...
ENVIRONMENT DIVISION.
DATA DIVISION.
PROCEDURE DIVISION.
```

In this book you will learn to write class definitions (programs) in which the structure is quite different from the above. So do not allow yourself to be confused by this apparent "radical" departure from all that we perceive as "good and true" about program structure. In object-oriented Cobol, we deal with two different types of objects: the **factory object** and the **instance object**. You will use the factory object in much the same way you use a subprogram. That is, you can think of the factory object as existing at load time with its procedures (and data) ready to be used. In contrast, the instance object is much like the rectangle of Chapter 2. It is a template from which a working instance must be created. Then you have access to data of the object through the procedures of the class's object definition.

As a class definition can define two different types of objects, each of which contains object data and associated procedures, you probably correctly guessed that its basic program structure, shown in Figure 3-5, is significantly different from that of a conventional Cobol program.

```
IDENTIFICATION DIVISION.
  CLASS-ID. class-name ...
ENVIRONMENT DIVISION.

IDENTIFICATION DIVISION.
FACTORY.
        (Factory object entries)
END FACTORY.

IDENTIFICATION DIVISION.
OBJECT.
        (Instance object entries)
END OBJECT.
```

Figure 3-5.
Class definition skeleton.

You can consider this definition as comprised of three components.

- For lack of a better term, the **class component** containing two divisions: Identification and Environment.
- An Identification Division containing the **Factory paragraph** defining the factory object of this class definition.
- An Identification Division containing the **Object paragraph** defining the instance object of this class definition.

In this chapter you will see the room data encapsulated in the factory object of the room class definition. In this form, you will observe relatively little difference between the driver program/class program and the program/subprogram pair of Chapter 1.

Note: The new Standard designates the header entry IDENTIFICATION DIVISION (not the Identification Division itself) as optional. As it provides no useful documentary value preceding the definition of the Factory and the Object, it is omitted in examples of this book.

```
        $set sourceformat "free"
 1 *>***************************************************
 2 *> Room Rental System
 3 *> W. Price August 30, 1999              R03-ROOM.CBL
 4 *> Net Express example
 5 *> This class contains the room data and the method
 6 *> "get-room-prices".
 7 *>    Input:  Discount switch
 8 *>    Output: Standard configuration price
 9 *>            Special configuration price
10 *>***************************************************
11
12 Identification Division.
13      Class-id.  RoomClass.
14
15 Environment Division.
16      Object Section.
17          Class-Control.
18              RoomClass is class "r03-room"
19              .
20 *>=================================================
21 FACTORY.
22
23   Data Division.
24     Object-Storage Section.
25       01  room-data.
26           10  room-number       pic X(03)  value "100".
27           10  std-config-price  pic 9(03)  value 225.
28           10  spec-config-price pic 9(03)  value 385.
29           10  room-discount     pic v9(02) value .05.
30           10  room-capacity     pic 9(02)  value 38.
31
32   Procedure Division.
33
34     *>-----------------------------------------------
35     Identification Division.
36       Method-id. get-room-prices.
37     *>-----------------------------------------------
38     Data Division.
39       Local-Storage Section.
40         01  lo-price-factor          pic 9(01)v9(02).
41
42       Linkage Section.
43         01  ls-apply-discount-sw  pic x(01).
44             88  ls-apply-discount    value "Y" "y".
45         01  ls-room-prices.
46             10  ls-std-config-price  pic 9(03).
47             10  ls-spec-config-price pic 9(03).
48
49     Procedure Division  Using ls-apply-discount-sw
50                         Returning ls-room-prices.
51       Move std-config-price to ls-std-config-price
52       Move spec-config-price to ls-spec-config-price
53       Evaluate TRUE
54         When ls-apply-discount
55           Subtract room-discount from 1.0
56                         giving lo-price-factor
57           Multiply lo-price-factor
58                         by ls-std-config-price
59           Multiply lo-price-factor
60                         by ls-spec-config-price
61       End-Evaluate *> TRUE
62       Exit method
63       .
64     End Method get-room-prices.
65     *>-----------------------------------------------
66 END FACTORY.
67 END CLASS RoomClass.
```

(a) Micro Focus dialect.

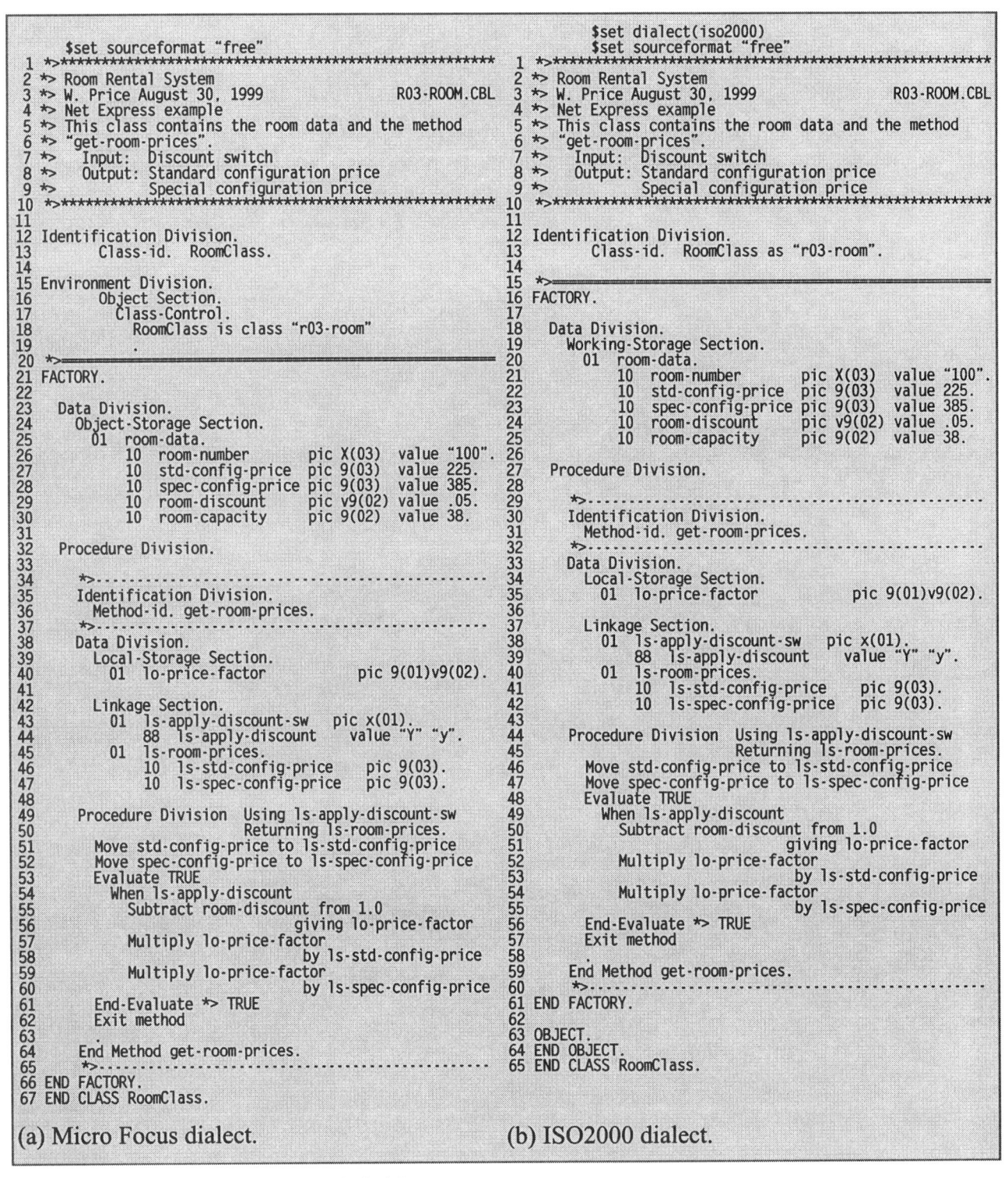

```
        $set dialect(iso2000)
        $set sourceformat "free"
 1 *>***************************************************
 2 *> Room Rental System
 3 *> W. Price August 30, 1999              R03-ROOM.CBL
 4 *> Net Express example
 5 *> This class contains the room data and the method
 6 *> "get-room-prices".
 7 *>    Input:  Discount switch
 8 *>    Output: Standard configuration price
 9 *>            Special configuration price
10 *>***************************************************
11
12 Identification Division.
13      Class-id.  RoomClass as "r03-room".
14
15 *>=================================================
16 FACTORY.
17
18   Data Division.
19     Working-Storage Section.
20       01  room-data.
21           10  room-number       pic X(03)  value "100".
22           10  std-config-price  pic 9(03)  value 225.
23           10  spec-config-price pic 9(03)  value 385.
24           10  room-discount     pic v9(02) value .05.
25           10  room-capacity     pic 9(02)  value 38.
26
27   Procedure Division.
28
29     *>-----------------------------------------------
30     Identification Division.
31       Method-id. get-room-prices.
32     *>-----------------------------------------------
33     Data Division.
34       Local-Storage Section.
35         01  lo-price-factor          pic 9(01)v9(02).
36
37       Linkage Section.
38         01  ls-apply-discount-sw  pic x(01).
39             88  ls-apply-discount    value "Y" "y".
40         01  ls-room-prices.
41             10  ls-std-config-price  pic 9(03).
42             10  ls-spec-config-price pic 9(03).
43
44     Procedure Division  Using ls-apply-discount-sw
45                         Returning ls-room-prices.
46       Move std-config-price to ls-std-config-price
47       Move spec-config-price to ls-spec-config-price
48       Evaluate TRUE
49         When ls-apply-discount
50           Subtract room-discount from 1.0
51                         giving lo-price-factor
52           Multiply lo-price-factor
53                         by ls-std-config-price
54           Multiply lo-price-factor
55                         by ls-spec-config-price
56       End-Evaluate *> TRUE
57       Exit method
58
59     End Method get-room-prices.
60     *>-----------------------------------------------
61 END FACTORY.
62
63 OBJECT.
64 END OBJECT.
65 END CLASS RoomClass.
```

(b) ISO2000 dialect.

Figure 3-6. The r02-room class definition.

Basic Elements

With this brief introduction, let's look at the Room class definition shown in Figure 3-6 where you see:

- Designation of the class name
- Association of referenced classes with corresponding physical files on disk
- Definition of the object data
- The class method (that allows you to operate on the object's data)

The Identification and Environment Divisions

In a conventional Cobol program, the first entry is like the following.

```
Identification Division.
Program-ID.  Room03Driver.
```

In contrast, in a class definition, the first entry you see is like this:

```
Identification Division.
Class-ID.  RoomClass
```

This is a simple correspondence: the Class-ID corresponds to the Program-ID. The name you select here is the class name. It is internal to the class (it has no meaning outside the class). Like Driver of Figure 3-4(b), the ISO2000 version includes the as clause identifying for the compiler the name to use for the executable.

For this example, the Micro Focus dialect requires an Environment Division with the entries shown in Figure 3-6(a), lines 15-18. The entry of line 18 is required to externalize the name of this file. It serves the same purpose as the as clause in the ISO2000 version.

In both versions you see the class name RoomClass, the name appearing in the Class-ID, related to the physical file room03c1 [line 18 in Figure 3-6(a) and line 13 in Figure 3-6(b)]. If you refer to both examples of Driver in Figure 3-4, you see that the same class name is used in both the driver and the class definition. However, they are *not* required to be identical. Each is local to its own source code unit; each is related to the external file through the appropriate entries.

The Factory Object Definition

Defining the Factory Object

At line 21 the keyword FACTORY designates the factory object paragraph. Under FACTORY you see Data and Procedure Divisions. You define data of the object under the Data Division; you define methods of the object under the Procedure Division. In essence this corresponds to the abstract data type described in Chapter 2: it consists of data and procedures to operate on the data.

According to ISO2000, the Working-Storage section of this Data Division defines object data of this factory object (lines 20-25). In Figure 3-6(a) you see Object Storage Section, the Micro Focus dialect syntax. [Personal COBOL includes a compiler directive allowing you to use Working-Storage Section here thereby complying with the Standard. However, I had some subtle problems using it that I could not resolve so I gave up and used Object-Storage Section in all my examples.]

Methods

Under the Procedure Division of the Factory paragraph, you define this object's methods. The first and only method in this class definition begins at line 35 [referring to Figure 3-6(a)]. One aspect of class definitions is the appearance of a complete program structure within the Procedure Division of the object. That is, each method can include each of the four Cobol divisions. Here you see the following.

- At lines 35 and 36, an Identification Division containing a Method-ID paragraph. Notice that you now have three ID categories: Program-ID, Class-ID, and Method-ID. Each falls under an Identification Division header. [Note: The Identification Division header is included in these two examples only to emphasize the four-division structure of a method. In all examples that follow, this header is omitted, consistent with that feature of the new Standard. Be aware that both Net Express and Personal COBOL allow omission of this header.]
- At lines 38-47, a Data Division consisting of a Local-Storage Section and a Linkage Section. The Local-Storage Section allows you to define non-persistent data items that are local to the method. The new standard does not permit a Working-Storage Section within a method although both Net Express and Personal COBOL do permit it.
- At lines 49-61, a Procedure Division with its required parameters listed in the division header.

> **Important note:** There are some subtle potential problems regarding Local-Storage and Working-Storage Sections with current Micro Focus software. Refer to the summary at the end of this chapter.

As is evident here, a method looks much like a subprogram in that it can: (1) include all four divisions, and (2) include parameters for interprogram communication. If it uses parameters, then it must include a Linkage Section and a Procedure Division header identifying the parameters. If you compare lines 40-63 of Figure 3-6(a) with lines 26-49 of the subprogram in Figure 1-10, you will see that they are almost identical

A significant difference is that the method definition Procedure Division header (lines 49 and 50) identifies one parameter with a Using clause and the other with a Returning clause. As you learned in studying the driver program, OOCobol uses:

Using   Data passed from the invoking program to the invoked program. (Data-items listed in the Using clause *can* be changed by the invoked method just as with subprograms.)

Returning   Data passed from the invoked program to the invoking program.

Rules for implementing the Using are identical to those for subprograms. That is, parameters listed in the Using must be 01 items; you cannot use non-01 elementary items. You should also be aware that the new Standard *restricts the Returning parameter to a single 01 entry.*

At line 62 you see an Exit statement that causes control to be returned to the invoking program. Actually, it is not needed in this case as control is returned to the invoking program after the last statement of a method is executed. With the exception of this example, programs in this book do not include the Exit statement.

End Markers

Within a class definition, you must end all definitions with **End markers**. For instance, the end of each method must be indicated with an End Method marker such as the following from line 64 of Figure 3-4(a).

    End Method get-room-prices

Similarly, you end the Factory Object with END FACTORY (line 66); notice that no name is associated with the object header (line 21) so none is included in the END FACTORY marker. You end the class definition with END CLASS which includes the class name.

Special ISO2000 Requirement

If you use the ISO2000 switch with Net Express Version 3 you will encounter a compiler error if your class definition does not include both the Factory and the Object paragraphs. Even though this example does not require an instance object definition, the OBJECT and END OBJECT entries are included [lines 63 and 64 of Figure 3-6(b)]. Presumably, future releases of Net Express will not require empty object definitions.

You *must* be aware that Net Express 3.0 uses a special technique for generating a table of both external class names and method names. This technique introduces case sensitivity (although that may change in later releases of Net Express). *You will save yourself a lot of grief if you religiously use lower case for:*

- Externalized class names. For instance, name the room class definition r03-room.cbl (all lower-case) then include the following in the Environment Division.

        Class-Control.
            RoomClass is class "r03-room"

- Method names. Make a habit of using only lower-case (hyphens are okay), for instance:

        Method-id. get-room-prices.

Multiple Methods in a Class

Expanding the Basic Room Class

If, at this point, if you sit back and compare the subprogram approach of Chapter 1 and the OO approach of this chapter you might wonder what's the big deal about OOCobol. You have nearly a direct mapping of the program/subprogram over to the driver/class. The response is that you've only scratched the surface of object orientation. As your first expansion of the room class, let's consider the pricing policy (full and discounted prices). In this example, providing the prices, whether full or discounted, is a relatively simple operation. However, in an actual application, pricing policies could be very complex, depending upon factors such as the day of the week, number of consecutive days required, and so on. Furthermore, determination of discounted prices could involve procedures completely different from those for determining full prices.

With these considerations, let's create two independent methods: one to return the full price and the other to calculate and return the discounted price. This keeps these actions independent of one another. It also offers another desirable feature. It eliminates the need for passing a switch for determining whether or not to apply the discount. Switches are great for many applications, but they tend to be error prone (to us, the programmers, not to the computer). While we're at it, let's include a method that returns the room capacity.

As before, let's first be class users and incorporate this new version of the room class into the driver. Then we can be class builders and look at the changes to the room class definition. Following is the description of the new room class that we require as class users.

Class Name   r04-room

Description   This class contains and manages room data.

Class methods
  get-discounted-room-prices
    Purpose
      Return discounted room prices from the room object.
    Input
      none
    Output
      A record containing
        Discounted standard room price   pic 9(03)
        Discounted special room price   pic 9(03)
  get-room-capacity
    Purpose
      Return room capacity from the room object.
    Input
      none
    Output
      Room capacity   pic 9(02)
  get-room-prices
    Purpose
      Return room prices from the room object.
    Input
      none
    Output
      A record containing
        Standard room price   pic 9(03)
        Special room price   pic 9(03)

```cobol
       $set sourceformat "free"
1  *>****************************************
2  *> Room Rental System
3  *> W. Price  30 August 1999           R04-DRVR.CBL
4  *>
5  *> This driver provides the user a menu allowing
6  *> for full room prices, discounted room prices,
7  *> or room capacity. It illustrates invoking
8  *> different methods of the room class.
9  *>****************************************
10
11 Identification Division.
12     Program-ID. Room04Driver.
13
14 Environment Division.
15     Object Section.
16         Class-control.
17             RoomClass is class "r04-room"
18
19 .
20 Data Division.
21     Working-Storage Section.
22
23     01 room-prices.
24         10 std-config-price       pic 9(03).
25         10 spec-config-price      pic 9(03).
26     01 room-capacity              pic 9(02).
27
28     01 menu-choice                pic X(01).
29         88 discounted-prices      value "D" "d".
30         88 standard-prices        value "S" "s".
31
32 Procedure Division.
33
34 000-process-room-data.
35     Perform 200-get-user-request

36     Evaluate TRUE
37         When discounted-prices
38             Invoke RoomClass
39                 "get-discounted-room-prices"
40                 Returning room-prices
41             Perform 900-display-room-prices
42         When standard-prices
43             Invoke RoomClass "get-room-prices"
44                 Returning room-prices
45             Perform 900-display-room-prices
46         When other
47             Invoke RoomClass "get-room-capacity"
48                 Returning room-capacity
49             Perform 950-display-room-capacity
50     End-evaluate *>TRUE
51     Stop run
52 .
53 200-get-user-request.
54     Display " "
55     Display "The options are:"
56     Display "  C - Room capacity (default)"
57     Display "  S - Standard room prices"
58     Display "  D - Discounted room prices"
59     Display " "
60     Display "Your choice <C,S,D>? " no advancing
61     Accept menu-choice
62 .
63 900-display-room-prices.
64     Display " "
65     Display "Standard configuration price: "
66                                std-config-price
67     Display "Special configuration price: "
68                                spec-config-price
69 .
70 950-display-room-capacity.
71     Display " "
72     Display "Room capacity: " room-capacity
73 .
```

Figure 3-7 The r04-drvr driver program.

Modifications to the Program Driver

By inspecting the r04-drvr listing of Figure 3-7, you can see the following differences from the preceding driver.

1. Because the user now has three options (full prices, discounted prices, and room capacity), the 200 module includes a short menu (lines 54-60).
2. At line 61 the user's response is accepted into the data item menu-choice (defined at line 28).
3. The menu-choice value is tested by the Evaluate statement (see lines 37, 42, and 46) using condition-names defined at lines 29 and 30.
4. To minimize code in this example, the room capacity option is treated as the default action (beginning line 46). Thus, any entry other than S or D is treated as if it were a C. In an actual application program, you would probably include an exit option and a loop requiring a valid entry.
5. At lines 38, 43, and 47 you see the room factory object invoked with the following form.

    Invoke RoomClass ...

   In each case, the appropriate method and arguments complete the Invoke statement.
6. Module 950 is added to display the room capacity.

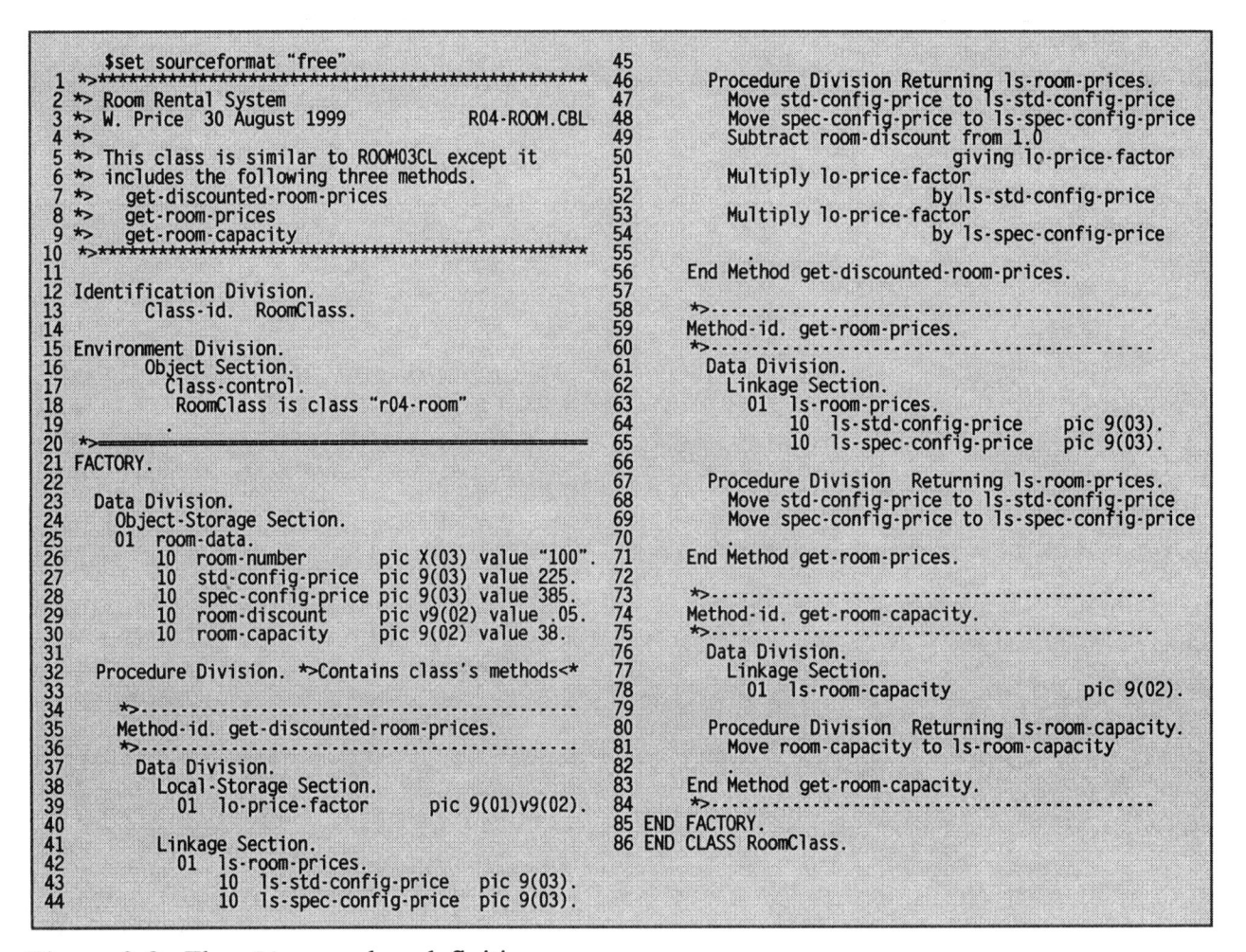

```
         $set sourceformat "free"
1  *>*******************************************
2  *> Room Rental System
3  *> W. Price   30 August 1999            R04-ROOM.CBL
4  *>
5  *> This class is similar to ROOM03CL except it
6  *> includes the following three methods.
7  *>     get-discounted-room-prices
8  *>     get-room-prices
9  *>     get-room-capacity
10 *>*******************************************
11
12 Identification Division.
13      Class-id.  RoomClass.
14
15 Environment Division.
16      Object Section.
17         Class-control.
18            RoomClass is class "r04-room"
19            .
20 *>===========================================
21 FACTORY.
22
23   Data Division.
24     Object-Storage Section.
25     01  room-data.
26         10   room-number       pic X(03) value "100".
27         10   std-config-price  pic 9(03) value 225.
28         10   spec-config-price pic 9(03) value 385.
29         10   room-discount     pic v9(02) value .05.
30         10   room-capacity     pic 9(02) value 38.
31
32   Procedure Division.  *>Contains class's methods<*
33
34 *>-------------------------------------------
35   Method-id. get-discounted-room-prices.
36 *>-------------------------------------------
37     Data Division.
38       Local-Storage Section.
39         01  lo-price-factor    pic 9(01)v9(02).
40
41       Linkage Section.
42         01  ls-room-prices.
43             10  ls-std-config-price   pic 9(03).
44             10  ls-spec-config-price  pic 9(03).
45
46     Procedure Division Returning ls-room-prices.
47       Move std-config-price to ls-std-config-price
48       Move spec-config-price to ls-spec-config-price
49       Subtract room-discount from 1.0
50                             giving lo-price-factor
51       Multiply lo-price-factor
52                             by ls-std-config-price
53       Multiply lo-price-factor
54                             by ls-spec-config-price
55       .
56   End Method get-discounted-room-prices.
57
58 *>-------------------------------------------
59   Method-id. get-room-prices.
60 *>-------------------------------------------
61     Data Division.
62       Linkage Section.
63         01  ls-room-prices.
64             10  ls-std-config-price   pic 9(03).
65             10  ls-spec-config-price  pic 9(03).
66
67     Procedure Division Returning ls-room-prices.
68       Move std-config-price to ls-std-config-price
69       Move spec-config-price to ls-spec-config-price
70       .
71   End Method get-room-prices.
72
73 *>-------------------------------------------
74   Method-id. get-room-capacity.
75 *>-------------------------------------------
76     Data Division.
77       Linkage Section.
78         01  ls-room-capacity         pic 9(02).
79
80     Procedure Division Returning ls-room-capacity.
81       Move room-capacity to ls-room-capacity
82       .
83   End Method get-room-capacity.
84 *>-------------------------------------------
85 END FACTORY.
86 END CLASS RoomClass.
```

Figure 3-8. The r04-room class definition.

Additions to the Class Definition

Figure 3-8 lists the new class definition r04-room that includes the three required methods. Each method is begun with a Method-ID and ended with an End Method. Each is totally independent of the other. The only thing they have in common is that they all have access to the object data of this class (lines 25-30).

The independence of one method from another is an important point—data defined in a method is local to that method. For instance, the method get-discounted-room-prices includes the Local-Storage Section data item lo-price-factor. This item is local to its method. If, for instance, you referred to it in the get-room-capacity method, you would receive a compiler error. Be aware Local-Storage Section data values are not carried over from one invocation of a method to another. Notice also that the same data names are used in the Linkage Sections of the different methods. Whether you use the same or different names from one method to another is completely immaterial. Again, these names are local to their individual methods.

Recall from earlier descriptions that each method of a class definition can include all four divisions: each has the form of a complete "mini-program." The method definition structure hierarchy is:

Introduction to Classes and Objects

```
Identification Division.
  Method-ID. ...
Environment Division.
  Environment Division entries...
Data Division.
  Data Division entries...
Procedure Division.
  Procedural code
End-method ...
```

Formalizing Some Principles

Terminology

When studying a new topic, it is easy to become bogged down in terminology—this is especially true with object technology. Here are some of the terms that you should recognize.

Program A conventional Cobol program; it includes a Program-ID paragraph in the Identification Division.

Class program or **Class definition** The source unit that defines a class. It includes a Class-ID paragraph in the Identification Division.

Factory definition That portion of code in the class program between the reserved words FACTORY and END FACTORY.

Factory object data The data definitions of the Object-Storage Section (Working-Storage Section in the ISO2000 dialect) immediately following the FACTORY header and preceding the method definitions.

Source unit In terms of the principles of this chapter, a complete program whether a conventional program or class definition. Technically, the ISO Standard defines a source unit as: "A sequence of statements beginning with an Identification Division and finishing with an end marker or the end of the compilation group, including any contained source units."

Recommended Styles

The following standard programming styles expand upon those introduced in Chapter 1. If you skipped Chapter 1, go back and read those recommendations.

Source program general format.

For all programs in this book, I use the following general program layout rules.

- Two-space successive indenting of elements as in Figure 3-8.
- Omit the Identification Division header from each method. For instance, the Method-ID paragraph header at line 35 of Figure 3-8 is not preceded by a division header.

- The Method-ID is bordered above and below with a row of hyphens to set it apart.
- All method entries below the Method-ID entry are indented (even though they are not syntactically subordinate to the Method-ID header). This clearly delineates the method for you.
- The End Method marker is positioned directly beneath its corresponding Method-ID header.

File Names for Programs

- If you are using Personal COBOL, use names of eight characters or fewer.
- Use a naming convention that indicates to you the class (such as the following).

    Examples: r03-room.cbl
    r03-mgr.cbl

    Where: r indicates the Room application
    03 identifies the project (example) number
    room (or mgr) identifies the particular class program.

- If you are using Net Express,
  (a) do not restrict yourself to eight characters, and
  (b) use lower-case.

Data Item Names

- Use all lower-case with words separated by hyphens, for instance, std-config-price.
- Prefix data names as follows (use Figure 3-8 as a guide):

    Linkage Section: ls-
    for instance, ls-std-config-price

    Local-Storage Section of methods: lo-
    for instance, lo-price-factor

    No prefix for Object-Storage Section of class definition
    for instance, std-config-price

Other Names within a Program

- For class names use uppercase for the first letter of each word comprising the name, do not use hyphens, for example: RoomClass.
- Use lowercase for method names—use hyphens to provide readability between words, for example, get-room-prices.
- Use lowercase for externalized class names, for example, r04-room in the following.

    Class RoomClass as "r04-room"

As you begin programming, you will find that adhering to these standards greatly improves the readability of your programs.

Other

- In the comments at the beginning of the driver, list all classes comprising the project.
- In the comments at the beginning of each class, list all methods of the class in alphabetic sequence (the order of the methods themselves can be whatever is meaningful to you). If your class incorporates both factory and instance methods, list them separately.

Micro Focus and ISO2000 Differences

This book focuses on the Micro Focus dialect which is common to both Net Express and Personal COBOL. Following is a summary of the differences between the Micro Focus and ISO2000 dialects using Room03 entries as examples.

Micro Focus	**ISO2000**
Program-ID entry.	
`Program-ID. Room04Driver.`	`Program-ID. Room03Driver` `              as "r03-drvr".`
Class identifier in class program.	

`Identification Division.`
`    Class-ID. RoomClass.`
 	
`Environment Division.`
`    Object Section.`
`        Class-Control.`
`            RoomClass is class "r03-room".`
	`Identification Division.`
	`    Class-ID. RoomClass`
	`              as "r03-room".`
	
	(Environment Division entry is not required for r03-room as it is designated in the Class-ID.)

Class declaration syntax.	

`Environment Division.`
`    Object Section.`
`        Class-Control.`
`            RoomClass is class "r03-room"`
	`Environment Division.`
	`    Configuration Section.`
	`        Repository.`
	`            Class RoomClass as "r03-room".`

Object data definition.	
`Data Division.` `    Object-Storage Section.`	`Data Division.` `    Working-Storage Section.`

Local-Storage and Working-Storage Sections

In all the examples of this book, I had used Working-Storage Section in methods instead of Local-Storage Section. As this second edition was ready to go to press, the Standards Committee voted to disallow the Working-Storage Section within methods (because of the manner in which it violated encapsulation). So I scrambled to update all examples. If you find Working-Storage Sections in some of the example methods, it's only because I missed them in the process.

Unfortunately, a few of my examples failed with this change because I had used Value clauses. Both Net Express and Personal COBOL appear to ignore Value clauses in the Local-Storage Section. This is contrary to the Standard which permits the use of Value clauses in Local Storage. In fact, a feature of the Value clause in Local Storage is that the data item is set to its initial value with each invocation of the method. This is in contrast to data items in Working Storage where values are retained from one invocation to another.

Summing Up

This chapter provides you with your first look at the nature of classes and objects. Following are the significant points of the chapter.
- A class program, or class definition, contains a data definition describing the object data and the methods that operate on this data.
- Methods of a class are executed using the Invoke statement (equivalent to the Call for subprograms).

Coming Up

Examples of this chapter are contrived in that they use Value clauses to define object data. In Chapter 4 you will learn how to use a database interface class to access data from an indexed file to place desired data into the object's data fields.

Assignments

Application #1 Description

Jennifer and Bartholemew are dessert connoisseurs. After tasting their latest creation they decide to form a business and market a variety of flavors. Following some discussion and a flip of the coin, they select a company name: Jen and Barry's Desserts.

Being a computer nut, Jen wants everything about the business computerized. Since Cobol is the language of business, she decides that OOCobol is the way to go for their company. You are in charge of the programming effort.

J&B's first product is the J&B Rope. To understand data needs, you need to know a little about how it is prepared and dispensed. After each dessert Rope is prepared, it is wound in a roll. Although some sales are by the full roll, most are through special J&B dispensing machines that dispense Rope by the inch. To satisfy customer and dispensing machines needs, rolls are produced in three lengths. One of Barry's idiosyncrasies relates to his dislike for weight measurements. "After all" he says, "we're not selling hamburger." So for pricing and inventory purposes, he designates quantity by the inch.

3-1

This assignment, based on Jen & Barry's, is essentially a parallel to the room example of this chapter. You are to create a driver and dessert inventory class program. For your source files and project name, use the same format as the examples of this book, for instance, j01-dsrt.cbl for the dessert inventory class program. (This way your notation will be consistent with name selections in Chapter 4's assignment.) The dessert inventory class must contain the following:

Object data.

Item	Size	Value
Dessert ID	3 characters	100
Flavor description	10 characters, alphanumeric	Mello Blue
Roll length	2 digits	36
Rolls onhand	3 digits	100
Per inch cost	Dollars and cents (less than $10)	.75

The class definition must include the following two methods.

Method 1.

Calculate the Number of inches onhand (Roll length times Rolls onhand)
Return:
    Flavor description
    Roll length
    Rolls onhand
    Inches onhand

Method 2.

Calculate the Inventory value (Roll length times Rolls onhand times Per inch cost)
Return
    Flavor description
    Inventory value

The driver must:

1. Display a brief announcement screen describing what the program does
2. Give the user the choice of accessing data from either of the two methods.
3. Display the data returned from execution of the selected method.
4. Terminate.

Application #2 Description

Charlie Fibb and Al Cheetum, are avid scuba divers with several years experience in the travel agency business. Finally reaching the point of total frustration with boring, run-of-the-mill vacations, they decide to open their own "extreme" vacation agency. Through an arrangement with Underwater Habitats, Incorporated, they will lease fully self-sufficient, relocatable ocean-floor luxury living habitats. In turn, they will provide vacation "event" packages to the adventurous through their newly-formed company named Fibb & Cheetum Ultimate Adventures (abbreviated F&B).

    In addition to vacation-scheduling experience, they have a belief in both the power and the longevity of Cobol for business applications. It doesn't take them long to recognize the value of implementing object methodology. After a detailed object-oriented analysis and design phase, they begin work on the facility portion of the system.

3-2

This assignment, based on F&B, is essentially a parallel to Room04. You are to create driver and event class programs. For your source files and project name, use the same format as the examples of this book, for instance, f01-even.cbl for the event class program. (This way your notation will be consistent with name selections in Chapter 4's assignment.) The event class must contain the following:

Object data.

Item	Size	Value
Event ID	4 characters	1001
Event description	20 characters	Basin Exploration
Facility	7 characters	MIR-3
Duration	2 digits	07
Site	2 characters	A1
Daily rate	4 digits	1800

The class definition must include the following two methods.

Method 1.

Return:
    Event ID
    Event description
    Facility
    Duration

Method 2.

Calculate the Event cost
    (Duration times Daily rate)
Return:
    Event ID
    Event description
    Event cost

The driver must:

1. Display a brief announcement screen describing what the program does
2. Give the user the choice of accessing data from either of the two methods.
3. Display the data returned from execution of the selected method.
4. Terminate.

Using a Database Interface Class

Chapter Contents

Processing With an Instance Object 66
    Some Basics 66
    The Driver Program—r05-drvr 68
    The Object Handle 69
    Invoking a Method of the Newly Created Object 70
    The Class Program—R05-room 70
About Object Data 70
    Reviewing Room05 70
    Populating an Object 72
Using a Database Interface Class 73
    Expanding Room05 73
    DBI Class Description—R06-dbi 75
    The DBI Class Definition 75
    The Room Class—R06-room 77
    The Driver Program—R06-drvr 79
    Final Comment on Room06 79
Commentary on Data Types 80
Creating Multiple Instances 81
    Two Instances of the Room Class 81
    Subscripting Object Handles 83
Providing for Repetition 84
    The Driver Program Room07dr 84
    Multiple Instantiations of a Class 84
Summing Up 87
    Project Summary 87
    General Summary 87
Coming Up 87
Assignments 88

Chapter 4

Chapter Introduction

The class program examples of Chapter 3 provide your first insight to classes and objects with OOCobol. This chapter expands the room application to illustrate the following concepts.

- The distinction between a class and an object.
- Reading data from in indexed file via a database interface class.
- Create an object from a class definition using the Invoke statement.
- Placing data in an object (populating an object).
- Creating multiple instances of the room class.
- Repetition in the room program.

Processing With an Instance Object

Some Basics

From Chapter 3 you saw that the class program appears to take on the same role as a subprogram of Chapter 1. For instance, the representation of Room04 shown in Figure 4-1 is virtually identical to that of the program/subprogram pair in Chapter 1—see Figure 1-10. Defining the room object in the Factory makes this possible. Although this technique simplifies your first look at OOCobol syntax, it is not the way in which one implements object methodology. This chapter's examples define the room object in the OBJECT paragraph, the technique used for Room for the remainder of this book. It is a versatile approach that provides the capability for working with data for more than one room at any given time. As you will see, you will be able create multiple room objects during a processing activity.

Like a factory object, an instance object contains data that is accessible to a invoking program only through methods of the class definition. However, there is a

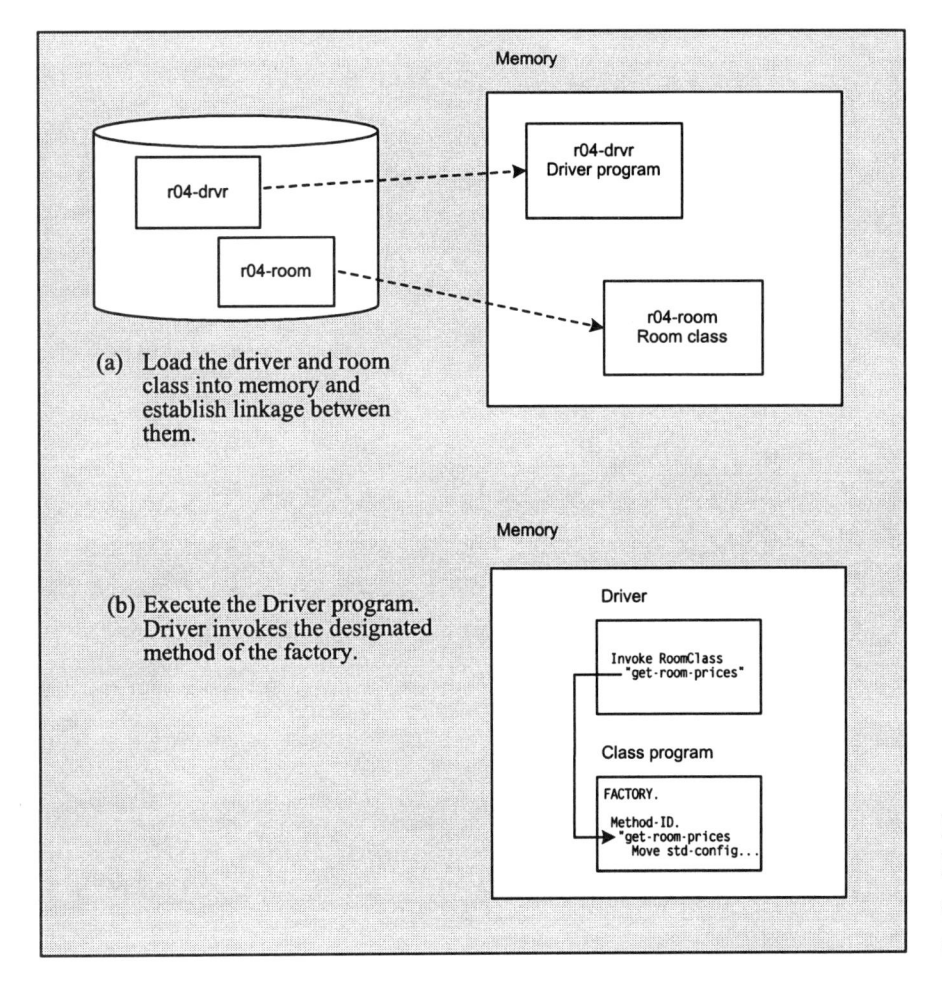

(a) Load the driver and room class into memory and establish linkage between them.

(b) Execute the Driver program. Driver invokes the designated method of the factory.

Figure 4-1. Loading and executing the driver/class pair.

significant difference: the definition of the instance object in the class program only serves as a template from which a "working" instance object can be created. The overall sequence of operation is illustrated by the depiction of Figure 4-2.

- In (a) Driver and Room are loaded into memory as with the program/subprogram pair.
- In (b) Driver creates an instance of Room (instantiates Room). The instance of the class is depicted by a six-sided box
- This instance, is then processed by Driver in (c).

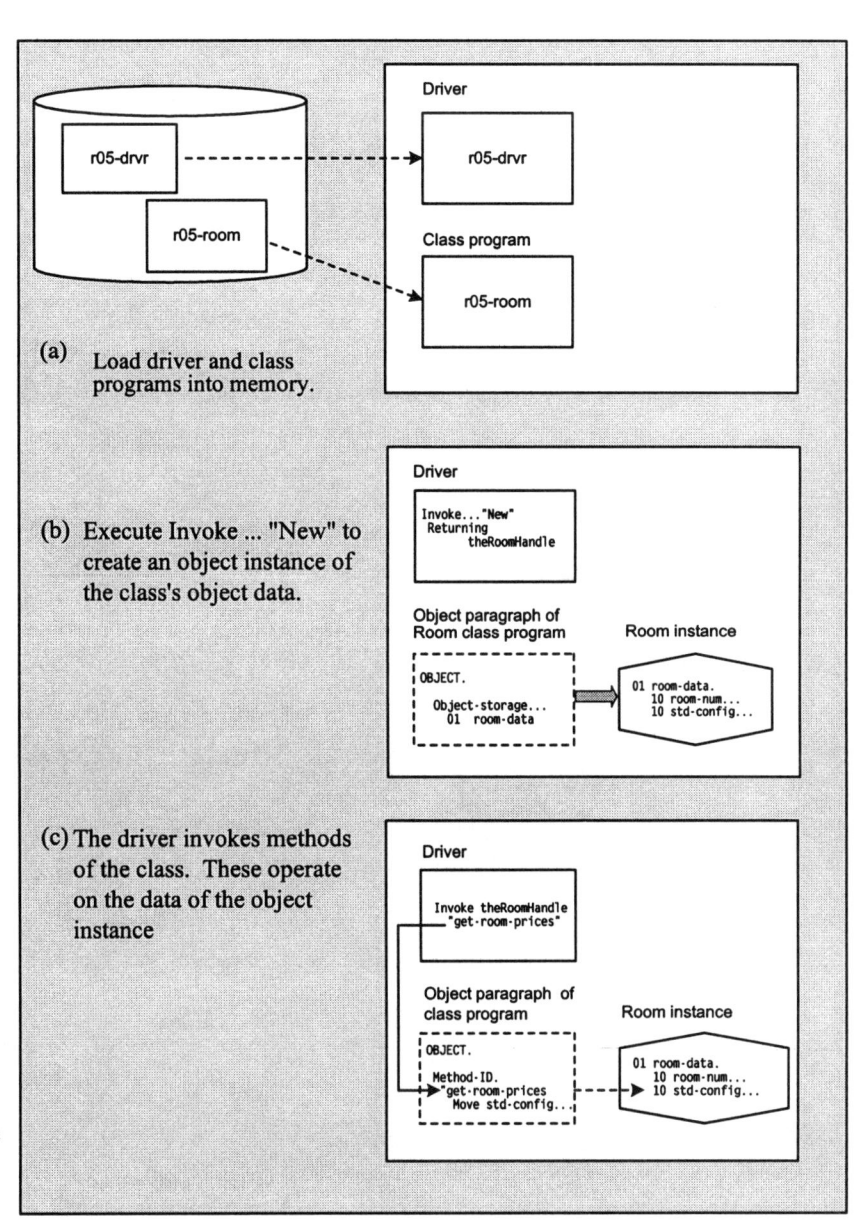

Figure 4-2. Processing with an instance object.

(a) Load driver and class programs into memory.

(b) Execute Invoke ... "New" to create an object instance of the class's object data.

(c) The driver invokes methods of the class. These operate on the data of the object instance

> To avoid "terminology confusion" regarding the words *factory* and *object*, usage in this book is as follows.
>
> **Factory definition**: Source code, located between the paragraph header FACTORY and its corresponding end marker END FACTORY.
>
> **Object definition**: Source code, located between the paragraph header OBJECT and its corresponding end marker END OBJECT.
>
> **Factory object**: The data items defined in the factory definition's Object-Storage Section. Also, includes File Section data items if the factory contains a file definition (Net Express only).
>
> **Instance object** or **Object**: A duplicate of the data items defined in the object definition's Object-Storage Section the result of instantiating a class. Also, includes File Section data items if the object contains a file definition (Net Express only).

The Driver Program—r05-drvr

Proj0401
Room05

The next example, Room05 stored in the folder Proj0401, illustrates creating an instance object. Let's first look at the following Invoke from Driver's lines 39 and 40 in Figure 4-3.

```
          $set sourceformat "free"
 1 *>*****************************************
 2 *> Room Rental System
 3 *> W. Price   Nov 23, 1999         R05-DRVR.CBL
 4 *>
 5 *> This driver provides the user a menu allowing
 6 *> for full room prices, discounted room prices,
 7 *> or room capacity.  It illustrates invoking
 8 *> different methods of the room class.
 9 *> The following classes comprise this project:
10 *>    r05-room    Room
11 *>*****************************************
12
13 Identification Division.
14       Program-ID.  Room05Driver.
15
16 Environment Division.
17       Object Section.
18          Class-control.
19             RoomClass is class "r05-room"
20             .
21 Data Division.
22    Working-Storage Section.
23
24       01 room-prices.
25          10 std-config-price      pic 9(03).
26          10 spec-config-price     pic 9(03).
27       01 room-capacity            pic 9(02).
28
29       01 menu-choice              pic X(01).
30          88 discounted-prices        value "D" "d".
31          88 standard-prices          value "S" "s".
32
33       01 theRoomHandle   usage object reference.
34
35 Procedure Division.
36    000-process-room-data.
37
38       *> Create an instance of the room object
39       Invoke RoomClass "new"
40                      Returning theRoomHandle
41       Perform 850-get-menu-selection
42       Evaluate TRUE
43          When discounted-prices
44             Invoke theRoomHandle
45                         "get-discounted-room-prices"
46                         Returning room-prices
47             Perform 900-display-room-prices
48          When standard-prices
49             Invoke theRoomHandle "get-room-prices"
50                         Returning room-prices
51             Perform 900-display-room-prices
52          When other
53             Invoke theRoomHandle "get-room-capacity"
54                         Returning room-capacity
55             Perform 950-display-room-capacity
56       End-evaluate *>TRUE
57       Stop run
58       .
59    850-get-menu-selection.
60       Display " "
61       Display "The options are:"
62       Display "   C - Room capacity (default)"
63       Display "   S - Standard room prices"
64       Display "   D - Discounted room prices"
65       Display " "
66       Display "Your choice <C,S,D>? " no advancing
67       Accept menu-choice
68       .
69    900-display-room-prices.
70       Display " "
71       Display "Standard configuration price: "
72                                     std-config-price
73       Display "Special configuration price: "
74                                     spec-config-price
75       .
76    950-display-room-capacity.
77       Display " "
78       Display "Room capacity: " room-capacity
```

Figure 4-3. Driver—r05-drvr.

```
Invoke RoomClass "new"
          Returning theRoomHandle
```

To instantiate the instance object definition of a class, you must make available three items of information.

1. The internal name you have designated to represent this class definition (RoomClass in this case, see line 19).
2. The word new, the name of a method for instantiating classes (creating the object). Be aware that new is not a method of RoomClass. It is available to RoomClass through one of the components of the class library furnished with every object-oriented Cobol compiler. Remember that in this book, class names use uppercase for the first letter of each word comprising the name; hyphens are not used.
3. A Returning parameter listing a data item that will contain the the newly created object's location and other information about.

The Object Handle

As defined in this program, RoomClass refers to the room class, see the entry at line 19 of Figure 4-3. When you create an instance of the class, that object is a separate entity from the class. You do *not* have access to it through the class name. Your access is through the **object handle** designated as a parameter in the Invoke statement that creates the instance as illustrated in Figure 4-4. In this example, the name of this identifier is theRoomHandle (refer to line 40 of the program). You see this data item defined in line 33 by the following:

```
01  theRoomHandle      usage is object reference.
```

Object reference is a new data type introduced with OOCobol specifically to give you access to objects you create. You will learn more about object handles later in this chapter. In this book, object-handle names follow the same rules as class names except letters of the first word are all lower case.

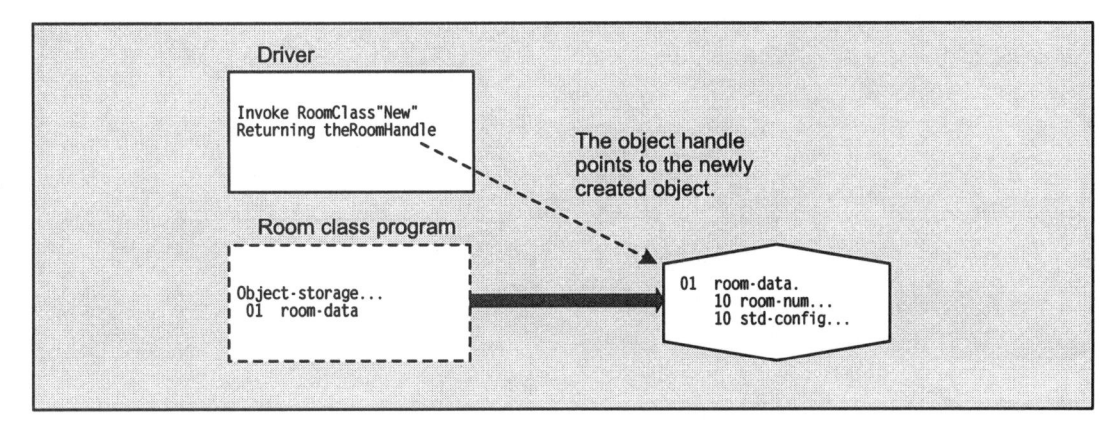

Figure 4-4. The object handle.

Invoking a Method of the Newly Created Object

Now let's compare any of the three Invoke statements from this program, in which the instance object is used, to its counterpart of the Chapter 3 example in which the factory object is used. For example, with the instance object (Figure 4-3's lines 49 and 50) you have:

```
Invoke theRoomHandle "get-room-prices"
                    Returning room-prices
```

Correspondingly with the factory object of Figure 3-7 you have:

```
Invoke RoomClass "get-room-prices"
                Returning room-prices
```

Remember from the general form description in Chapter three that the entry following the keyword Invoke must be either an object handle or a class name. The former causes a method of the Object paragraph to be executed; the latter causes a method of the Factory paragraph to be executed. Be aware that the Factory and the Object are totally independent of one another. If you use the naming technique of this book, a glance at your code tells you which type of object you are referencing, factory or instance. That is,

- theRoomHandle in which the first letter of the first word is lower case, immediately identifies (for you, not the system) that this is an instance method.
- RoomClass in which the first letter of every word is upper case, immediately identifies (for you, not the system) that this is a factory method.

The Class Program—R05-room

In the class program of Figure 4-5 you see that the only change from the corresponding class program of Chapter 3 is placement of the object definition under the OBJECT paragraph.

About Object Data

Reviewing Room05

Before proceeding, let's view the driver and the class of Room05 from the perspective of the actions taken by each program.

Driver
    Provide overall program control
    Query user
    Create a room object
    Access room data
    Display results

Using a Database Interface Class

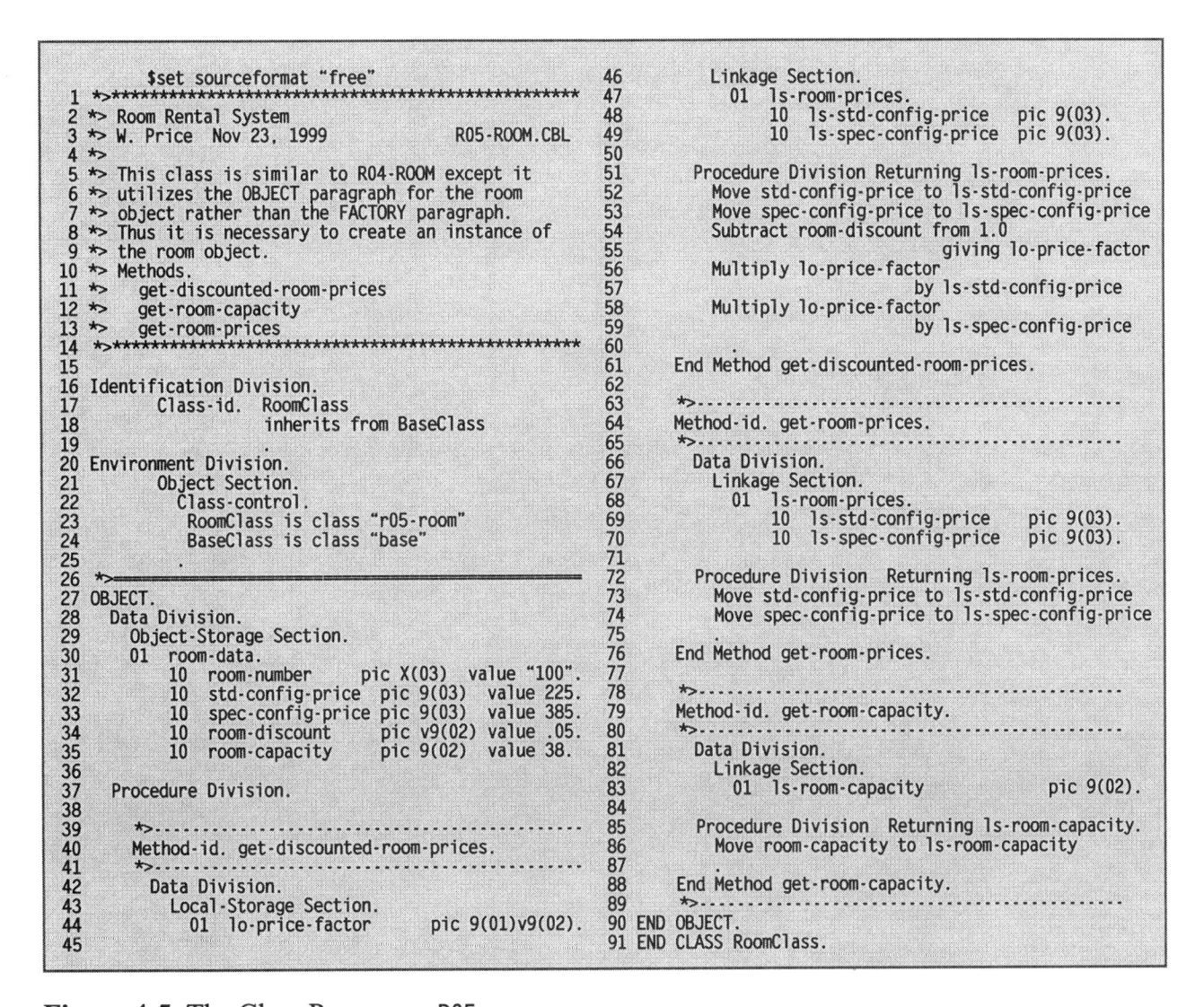

```
            $set sourceformat "free"
1  *>***************************************************
2  *> Room Rental System
3  *> W. Price  Nov 23, 1999            R05-ROOM.CBL
4  *>
5  *> This class is similar to R04-ROOM except it
6  *> utilizes the OBJECT paragraph for the room
7  *> object rather than the FACTORY paragraph.
8  *> Thus it is necessary to create an instance of
9  *> the room object.
10 *> Methods.
11 *>    get-discounted-room-prices
12 *>    get-room-capacity
13 *>    get-room-prices
14 *>***************************************************
15
16 Identification Division.
17      Class-id. RoomClass
18                inherits from BaseClass
19           .
20 Environment Division.
21      Object Section.
22         Class-control.
23            RoomClass is class "r05-room"
24            BaseClass is class "base"
25            .
26 *>═══════════════════════════════════════════════════
27 OBJECT.
28   Data Division.
29     Object-Storage Section.
30      01 room-data.
31         10 room-number      pic X(03)   value "100".
32         10 std-config-price pic 9(03)   value 225.
33         10 spec-config-price pic 9(03)  value 385.
34         10 room-discount    pic v9(02)  value .05.
35         10 room-capacity    pic 9(02)   value 38.
36
37   Procedure Division.
38
39      *>.............................................
40      Method-id. get-discounted-room-prices.
41      *>.............................................
42        Data Division.
43          Local-Storage Section.
44            01 lo-price-factor    pic 9(01)v9(02).
45
46          Linkage Section.
47            01 ls-room-prices.
48               10 ls-std-config-price   pic 9(03).
49               10 ls-spec-config-price  pic 9(03).
50
51        Procedure Division Returning ls-room-prices.
52          Move std-config-price to ls-std-config-price
53          Move spec-config-price to ls-spec-config-price
54          Subtract room-discount from 1.0
55                            giving lo-price-factor
56          Multiply lo-price-factor
57                            by ls-std-config-price
58          Multiply lo-price-factor
59                            by ls-spec-config-price
60          .
61      End Method get-discounted-room-prices.
62
63      *>.............................................
64      Method-id. get-room-prices.
65      *>.............................................
66        Data Division.
67          Linkage Section.
68            01 ls-room-prices.
69               10 ls-std-config-price   pic 9(03).
70               10 ls-spec-config-price  pic 9(03).
71
72        Procedure Division  Returning ls-room-prices.
73          Move std-config-price to ls-std-config-price
74          Move spec-config-price to ls-spec-config-price
75          .
76      End Method get-room-prices.
77
78      *>.............................................
79      Method-id. get-room-capacity.
80      *>.............................................
81        Data Division.
82          Linkage Section.
83            01 ls-room-capacity          pic 9(02).
84
85        Procedure Division  Returning ls-room-capacity.
86          Move room-capacity to ls-room-capacity
87          .
88      End Method get-room-capacity.
89      *>.............................................
90 END OBJECT.
91 END CLASS RoomClass.
```

Figure 4-5. The Class Program—R05-room.

Room Class
Return room prices
Return discounted room prices
Return room capacity

We can think of these as the **responsibilities** of each of these two components. Communication between the two components is illustrated in Figure 4-6.

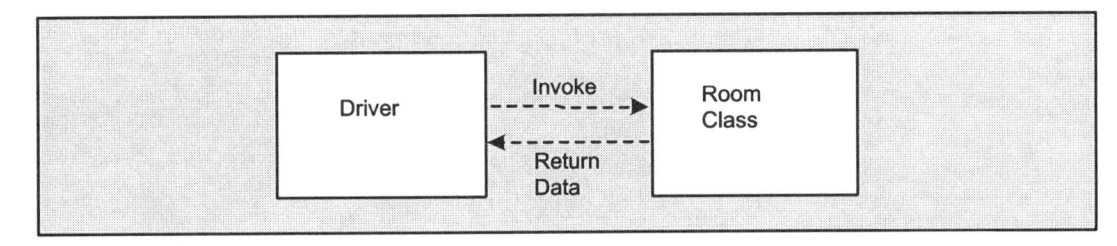

Figure 4-6. Relationship between the driver and the room class.

There are two important points regarding this example that have significant implications for the next example. First, neither Driver nor any other program can directly access the data of the room object. The only access is through methods of the room class. That is, if you must read or change any of the object's data, the class from which the object was created must include a method to perform the action. Second, access to the object is through the object handle. Since Driver created the room object (by invoking the method new), the object handle was returned to Driver. In other words, Driver "owns" the handle and thus "knows" where the object is located in memory.

Populating an Object

Declaring the data with Value clauses in the previous examples is a good way to get a first look at OOCobol. However, that technique has little practical value for most applications. Usually you will create an object and then **populate** it (place data in it). The data to populate an object may be data entered from the keyboard or it may be data from files. In fact, data you often see in an object has the appearance of a single record or part of a record from a data file. (Or it may even be data from two or more records.)

Remember from the previous example (r05-room) that you access an object's data through methods of the class from which the object was created. This is illustrated in code segments of Figure 4-7 extracted from the programs of Room05.

As you might suspect, the technique for populating an object is much the same as that for accessing data from an object. That is, you must include a method in the

```
Driver

Working-Storage Section.
01  room-prices.
    10  std-config-price      pic 9(03).
    10  spec-config-price     pic 9(03).
...
Invoke theRoomHandle "get-room-prices"
       Returning room-prices
```

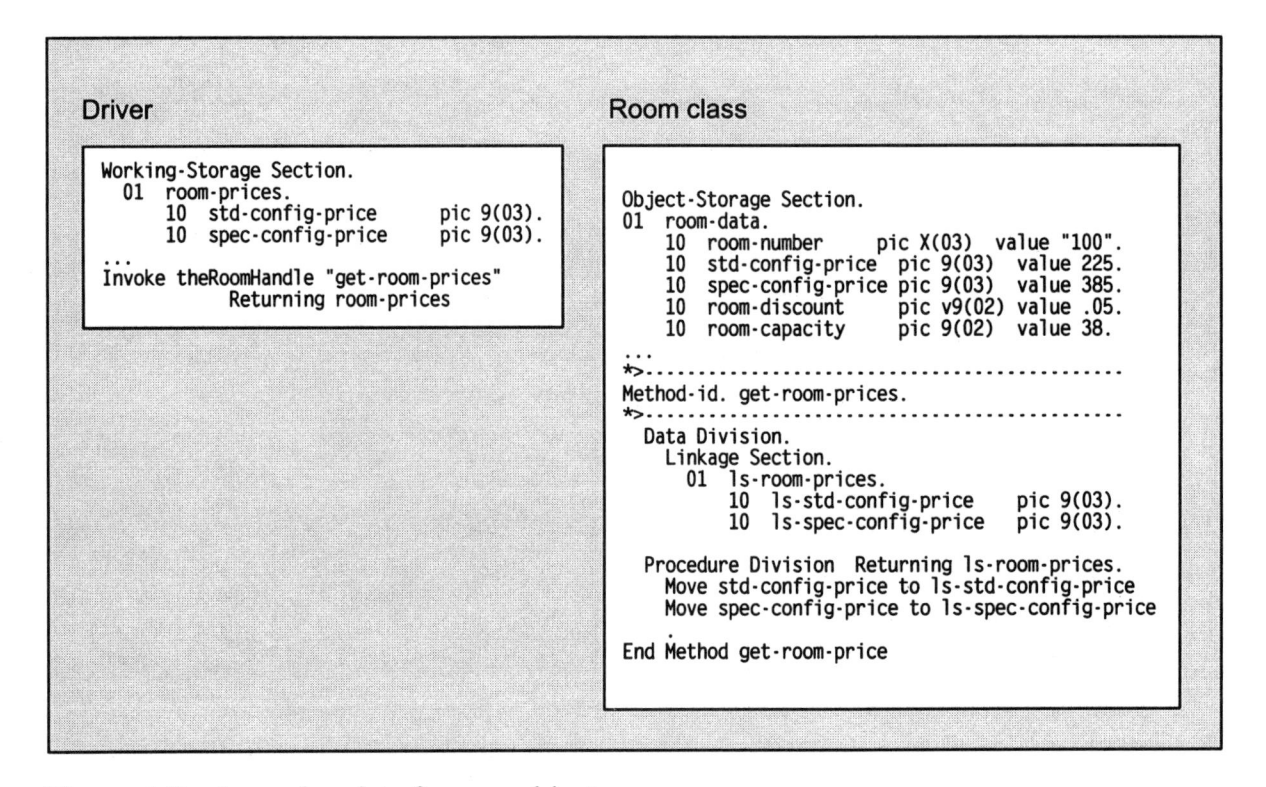

```
Room class

Object-Storage Section.
01  room-data.
    10  room-number       pic X(03)  value "100".
    10  std-config-price  pic 9(03)  value 225.
    10  spec-config-price pic 9(03)  value 385.
    10  room-discount     pic v9(02) value .05.
    10  room-capacity     pic 9(02)  value 38.
...
*>...........................................
Method-id. get-room-prices.
*>...........................................
    Data Division.
        Linkage Section.
        01  ls-room-prices.
            10  ls-std-config-price   pic 9(03).
            10  ls-spec-config-price  pic 9(03).

    Procedure Division Returning ls-room-prices.
        Move std-config-price to ls-std-config-price
        Move spec-config-price to ls-spec-config-price
.
End Method get-room-price
```

Figure 4-7. Accessing data from an object.

class definition that can be invoked by another program. In Figure 4-8 you see code segments that illustrate how you might populate price data of the room object with data entered from the keyboard of a driver program.

Using a Database Interface Class

Expanding Room05

The skeleton of Figure 4-8's Driver uses data entered from the keyboard to populate the object. If you inspect Room's method, you will see that it "doesn't care" where the data comes from. That is, the method populate-the-room-object could be invoked by Driver or by any other program of the project. The source could be the keyboard or a file or from program computations.

This chapter expands the room application to include populating the room object with data from an indexed file. The sequence of events in processing a user request now becomes something like the following.

1. Accept a room number from the user.
2. Read the file to obtain the room record for the requested room.
3. Extract the data needed for the room object from the record.
4. Create a room object (instantiate Room).
5. Populate the room object with data obtained from the room record.
6. Access user-requested data from the object.
7. Display the results for the user.

```
Driver

Working-Storage Section.
  01 room-prices.
     10 std-config-price     pic 9(03).
     10 spec-config-price    pic 9(03).
     ...

Invoke RoomClass "new"
       Returning theRoomHandle

Display "Enter the standard config price "
Accept std-config-price
Display "Enter the special config price "
Accept spec-config-price

Invoke theRoomHandle
       "populate-room-object-prices"
       Using room-prices
```

```
Room class

Object-Storage Section.
  01 room-data.
     10 room-number       pic X(03) value "100".
     10 std-config-price  pic 9(03) value 225.
     10 spec-config-price pic 9(03) value 385.
     10 room-discount     pic v9(02) value .05.
     10 room-capacity     pic 9(02) value 38.
  ...
*>......................................
Method-id. populate-room-object-prices.
*>......................................
  Data Division.
    Linkage Section.
      01 ls-room-prices.
         10 ls-std-config-price   pic 9(03).
         10 ls-spec-config-price  pic 9(03).

  Procedure Division Returning ls-room-prices.
    Move ls-std-config-price to std-config-price
    Move ls-spec-config-price to spec-config-price
  .
End Method populate-room-object-prices
```

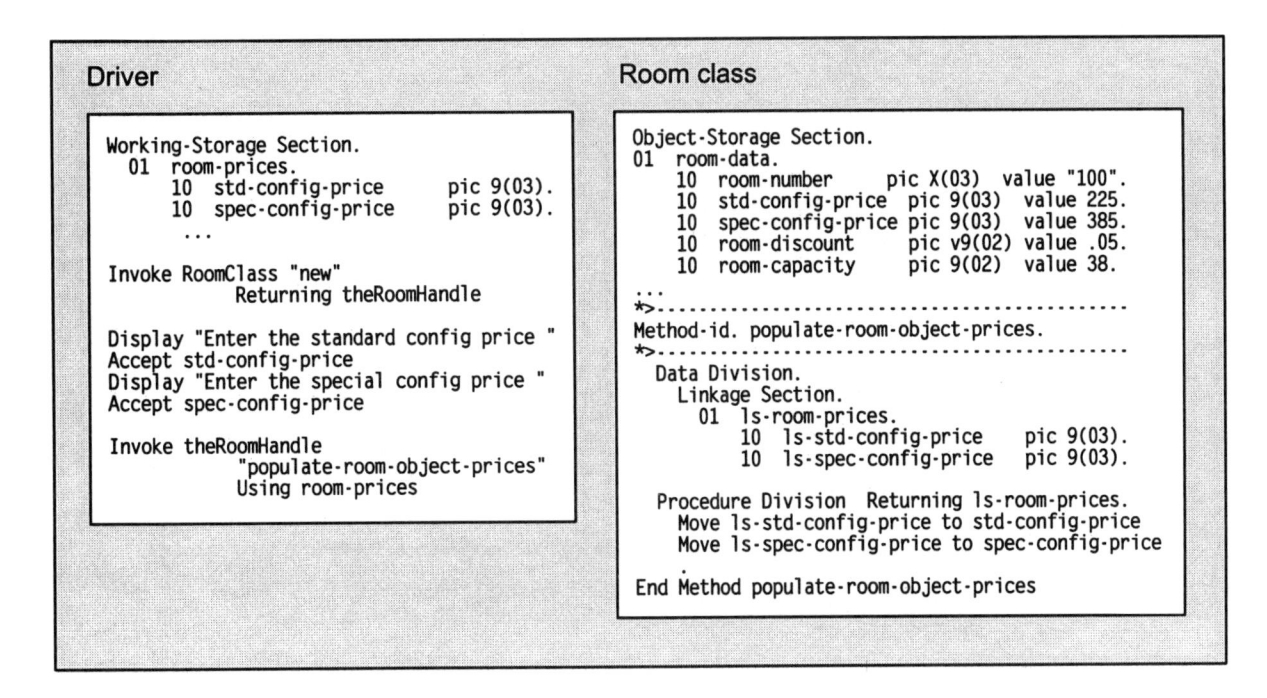

Figure 4-8. Populating an object.

As you will learn in Chapter 6, good design suggests creating another class for the purpose of accessing files (or databases) for data required by the application. Accordingly, the next example consists of three components: Driver, the room class Room, and a **database interface** class DBI. In addition to the tasks of Room05's driver, this driver will also instantiate Room and populate the room object. [Note: In the first edition of this book I assigned that responsibility to DBI. I now consider that a poor design decision. Chapter 6 discusses the design considerations.] Responsibilities of the various components of Room06 will be something like the following.

Driver
> Provide overall program control
> Query user for a room number
> Instantiate Room (create a room object)
> Populate room object
> Query user for information request
> Access room data
> Display results

Room class
> Accept room data from DBI
> Return room prices
> Return discounted room prices
> Return room capacity

DBI class
> Open and close room file
> Read the designated record
> Return data needed for room object

Relationships between these three components of Room06 are illustrated in Figure 4-9

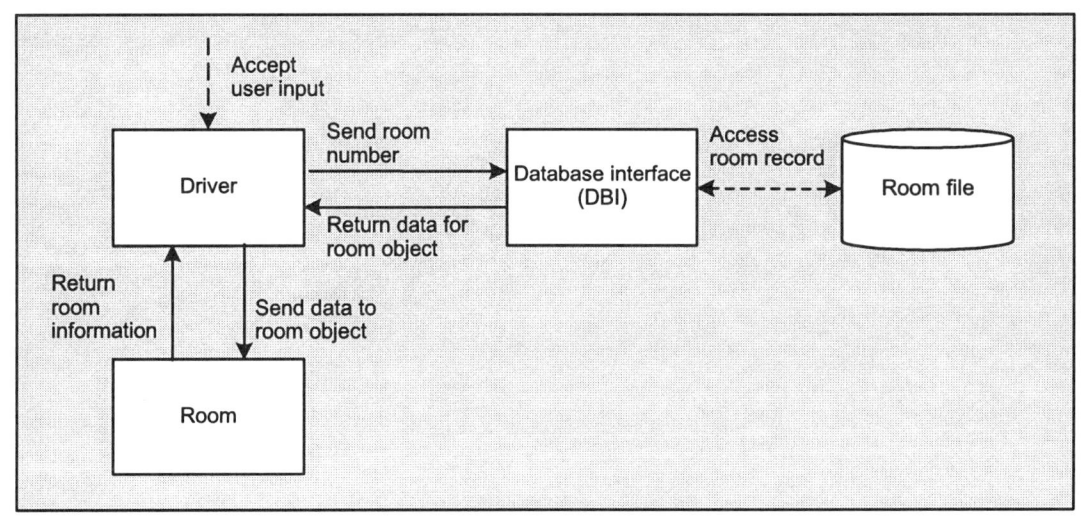

Figure 4-9. Relationships between Driver, Room, and DBI.

DBI Class Description—R06-dbi

Before analyzing the DBI class program, read the following description of this class.

Class   r06-dbi

Description   This class provides access to the room indexed file. It accepts a requested room number and searches for the desired record. If the record is found, it is stored as the factory's object data.

Class methods

open-file Opens the file for random access.
   Input: None
   Output: None

close-file Closes the file.
   Input: None
   Output: None

read-room-file
   Input
      Room number   pic X(03)
   Output
      A record-found switch   pic X(01)
         Record found   Value: Y
         Record not found   Value: N

get-room-data
   Input: None
   Output
      A data item containing the following.
         room number   pic X(03)
         standard configuration price pic 9(03)
         special configuration price   pic 9(03)
         room discount   pic v9(02)
         room capacity   pic 9(02)

The DBI Class Definition

The database interface class definition (DBI) in Figure 4-10 processes the indexed file room.di. File processing in class programs is described in Chapter 7, so do not be concerned with details of the file definition entries here: the important program elements for this discussion are as follows.

1. This class has no Instance Object code; everything is defined in the Factory.
2. The class includes four methods: close-file, open-file, and read-room-file, and get-room-data.
3. The open-file and close-file methods include no input or output parameters—see the respective Procedure Division headers (lines 93 and 59).

```
          $set sourceformat "free"
 1 *>***************************************************
 2 *> Room Rental System
 3 *> W. Price  Nov 22, 1999              R06-DBI.CBL
 4 *>
 5 *> This class definition is the database
 6 *> interface for the ROOM system.  It reads a
 7 *> requested record from the indexed file ROOM.DI
 8 *> Object methods
 9 *>    close-file
10 *>    get-room-data
11 *>    open-file
12 *>    read-room-file
13 *>***************************************************
14
15 Identification Division.
16       Class-ID.  RoomDatabaseInterface
17                  inherits from BaseClass.
18
19 Environment Division.
20       Object Section.
21       Class-control.
22           RoomDatabaseInterface is class "r06-dbi"
23           BaseClass             is class "base"
24           .
25
26 *>=
27 FACTORY.
28
29     Environment Division.
30        Input-Output Section.
31        File-Control.
32          Select room-file
33               assign to "c:\eooc2\eData\room.di"
34               organization is indexed
35               access is random
36               record key is rr-room-number.
37
38     Data Division.
39       File Section.
40       FD Room-File.
41       01 room-record.
42          10 rr-room-number            pic x(03).
43          10 rr-acctg-code             pic x(10).
44          10 rr-room-type              pic x(03).
45          10 rr-std-config-price       pic 9(03).
46          10 rr-spec-config-price      pic 9(03).
47          10 rr-pricing-code           pic 9(01).
48          10 rr-room-discount          pic v9(02).
49          10 rr-room-capacity          pic 9(02).
50          10 rr-room-width             pic 9(02).
51          10 rr-room-length            pic 9(02).
52          10 rr-work-stations          pic 9(02).
53          10 rr-work-station-capacity  pic 9(01).
54
55     Procedure Division.
56 *>.................................................
57     Method-ID. close-file.
58 *>.................................................
59     Procedure Division.
60        Close room-file
61        .
62     End Method close-file.
63
64 *>.................................................
65 Method-ID. get-room-data.
66 *>.................................................
67    Data Division.
68      Linkage Section.
69      01 ls-room-object-data.
70         10 ls-room-number            pic x(03).
71         10 ls-std-config-price       pic 9(03).
72         10 ls-spec-config-price      pic 9(03).
73         10 ls-room-discount          pic v9(02).
74         10 ls-room-capacity          pic 9(02).
75
76    Procedure Division
77                Returning ls-room-object-data.
78       Move rr-room-number to ls-room-number
79       Move rr-std-config-price
80               to ls-std-config-price
81       Move rr-spec-config-price
82               to ls-spec-config-price
83       Move rr-room-discount
84               to ls-room-discount
85       Move rr-room-capacity
86               to ls-room-capacity
87       .
88    End Method get-room-data.
89
90 *>.................................................
91 Method-ID. open-file.
92 *>.................................................
93    Procedure Division.
94       Open input room-file
95       .
96    End Method open-file.
97
98 *>.................................................
99 Method-ID. read-room-file.
100 *>.................................................
101    Data Division.
102      Linkage Section.
103      01 ls-room-number              pic x(03).
104      01 ls-record-found-sw          pic X(01).
105         88 ls-record-found          value "Y".
106         88 ls-record-not-found      value "N".
107
108    Procedure Division Using ls-room-number
109                 Returning ls-record-found-sw.
110       Move ls-room-number to rr-room-number
111       Read Room-File
112          Invalid key
113              Set ls-record-not-found to true
114          Not invalid key
115              Set ls-record-found to true
116       End-Read *>Room-File
117       .
118    End Method read-room-file.
119 *>.................................................
120 END FACTORY.
121 END CLASS RoomDatabaseInterface.
```

Figure 4-10. The database interface class—r06-dbi.

4. From the Procedure Division header (lines 108 and 109) you see that the read-room-file method requires one input item (ls-room-number defined at line 103) and one output item defined (ls-record-found-sw defined at line 104). The file is read at line 111 of the read-room-file method.
   • If the requested room does not exist, the Invalid key option is executed and the output parameter is set to ls-record-not-found (value N).

- If the requested room exists, the Not invalid key option is executed and the output parameter is set to ls-record-found (value Y).
4. The method get-room-data (beginning line 65) provides access to fields of the file record required to populate the room object.

The Room Class—R06-room

Following is a description of r06-room, the room class program for this project. You now see four methods: three for accessing data from the object (same as r05-room) and the new one populate-the-room-object.

Class   r06-room

Description   This class contains and manages data for one room.

Class methods

   get-discounted-room-prices
      Purpose
         Return discounted room prices from the room object.
      Output
         A data item containing:

Standard room price	pic 9(03)
Special room price	pic 9(03)

   get-room-capacity
      Purpose
         Return room capacity from the room data of the object.
      Output

Room capacity	pic 9(02)

   get-room-prices
      Purpose
         Return room prices from the room object.
      Output
         An 01 data-item containing

Standard room price	pic 9(03)
Discounted room price	pic 9(03)

   populate-the-room-object
      Purpose
         Accept data from the invoking program and populate the class's object data.
      Input
         A data item containing

Room number	pic X(03)
Standard configuration room price	pic 9(03)
Special configuration room price	pic 9(03)
Room discount	pic v9(03)
Room capacity	pic 9(02)

Compare the program listing of Figure 4-11 for this version of Room to that of r05-room (Figure 4-5) and you will see that the first three methods are identical. The new method, populate-the-room-object, is at lines 90-104. As data is now placed into the object by this method, the Value clauses have been removed from these data items (see lines 32-36).

```
 1         $set sourceformat "free"
 2  *>***********************************************
 3  *> Room Rental System
 4  *> W. Price  Nov 22, 1999                R06-ROOM.CBL
 5  *>
 6  *> This class is same as  R05-ROOM except:
 7  *>    Value clauses are eliminated from the
 8  *>    object data.
 9  *> Methods.
10  *>    get-discounted-room-prices
11  *>    get-room-capacity
12  *>    get-room-prices
13  *>    populate-the-room-object
14  *>
15  *>***********************************************
16  Identification Division.
17       Class-id.   RoomClass
18                   inherits from BaseClass
19
20  Environment Division.
21       Object Section.
22          Class-control.
23             RoomClass is class "r06-room"
24             BaseClass is class "base"
25             .
26  *>==================================================
27
28  OBJECT.
29    Data Division.
30       Object-Storage Section.
31       01  room-data.
32           10  room-number       pic X(03).
33           10  std-config-price  pic 9(03).
34           10  spec-config-price pic 9(03).
35           10  room-discount     pic v9(02).
36           10  room-capacity     pic 9(02).
37
38    Procedure Division.
39  *>--------------------------------------------------
40       Method-id. get-discounted-room-prices.
41  *>--------------------------------------------------
42       Data Division.
43          Local-Storage Section.
44          01  lo-price-factor     pic 9(01)v9(02).
45          Linkage Section.
46          01  ls-room-prices.
47              10  ls-std-config-price  pic 9(03).
48              10  ls-spec-config-price pic 9(03).
49
50       Procedure Division Returning ls-room-prices.
51          Subtract room-discount from 1.0
52                            giving lo-price-factor
53          Multiply lo-price-factor
54                            by std-config-price
55                            giving ls-std-config-price
56          Multiply lo-price-factor
57                            by spec-config-price
58                            giving ls-spec-config-price
59          .
60       End Method get-discounted-room-prices.
61
62  *>--------------------------------------------------
63       Method-id. get-room-prices.
64  *>--------------------------------------------------
65       Data Division.
66          Linkage Section.
67          01  ls-room-prices.
68              10  ls-std-config-price   pic 9(03).
69              10  ls-spec-config-price  pic 9(03).
70
71       Procedure Division  Returning ls-room-prices.
72          Move std-config-price to ls-std-config-price
73          Move spec-config-price to ls-spec-config-price
74          .
75       End Method get-room-prices.
76
77  *>--------------------------------------------------
78       Method-id. get-room-capacity.
79  *>--------------------------------------------------
80       Data Division.
81          Linkage Section.
82          01  ls-room-capacity          pic 9(02).
83
84       Procedure Division  Returning ls-room-capacity.
85          Move room-capacity to ls-room-capacity
86          .
87       End Method get-room-capacity.
88
89  *>--------------------------------------------------
90       Method-id. populate-the-room-object.
91  *>--------------------------------------------------
92       Data Division.
93          Linkage Section.
94          01  ls-room-data.
95              10  ls-room-number       pic X(03).
96              10  ls-std-config-price  pic 9(03).
97              10  ls-spec-config-price pic 9(03).
98              10  ls-room-discount     pic v9(02).
99              10  ls-room-capacity     pic 9(02).
100
101      Procedure Division  Using ls-room-data.
102         Move ls-room-data to room-data
103         .
104      End Method populate-the-room-object.
105 *>--------------------------------------------------
106 END OBJECT.
107 END CLASS RoomClass.
```

Figure 4-11. The room class—r06-room.

The Driver Program—R06-drvr

From an earlier description, you know that Driver for this application has the following responsibilities.

> Provide overall program control
> Query user for a room number
> Instantiate Room (create a room object)
> Populate room object
> Query user for information request
> Access room data
> Display results

Now look at Figure 4-12 and notice the following features of this driver.

- As Driver will communicate with DBI as well as Room, the DBI class program is identified in the Class-control paragraph (see line 20).
- The 000 module (beginning line 46) opens the file, processes the user request, closes the file, and terminates processing.
- The user is queried for the desired room number in the 800 module (performed from line 53).
- Look at the Invoke at lines 54-56. The room number is the input parameter to the DBI. The returned parameter (record-found-sw defined at line 36) indicates whether of not the requested record was found.
    - If the record was found, Room is instantiated and populated (refer to lines 58 and 65-71) and the request is processed (line 59).
    - If the record was not found, the program displays an error message (line 61). Execution returns to the 000 module whereby the file is closed and processing terminated.
- The 250 module accesses data required for the room object (lines 65 and 66), instantiates Room (lines 67 and 68) and populates the room object (lines 69-71).

Final Comment on Room06

If you sit back and review the three components of this application, you could easily reach the conclusion that a room class is not unnecessary. You only need look at lines 26-31 of Figure 4-12's Driver (they define data needed for the room object) to realize that all data necessary to process the user request is available within Driver. You could argue that the room object adds nothing but complexity to the example. However, that approach is very limited in its scope and subverts the many powerful of object methodology. For instance, the next example illustrates concurrently having information on more than one room available. Furthermore, in later chapters you will see some of the many benefits of this approach.

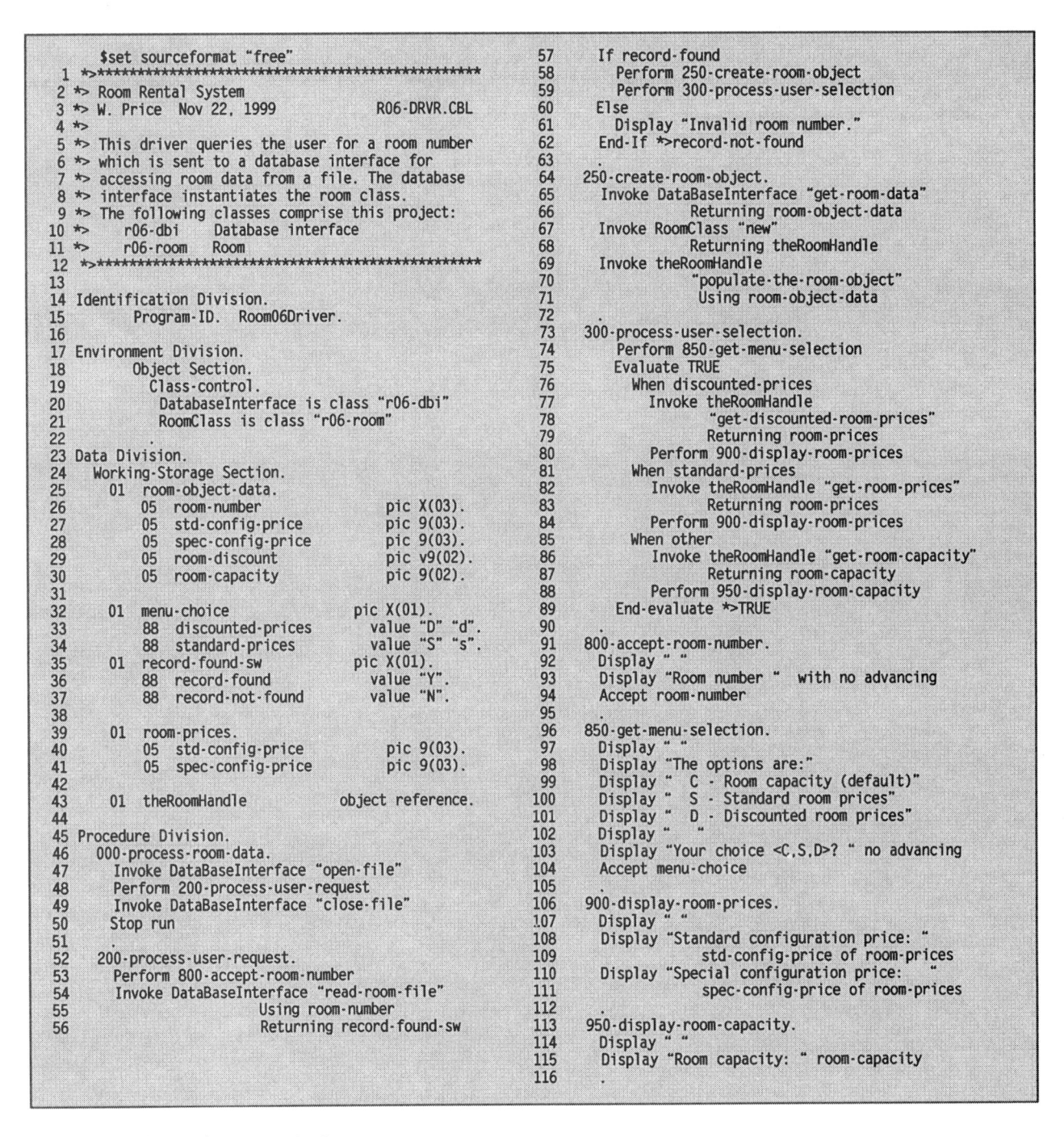

```cobol
       $set sourceformat "free"
1  *>*****************************************
2  *> Room Rental System
3  *> W. Price  Nov 22, 1999          R06-DRVR.CBL
4  *>
5  *> This driver queries the user for a room number
6  *> which is sent to a database interface for
7  *> accessing room data from a file. The database
8  *> interface instantiates the room class.
9  *> The following classes comprise this project:
10 *>     r06-dbi    Database interface
11 *>     r06-room   Room
12 *>*****************************************
13
14 Identification Division.
15      Program-ID.  Room06Driver.
16
17 Environment Division.
18      Object Section.
19         Class-control.
20            DatabaseInterface is class "r06-dbi"
21            RoomClass is class "r06-room"
22
23 Data Division.
24      Working-Storage Section.
25      01  room-object-data.
26          05  room-number          pic X(03).
27          05  std-config-price     pic 9(03).
28          05  spec-config-price    pic 9(03).
29          05  room-discount        pic v9(02).
30          05  room-capacity        pic 9(02).
31
32      01  menu-choice              pic X(01).
33          88  discounted-prices    value "D" "d".
34          88  standard-prices      value "S" "s".
35      01  record-found-sw          pic X(01).
36          88  record-found         value "Y".
37          88  record-not-found     value "N".
38
39      01  room-prices.
40          05  std-config-price     pic 9(03).
41          05  spec-config-price    pic 9(03).
42
43      01  theRoomHandle            object reference.
44
45 Procedure Division.
46      000-process-room-data.
47          Invoke DataBaseInterface "open-file"
48          Perform 200-process-user-request
49          Invoke DataBaseInterface "close-file"
50          Stop run
51          .
52      200-process-user-request.
53          Perform 800-accept-room-number
54          Invoke DataBaseInterface "read-room-file"
55                  Using room-number
56                  Returning record-found-sw
57          If record-found
58              Perform 250-create-room-object
59              Perform 300-process-user-selection
60          Else
61              Display "Invalid room number."
62          End-If *>record-not-found
63          .
64      250-create-room-object.
65          Invoke DataBaseInterface "get-room-data"
66                  Returning room-object-data
67          Invoke RoomClass "new"
68                  Returning theRoomHandle
69          Invoke theRoomHandle
70                  "populate-the-room-object"
71                  Using room-object-data
72          .
73      300-process-user-selection.
74          Perform 850-get-menu-selection
75          Evaluate TRUE
76              When discounted-prices
77                  Invoke theRoomHandle
78                          "get-discounted-room-prices"
79                          Returning room-prices
80                  Perform 900-display-room-prices
81              When standard-prices
82                  Invoke theRoomHandle "get-room-prices"
83                          Returning room-prices
84                  Perform 900-display-room-prices
85              When other
86                  Invoke theRoomHandle "get-room-capacity"
87                          Returning room-capacity
88                  Perform 950-display-room-capacity
89          End-evaluate *>TRUE
90          .
91      800-accept-room-number.
92          Display " "
93          Display "Room number " with no advancing
94          Accept room-number
95          .
96      850-get-menu-selection.
97          Display " "
98          Display "The options are:"
99          Display "   C - Room capacity (default)"
100         Display "   S - Standard room prices"
101         Display "   D - Discounted room prices"
102         Display " "
103         Display "Your choice <C,S,D>? " no advancing
104         Accept menu-choice
105         .
106     900-display-room-prices.
107         Display " "
108         Display "Standard configuration price: "
109                  std-config-price of room-prices
110         Display "Special configuration price:  "
111                  spec-config-price of room-prices
112         .
113     950-display-room-capacity.
114         Display " "
115         Display "Room capacity: " room-capacity
116         .
```

Figure 4-12. Driver—r06-drvr.

Commentary on Data Types

On first exposure to object handles it is easy to view them as something completely different from anything you've seen before. But don't be confused, they are simply identifiers of a particular usage type that allow you to refer to an object. For a broader view of data types, consider the following four examples.

```
10   sample-number       pic 9(04)   usage packed-decimal.
10   sample-alpha        pic X(04)   usage display.
10   sample-index                    usage index.
10   sampleObjectHandle              usage object reference.
```

Here you see four data items, each different from the other in type. You are quite familiar with the "ordinary" X and 9 data types. The item `sample-number` is a four-digit number with an internal packed-decimal data format. You can you place data in it with a Move or an arithmetic operation, or you can copy its contents to another data item, or you can display its value. In spite of its internal format, you see it as simply a numeric item. The item `sample-alpha` is a four-character field with an internal format that corresponds to the code set of the computer (ASCII or EBCDIC). Like `sample-number`, you can use it in statements such as Move and Display, but you cannot use it in arithmetic statements.

The third example, `sample-index`, is an altogether different data type. It is specifically intended for table indexing and is only for internal program usage. In table processing, its value "points to" a given table entry. You cannot use Move and arithmetic statements on it nor can you display its value. To change its contents, you must use the Set statement.

The last example, `sampleObectHandle`, is similar to `sample-index` in that its use is very specialized. It contains two basic pieces of information: the location of an object and the identity of the class from which the object was created. You cannot use Move and arithmetic statements on it nor can you display its value. You normally give a value by invoking the method "new". But you can also give it a value with the Set statement, as you will see in later examples.

Creating Multiple Instances

Two Instances of the Room Class

Suppose you have a processing need in which you must have concurrent access to the data from two rooms of the room file. That's no problem as an object definition (as opposed to a factory definition) includes the capability for you to create as many instances as you need. If you need two different room objects, you declare two object handles, then you create an instance using each handle as done in Figure 4-13's Driver. This example arbitrarily uses the two room numbers 103 and 107, but any two could have been used. (In order to minimize the program size for this illustration, no error checking is performed.) At lines 50-59 and 61-70 data is accessed and the two instances are created and populated. Thus, after execution of these Invoke statements, two independent room objects exist. Driver has access to the first via the object handle `firstRoomHandle` and the second via the handle `secondRoomHandle`. At lines 75 and 81, Room's method `get-room-prices` is invoked for each of the two objects. The same method returns data that depends upon the object referenced in the Invoke.

```cobol
              $set sourceformat "free"
1  *>****************************************************
2  *> Room Rental System
3  *> W. Price     Nov 22, 1999              R06-DRV2.CBL
4  *>
5  *> This driver illustrates creating two independent
6  *> objects from the class definition R06-ROOM.
7  *> Its actions are as follows:
8  *>    Create two instances
9  *>    Read pricing data from the database into each
10 *>    instance (arbitrarily using Rooms 103 & 107)
11 *>    Access data from each object and display it.
12 *> The following classes comprise this project:
13 *>    r06-dbi    Database interface
14 *>    r06-room   Room
15 *>****************************************************
16
17 Identification Division.
18        Program-ID. Room06Driver2.
19
20 Environment Division.
21        Object Section.
22          Class-control.
23             DatabaseInterface is class "r06-dbi"
24             RoomClass         is class "r06-room"
25             .
26 Data Division.
27
28      Working-Storage Section.
29
30        01 room-object-data.
31           05 room-number              pic X(03).
32           05 room-prices.
33              10 std-config-price      pic 9(03).
34              10 spec-config-price     pic 9(03).
35           05 room-discount            pic v9(02).
36           05 room-capacity            pic 9(02).
37        01 record-found-sw             pic X(01).
38
39        01 firstRoomHandle  object reference.
40        01 secondRoomHandle object reference.
41
42 Procedure Division.
43
44 000-process-room-data.
45     *> Access data from two records thereby
46     *> creating two instances of the room object
47     *> (using Rooms 103 & 107)
48     Invoke DataBaseInterface "open-file"
49     Move "103" to room-number
50     Invoke DataBaseInterface "read-room-file"
51                     Using room-number
52                     Returning record-found-sw
53     Invoke DataBaseInterface "get-room-data"
54                     Returning room-object-data
55     Invoke RoomClass "new"
56                     Returning firstRoomHandle
57     Invoke firstRoomHandle
58                     "populate-the-room-object"
59                     Using room-object-data
60     Move "107" to room-number
61     Invoke DataBaseInterface "read-room-file"
62                     Using room-number
63                     Returning record-found-sw
64     Invoke DataBaseInterface "get-room-data"
65                     Returning room-object-data
66     Invoke RoomClass "new"
67                     Returning secondRoomHandle
68     Invoke secondRoomHandle
69                     "populate-the-room-object"
70                     Using room-object-data
71     Invoke DataBaseInterface "close-file"
72
73     *> Retrieve the data from the first object
74     *> and display it on the screen
75     Invoke firstRoomHandle "get-room-prices"
76                     Returning room-prices
77     Perform 300-display-room-data
78
79     *> Retrieve the data from the first object
80     *> and display it on the screen
81     Invoke secondRoomHandle "get-room-prices"
82                     Returning room-prices
83     Perform 300-display-room-data
84     Stop run
85     .
86 300-display-room-data.
87     Display " "
88     Display "Standard configuration price: "
89                     std-config-price
90     Display "Special configuration price:  "
91                     spec-config-price
92     .
```

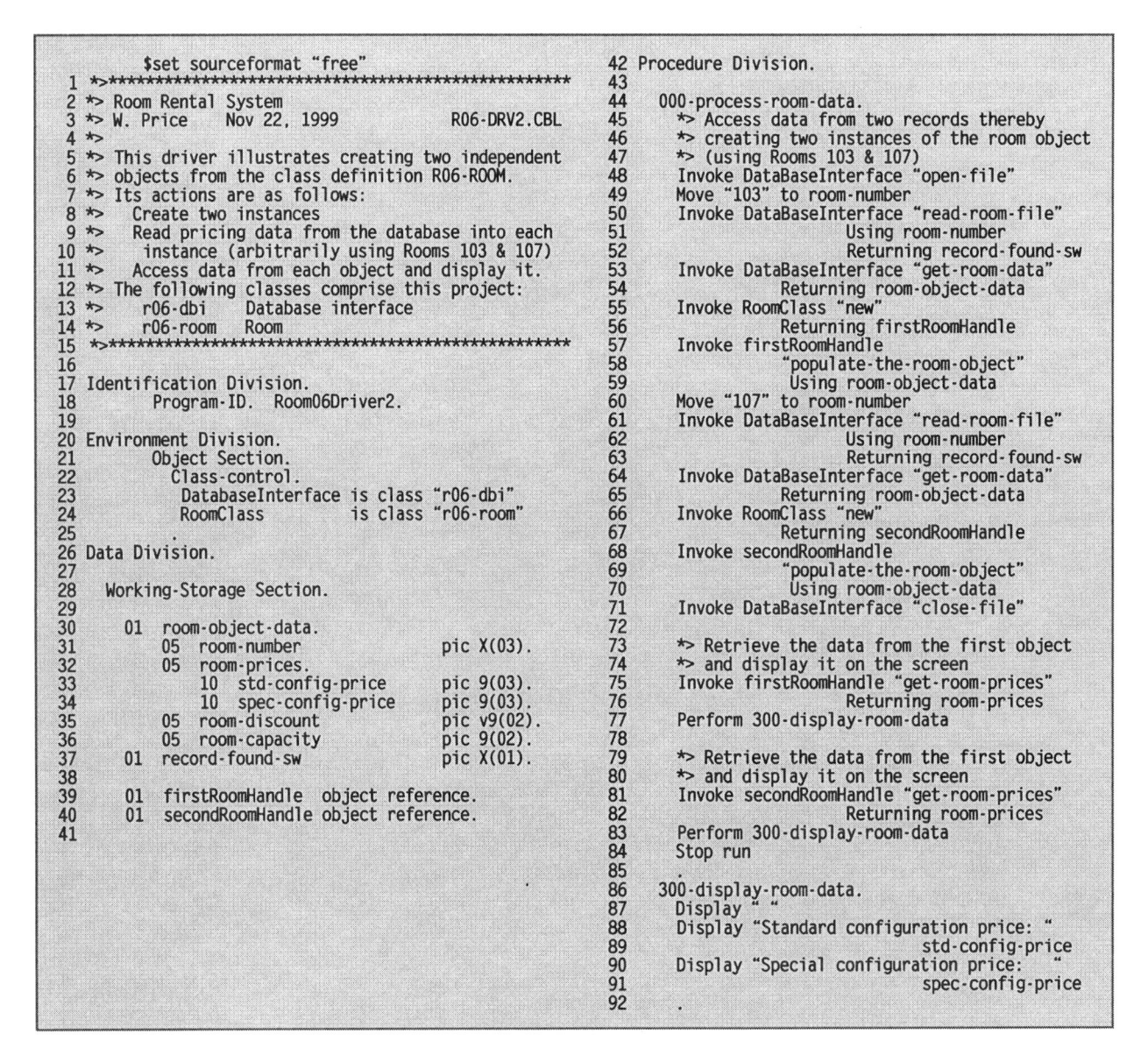

Figure 4-13. Driver r06-drv2 to create two instances.

In object technology, you will commonly encounter the term **polymorphism**, a word with Greek origins meaning "many forms." Here you see a simple form of polymorphism: the same message to two different objects produces different results. You will see more of this as you progress in this book.

The three drivers, r06-drvr, r06-drv2 and r6-drv3 (described next), are designated as part of the Room06 project. If you wish to run either example, proceed as follows.

- Net Express: Click the run icon and from the popup window change DEBUG\r06-drvr to DEBUG\r06-dvr2 and click OK.
- Personal COBOL: From the browser screen, highlight Room06Driver2 and run.

Subscripting Object Handles

Sometimes you need to create several instances of an object and have them all available for processing at the same time. You can do this by subscripting object handle data items in exactly the same way you subscript ordinary data items. To illustrate this, the next driver, r06-drv3, creates five instances of the room class. To minimize the code so you can focus on subscripted object handles, five consecutive rooms are accessed (103 through 107). The relatively simple approach used in the example is possible because the example room file contains consecutive room numbers.

In Figure 4-14 the object handles are declared at lines 39 and 40; the result is theRoomHandle(1) through theRoomHandle(5). The five instances (objects) are created by repeated sequence of invokes in lines 53-62. Under control of the Perform varying, the subscript object-sub progresses from 1 through 5. Note that the room number is tied to the subscript by the Compute at line 52, a convenient device for this illustration. Another loop at lines 75-85 displays data from the five instances.

```
           $set sourceformat "free"                       43  Procedure Division.
 1  *>*********************************************       44
 2  *> Room Rental System                                  45      000-demo-multiple-instances.
 3  *> W. Price   Nov 22, 1999          R06-DRV3.CBL      46         Invoke DatabaseInterface "open-file"
 4  *>                                                    47         *> Create and populate the five instances
 5  *> This driver illustrates creating 5 independent     48         Perform varying object-sub
 6  *> objects from the class definition R06-ROOM.        49                  from 1 by 1 until object-sub > 5
 7  *> Its actions are as follows:                        50            *> Arbitrarily use object-sub to get a room
 8  *>    Create five instances                           51            *> num. The following gives Rooms 103-107.
 9  *>    Read pricing data from the database into each   52            Compute room-number-9 = object-sub + 102
10  *>       instance (arbitrarily using Rooms 103-107)   53            Invoke DataBaseInterface "read-room-file"
11  *>    Access data from each object and display it.    54                     Using room-number
12  *> The following classes comprise this project:       55                     Returning record-found-sw
13  *>    r06-dbi      Database interface                 56            Invoke DataBaseInterface "get-room-data"
14  *>    r06-room     Room                               57                     Returning room-object-data
15  *>*********************************************       58            Invoke RoomClass "new"
16                                                        59                     Returning theRoomHandle(object-sub)
17  Identification Division.                              60            Invoke theRoomHandle(object-sub)
18      Program-ID.  Room06Driver3.                       61                     "populate-the-room-object"
19  Environment Division.                                 62                     Using room-object-data
20      Object Section.                                   63         End-perform *> varying object-sub
21         Class-control.                                 64         Invoke DatabaseInterface "close-file"
22            DataBaseInterface is class "r06-dbi"        65         Perform 900-display-all-data
23            RoomClass is class "r06-room"               66         Stop run
24            .                                           67         .
25  Data Division.                                        68      900-display-all-data.
26      Working-Storage Section.                          69         Display " "
27                                                        70         Display "Five instances have been created."
28      01  room-object-data.                             71         Display " "
29          05  room-number              pic X(03).       72         Display "  Room   Standard    Special"
30          05  room-number-9 redefines                   73         Display "  Num    Price      Price"
31                         room-number   pic 9(03).       74         Display " "
32          05  room-prices.                              75         Perform varying object-sub
33              10  std-config-price     pic 9(03).       76                  from 1 by 1 until object-sub > 5
34              10  spec-config-price    pic 9(03).       77            Invoke theRoomHandle(object-sub)
35          05  room-discount            pic v9(02).      78                     "get-room-prices"
36          05  room-capacity            pic 9(02).       79                     Returning room-prices
37      01  record-found-sw              pic X(01).       80            *> Display each of the five instances
38                                                        81            Compute room-number-9 = object-sub + 102
39      01  theRoomHandle       object reference          82            Display "  " room-number with no advancing
40                              occurs 5 times.           83            Display "     " std-config-price no advancing
41      01  object-sub                   pic 9(01).       84            Display "        " spec-config-price
42                                                        85         End-perform *> varying object-sub
                                                          86         .
```

Figure 4-14. Room driver r06-drv3 using subscripted object handles.

Providing for Repetition

The Driver Program Room07dr

Proj0403
Room07

If you've run the example programs, you've probably not found them very gratifying in that each program makes only one pass. To test different aspects of the program, you must make repeated runs. Before progressing to Chapter 5, let's provide for repetition.

The driver program shown in Figure 4-15 is reasonably straightforward—you might find it helpful to run it for a feel of how it works. Portions of code that you can focus on are the following.

1. Repetition is controlled by the user-entered room number—a blank value entered via line 100 triggers termination.
2. Loop control is via the Perform (lines 48-50) which refers to room-number via its 88 entry finished (lines 25 and 26).
3. If the user makes no entry for the room number the code of lines 58-66 is skipped and control is returned to line 48. As room-number contains spaces (finished of line 26 is true), execution continues to line 51.

Multiple Instantiations of a Class

One subtle aspect of project Room07 is that Driver creates a new instance of Room for each user request of room data. Assume that in response to a user request, Driver has just created and populated a room object. Upon receiving another request, Driver instantiates room again. What happens to the previous object? To understand that, look at Figure 4-4 and remember that creation of an object is a two-step process: the object data is replicated in memory, and the memory address of that data area is returned as a handle. That is, the object handle "points to" the newly created object. Thus if you have processed, for instance, four user requests, the memory contents would appear as shown in Figure 4-16. You see that the single object handle, theRoomHandle, points to the most recently created object and that the other three have been "cast loose." They are no longer accessible to the program (because they no longer have object handles) *but* they remain in memory. Therefore, you might conclude that you can lose memory in a repetitious environment (this loss of memory is called **memory leakage**). One way of avoiding a problem is through the method

Using a Database Interface Class

```cobol
       $set sourceformat "free"
1  *>****************************************
2  *> Room Rental System
3  *> W. Price  Nov 22, 1999         R07-DRVR.CBL
4  *>
5  *> This driver is an expansion of ROOM06DR. It
6  *> provides for program repetition until the
7  *> user decides to terminate.
8  *> The following classes comprise this project:
9  *>    r06-dbi    Database interface
10 *>    r06-room   Room
11 *>****************************************
12
13 Identification Division.
14     Program-ID.  Room07Driver.
15
16 Environment Division.
17     Object Section.
18        Class-control.
19           DatabaseInterface is class "r06-dbi"
20           RoomClass is class "r06-room"
21           .
22 Data Division.
23    Working-Storage Section.
24       01 room-object-data.
25          05   room-number            pic X(03).
26             88 finished              value spaces.
27          05   std-config-price       pic 9(03).
28          05   spec-config-price      pic 9(03).
29          05   room-discount          pic v9(02).
30          05   room-capacity          pic 9(02).
31
32       01 menu-choice                 pic X(01).
33             88 discounted-prices     value "D" "d".
34             88 standard-prices       value "S" "s".
35       01 record-found-sw             pic X(01).
36             88 record-found          value "Y".
37             88 record-not-found      value "N".
38
39       01 room-prices.
40          05   std-config-price       pic 9(03).
41          05   spec-config-price      pic 9(03).
42
43       01 theRoomHandle               object reference.
44
45 Procedure Division.
46    000-process-room-data.
47       Invoke DataBaseInterface "open-file"
48       Perform 200-process-user-requests
49                   with test after
50                   until finished
51       Invoke DataBaseInterface "close-file"
52       Display "Processing complete"
53       Stop run
54       .
55    200-process-user-requests.
56       Perform 800-accept-room-number
57       If NOT finished
58          Invoke DataBaseInterface "read-room-file"
59                      Using room-number
60                      Returning record-found-sw
61          If record-found
62             Perform 250-create-room-object
63             Perform 300-process-user-selection
64          Else
65             Display "Invalid room number."
66          End-If *>record-not-found
67       End-If *>NOT finished
68       .
69    250-create-room-object.
70       Invoke DataBaseInterface "get-room-data"
71                      Returning room-object-data
72       Invoke RoomClass "new"
73                      Returning theRoomHandle
74       Invoke theRoomHandle
75                "populate-the-room-object"
76                      Using room-object-data
77       .
78    300-process-user-selection.
79       Perform 850-get-menu-selection
80       Evaluate TRUE
81          When discounted-prices
82             Invoke theRoomHandle
83                 "get-discounted-room-prices"
84                      Returning room-prices
85             Perform 900-display-room-prices
86          When standard-prices
87             Invoke theRoomHandle "get-room-prices"
88                      Returning room-prices
89             Perform 900-display-room-prices
90          When other
91             Invoke theRoomHandle "get-room-capacity"
92                      Returning room-capacity
93             Perform 950-display-room-capacity
94       End-evaluate *>TRUE
95       .
96    800-accept-room-number.
97       Display " "
98       Display "Room number (no entry to terminate) "
99                with no advancing
100      Accept room-number
101      .
102   850-get-menu-selection.
103      Display " "
104      Display "The options are:"
105      Display "  C - Room capacity (default)"
106      Display "  S - Standard room prices"
107      Display "  D - Discounted room prices"
108      Display " "
109      Display "Your choice <C,S,D>? " no advancing
110      Accept menu-choice
111      .
112   900-display-room-prices.
113      Display " "
114      Display "Standard configuration price: "
115                std-config-price of room-prices
116      Display "Special configuration price:  "
117                spec-config-price of room-prices
118      .
119   950-display-room-capacity.
120      Display " "
121      Display "Room capacity: " room-capacity
122      .
```

Figure 4-15. The driver r07-drvr—allowing for repetition.

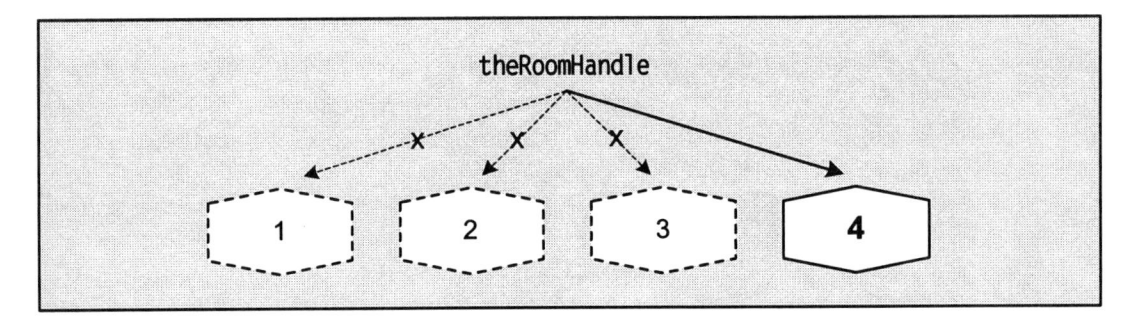

Figure 4-16. Inaccessible objects.

finalize (a method of the base class). The following Invoke frees up the memory used by the object and sets the room handle to a value null.

```
Invoke theRoomHandle "finalize"
         Returning theRoomHandle
```

However the new Standard designates a superior technique to periodically search for objects that are no longer accessible (no longer have handles pointing to them) and delete them thereby freeing up their occupied memory. This is called automatic **garbage collection**, a feature that would free you from the need to finalize an object. However, as of the publication date of this book, automatic garbage collection had not been implemented by Micro Focus.

Summing Up

Project Summary

Proj0401 (Room05) is a variation of Chapter 3's Room04 in which the room object is defined in the Object paragraph rather than the Factory paragraph. As such, the room class must be instantiated thereby yielding an instance object for processing.

Proj0402 (Room06) incorporates a database interface class from which data is accessed to populate the room object. Two alternate drivers illustrate creating multiple instances of the room class.

Proj0403 (Room07) introduces repetition whereby DBI creates a new instance object for each user request.

General Summary

This chapter focuses on employing a database interface in a system to provide access to data in a file. Following are significant points of the chapter.

- Introduction of a second class yields a three-part system in which components must collaborate with one another to accomplish their responsibilities; refer to Figure 4-9. In such an environment, visibility between classes (or a class and the driver) is a critical consideration.
- For a simple application in which object data is read from an indexed file, one could argue that data access could easily be built into the room class. In general, that is a poor practice as it yields a class that begins to lose some of its cohesiveness. Room has the responsibility to manage its data. DBI has the responsibility of providing access to external data as required by room. These are separate, independent functions
- There is no limit to the number of times a class can be instantiated within a loop.

Coming Up

You've seen how the responsibility for instantiating and populating a room object has been given to a separate class: the database interface class. If you inspect Driver of this chapter, you will see that it has many responsibilities. In fact, it looks much like a conventional Cobol program with good "structure." In Chapter 5 you will see how functions of Driver are identified and delegated to new classes. In the end, Driver will do no more than get things started.

Assignments

4-1

This assignment involves modifying Assignment 3-1 to:

- include the database interface j02-dbi.cbl stored in the folder aProgs included CD accompanying this book (if you are using Personal COBOL, obtain j02-dbi.cbl from the folder aProgsPC), and
- provide for repetition under user control.

Following are features of the database interface class definition

    File name   j02-dbi.cbl

    Class-ID   DessertDatabaseInterface

    Description   This class accesses the indexed file dessert.di.

Class methods
    open-file
        Purpose
            Open the dessert file.
    close-file
        Purpose
            Close the dessert file.
    read-dessert-record
        Purpose
            Access a designated data record into the FD defined dessert record.
        Input
            Dessert ID   pic X(03)
        Output
            Record-found switch   pic X(01)
                Value: Record found   Y
                       Record not found   N

You will need to add your own method for accessing data needed to populate the dessert object.

When you inspect the file's record description, you will see several fields that do not pertain to this application. Your dessert object data must contain only those fields needed to produce the requested output (the same as 3-1).

Room object data.

    Dessert ID
    Flavor description
    Roll length
    Rolls onhand
    Per inch cost

4-2

This assignment involves modifying Assignment 3-2 to:

- include the database interface f02-dbi.cbl stored on the disk included with this book (if you are using Personal COBOL, obtain f02-dbi.cbl from the folder aProgsPC), and
- provide for repetition under user control.

Following are features of the database interface class definition

    File name   f02-dbi.cbl

    Class-ID   EventDatabaseInterface

    Description   This class accesses the indexed file event.di.

Class methods
```
    open-file
        Purpose
            Open the event file.
    close-file
        Purpose
            Close the event file.
    read-event-record
        Purpose
            Access a designated data record into the FD defined event record.
        Input
            Event ID                              pic X(04)
        Output
            Record-found switch                   pic X(01)
                Value: Record found                 Y
                       Record not found             N
```

You will need to add your own method for accessing data needed to populate the event object.

When you inspect the file's record description, you will see several fields that do not pertain to this application. Your room object data must contain only those fields needed to produce the requested output (the same as 3-2).

Room object data.

    Event ID
    Event description
    Facility
    Duration
    Site
    Daily rate

Full Object Orientation of the Room Example

Chapter Contents

Creating a User Interface Class 92
   Reviewing the Driver R07-drvr 92
   A User Interface Class 94
   The Class User Perspective of the User Interface Class 96
   The Driver Program 96
   Component Reusability 98
Final Conversion of Room System to Object Orientation 98
   A Room Manager Class 98
   The Driver and Room Manager—Room09 98
   The Notion of Public and Private Methods 100
Creating All Classes with Instance Object Definitions 100
   About this Example 100
   Instantiating all Objects in Driver 102
   Instantiating the Classes in Room Manager's Factory 106
Summing Up 108
   Project Summary 108
   General Summary 108
Coming Up 109
Assignment 109

Chapter 5

Chapter Introduction

Chapters 3 and 4 introduced you to classes, objects, and object-oriented programs. This chapter continues by creating new classes to handle the processing activities of Driver. From this chapter you will learn about the following.

- A user interface class that handles all interaction with the user.
- A manager class to handle overall control functions
- Communication between classes.
- Storing object handles as object data.
- More about viewing programming applications from a responsibilities/ collaborations perspective.

Creating a User Interface Class

Object orientation is a powerful programming tool. However, you cannot realize the full potential of OO merely by using an OO language. You must use object-oriented analysis (OOA) and object-oriented design (OOD) during the planning and design phases. For an experienced programmer, it is tempting to carry over structured methodology when moving from structural design and programming to object orientation. This is a mistake of disastrous consequences. You must think object orientation throughout. You must analyze an application from the perspective of potential classes and the responsibilities/collaborations of each class.

The preceding chapters place relatively little emphasis on program design for a good reason—to maintain the focus on basic OOCobol principles. Consequently, you've seen an application in which a considerable portion of the logic and code reside in the driver (see r07-drvr, Figure 4-15). As a result, you have an application that is half conventional methodology and half object methodology. This is an easy trap into which you can fall. A good OO design results in relatively little code in the driver: only that which is necessary to get the application started.

Reviewing the Driver R07-drvr

Inspect r07-drvr's Procedure Division, repeated here in Figure 5-1, for elements performing a similar type function that might be removed and placed in separate class. Perhaps most obvious are the interactive input and output actions—those elements that interface with the user. Consisting of modules 800, 850, 900, and 950 and the Display statements of lines 52 and 65, this collection comprises a **user interface**.

As a first step, let's remove this user interface code from the driver and create a user interface class. This new user interface class will fit into the overall structure as illustrated in Figure 5-2. Notice that this project uses the DBI and Room classes of Room06 as did the project Room07. Responsibilities of the various components of Room08 will be something like the following.

Driver
   Provide overall program control
   Instantiate Room (create a room object)
   Populate room object
   Access room data

User interface
   Query user for a room number
   Query user for information request
   Display results

Full Object Orientation of the Room Example

```
45  Procedure Division.
46  000-process-room-data.
47     Invoke DataBaseInterface "open-file"
48     Perform 200-process-user-requests
49                          with test after
50                          until finished
51     Invoke DataBaseInterface "close-file"
52     Display "Processing complete"
53     Stop run
54     .
55  200-process-user-requests.
56     Perform 800-accept-room-number
57     If NOT finished
58        Invoke DataBaseInterface "read-room-file"
59                       Using room-number
60                       Returning record-found-sw
61        If record-found
62           Perform 250-create-room-object
63           Perform 300-process-user-selection
64        Else
65           Display "Invalid room number."
66        End-If *>record-not-found
67     End-If *>NOT finished
68     .
69  250-create-room-object.
70     Invoke DataBaseInterface "get-room-data"
71                    Returning room-object-data
72     Invoke RoomClass "New"
73                    Returning theRoomHandle
74     Invoke theRoomHandle
75            "populate-the-room-object"
76              Using room-object-data
77     .
78  300-process-user-selection.
79     Perform 850-get-menu-selection
80     Evaluate TRUE
81        When discounted-prices
82           Invoke theRoomHandle
83              "get-discounted-room-prices"
84              Returning room-prices
85           Perform 900-display-room-prices
86        When standard-prices
87           Invoke theRoomHandle "get-room-prices"
88              Returning room-prices
89           Perform 900-display-room-prices
90        When other
91           Invoke theRoomHandle "get-room-capacity"
92              Returning room-capacity
93           Perform 950-display-room-capacity
94     End-evaluate *>TRUE
95     .
96  800-accept-room-number.
97     Display " "
98     Display "Room number (no entry to terminate) "
99             with no advancing
100    Accept room-number
101    .
102 850-get-menu-selection.
103    Display " "
104    Display "The options are:"
105    Display "  C - Room capacity (default)"
106    Display "  S - Standard room prices"
107    Display "  D - Discounted room prices"
108    Display " "
109    Display "Your choice <C,S,D>? " no advancing
110    Accept menu-choice
111    .
112 900-display-room-prices.
113    Display " "
114    Display "Standard configuration price: "
115            std-config-price of room-prices
116    Display "Special configuration price: "
117            spec-config-price of room-prices
118    .
119 950-display-room-capacity.
120    Display " "
121    Display "Room capacity: " room-capacity
122    .
```

Figure 5-1. Procedure Division from r07-drvr.

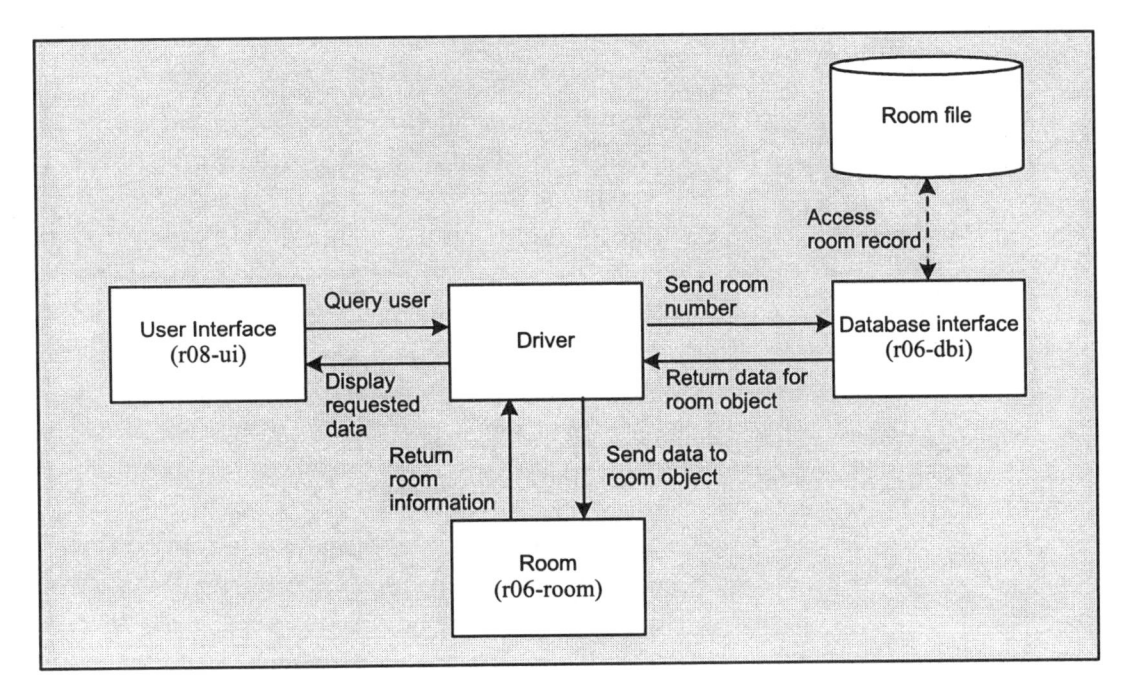

Figure 5-2. Class relationships for Room08.

Room class
   Accept room data from DBI
   Return room prices
   Return discounted room prices
   Return room capacity

DBI class
   Open and close room file
   Read the designated record
   Return data needed for room object

A User Interface Class

In the broad context of the room application you know that the user interface program must have the following interaction with the user.

1. Query for room number; return the room number to the calling component.
2. Query regarding whether or not to apply a discount; return the discount query result to the calling component.
3. Display an error message for invalid room.
4. Display room capacity.
5. Display room prices.

[Proj0501 Room08]

The **user interface** class program, or simply **UI**, depicted in Figure 5-2 is stored in the folder Proj0501 as r08-ui.cbl. In its listing of Figure 5-3 you see that all of the code is included as a factory definition. Like DBI, only one copy of UI is required and that copy will exist for the duration of the run. Let's look at each of its five methods in the order they are listed above.

Object Method query-for-room-number. This method (lines 96-109) accepts the user-response for the requested room number and returns it to the invoking program. It corresponds to r07-drvr's 800 module—see Figure 5-1

Object Method get-menu-selection. This method (lines 30-49) displays the menu. Its procedural code corresponds to the 850 module of r07-drvr—see Figure 5-1. The user can select room capacity, standard room prices, or discounted room prices. The choice is returned to the calling program via the data-item ls-menu-choice. Notice line 46 where the user's choice is converted to upper-case using the upper-case function. (This is one of the 1989 intrinsic function additions to Cobol-85.) In all earlier programs, the condition names allowed for either upper- or lower-case entries. With the menu code now hidden from the driver programmer, it is good idea to do this conversion and remove the burden from the programmer. Now the invoking program need only designate condition names for D and S (d and s are no longer needed).

Object Method display-message. When the user enters an invalid room number, the program displays an error message. This method (lines 52-62) is generalized so that any message up to 40 characters in length can be sent to it for display through the parameter ls-message. This method corresponds to the Display statements at lines 52 and 65 in r07-drvr.

Full Object Orientation of the Room Example

```
        $set sourceformat "free"
1  *>***********************************************
2  *> Room Rental System
3  *> W. Price   Sept 20 1999              R08-UI.CBL
4  *>
5  *> This UI class handles all communication with
6  *> the user.  The method code has been extracted
7  *> from the preceding driver program.
8  *> Object Methods are:
9  *>       display-message
10 *>       display-room-capacity
11 *>       display-room-prices
12 *>       get-menu-selection
13 *>       query-for-room-number
14 *>***********************************************
15
16 IDENTIFICATION DIVISION.
17     Class-id.  UserInterface.
18
19 Environment Division.
20     Object Section.
21       Class-control.
22          UserInterface is class  "r08-ui"
23          .
24 *>=================================================
25 FACTORY.
26
27   Procedure Division.
28
29     *>..............................................
30     Method-id. get-menu-selection.
31     *>..............................................
32       Data Division.
33         Linkage Section.
34           01 ls-menu-choice           pic x(01).
35
36       Procedure Division Returning ls-menu-choice.
37         Display " "
38         Display "The options are:"
39         Display "  C - Room capacity (default)"
40         Display "  S - Standard room prices"
41         Display "  D - Discounted room prices"
42         Display " "
43         Display "Your choice <C,S,D>? "
44                            with no advancing
45         Accept ls-menu-choice
46         Move function upper-case(ls-menu-choice)
47                            to ls-menu-choice
48         .
49     End Method get-menu-selection.
50
51     *>..............................................
52     Method-id. display-message.
53     *>..............................................
54       Data Division.
55         Linkage Section.
56           01 ls-message               pic x(40).
57
58       Procedure Division Using ls-message.
59         Display " "
60         Display ls-message
61         .
62     End Method display-message.
63
64     *>..............................................
65     Method-id. display-room-capacity.
66     *>..............................................
67       Data Division.
68         Linkage Section.
69           01 ls-room-capacity         pic 9(02).
70
71       Procedure Division Using ls-room-capacity.
72         Display " "
73         Display "Room capacity: " ls-room-capacity
74         .
75     End Method display-room-capacity.
76
77     *>..............................................
78     Method-id. display-room-prices.
79     *>..............................................
80       Data Division.
81         Linkage Section.
82           01 ls-room-prices.
83             10 ls-std-config-price    pic 9(03).
84             10 ls-spec-config-price   pic 9(03).
85
86       Procedure Division Using ls-room-prices.
87         Display " "
88         Display "Standard configuration price: "
89                             ls-std-config-price
90         Display "Special configuration price:  "
91                             ls-spec-config-price
92         .
93     End Method display-room-prices.
94
95     *>..............................................
96     Method-id. query-for-room-number.
97     *>..............................................
98       Data Division.
99
100      Linkage Section.
101        01 ls-room-number            pic X(03).
102
103    Procedure Division Returning ls-room-number.
104      Display " "
105      Display "Room number (blank if finished) "
106                          with no advancing
107      Accept ls-room-number
108      .
109   End Method query-for-room-number.
110   *>..............................................
111 END FACTORY.
112 END CLASS UserInterface.
```

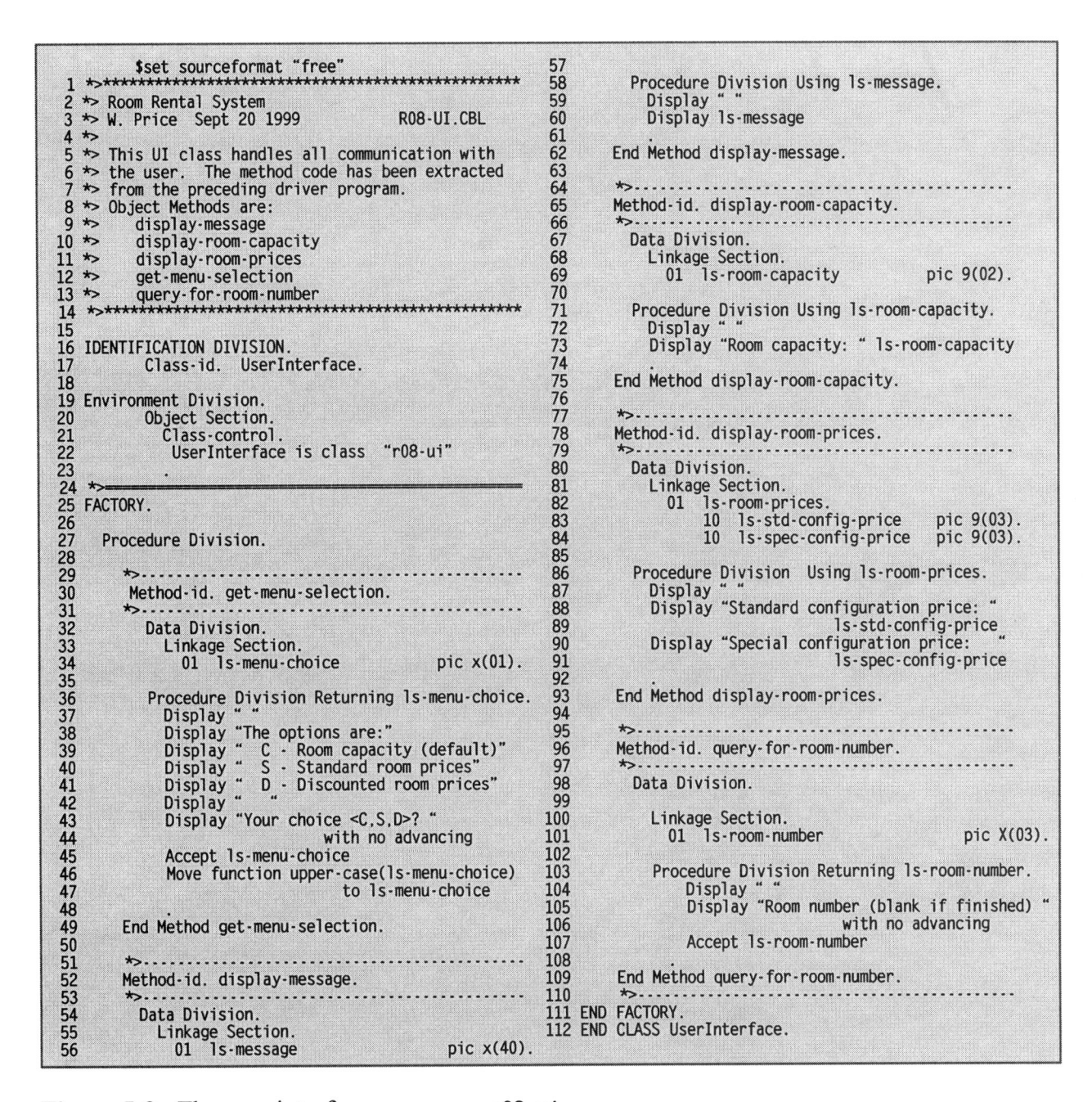

Figure 5-3. The user interface program—r08-ui.

Object method `display-room-capacity`. This method (lines 65-75) is straightforward. It simply displays the room capacity sent to it by the invoking program. It corresponds to the 950 module of r07-drvr.

Object method `display-room-prices`. The procedural code of this method (lines 78-93) corresponds to the 900 module of r07-drvr.

The Class User Perspective of the User Interface Class

Before focusing on the driver program, you should inspect the following description of the user interface class.

Class   r06-ui

Description   This class manages all interactive input and output operations with the user.

Class methods
```
get-menu-selection
```
    Purpose

        Present the menu selection to the user and accept a response.

    Output

Menu selection	`pic X(01)`	
Room capacity	`value C`	
Standard room prices	`value S`	
Discounted room prices	`value D`	

```
display-message
```
    Purpose

        Display a selected message.

    Input

        Message to be displayed   `pic X(40)`

```
display-room-capacity
```
    Purpose

        Display the room capacity.

    Input

        Room capacity   `pic 9(02)`

```
display-room-prices
```
    Purpose

        Display the standard and discounted room prices.

    Input

        An 01 item containing

            Standard configuration room price   `pic 9(03)`

            Special configuration room price   `pic 9(03)`

```
query-for-room-number
```
    Purpose

        Query the user for the desired room number.

    Output

        Room number entered by user   `pic X(03)`

The Driver Program

As you can see by inspecting Figure 5-4, the progression from r07-drvr to r08-drvr involves no major changes in the overall logic of the 000, 200 and 250 modules.

1. All input/output modules (800, 850, 900, and 950) are removed as these functions are now handled by UI.

Full Object Orientation of the Room Example

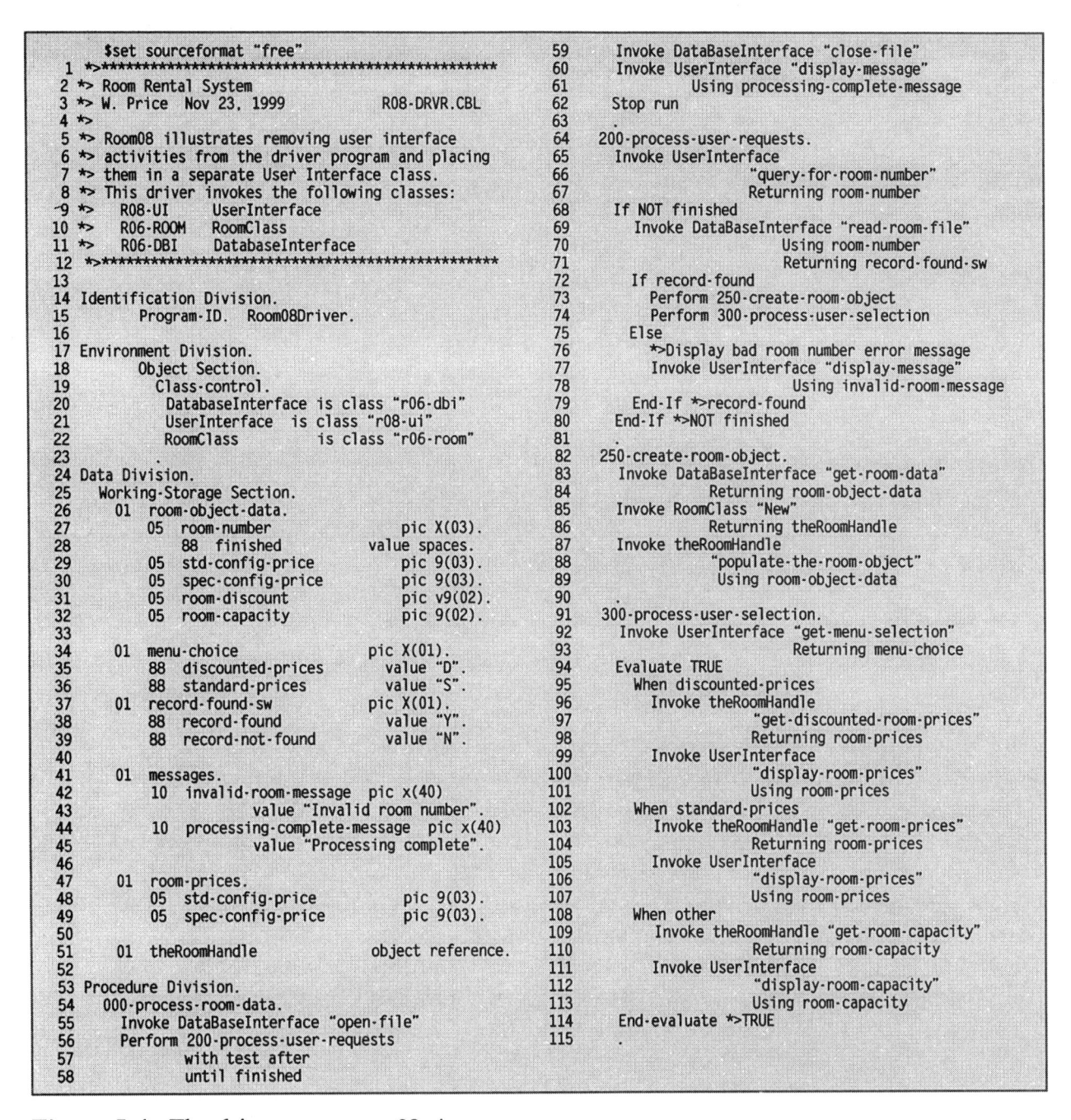

```cobol
      $set sourceformat "free"
1  *>*******************************************
2  *> Room Rental System
3  *> W. Price  Nov 23, 1999           R08-DRVR.CBL
4  *>
5  *> Room08 illustrates removing user interface
6  *> activities from the driver program and placing
7  *> them in a separate User Interface class.
8  *> This driver invokes the following classes:
9  *>    R08-UI     UserInterface
10 *>    R06-ROOM   RoomClass
11 *>    R06-DBI    DatabaseInterface
12 *>*******************************************
13
14 Identification Division.
15     Program-ID. Room08Driver.
16
17 Environment Division.
18     Object Section.
19         Class-control.
20             DatabaseInterface is class "r06-dbi"
21             UserInterface  is class "r08-ui"
22             RoomClass      is class "r06-room"
23
24 Data Division.
25     Working-Storage Section.
26     01  room-object-data.
27         05  room-number              pic X(03).
28             88  finished             value spaces.
29         05  std-config-price         pic 9(03).
30         05  spec-config-price        pic 9(03).
31         05  room-discount            pic v9(02).
32         05  room-capacity            pic 9(02).
33
34     01  menu-choice                  pic X(01).
35         88  discounted-prices        value "D".
36         88  standard-prices          value "S".
37     01  record-found-sw              pic X(01).
38         88  record-found             value "Y".
39         88  record-not-found         value "N".
40
41     01  messages.
42         10  invalid-room-message     pic x(40)
43                     value "Invalid room number".
44         10  processing-complete-message  pic x(40)
45                     value "Processing complete".
46
47     01  room-prices.
48         05  std-config-price         pic 9(03).
49         05  spec-config-price        pic 9(03).
50
51     01  theRoomHandle                object reference.
52
53 Procedure Division.
54     000-process-room-data.
55         Invoke DataBaseInterface "open-file"
56         Perform 200-process-user-requests
57             with test after
58             until finished
59         Invoke DataBaseInterface "close-file"
60         Invoke UserInterface "display-message"
61                 Using processing-complete-message
62         Stop run
63         .
64     200-process-user-requests.
65         Invoke UserInterface
66                         "query-for-room-number"
67                         Returning room-number
68         If NOT finished
69             Invoke DataBaseInterface "read-room-file"
70                         Using room-number
71                         Returning record-found-sw
72             If record-found
73                 Perform 250-create-room-object
74                 Perform 300-process-user-selection
75             Else
76                 *>Display bad room number error message
77                 Invoke UserInterface "display-message"
78                         Using invalid-room-message
79             End-If *>record-found
80         End-If *>NOT finished
81         .
82     250-create-room-object.
83         Invoke DataBaseInterface "get-room-data"
84                         Returning room-object-data
85         Invoke RoomClass "New"
86                         Returning theRoomHandle
87         Invoke theRoomHandle
88                         "populate-the-room-object"
89                         Using room-object-data
90         .
91     300-process-user-selection.
92         Invoke UserInterface "get-menu-selection"
93                         Returning menu-choice
94         Evaluate TRUE
95             When discounted-prices
96                 Invoke theRoomHandle
97                         "get-discounted-room-prices"
98                         Returning room-prices
99                 Invoke UserInterface
100                        "display-room-prices"
101                        Using room-prices
102            When standard-prices
103                Invoke theRoomHandle "get-room-prices"
104                        Returning room-prices
105                Invoke UserInterface
106                        "display-room-prices"
107                        Using room-prices
108            When other
109                Invoke theRoomHandle "get-room-capacity"
110                        Returning room-capacity
111                Invoke UserInterface
112                        "display-room-capacity"
113                        Using room-capacity
114        End-evaluate *>TRUE
115        .
```

Figure 5-4. The driver program r08-drvr.

2. The Perform statements for input/output operations are replaced with Invokes to the corresponding methods of UI. For instance, compare line 85 of Figure 5-1 to lines 99-101 of Figure 5-4.
3. The user interface class definition is identified in the Class-control paragraph—see line 21. Note that each invoke of UI designates this class name, thereby causing the system to look for a factory method.

There is one other item to notice. At lines 35 and 36 the lower-case letters are no longer needed in the condition names. Remember, the UI class converts the user's input to upper-case.

Component Reusability

You can see that Room08 is basically an expansion of Room07 which, in turn, is a extension of Room06. In expanding these applications, r06-room and r06-dbi are used without change. In other words, the tested and proven code from one application was reused in another application.

One of the selling features of object orientation is **component reusability**. For an insight to the concept of reusability, consider the date intrinsic functions added to the Standard in 1989. We no longer need to write date calculation code for every application we design because we can now use the generalized date functions—that is, we no longer need to reinvent the wheel. Notice the basic idea behind the intrinsic functions: write generalized *reusable* code to perform specific commonly encountered operations. Classes of the object world offer the same advantages. Most application areas have numerous actions common to that area. For example, a lending institution has numerous methods for calculating interest; an educational institution has numerous methods for processing student records. These can be coded as class libraries and made available within and without an organization.

Final Conversion of Room System to Object Orientation

A Room Manager Class

Proj0502
Room09

Room08's driver r08-drvr provides overall control of the room application. As a rule, the driver will normally consist of only a few lines to code to start the process. At most, it might create one or more needed objects then invoke a method of some controlling class program. To that end, project Room09's Driver is virtually eliminated from the conceptual scheme by placing its activities in a new Room Manager class. Notice in the class diagram of Figure 5-5 that Driver is no longer a major component. As you will see when you look at the code, it performs no function other than starting the process. Also, you see that this application incorporates the same three classes (UI, Room, and DBI) used in the preceding project (refer to Figure 5-2).

The Driver and Room Manager—Room09

As you see in Figure 5-6 Driver for this project performs no processing. It simply turns control over to Room Manager to begin processing and terminates the run when control is returned. Since Driver must access Room Manager, the Room Manager class is identified in Driver's Class-control paragraph.

All of the code from r08-drvr (see Figure 5-4) is incorporated into the new class Room Manager of Figure 5-7. Notice the following about this class definition.

Full Object Orientation of the Room Example

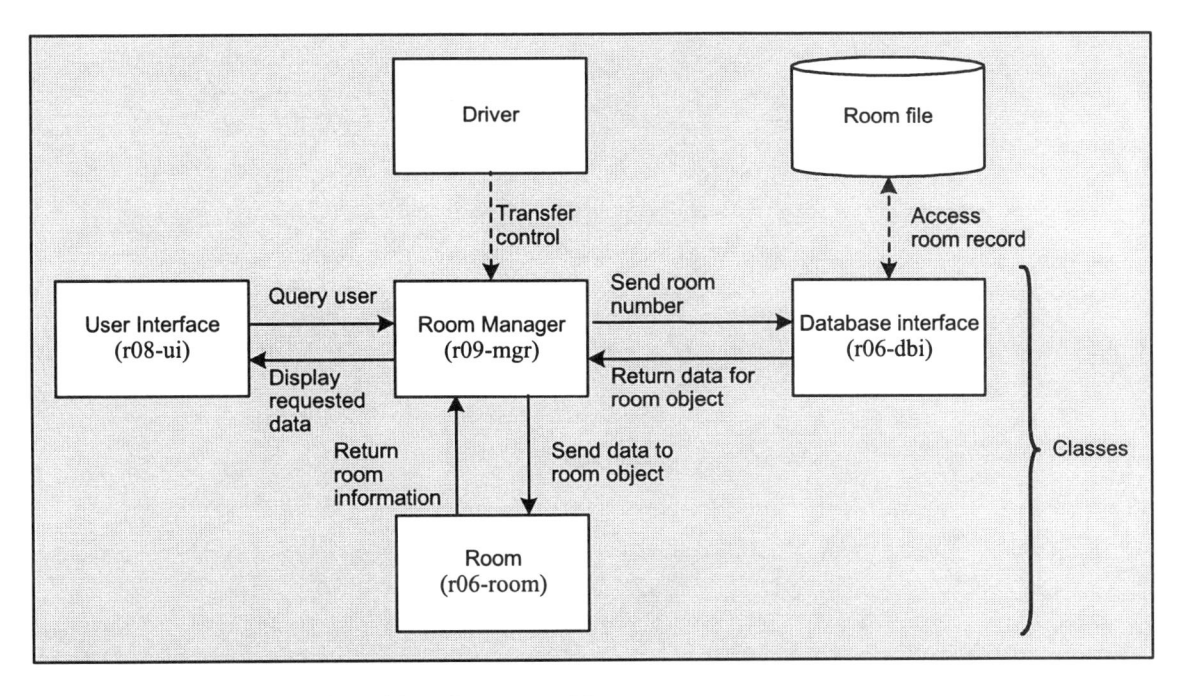

Figure 5-5. Class relationships for Room09.

Figure 5-6. Driver for Room09—r09-drvr.

```
          $set sourceformat "free"
1  *>*************************************************
2  *> Room Rental System
3  *> W. Price  Sept 21, 1999        R09-DRVR.CBL
4  *> Room09 expands Room08 by removal of processing
5  *> code from the driver and placing it in a new
6  *> class definition—a room manager. The driver
7  *> simply transfers control to the Room Manager.
8  *> The following classes comprise this project:
9  *>    R08-UI     UserInterface
10 *>    R09-MGR    RoomManager
11 *>    R06-ROOM   RoomClass
12 *>    R06-DBI    DatabaseInterface
13 *>*************************************************
14
15 Identification Division.
16      Program-ID.  Room09Driver.
17
18 Environment Division.
19      Object Section.
20         Class-control.
21            RoomManager is class "r09-mgr"
22            .
23
24 Procedure Division.
25
26   *> Turn control over to the room manager
27   Invoke RoomManager "process-user-requests"
28   Stop run
29   .
```

- The method process-user-requests controls repetition. It includes the code from r08-drvr's 000 module and a portion of the code from the 200 module.
- The procedural portion of the method process-this-request includes a portion of the code of r08-drvr's 200 module and the 250 module code.
- For each room request, the control method (process-user-requests) invokes another method of this class (process-this-request) using the predefined object identifier Self.

Upon exit from the loop (lines 67-78), the file is closed, a message displayed, and control is returned to the driver where processing is terminated.

The Notion of Public and Private Methods

There is an important difference between the way the methods of this class are used. That is, in this application process-user-requests is the only method invoked by a class user from another program module. The other three methods (create-room-object, process-this-request, and process-user-selections) are invoked from within this class—see lines 75, 103, and 104. Consequently, they are called **private methods** as they are "privately" invoked from other methods of this class. The method process-user-requests is called a **public method** in that it is intended to be invoked from other program modules. On one hand, Cobol does not include capabilities for you to identify a method as private thereby prohibiting invoking it from another module. On the other hand, Cobol does allow you to define interfaces (separate modules) that can restrict the user's "view" of a class's methods. Interfaces are described in Chapter 10. Documentation procedures used in this book (described in Chapter 6) distinguish between public and private methods.

Creating All Classes with Instance Object Definitions

About this Example

In all the preceding examples, objects that will exist for the duration of a run are defined in the Factory paragraph (Room Manager, UI, and DBI). Objects that are recreated (or for which there may be more than one during a run) are defined in the Object paragraph thereby requiring instantiation (Room).

A factory object that can be used as is the factory in this book is unique to Cobol's implementation of object orientation. In fact, all other object-oriented languages require that all objects of an application be instantiated from instance object definitions.

Actually some practitioners prefer to define all objects in the Object paragraph and use the Factory only for creating and finalizing objects and for some other specialized operations (you will see examples later in this chapter and in Chapter 9). The next project, Room10, provides you an example of that approach and also illustrates some important principles not illustrated by other projects of this book. This project consists of the following components.

Full Object Orientation of the Room Example

```cobol
       $set sourceformat "free"
1  *>****************************************************
2  *> Room Rental System
3  *> W. Price  Nov 25 1999           R09-MGR.CBL
4  *>
5  *> RoomManager handles access to the classes of
6  *> the Room system.
7  *> Methods:
8  *>    create-room-object
9  *>    process-user-requests
10 *>    process-this-request
11 *>    process-user-selections
12 *>****************************************************
13
14 Identification Division.
15     Class-ID.  RoomManager.
16
17 Environment Division.
18     Object Section.
19       Class-control.
20         UserInterface      is class "r08-ui"
21         DatabaseInterface  is class "r06-dbi"
22         RoomClass          is class "r06-room"
23         RoomManager        is class "r09-mgr"
24         .
25 *>=========================================================
26 FACTORY.
27   Data Division.
28     Object-Storage Section.
29       01 theRoomHandle    object reference.
30
31   Procedure Division.
32 *>-------------------------------------------------
33   Method-id. create-room-object.
34 *>-------------------------------------------------
35     Data Division.
36       Local-Storage Section.
37         01 lo-room-object-data.
38           10 lo-room-number          pic X(03).
39           10 lo-std-config-price     pic 9(03).
40           10 lo-spec-config-price    pic 9(03).
41           10 lo-room-discount        pic v9(02).
42           10 lo-room-capacity        pic 9(02).
43
44     Procedure Division.
45         Invoke DataBaseInterface "get-room-data"
46                 Returning lo-room-object-data
47         Invoke RoomClass "New"
48                 Returning theRoomHandle
49         Invoke theRoomHandle
50                 "populate-the-room-object"
51                 Using lo-room-object-data
52     End Method create-room-object.
53
54 *>-------------------------------------------------
55   Method-id. process-user-requests.
56 *>-------------------------------------------------
57     Data Division.
58       Local-Storage Section.
59         01 lo-room-number           pic x(03).
60           88 lo-no-more-room-requests
61                       value spaces.
62         01 lo-process-complete-message pic X(40)
63                       value "Processing complete".
64
65     Procedure Division.
66         Invoke DatabaseInterface "open-file"
67         Perform with test after
68             until lo-no-more-room-requests
69           Invoke UserInterface
70                 "query-for-room-number"
71                 Returning lo-room-number
72           If lo-no-more-room-requests
73             Continue
74           Else
75             Invoke Self "process-this-request"
76                 Using lo-room-number
77           End-If *>no-more-room-requests
78         End-Perform *>with test after
79         Invoke DatabaseInterface
80                 "close-file"
81         Invoke UserInterface "display-message"
82                 Using lo-process-complete-message
83         .
84     End Method process-user-requests.
85
86 *>-------------------------------------------------
87   Method-id. process-this-request.
88 *>-------------------------------------------------
89     Data Division.
90       Local-Storage Section.
91         01 lo-record-found-sw       pic X(01).
92           88 lo-record-found        value "Y".
93         01 lo-invalid-room-message  pic X(40)
94                 value "Invalid room number".
95       Linkage Section.
96         01 ls-room-number           pic X(03).
97
98     Procedure Division Using ls-room-number.
99         Invoke DataBaseInterface "read-room-file"
100                Using ls-room-number
101                Returning lo-record-found-sw
102        If lo-record-found
103          Invoke Self "create-room-object"
104          Invoke Self "process-user-selections"
105        Else
106          Invoke UserInterface "display-message"
107                  Using lo-invalid-room-message
108        End-If *>lo-record-found
109    End Method process-this-request.
110
111 *>-------------------------------------------------
112  Method-id. process-user-selections.
113 *>-------------------------------------------------
114    Data Division.
115      Local-Storage Section.
116        01 lo-room-prices.
117          10 lo-std-config-price     pic 9(03).
118          10 lo-spec-config-price    pic 9(03).
119        01 lo-room-capacity          pic 9(02).
120        01 lo-menu-choice            pic X(01).
121          88 lo-discounted-prices    value "D".
122          88 lo-standard-prices      value "S".
123
124    Procedure Division.
125        Invoke UserInterface
126               "get-menu-selection"
127               Returning lo-menu-choice
128        Evaluate TRUE
129        When lo-discounted-prices
130          Invoke theRoomHandle
131                 "get-discounted-room-prices"
132                 Returning lo-room-prices
133          Invoke UserInterface
134                 "display-room-prices"
135                 Using lo-room-prices
136        When lo-standard-prices
137          Invoke theRoomHandle "get-room-prices"
138                 Returning lo-room-prices
139          Invoke UserInterface
140                 "display-room-prices"
141                 Using lo-room-prices
142        When other
143          Invoke theRoomHandle "get-room-capacity"
144                 Returning lo-room-capacity
145          Invoke UserInterface
146                 "display-room-capacity"
147                 Using lo-room-capacity
148        End-evaluate *>TRUE
149        .
150    End Method process-user-selections.
151 *>-------------------------------------------------
152 END FACTORY.
153 END CLASS RoomManager.
```

Figure 5-7. Room manager for Room09—r09-mgr.

- Driver—r10-drvr: involves significant new code, a focus of this example.
- Room Manager—r10-mgr: involves significant new code, a focus of this example.
- User Interface (UI)—r10-ui: code is moved from the Factory paragraph to the Object paragraph with no change.
- Database Interface (DBI)—r10-dbi: code is moved from the Factory paragraph to the Object paragraph with no change.
- Room—r06-room: this is Chapter 4's Room class.

Compare the DBI r10-dbi of Figure 5-8 to r06-dbi of Figure 4-10 and you will see that object code for the two are identical. However, the two class definitions differ in that r10-dbi includes the code under the Object paragraph whereas r06-dbi includes the code under the Factory paragraph. If you inspect r10-ui stored in the folder Proj0503 (compare it to r08-ui) you will see that it also includes its object code within the Object paragraph. Similarly, Room Manager contains its control code in the Object paragraph. Therefore, any application using these classes must include code to instantiate them before processing can begin. The next two examples illustrate two techniques for accomplishing this.

Instantiating all Objects in Driver

One way to handle this is instantiate Room Manager, UI, and DBI in Driver. Then responsibilities of Driver and Room Manager become:

Driver
  Instantiate Room Manager, UI, and DBI

Room Manager
  Provide overall program control
  Communicate with DBI for file access
  Instantiate Room (create a room object)
  Communicate with Room to populate room object
  Communicate with Room to access room data
  Communicate with UI for user input and output

This is a reasonable approach but it introduces a problem regarding communication between classes. That is, Room Manager must communicate with both DBI and UI. However, as Driver instantiated these two classes, it has the handles needed by Room Manager, for instance, refer to Figure 5-9.

Full Object Orientation of the Room Example

```cobol
       $set sourceformat "free"
1  *>***************************************************
2  *> Room Rental System
3  *> W. Price  Nov 25, 1999                 R10-DBI.CBL
4  *>
5  *> This class definition is identical to R06-DBI
6  *> except the entire object definition is in the.
7  *> OBJECT paragraph rather than the FACTORY para.
8  *> Object methods
9  *>    close-file
10 *>    get-room-data
11 *>    open-file
12 *>    read-room-file
13 *>***************************************************
14
15 Identification Division.
16      Class-ID.  DatabaseInterface
17                 inherits from BaseClass.
18
19 Environment Division.
20      Object Section.
21        Class-control.
22          DatabaseInterface is class "r10-dbi"
23          RoomClass is class "r06-room"
24          BaseClass is class "base"
25          .
26
27 *>=
28 OBJECT.
29    Environment Division.
30       Input-Output Section.
31       File-Control.
32         Select room-file
33              assign to "c:\Eooc2\eData\room.di"
34              organization is indexed
35              access is random
36              record key is rr-room-number.
37
38    Data Division.
39      File Section.
40      FD  Room-File.
41      01  room-record.
42          10  rr-room-number            pic x(03).
43          10  rr-acctg-code             pic x(10).
44          10  rr-room-type              pic x(03).
45          10  rr-std-config-price       pic 9(03).
46          10  rr-spec-config-price      pic 9(03).
47          10  rr-pricing-code           pic 9(01).
48          10  rr-room-discount          pic v9(02).
49          10  rr-room-capacity          pic 9(02).
50          10  rr-room-width             pic 9(02).
51          10  rr-room-length            pic 9(02).
52          10  rr-work-stations          pic 9(02).
53          10  rr-work-station-capacity  pic 9(01).
54      Working-Storage Section.
55
56    Procedure Division.
57 *>---------------------------------------------------
58    Method-ID. close-file.
59 *>---------------------------------------------------
60       Procedure Division.
61         Close room-file
62         .
63    End Method close-file.
64
65 *>---------------------------------------------------
66 Method-ID. get-room-data.
67 *>---------------------------------------------------
68    Data Division.
69      Linkage Section.
70      01  ls-room-object-data.
71          10  ls-room-number            pic x(03).
72          10  ls-std-config-price       pic 9(03).
73          10  ls-spec-config-price      pic 9(03).
74          10  ls-room-discount          pic v9(02).
75          10  ls-room-capacity          pic 9(02).
76
77    Procedure Division
78                 Returning ls-room-object-data.
79       Move rr-room-number to ls-room-number
80       Move rr-std-config-price
81                           to ls-std-config-price
82       Move rr-spec-config-price
83                           to ls-spec-config-price
84       Move rr-room-discount
85                           to ls-room-discount
86       Move rr-room-capacity
87                           to ls-room-capacity
88       .
89    End Method get-room-data.
90
91 *>---------------------------------------------------
92 Method-ID. open-file.
93 *>---------------------------------------------------
94       Procedure Division.
95         Open input room-file
96         .
97    End Method open-file.
98
99 *>---------------------------------------------------
100 Method-ID. read-room-file.
101 *>---------------------------------------------------
102    Data Division.
103      Linkage Section.
104      01  ls-room-number             pic x(03).
105      01  ls-record-found-sw         pic X(01).
106          88  ls-record-found        value "Y".
107          88  ls-record-not-found    value "N".
108
109    Procedure Division Using ls-room-number
110                 Returning ls-record-found-sw.
110       Move ls-room-number to rr-room-number
111       Read Room-File
112       Invalid key
113           Set ls-record-not-found to true
114       Not invalid key
115           Set ls-record-found to true
116       End-Read  *>Room-File
117       .
118
119    End Method read-room-file.
120 *>---------------------------------------------------
121 END OBJECT.
122 END CLASS DatabaseInterface.
```

Figure 5-8. Database interface class—r10-dbi.

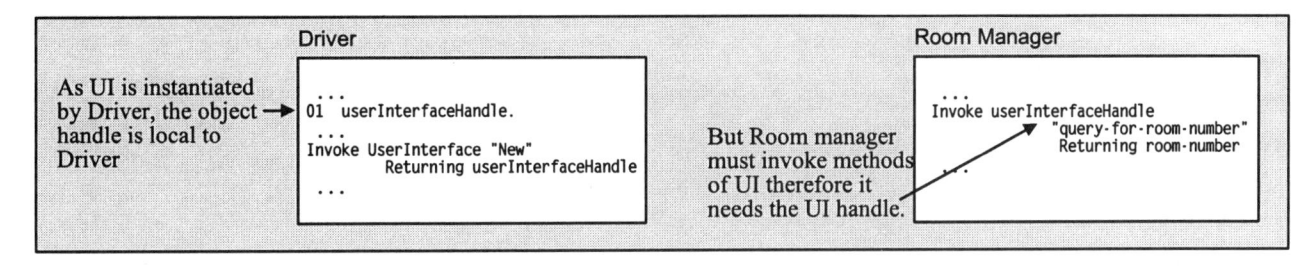

Figure 5-9. An object handle created in one module and required in another.

Driver:
As UI is instantiated by Driver, the object handle is local to Driver
```
01  userInterfaceHandle.
...
Invoke UserInterface "New"
            Returning userInterfaceHandle
...
```

Room Manager:
But Room manager must invoke methods of UI therefore it needs the UI handle.
```
...
Invoke userInterfaceHandle
            "query-for-room-number"
            Returning room-number
...
```

```
        $set sourceformat "free"
 1 *>***********************************************
 2 *> Room Rental System
 3 *> W. Price  Nov 25, 1999            R10-DRVR.CBL
 4 *> Room10 contains the same components as Room09.
 5 *> However, in Room10 all objects are defined
 6 *> as instance objects (in the OBJECT paragraph).
 7 *> The UI, Room Manager, and and DBI classes are
 8 *> instantiated in the factory of Room Manager.
 9 *>
10 *> The following classes comprise this project:
11 *>    R10-UI      UserInterface
12 *>    R10-MGR     RoomManager
13 *>    R10-ROOM    RoomClass
14 *>    R10-DBI     DatabaseInterface
15 *>***********************************************
16
17 Identification Division.
18        Program-ID.  Room10Driver.
19
20 Environment Division.
21        Object Section.
22          Class-control.
23            DatabaseInterface   is class "r10-dbi"
24            RoomManager         is class "r10-mgr"
25            UserInterface       is class "r10-ui"
26            .
27 Data Division.
28     Working-Storage Section.
29       *> object-handles.
30         01 roomManagerHandle       object reference.
31         01 userInterfaceHandle     object reference.
32         01 dataBaseInterfaceHandle object reference.
33
34 Procedure Division.
35    *> Create a room-manager object.
36       Invoke RoomManager "new"
37                   Returning roomManagerHandle
38
39    *> Create a user-interface object.
40       Invoke UserInterface "new"
41                   Returning userInterfaceHandle
42    *> Pass UI handle to room-manager instance
43       Invoke roomManagerHandle "pass-ui-handle"
44                   Using userInterfaceHandle
45
46    *> Create a data-base interface object.
47       Invoke DatabaseInterface "new"
48                   Returning dataBaseInterfaceHandle
49    *> Pass DBI handle to room-manager instance
50       Invoke roomManagerHandle "pass-dbi-handle"
51                   Using dataBaseInterfaceHandle
52
53    *> Give control to Room Manager
54       Invoke roomManagerHandle
55                      "process-user-requests"
56
57    Stop run
58    .
```

Figure 5-10. Driver for Room10—r10-drvr.

You see the solution to this dilemma in Figures 5-10 (Driver) and 5-11 (Room Manager). Driver's Invoke statements at lines 36, 40 and 47 instantiate each of these three classes (the handles are defined at lines 30-32). At Driver's line 43, Room Manager's method pass-ui-handle is invoked with the UI handle identified as the parameter.

Now look at Room Manager in Figure 5-11 where you see the UI and DBI handles defined as object data (lines 37 and 38) and the methods pass-dbi-handle (line 43) and pass-ui-handle (line 58). Focusing on the latter, you see that it accepts the object handle and stores it in its object data with the following statement (lines 66 and 67).

```
Set userInterfaceHandle
    to ls-userInterfaceHandle
```

Notice that this data is moved using the Set statement. As with index data items (refer to the discussion "Commentary on Data Types" in Chapter 4) you cannot use the Move. Being object data, it is available to all instance methods of the class.

You can see that the pass-dbi-handle method beginning line 43 performs the same action for DBI.[*]

---

[*] You could write a single method to accept both handles thereby requiring only one Invoke to pass them. However, the technique used here is preferred as it is simpler to maintain. For instance, if you restructured the application and removed all reference to, for instance, DBI from this class you simply remove the existing method as opposed to modifying a "multi-purpose" method.

Full Object Orientation of the Room Example

```cobol
       $set sourceformat "free"
1  *>***************************************************
2  *> Room Rental System
3  *> W. Price  Nov. 25, 1999              R10-MGR.CBL
4  *>
5  *> RoomManager handles access to the classes of
6  *> the Room system.
7  *> Processing code is placed in the OBJECT
8  *> paragraph. This class as well as UI and DBI
9  *> are instantiated by Driver. Access to the UI
10 *> and DBI are via handles passed from Driver.
11 *> Object methods
12 *>    create-room-object
13 *>    pass-dbi-handle
14 *>    pass-ui-handle
15 *>    process-this-request
16 *>    process-user-requests
17 *>    process-user-selections
18 *>***************************************************
19
20 Identification Division.
21        Class-ID.  RoomManager
22                   inherits from BaseClass
23                   .
24
25 Environment Division.
26        Object Section.
27        Class-control.
28            RoomClass              is class "r06-room"
29            RoomManager            is class "r10-mgr"
30            BaseClass              is class "base"
31            .
32 *>========================================================
33 OBJECT.
34
35   Data Division.
36      Object-Storage Section.
37         01  userInterfaceHandle       object reference.
38         01  dataBaseInterfaceHandle   object reference.
39         01  theRoomHandle             object reference.
40
41   Procedure Division.
42 *>-----------------------------------------------
43   Method-id. pass-dbi-handle.
44 *>-----------------------------------------------
45      Data Division.
46         Linkage Section.
47            01 ls-dataBaseInterfaceHandle
48                                       object reference.
49
50      Procedure Division
51                Using ls-dataBaseInterfaceHandle.
52         Set dataBaseInterfaceHandle
53                to ls-dataBaseInterfaceHandle
54         .
55   End Method pass-dbi-handle.
56
57 *>-----------------------------------------------
58 Method-id. pass-ui-handle.
59 *>-----------------------------------------------
60      Data Division.
61         Linkage Section.
62            01 ls-userInterfaceHandle object reference.
63
64      Procedure Division
65                Using ls-userInterfaceHandle.
66         Set userInterfaceHandle
67                to ls-userInterfaceHandle
68         .
69 End Method pass-ui-handle.
70
71 *>-----------------------------------------------
72 Method-id. process-user-requests.
73 *>-----------------------------------------------
74      Data Division.
75         Local-Storage Section.
76            01 lo-room-number                pic x(03).
77               88 lo-no-more-room-requests
78                                          value spaces.
79            01 lo-process-complete-message pic X(40)
80                      value "Processing complete".
81
82      Procedure Division.
83         Invoke dataBaseInterfaceHandle "open-file"
84         Perform with test after
85                until lo-no-more-room-requests
86            Invoke userInterfaceHandle
87                   "query-for-room-number"
88                   Returning lo-room-number
89            If lo-no-more-room-requests
90               Continue
91            Else
92               Invoke Self "process-this-request"
93                      Using lo-room-number
94            End-If *>no-more-room-requests
95         End-Perform *>with test after
96         Invoke dataBaseInterfaceHandle
97                   "close-file"
98         Invoke userInterfaceHandle "display-message"
99                Using lo-process-complete-message
100        .
101 End Method process-user-requests.
...
195 END CLASS RoomManager.
```

Figure 5-11. Room manager for Room10—r10-mgr.

Instantiating the Classes in Room Manager's Factory

[Proj0504 Room11]

Another approach is to place the instance creation code of Figure 5-10 in the Factory of Room Manager as done in Figure 5-12. Execution now proceeds as follows.

1. Processing is begun in Driver which contains the statement:

   Invoke RoomManager "start-up"

   Use of the class name RoomManager (as opposed to an object handle) causes the system to look for the factory method start-up.
2. The three classes, Room Manager, UI, and DBI are instantiated and the handles are passed on to the Room Manager instance. This code (lines 50-65) is nearly identical to the corresponding code of the preceding project's driver (Figure 5-10). The only difference is the identifier Super (line 50) as the factory is instantiating its own instance object. [Note: The object identifier Super forces the system to move "up" to the Base class for the method new. You will learn details of this in Chapter 8.]
3. Control is passed to the instance object via the Invoke of line 67.

When you look at a class definition such as r11-mgr you see a single source module. However, you must recognize that the Factory and Object are quite independent of one another. Consequently, *data of the Factory paragraph is not visible to methods of the Object paragraph and conversely, object data of the instance created from the Object paragraph is not visible to methods of the Factory paragraph*. It is almost as if they are two separate source modules.

Now look at the Invoke of lines 50 and 51, located in the Factory paragraph of this class, to create an instance of the Object paragraph of this class. It creates an instance of Room Manager exactly the same as if it were executed from another program (for example, the Driver of Figure 5-10). Then the resulting room handle, roomManagerHandle, is used as the object reference in the Invoke statements of lines 57, 64, and 67.

Lines 57 and 64 pass the needed object handles to the instance object exactly as before. Do not get the idea that you could define these handles (lines 44-46) as Factory object data and therefore have them visible to the instance object. It bears repeating that *object data of the Factory paragraph is not visible to methods of the Object paragraph and conversely, object data of the instance created from the Object paragraph is not visible to methods of the Factory paragraph*.

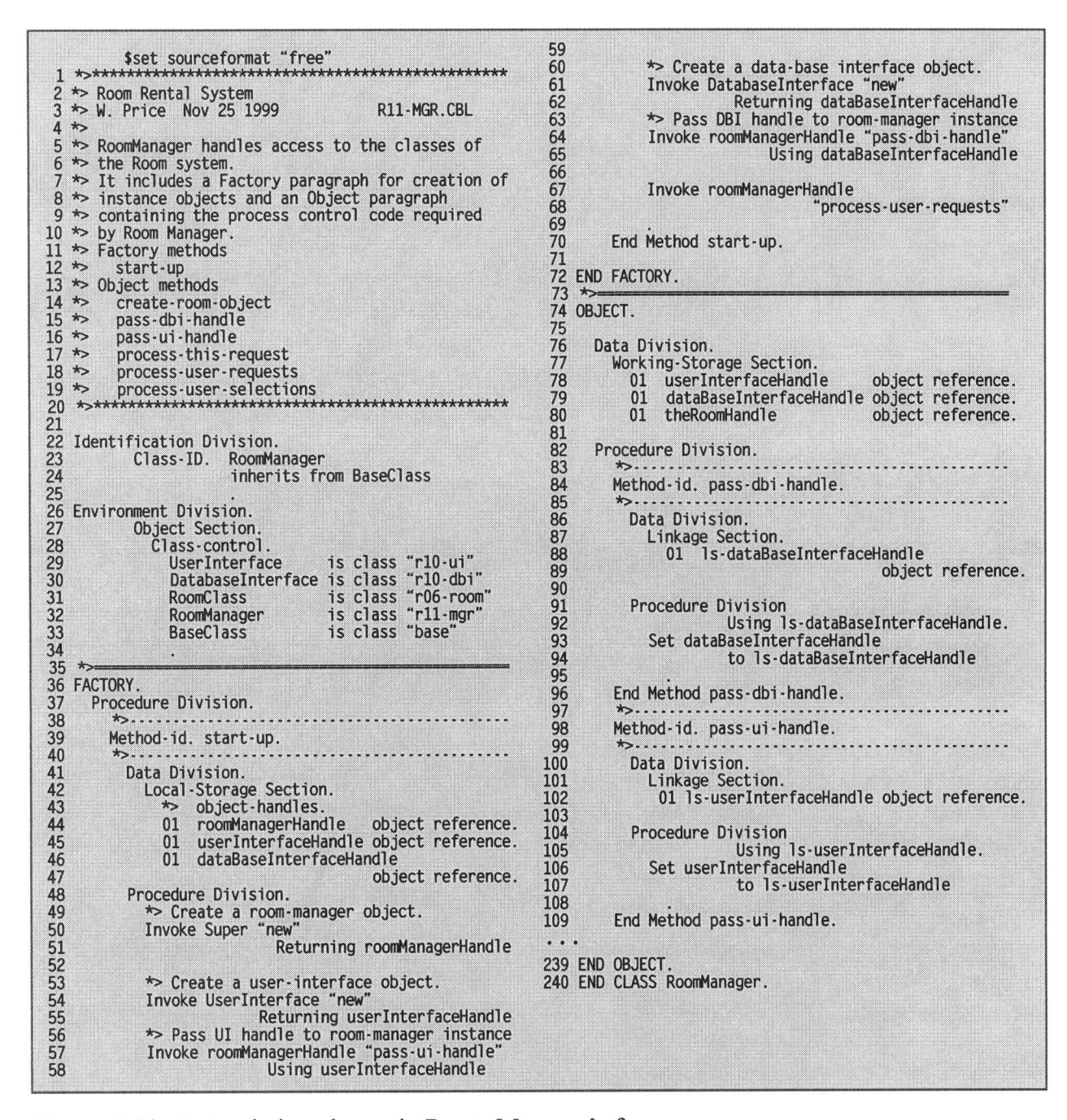

```cobol
        $set sourceformat "free"
1  *>*****************************************************
2  *> Room Rental System
3  *> W. Price  Nov 25 1999               R11-MGR.CBL
4  *>
5  *> RoomManager handles access to the classes of
6  *> the Room system.
7  *> It includes a Factory paragraph for creation of
8  *> instance objects and an Object paragraph
9  *> containing the process control code required
10 *> by Room Manager.
11 *> Factory methods
12 *>    start-up
13 *> Object methods
14 *>    create-room-object
15 *>    pass-dbi-handle
16 *>    pass-ui-handle
17 *>    process-this-request
18 *>    process-user-requests
19 *>    process-user-selections
20 *>*****************************************************
21
22 Identification Division.
23       Class-ID.  RoomManager
24                  inherits from BaseClass
25                  .
26 Environment Division.
27       Object Section.
28          Class-control.
29             UserInterface       is class "r10-ui"
30             DatabaseInterface   is class "r10-dbi"
31             RoomClass           is class "r06-room"
32             RoomManager         is class "r11-mgr"
33             BaseClass           is class "base"
34             .
35 *>==========================================================
36 FACTORY.
37    Procedure Division.
38       *>..............................................
39       Method-id. start-up.
40       *>..............................................
41          Data Division.
42          Local-Storage Section.
43             *> object-handles.
44             01 roomManagerHandle   object reference.
45             01 userInterfaceHandle object reference.
46             01 dataBaseInterfaceHandle
47                                    object reference.
48          Procedure Division.
49             *> Create a room-manager object.
50             Invoke Super "new"
51                         Returning roomManagerHandle
52
53             *> Create a user-interface object.
54             Invoke UserInterface "new"
55                         Returning userInterfaceHandle
56             *> Pass UI handle to room-manager instance
57             Invoke roomManagerHandle "pass-ui-handle"
58                         Using userInterfaceHandle
59
60             *> Create a data-base interface object.
61             Invoke DatabaseInterface "new"
62                         Returning dataBaseInterfaceHandle
63             *> Pass DBI handle to room-manager instance
64             Invoke roomManagerHandle "pass-dbi-handle"
65                         Using dataBaseInterfaceHandle
66
67             Invoke roomManagerHandle
68                                  "process-user-requests"
69             .
70       End Method start-up.
71
72 END FACTORY.
73 *>==========================================================
74 OBJECT.
75
76    Data Division.
77       Working-Storage Section.
78          01 userInterfaceHandle      object reference.
79          01 dataBaseInterfaceHandle  object reference.
80          01 theRoomHandle            object reference.
81
82    Procedure Division.
83       *>..............................................
84       Method-id. pass-dbi-handle.
85       *>..............................................
86          Data Division.
87          Linkage Section.
88             01 ls-dataBaseInterfaceHandle
89                                        object reference.
90
91          Procedure Division
92                     Using ls-dataBaseInterfaceHandle.
93             Set dataBaseInterfaceHandle
94                     to ls-dataBaseInterfaceHandle
95             .
96       End Method pass-dbi-handle.
97       *>..............................................
98       Method-id. pass-ui-handle.
99       *>..............................................
100         Data Division.
101         Linkage Section.
102            01 ls-userInterfaceHandle object reference.
103
104         Procedure Division
105                    Using ls-userInterfaceHandle.
106            Set userInterfaceHandle
107                    to ls-userInterfaceHandle
108            .
109      End Method pass-ui-handle.
...
239 END OBJECT.
240 END CLASS RoomManager.
```

Figure 5-12. Instantiating classes in Room Manager's factory.

Summing Up

Project Summary

Room08 (Proj0501) is an expansion of Room07 in which all user interaction code is removed from Driver and placed in a separate User Interface (UI) class. As UI exists for the duration of the run, it is defined in the class's Factory paragraph.

Room09 (Proj0502) is the final step in converting previous versions to full object methodology. Room08 is modified by removing all processing code from Driver and placing it in a Room Manager class. As Room Manager exists for the duration of the run, it is defined in the class's Factory paragraph. Driver now does nothing more than begin and end the process.

Room10 (Proj0503) is a variation of Room09 in which all objects are defined as instance objects. Driver now has the responsibilities of instantiating Room Manager, UI, and DBI, then passing handles of UI and DBI to the Room Manager object.

Room11 (Proj0504) is identical to Room10 except that instantiation of the three classes is now performed in the factory of Room Manager.

General Summary

The focus of this chapter has been on moving your thinking from the structured approach to the object approach. Examples of Chapter 4 are based partially on structured methodology (Driver) and partially on object methodology (Room and DBI). When the structured-trained programmer finds the "going getting tough" in identifying classes of an application, the tendency is to fall back into the structured mindset (our perceived safety net). Avoid that pitfall! Focus on "things," their responsibilities, and their collaborators. From examples of this chapter you've learned about the following.

- Breaking an application down into four basic classes:
    User interface
    Overall control (Room Manager)
    Application specific (Room)
    Database interface
- Communication between classes of an application.
- Creating an application in which all objects of the system are defined as instance objects. This approach does not take advantage of Cobol's unique factory features.

Coming Up

Chapter 1 reviews the structured program cycle: analysis, design, and programming. Object technology, although a major change in programming methodology, still requires these three steps. A problem must still be analyzed, and a design developed, and that design programmed. One beauty of object technology is that the same representation tool is used throughout the process: the focus is on objects. Chapter 6 explores those representation tools.

Assignment

5-1
Expand the application of Assignment 4-1 to include the following two classes:
   A user interface to handle all communication with the user
   A system manager class to provide overall control.
The sole function of the driver program is to create needed objects and pass control to the appropriate class program.

5-2
Expand the application of Assignment 4-2 to include the following two classes:
   A user interface to handle all communication with the user
   A system manager class to provide overall control.
   The sole function of the driver program is to create needed objects and pass control to the appropriate class program.

Object-Oriented Analysis & Design

Chapter Contents

Some Basic Concepts 112
    Analysis and Design 112
    Categories of Classes 113
Object-Oriented Design Tools 113
    Object Think 114
    Use-Case Scenarios 114
    Identifying Classes from a Problem Statement 115
    Responsibility-driven design 115
    CRC Cards (Class-Responsibility-Collaborator) 117
    Class Diagrams 118
Phase I: Analysis and Modeling 119
    Finding Candidate Classes 119
    Use-Case Scenarios 119
    Problem Statement Analysis 121
    CRC Cards 122
Phase II—High-Level Design 122
    Activities of Phase II 122
    More on Classes and Class Diagrams 123
Phase III—Low-Level Design 124
    About Modeling and Documentation 124
About Documentation 125
    An Example Documentation Form 125
    A Documentation Template 128
    Setting Up and Using the Template 131
Summing Up 132
Coming Up 132
Design Assignments 133

Chapter 6

Chapter Introduction[*]

The focus of Chapters 2, 3, and 4 is on the very basics of object orientation and OOCobol syntax. Chapter 5 begins to scratch the surface of the object-oriented design mind-set and truly "objectifying" an application. This chapter is devoted to introducing object-oriented analysis and design techniques. From this chapter you will learn the following.

- Categorizing classes by stereotype
- Mind tools such as "object think" and "responsibility-driven design."
- Class diagrams to show an application's classes and their relationships to one another.
- Usage scenarios to explore and better understand a system.
- Using CRC (Class-Responsibility-Collaborator) cards in the analysis and design process.
- A documentation process for use in this book.

[*] Some significant changes to this chapter (over the first edition) were suggested by my good friend and respected colleague Michael Turk of the University of Western Sidney, MacArthur.

Some Basic Concepts

Analysis and Design

Chapters 1 and 2 furnished you a brief design and analysis contrast between structured methodology and object-oriented methodology. Although object-oriented analysis and design (OOA&D) differ in approach from traditional methods, OO analysis is still analysis, OO design is still design. The objective is still to go from the often fuzzy world of user expectations to the concrete world of programs. Analysis still defines "what" the system must do and design still designates "how" the system will do it.

OOA&D methods differ from structured methods in several ways. First, OO methods focus on objects throughout the entire software development life cycle, thereby providing a unified theme throughout the cycle. Second, OO methods support incremental development, which allows applications to be tested earlier in the life cycle than with conventional methods. In OO development, functionality is gradually accrued as a working system is constructed. A principal notion of OO methodology is the emphasis on **iteration**: the process of successive refinement of the system by application of experience and results gained from one level of analysis and design to the next level. This is clearly illustrated by the spiral representation described in Chapter 2 and repeated here in Figure 6-1.

Because class descriptions are the fundamental units of object-oriented construction, iteration provides early testing and feedback. As Peter Coad describes it, one does some analysis, some design, and some coding, then stands back to assess progress and repeats the cycle. However, this is not to suggest a general maxim "go forth and iterate." Object-oriented methodology does not render planning and thinking obsolete.

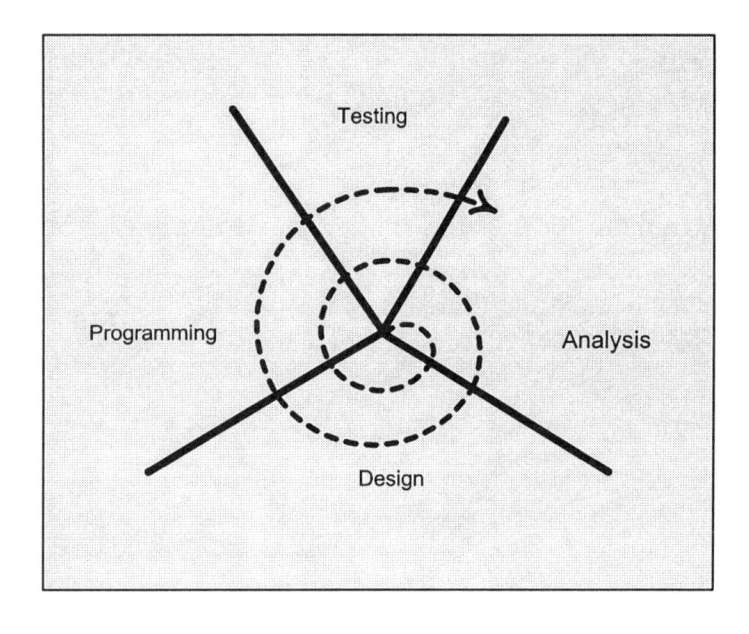

Figure 6-1.
The spiral model.

Categories of Classes

Through the process of exploration and discovery in the preceding chapter, you saw the room example expanded to following four basic classes.

- User interface (presentation)
- Room manager (control)
- Room (application domain)
- Database interface (data management)

In your reading about object technology, you will encounter the term **class stereotype**. Stereotyping is the grouping of classes according to type. One commonly encountered stereotyping scheme uses the above four classifications that grew out of the room application.

- **Presentation/Interface:** Responsible for presenting information to and retrieving input from users. These classes/objects are typically responsible for displaying graphical user interfaces or retrieving information.
- **Control:** Responsible for coordinating the services provided by different classes and objects. This category manages many of the operations in an application, acting as a go-between or middleman in carrying out requests for service.
- **Application Domain:** Perform tasks or contain information specific to an application.
- **Data Management:** Responsible for managing data structures. They hide the details of data structures thereby allowing the structures to change without affecting the other classes and objects in the system.

Each class contains its specialized data and provides relevant services. You will discover that most of your applications require each of the four categories. As you proceed with development of a system, you will find it helpful to view each potential type from the perspective of its stereotype.

Object-Oriented Design Tools

As with structured methodology, you will find numerous tools and techniques to aid with object-oriented design/analysis. Although this book focuses on using the object capabilities of Cobol, you must not become so involved with actual Cobol syntax that you overlook design aspects. To this end, this chapter describes the following basic tools.

- Object think
- Use-case scenarios
- Responsibility-driven design
- CRC cards (Class-Responsibility-Collaboration)
- Class diagrams
- Class documentation

Object Think

A common way of viewing an application is to identify "objects" of the system. As used here, the word *object* has a broader meaning than an instance of a class. An object can be anything to which action or thought can be directed, for instance, person, machine, organization, substance, parking lot, or airplane flight (event). Peter Coad has suggested an approach he calls **object think** in which he views each object as knowing things and knowing how to do things. A good approach is to personalize what you are modeling—that is, play the roll of an object. For instance, play the part of "room."

- I am a Room.
- I know my:
  - number
  - prices
  - discount
  - capacity
- I know how to:
  - tell you my prices
  - compute and tell you my discounted prices
  - tell you my capacity

Use-Case Scenarios

Analysis and design almost always involve two groups: users who understand the application (the **domain experts**) and analysts/designers who understand design techniques and computers. A small application may involve only one user and one designer whereas a large application may involve teams of users and designers. Whatever the situation, the "sides" must work together to go from the often fuzzy user expectations to the concrete world of a data processing system that will produce required results.

One tool for getting started is a **use-case analysis**. In a nutshell, a **use case** is a sequence of activities that produces something of value to an external entity or a user). For instance, placing a reservation for a room on a particular date yields something of value to the customer: the right to access of the room. Use cases view the system from an external perspective in describing what will happen in response to an event. In a complete room reservation system (beyond the scope of this book) the analysis phase would yield many **use-case scenarios** such as the following.

- A customer requests room information (the example of this book).
- A customer attempts to reserve a selected room for a particular date.
- The organization bills a customer for room rental.
- The organization receives a check from a customer for room rental.

Notice that these scenarios, which collectively describe the functions of the application, begin with some user (or other external entity) initiating a transaction or sequence of events.

Identifying Classes from a Problem Statement

Another approach to object-oriented analysis is prepare an English description of the problem (or part of the problem) as the starting point. Then proceed through the document highlighting nouns, which are potential classes. Verbs can also be highlighted as they serve to indicate operations that will be required on the object. This approach is useful because of its simplicity. It has the hidden benefit that it forces the domain experts and developers to focus on the vocabulary of the application and better crystallize the objectives of the application.

Following is a preliminary problem statement that could be used to begin analysis of the room rental application. In a later section of this chapter, you will see the "noun-identification" approach applied to this statement.

Room Rental Information System

The Scheduling Department of Object Training Centers rents both lecture rooms and computer lab rooms to its customers. A new interactive information system must allow customers to log on to access basic data including room prices and capacity and to reserve rooms. Data will be stored in four indexed files: room file, room tax rate file, customer file, and reservation calendar file.

Responsibility-driven design

Responsibility-driven design, based on the work of Rebecca Wirfs-Brock, is another "mind tool" used in object-oriented software development. You've already had an informal introduction to this technique in preceding chapters where you've seen each class identified together with its "responsibilities." For instance, one of Room's responsibilities is calculating and returning the discounted room rates. Of course, there is a limit to what an object knows and can do. Objects only know as much as they need in order to carry out their assigned tasks, and nothing more. In this world of responsible objects, it is collaboration between objects that moves the process forward and accomplishes work. Objects "talk" to one another by sending messages. (In OOCobol, the message—name of a method—is "sent" by the Invoke statement.) In this chapter you will take this approach one step further by identifying other classes with which a class must collaborate to dispense its responsibilities. A list of classes and their responsibilities/collaborators for Room09 of Chapter 5 is shown in Figure 6-2. For an insight to the terms "responsibilities" and "collaborators" let's focus on the method create-room-object from Room09's room manager (r09-mgr) included here as Figure 6-3.

```
UI
    Responsibilities                    Collaborators
        display-message
        display-room-capacity
        display-room-prices
        get-menu-selection
        query-for-room-number
Room Manager
    Responsibilities                    Collaborators
        Create room object                  DBI, Room
        Process user requests               DBI, UI
        Process this request                DBI, UI
        Process user selections             UI, Room
Room
    Responsibilities                    Collaborators
        get-discounted-room-prices
        get-room-capacity
        get-room-prices
        populate-the-room-object
DBI
    Responsibilities                    Collaborators
        close-file
        get-room-data
        open-file
        read-room-file
```

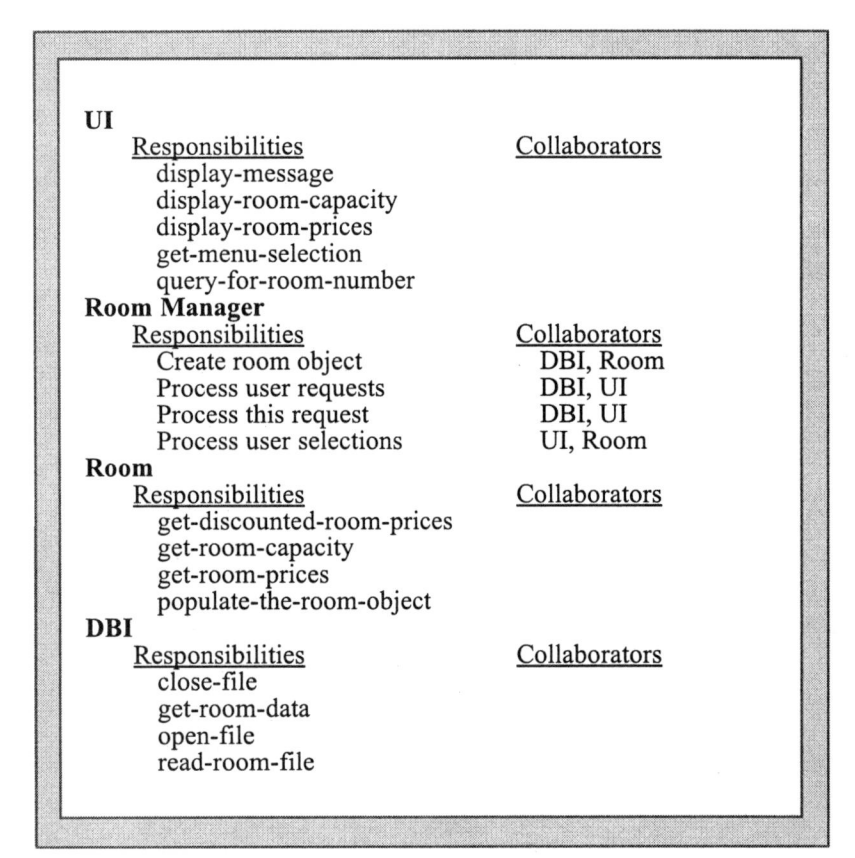

Figure 6-2.
Class responsibilities and collaborators for Room09.

- **Responsibilities** of a class correspond to methods of the class. For instance, the create-room-object method is identified as one of the responsibilities of Room Manager in Figure 6-2. This method performs the services of instantiating Room and populating it with data obtained from DBI.

```
*>-------------------------------------------
Method-id. create-room-object.
*>-------------------------------------------
Data Division.
    Working-Storage Section.
        01 ws-room-object-data.
            10 ws-room-number         pic X(03).
            10 ws-std-config-price    pic 9(03).
            10 ws-spec-config-price   pic 9(03).
            10 ws-room-discount       pic v9(02).
            10 ws-room-capacity       pic 9(02).

Procedure Division.
    Invoke DataBaseInterface "get-room-data"
           Returning ws-room-object-data
    Invoke RoomClass "New"
           Returning theRoomHandle
    Invoke theRoomHandle
           "populate-the-room-object"
           Using ws-room-object-data
End Method create-room-object.
```

Figure 6-3.
The method create-room-object from Room09's Room Manager.

- To perform these services, this method must invoke methods of other classes, in this case, DBI and Room. Thus, its collaborators are DBI and Room. If fulfilling a responsibility requires invoking another method of its own class (using the identifier Self), or a method of a superclass (the topic of Chapter 8) then that fact should be recorded.

Summarizing, a class's responsibilities correspond to methods of the class, and its collaborators are other classes containing methods that it invokes.

CRC Cards (Class-Responsibility-Collaborator)

The class-responsibility-collaborator summary of Figure 6-2 is actually a take-off of a responsibility-driven design tool called the **CRC card** (CRC is short for Class-Responsibility-Collaborator). A CRC card is nothing more than an index card illustrated in Figure 6-4. The front of the card is divided as follows.

- The class name is written at the top of the card.
- The left column contains the class's responsibilities.
- The right column contains the class's collaborators.

The back of the card contains a brief description of the class and a list of the class's attributes.

Class: Room Manager	
Responsibilities	**Collaborators**
1. Create room object.	1. DBI, Room.
2. Process user requests.	2. DBI, UI, Self.
3. Process this request.	3. DBI, UI, Self.
4. Process user selection.	4. Room, UI.

Room Manager: The object in the system that provides overall control of the process.

Attributes:
room handle

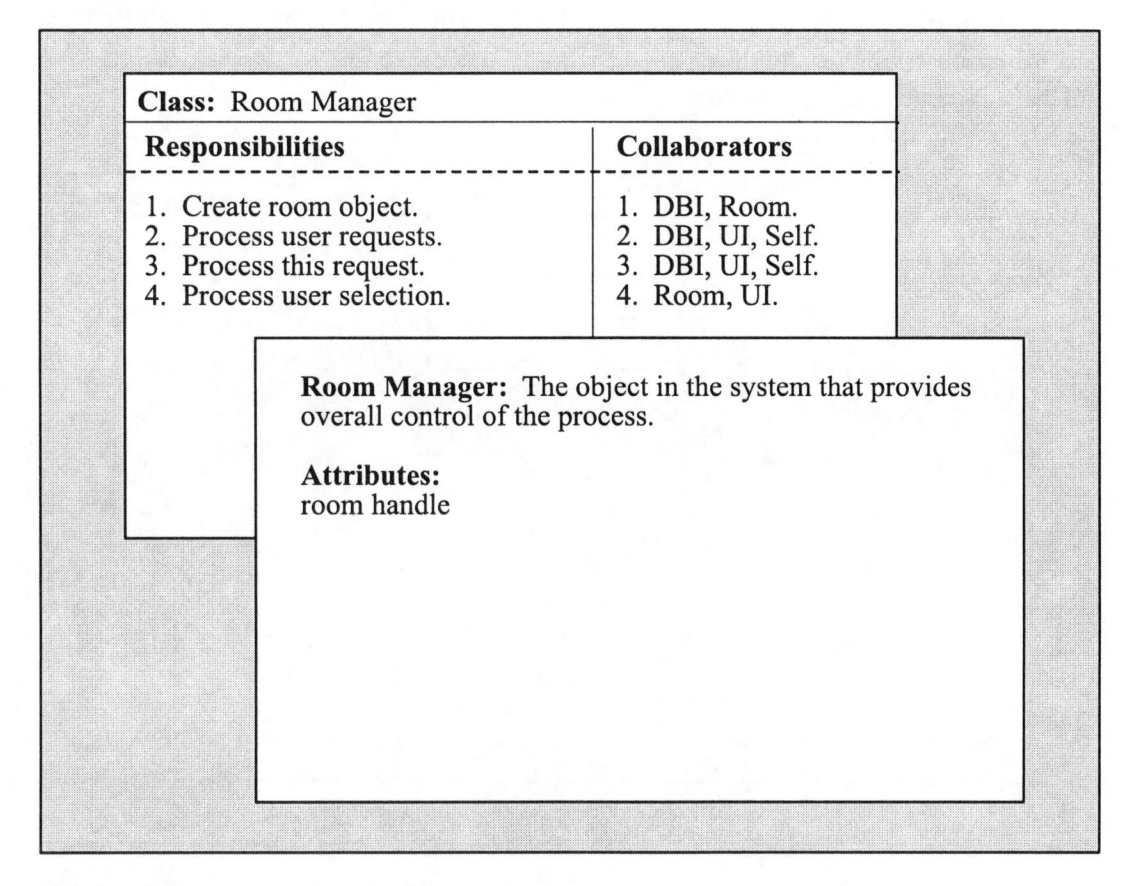

Figure 6-4. A CRC card for Room Manager.

CRC cards have emerged as a highly effective design tool in facilitating brainstorming and enhancing communication between all participants in the design activity. They are inexpensive, relatively informal, and convenient to manipulate as a system's characteristics evolve during design activities.

Class Diagrams

The **class diagram*** is a tool for illustrating a system's classes and the relationships between those classes. The diagrams of Chapter 5 (for instance, Figure 5-5) are essentially class diagrams. The **Unified Modeling Language (UML)** suggests the following structure for the class diagram.

- A class is represented by a rectangle divided horizontally into three parts as shown by the figure to the right.
    The top section contains the class name (in boldface).
    The middle section identifies attributes of the class (the object data).
    The bottom section identifies methods of the class.

ClassName
Attributes
Methods

- Related classes are connected by solid lines.
- Adjacent to each connecting line is a label indicating the association between the two classes. Optionally, an arrowhead can be included indicating the direction of the association.

Figure 6-5 is a basic class diagram for Room09 from Chapter 5. Notice that factory elements, both methods and attributes, are preceded with a dollar sign ($) to clearly indicate they are factory entries.

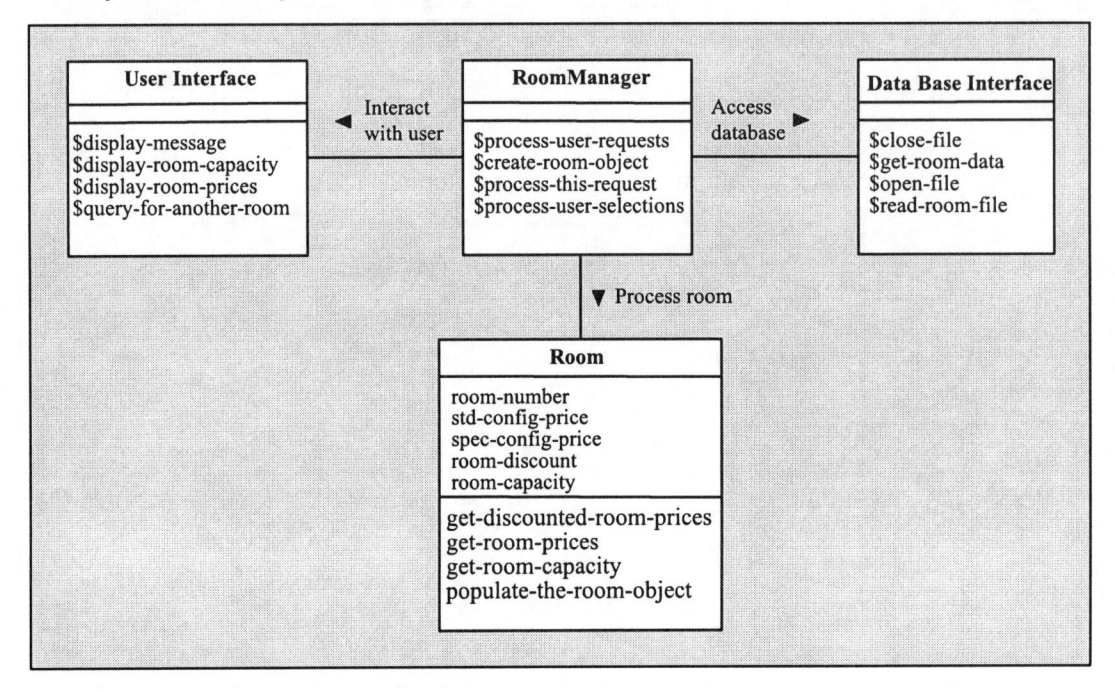

Figure 6-5. Class diagram for Room09.

---

* Class diagrams used in this book are taken from the Unified Modeling Language (UML), a widely used language for specifying, visualizing, constructing, and documenting the artifacts of software systems. It simplifies the complex process of software design, making a "blueprint" for construction.

Phase I: Analysis and Modeling

Finding Candidate Classes

The first phase of an object-oriented development effort is concerned with modeling the business application. The deliverables of this phase are:

- A problem description that defines what the intended software is expected to do.
- Usage scenarios that will be used to drive design and establish a basis for later testing.
- A list of candidate classes required to satisfy system needs; a class diagram serves to identify relationships between classes.

One of the more difficult tasks of OOA&D is finding the right classes of an application. Two techniques you can utilize are use-case analysis and noun-search of the application description (or a combination of the two). Let's look at each of these from the perspective of the room system.

Use-Case Scenarios

The first step in a use-case analysis is to enumerate primary use cases from the perspective of the overall functional elements of the system. For instance, the results of the initial brainstorming session might include the following.

- The customer logs on to our site to obtain room-pricing information.
- The customer logs on to our site to make a room reservation.
- The customer logs on to change a reservation (can be a cancellation).
- The customer phones to make a reservation.
- The customer phones to change a reservation (can be a cancellation).
- Business office prepares a customer invoice.
- Business office performs monthly billing.
- Business office prepares a monthly room utilization summary.
- Business office reviews each customer whose account is overdue to determine whether or not to revoke access rights.
- Rooms must be locked except when in use. Facilities management unlocks and locks rooms for renting customers.
- Facilities management schedules room cleanup around usage.
- And so on.

Each of the primary use cases will commonly break down into a number of secondary use scenarios. In constructing scenarios, keep them simple; a compound sentence usually should be broken into two separate scenarios. For instance, consider a customer logging on to reserve a room.

- The customer is not allowed to make a reservation because online reservation access rights have been revoked.
- The customer enters a room number that does not exist.
- The customer requests a room that is not available at the requested time.

You can summarize this use-case scenario on a use-case card (Figure 6-6) using either the form of the top card containing a numbered list of actions or the bottom card containing a semi-pseudocode description format.

Simple scenarios can help you identify candidate classes ("objects" that you should consider as possible classes) of the application as illustrated by the following.

1. The customer interacts with the system; therefore a **customer class** will be required.
2. Interaction with a user requires a **user interface class**.
3. Access to data from the customer database requires a **customer database interface class**.
4. Access to data from the room database requires a **room database interface class**.

The customer logs on to our site to make a room reservation.

1. Access the customer database for customer data.
2. If customer does not have access right, deny access.
3. Accept room number and date from customer.
4. Access the room database for the requested room record.
5. Room not found, display error message and ask for another room number.
6. Room not available requested date; give user option of another room or another date.
7. Room available, make reservation.

The customer logs on to our site to make a room reservation.

Access the customer database for customer data.
If customer does not have access right,
   deny access and terminate session.
Accept room number and date from customer.
Access the room database for the requested room record.
If room not found
   display error message and ask for another room number
Else
   If room available requested date
     make reservation
   Else
     give user option of another room or another date.

Figure 6-6. Use-case cards.

Overall, the list of scenarios developed during a use-case analysis serves three valuable purposes.

- Help uncover information about the system under development.
- Serve as input to CRC sessions of the next phase.
- Provide test cases to validate the system's operation.

Problem Statement Analysis

The other technique you might use in this preliminary phase of the analysis is preparing and analyzing the problem statement. Working with the problem statement from an earlier section of this chapter you might end up with the following underscored words as your "first cut" at candidate classes.

> The Scheduling Department of Object Training Centers rents both lecture rooms and computer lab rooms to its customers. A new interactive information system must allow customers to log on to access basic data including room prices and capacity and to reserve rooms. Data will be stored in four indexed files: room file, room tax rate file, customer file, and reservation calendar file.

Upon later scrutiny, you will probably delete some that you've identified as potential classes. But at this early stage, do not attempt to analyze them, simply identify them or else you'll probably become bogged down in details.

The next step is to ascertain whether or not each of your candidate classes is needed to accomplish goals of this application. Upon examining the application statement, notice that the goal of this system is to "allow customers to log on to access basic data and to reserve rooms." Let's consider each of the identified candidate classes.

1. As this is an online reservation system, the *Scheduling Department* would not be an appropriate class. However, the designer should inquire about other aspects of the system as reservation processing might require such a class.
2. *Object Training Centers* and *interactive information system* are general references and not potential classes.
3. Notice the word *room* occurs in several forms: *room facilities*, *lecture rooms*, *computer laboratory rooms*, and just plain *rooms*. As this problem statement provides no distinction between lecture and laboratory rooms, a single **room class** would likely suffice. However, the designer should inquire of the domain expert regarding the distinction between lecture room and laboratory room.
4. The *customer* is the external user of the system—a **customer class** is definitely required.
5. *Basic data* and *data* generically refer to attributes of the room class, not potential classes.
6. *Room prices* and *capacity* are attributes of room.

7. *Indexed files* is a general reference and is more appropriately addressed by considering the specific file types.
8. Access is required to both customer and room data. Therefore, the application will require **customer database interface** and **room database interface classes**.
9. The customer must have access to room pricing data thus requiring access to the room tax rate file via a **tax database interface class.**
10. For reserving rooms, the access to the reservation calendar file is needed. For this, you might need a separate **reservation calendar database interface class** or you might include a room reservation calendar as an attribute of the room class. (You will learn more about this in a later chapter.)

As you become experienced in object-oriented methodology, you will usually see the distinction between data items (potential attributes) and candidate classes immediately. As you spot attributes of a class; list them together with the appropriate class. For instance, prices and room capacity are obvious attributes of room.

CRC Cards

Further consideration of scenarios of the analysis phase provide input to the CRC sessions. During a CRC session, participants record candidate classes on these cards. As participants gain an understanding of the system, responsibilities and collaborations become evident and are recorded on appropriate cards.

Phase II—High-Level Design

Activities of Phase II

Phase II, high-level design, builds on the scenarios and candidate classes delivered from Phase I by allocating responsibilities to individual classes. Class and object definitions developed from analysis are often refined to meet constraints of the implementation. Activities of this phase include the following.

- Determine whether you will use factory objects for classes that exist for the run lifetime or instance objects for all.
- Assign a name to each class that reflects its function, for instance, User Interface, Room, Calendar, and Database Interface.
- Identify other needed classes such as a control class and intermediate service classes to coordinate services between components of the system. Although their placement in the overall scheme might not be obvious at first, it will become apparent as you learn more about the emerging system.
- Identify classes to serve as needed go-betweens to isolate application logic from machine and/or external dependencies. You will see an example of this in Chapter 7 where file handling is separated from DBI and placed in a separate file-handling class.

- Document the preceding by expanding and detailing the CRC cards, use-case cards, and class diagrams. These constitute the deliverables of this phase.

At this stage in the development of a system, you probably have not identified all of the methods your classes will require, but you now have a good idea of what must be done.

More on Classes and Class Diagrams

During high-level design, relationships between classes begin to crystallize. Class visibility, the requirement that one class knows or doesn't know about another, also begins to take form. By limiting visibility of each class to others, you limit coupling between classes thereby providing greater independence of classes.

Sometimes you will discover classes that differ only in a few attributes. For instance, assume that during a "question-and-answer" period, you learn that lecture rooms and lab rooms must be treated differently. So you decide on two classes as illustrated in Figure 6-7. As you can see, both the object data and the methods are almost the same. LectureRoom includes the room capacity; LabRoom includes the number of workstations and the seats per workstation. At first glance, methods appear to be the same. However, room capacity for LabRoom must be computed (number of stations time seats per station) so that method will differ from the same method of LectureRoom. Also, because the object data is different for the two classes, the methods to populate the object will differ. Implementing two classes as illustrated in Figure 6-7 introduces redundancy—highly undesirable. For instance, a change in the algorithm for calculating the discounted prices would require changes in the identical code of two different classes.

Object technology resolves this problem with a **hierarchy structure** that, when applied to this model, yields the form of Figure 6-8. Data and methods common to both LectureRoom and LabRoom are moved to a separate class entitled Room. Data and methods unique to each specialized class remain in that class. Room is called the **superclass** and LectureRoom and LabRoom are called **subclasses**. However, through a feature called **inheritance**, methods of the superclass are available to the subclasses. In using the subclasses, the programmer sees each subclass as if it were of the form shown in Figure 6-7. The arrow at the end of the connecting line in

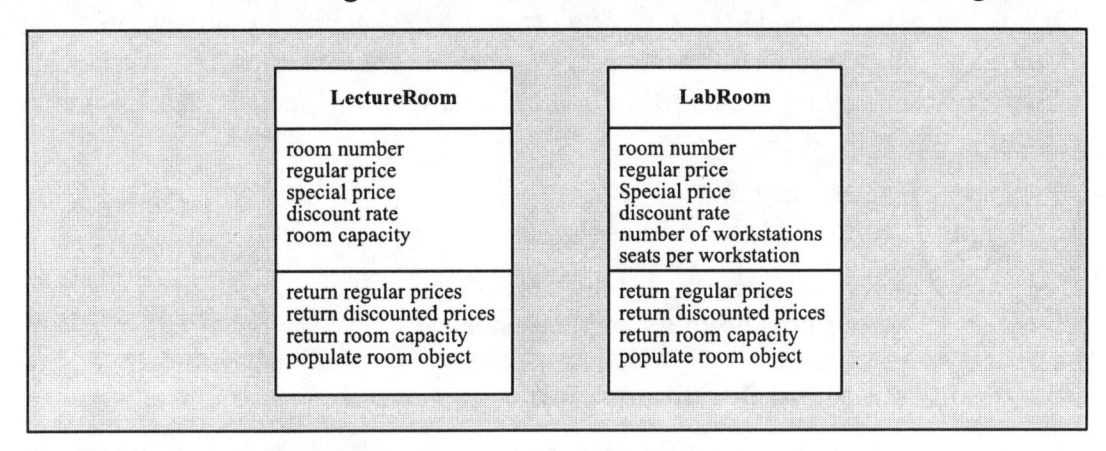

LectureRoom	LabRoom
room number regular price special price discount rate room capacity	room number regular price Special price discount rate number of workstations seats per workstation
return regular prices return discounted prices return room capacity populate room object	return regular prices return discounted prices return room capacity populate room object

Figure 6-7. Two similar classes.

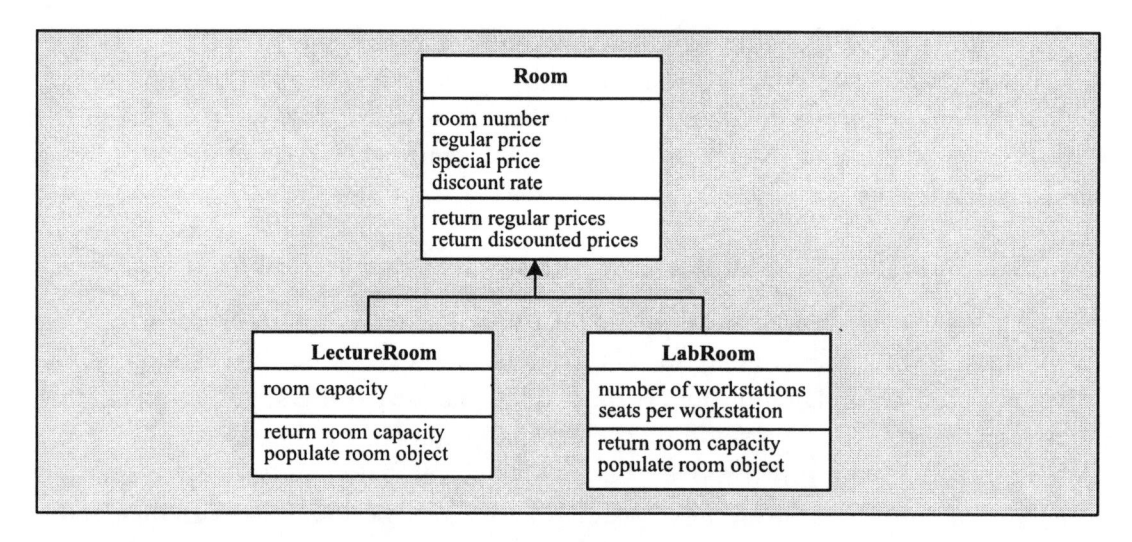

```
                        ┌─────────────────────────┐
                        │          Room           │
                        ├─────────────────────────┤
                        │ room number             │
                        │ regular price           │
                        │ special price           │
                        │ discount rate           │
                        ├─────────────────────────┤
                        │ return regular prices   │
                        │ return discounted prices│
                        └─────────────────────────┘
                                     △
                            ┌────────┴────────┐
                            │                 │
        ┌───────────────────────┐   ┌───────────────────────┐
        │      LectureRoom      │   │        LabRoom        │
        ├───────────────────────┤   ├───────────────────────┤
        │ room capacity         │   │ number of workstations│
        │                       │   │ seats per workstation │
        ├───────────────────────┤   ├───────────────────────┤
        │ return room capacity  │   │ return room capacity  │
        │ populate room object  │   │ populate room object  │
        └───────────────────────┘   └───────────────────────┘
```

Figure 6-8. Class diagram illustrating the inheritance relationship.

Figure 6-8 represents an inheritance hierarchy. You will learn about inheritance in Chapter 8.

Another type of structure encountered in object technology is the **aggregate**: basically an object that has been decomposed into its component parts. For instance, in preparing a graphic user interface system you might break a window into the four parts: title bar, pane, scrollbar, and border. The class diagram of Figure 6-9 uses a small diamond to show an aggregate relationship. In this example, you see that the class blocks do not contain each of the three areas (class name, attributes, and methods). There is no hard, fast rule that says you must display all three areas. So you can omit the attribute and method boxes if you are at a stage where you are showing neither the attributes nor the methods. You will see an example of aggregate structures in Chapter 9.

Phase III—Low-Level Design

During Phase III you add necessary detail to turn a design into an application. Class definitions must have a sufficient level of detail to describe messages, attributes, object creation, and relationships. Deliverables of Phase III include the following.

- Completed CRC cards
- Completed class diagrams
- A full set of use cards to serve as the basis for testing.

Together, these deliverables specify sufficient detail so that a programmer can generate code that tests both usability and performance.

About Modeling and Documentation

In the real world of programming, documentation is often a task that falls by the wayside because of pressure to get the programs up and running. In such cases, if the disaster doesn't strike during programming and testing, it most certainly strikes

```
                    ┌──────────┐
                    │  Window  │
                    └────◇─────┘
        ┌──────────┬─────┴─────┬──────────┐
   ┌────────┐ ┌────────┐ ┌──────────┐ ┌────────┐
   │TitleBar│ │  Pane  │ │ ScrollBar│ │ Border │
   └────────┘ └────────┘ └──────────┘ └────────┘
```

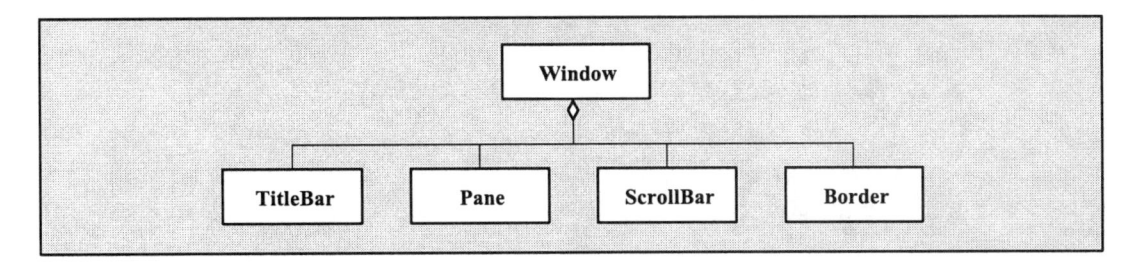

Figure 6-9. An aggregate structure.

during maintenance/upgrading. We all know the value of documentation, even though we may give it lip service at times.

In object technology, documentation is even more significant. Remember, documentation from the design phase is a refinement and extension of that same documentation of the analysis phase. There is no longer a complete shift of representation: we continue refining our object view. The user and the programmer both understand the model. So with object technology, we have representations that follow the entire cycle.

About Documentation

An Example Documentation Form

Thus far in this book you've seen a variety of techniques for documenting and illustrating your work: CRC cards, use-case cards, class diagrams, and a class/collaborator form. As a rule, you can consider documentation at two levels.

- For the class user who must be able to peruse the documentation to determine if it includes features needed in his/her application and how to use them. This boils down to a brief description of the class and details of using each public method. At this level, the user probably does not need to know details of the object data comprising the class.
- For the class writer who must maintain the class. This requires detail such as identification of object data and descriptions of all methods, both public and private.

I've included with this book a documentation template that I've found useful for both of the above needs. Its use is illustrated by the example of Figure 6-10 that has the following features.

1. The name of the class and both its super class and sub classes are identified with the general name by which the class is referenced and by its file name. This class has no super classes (other than Base) and no subclasses.
2. A description line, taken from the back of the CRC card, provides a brief description of the class. In addition, for some classes a "Special note" line describing any idiosyncrasy of the class might be appropriate. You'll see an example of this for a file-processing class in the next chapter.

Class: **Room Manager (r09-mgr.cbl)**
Description: The general control class that handles access to other classes of the room system.

FACTORY	Object Data: Room object handle	
Public Methods	*Parameters*	*Description*
process-user-requests		Provides overall process control. Collaborators: Self, UI, DBI
Private Methods	*Parameters*	*Description*
create-room-object		Creates and populates room object. Collaborators: Room, DBI Invoked by: process-this-request
process-this-request	Using: Room number pic X(03)	Handles processing for each room request. Collaborators: Self, DBI, UI Invoked by: process-user-requests
process-user-selections		Evaluates user data request and displays the requested information. Collaborators: UI, Room Invoked by: process-this-request

Figure 6-10. Sample class documentation—Room Manager.

3. Methods are grouped as either public or private.
4. The first row of this table identifies rows that follow as methods of the Factory. The second column of this row lists the factory's object data.
6. For subsequent rows, the first column identifies each method of the class by the actual class name (as required by a class user). As you see, methods are identified as either public or private, private being classes that are accessed only by other methods of this class.
6. The second column identifies data items. Each method entry identifies parameters and their characteristics, for instance, refer to the sixth row of this table containing the Using entry.
7. The third column contains the following for each method:
   - a description of the method,
   - a list of collaborators associated with the method (other methods it invokes), and
   - for private methods, the name of the method of the class that invokes the method.
8. Notice that data items in the second column are not identified by their Cobol data names but rather by a combination of words that suggest the nature of the field itself. Remember that to invoke a method, the name you use is your choice—it need not be the same name as that used in the method. Of course, you must know the picture clause.
9. Different fonts distinguish between actual Cobol items and descriptions. For instance, process-user-request (in 9-point Letter Gothic type) and pic X(03) are actual Cobol entries; Room number is a description of the data item.

Documentation for the remaining three classes of the Room09 application, is included on pages 127 and 128.

Class: User Interface (r08-ui.cbl)
Description: This class handles all interaction with the user.

FACTORY	Object Data: None	
Public Methods	*Parameters*	*Description*

get-menu-selection	Returning:
	  menu choice pic X(01)
	    C—Room capacity
	    S—Standard room prices
	    D—Discounted room prices
		Queries user for data display option. Menu choices are as shown.

display-message	Using: message pic X(40)	Displays transmitted message on user's screen.
display-room-capacity	Using: room capacity pic 9(02)	Displays room-capacity.

display-room-prices	Using:
	  Group item consisting of:
	    std config price pic 9(03)
	    spec config price pic 9(03)	

query-for-another-room	Returning: room number pic X(03)	Queries user for a room number. An empty entry terminates processing.

Figure 6-11. Class documentation for User Interface (r08-ui)

Class: Room (r06-room.cbl)
Description: Manages object data for a room.

OBJECT	Object Data:
	  room number
	  std config price
	  spec config price
	  room discount
	  room capacity	

Public Methods	**Parameters**	*Description*

get-discounted-room-prices	Returning:
	  room prices
	    std config price pic 9(03)
	    spec config price pic 9(03)
		Computes and returns discounted room prices as a group item.

get-room-prices	Returning:
	  room prices
	    std config price pic 9(03)
	    spec config price pic 9(03)
		Returns room prices as a group item.

get-room-capacity	Returning room capacity pic 9(02)	Returns room capacity.

populate-the-room-object	Using:
	  room data (group item)
	    room number pic X(03)
	    std config price pic 9(03)
	    spec config-price pic 9(03)
	    room discount pic 9V9(02)
	    room capacity pic 9(02)
		Populates the room object using data transmitted as a group item.

Figure 6-12. Class documentation for Room (r06-room).

Class: **Database Interface (r06-dbi.cbl)**
Description: This class provides read access to data of the indexed file room.di.

FACTORY	Object Data:
	  Room-file record
	    room number
	    accounting code
	    room type
	    std config price
	    spec config price
	    pricing code
	    room discount
	    room capacity
	    room width
	    room length	

Public Methods	*Parameters*	*Description*
`close-file`		Closes the room file.

`get-room-data`	Returning:
	  room object data (group item)
	    room number pic x(03)
	    std config price pic 9(03)
	    spec config price pic 9(03)
	    room discount pic v9(02)
	    room capacity pic 9(02)
		Returns room data required to populate the room object.

`open-file`	No parameters	Opens the room file.

`read-room-file`	Using:
	  room number pic X(03)
	Returning
	  record-found switch pic X(01)
	    Y—Record successfully read
	    N—Record not found
		Reads a room record using the input room number as the key. Returned value indicates whether or not record successfully read.

Figure 6-13. Class documentation for Database Interface (r06-dbi).

    User Interface (r08-ui)   Figure 6-11
    Room (r06-room)   Figure 6-12
    Database Interface (r06-dbi) Figure 6-13

Recall that Room11 (in the Proj0504 folder) illustrates using instance objects for all classes of the application. Figure 6-14 is the class documentation for Room Manager of this example. You should study each of these to see how various documentation features are implemented.

A Documentation Template

At first thought, formatting your documentation this way might appear to be a formidable task. However, the Examples CD included with this book contains the Microsoft Word template shown in Figure 6-15 that will allow you to simply fill in the blanks. Features of this form, beyond those discussed regarding Figure 6-10 follow.

1. The form includes two primary components: Factory and Object (corresponding to the Factory paragraph and the Object paragraph).

Class: Room Manager (r11-mgr.cbl)
Description: The general control class that handles access to other classes of the room system.

FACTORY	Object Data: None	
Public Methods	*Parameters*	*Description*
start-up		Creates instances of Room Manager (its own class), UI, and DBI then turns control over to the instance method. Collaborators: Self, UI, DBI
OBJECT	**Object Data:** User interface object handle Database interface object handle Room object handle	
Public Methods	*Parameters*	*Description*
process-user-requests		Provides overall process control. Collaborators: Self, UI, DBI
Private Methods	*Parameters*	*Description*
create-room-object		Creates and populates room object. Collaborators: Room, DBI Invoked by: process-this-request
pass-dbi-handle	Using: DBI handle object reference	Accepts DBI handle and stores it as object data for availability to other methods. Invoked by: start-up.
pass-ui-handle	Using: UI handle object reference	Accepts UI handle and stores it as object data for availability to other methods. Invoked by: start-up.
process-this-request	Using: Room number pic X(03)	Handles processing for each room request. Collaborators: Self, UI Invoked by: process-user-requests
process-user-selections		Evaluates user data request and displays the requested information. Collaborators: UI, Room Invoked by: process-this-request.

Figure 6-14. Class documentation for Room Manager (r11-mgr).

2. You replace items enclosed in parentheses with appropriate entries.
3. For entries not appropriate to a particular class, simply delete it. Use Figures 6-11 through 6-15 as guidelines.
4. If you bring this form up in Word, you will see tab settings for the indent levels in the examples.

Almost all examples in the book utilize Using for input parameters and Returning for the output parameter. If a method returns data through parameter listed under Using, you should explicitly so indicate. (Remember, Returning can list only one parameter.) For instance, assume you have a method with the following Procedure Division header.

```
Procedure Division Using room-number, c-factor, tax-code
```

Class:
Superclass:
Subclasses:
Description:
Special note:

FACTORY	**Object Data:** (list)	
Public Methods	*Parameters*	*Description*

(method name)	Using
	    (list)
	Returning
	    (list)
		(Description)
		Collaborators: (list)

Private Methods	*Parameters*	*Description*

(method name)	Using
	    (list)
	Returning
	    (list)
		(Description)
		Collaborators: (list)
		Invoked by: (method list)

OBJECT	**Object Data:** (list)	
Public Methods	*Parameters*	*Description*

(method name)	Using
	    (list)
	Returning
	    (list)
		(Description)
		Collaborators: (list)

Private Methods	*Parameters*	*Description*

(method name)	Using
	    (list)
	Returning
	    (list)
		(Description)
		Collaborators: (list)
		Invoked by: (method list)

Figure 6-15. A class documentation template.

> where: room-number is method input
>   c-factor (cost factory) is method output
>   tax-code is method output

Here you should include that information in the parameters entry, for instance:

> Using
>   Room number (I)   pic X(03)
>   Cost factor (O)   pic 9V99
>   Tax code (O)   pic X(07)

The Invoke, as does the familiar Call, allows parameter to be identified as available By reference or By content. Since By reference is the Cobol default, I do not include that information in the documentation. However, for any parameters specifically identified as By content, indicate that information as illustrated by the following (assuming Room number is by content).

Object-Oriented Analysis & Design

Using
    Room number (C)   pic X(03)
    Cost factory (O)   pic 9V99
    Tax code (O)   pic X(07)

You need not designate this field as input as By content allows only input.

Setting Up and Using the Template

The filename of the template is Class-doc.doc. If you loaded according to the instructions in the Preface of this book, you will find the file in the aData folder. To use it, you only need to open it and save it with another name in your working directory.

A better way is to save it as a Word dot file thereby making it readily available whenever you want to create a new one.

1. Bring up Microsoft Word.
2. Open the file Class-doc.doc.
3. Click File/Save As.
4. Following is the default display you will see at the bottom of your Save As window.

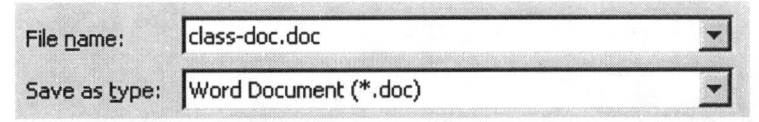

File name:	class-doc.doc
Save as type:	Word Document (*.doc)

5. You want to save this as Document Template (dot file). Expand the Save as type box and make that selection. This portion of the window should now appear as shown on the following page.

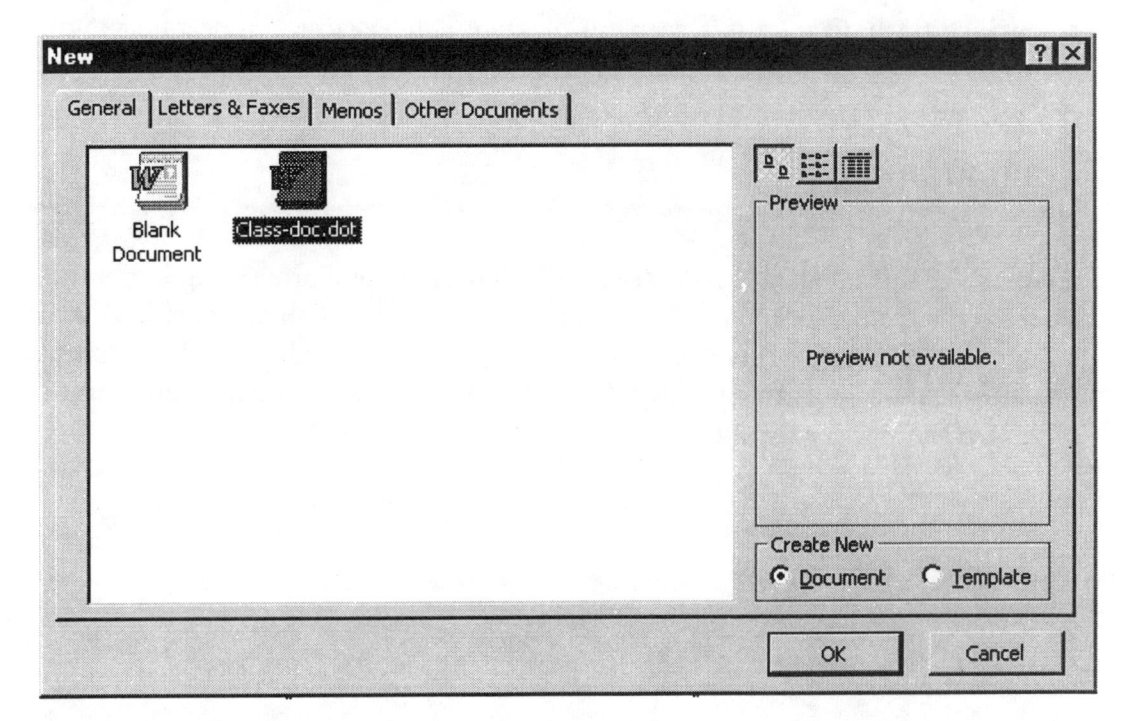

Figure 6-16. Creating a new document.

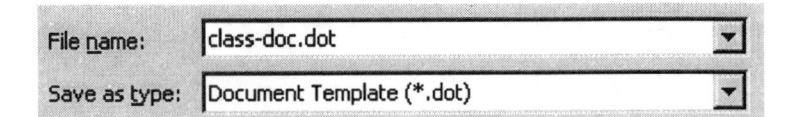

Now whenever you click File/New your New window will include the highlighted option shown in Figure 6-16. Select it (as shown), click the OK button, and the template will be loaded as a conventional Word document. You can then proceed to delete rows not applicable to your class and fill in entries as appropriate. As a wise man once said: "Simple as falling off a log."

Summing Up

Classes are commonly stereotyped as presentation/interface, control, application domain, and data management.

Object-oriented development emphasizes iteration: the process of successive refinement of a system by application of experience and results gained from one level of analysis and design to the next level.

A use-case scenario is a description of the sequence of events occurring within a system in response to a given event.

A class diagram is a tool for illustrating a system's classes and the relationships between those classes.

An object message diagram is a scenario diagram showing the sequence of messages to implement an operation or transaction.

A message trace diagram is a scenario diagram emphasizing time sequencing of events.

Coming Up

Examples to this point have included all file definitions and processing in the database interface class, adequate for the relatively simple examples considered thus far. However, as applications grow more complex and include access to multiple files, this approach become clumsy. Chapter 7 breaks file processing activities out of the DBI and places them in special file processing classes.

Design Assignments

5-1

Perform a CRC analysis on the following expanded version of the room rental application. Without a user to interview, you will need to make assumptions regarding the extent of this application. Clearly state your assumptions. Be aware that this statement includes superfluous descriptions that will have little or no bearing on the design. A significant purpose of the preliminary CRC session is to "separate the wheat from the chaff."

5-1 Problem Statement

One of the divisions of Object Technology Training handles room rental of its training facilities. Through its Facilities Management Office, a customer can reserve a room up to six months in advance. There is no limit on the number of days for a single reservation but the norm seems to be about three days. A reservation of more than two weeks is rare. Several categories of rooms are available for rent: lecture rooms, lab rooms, and so on.

Certain established customers receive a standard discount. Company policy requires a 25% deposit upon making the reservation with the balance due prior to the first day of the reservation. Special services provided during the rental period are billed separately with payment due in 30 days. No reservation will be made for a customer with an past-due balance.

OTC has a working agreement with several agencies that direct room-rental business to OTC for which OTC pays a referral fee of 3% the total rental fee. Referral fee conditions are clearly defined in a referral contract between OTC and the outside agencies.

5-2

You must describe the courtroom trial process to someone who has never heard of it. To do this, you've decided upon an object-oriented approach. That is, you must describe significant objects and, for each, list its responsibilities and collaborators. Work from the following description. Be aware that you must NOT represent every detail included in the description—some of it is extraneous and is there only to cloud the issue. Your object summary must describe the trial process (the standard American process that most of us have seen on TV numerous time). It *must exclude* any details not essential to the process.

5-2 Problem Statement

The local court tries felony cases Monday through Thursday beginning 9:00 AM with a one-hour lunch break at noon. Each of the three courtrooms includes spectator seats and has provisions for television coverage. A special seating area is reserved for the news media. Each court is permanently assigned a judge. If a defendant cannot afford an attorney, one is assigned by the court. The prosecuter is selected at random from the local district attorney's office. The jury is made up of registered voters from the local jurisdiction. Statistical studies have indicated that approximately 60% of jurors are women, many of whom list their occupation as homemakers.

5-3

Using the template of Figure 6-15, prepare documentation for each of the classes of your Chapter 4 assignment.

Processing Indexed Files

Chapter Contents

Using a File-Processing Class 138
    The Basic Concept 138
    The Room11 Project 140
    Room Manager—R11-mgr 140
    The Database Interface 142
    The Room File Processor—r11-r-fp 143
Updating Records of a File 146
    Some Program Design Considerations 146
    Additions to Room and Room Manager—Room12 148
    The Room Class—R12-room 150
Room Manager—R12-mgr 150
    The Room File Processor—R12-r-fp 154
    The DBI—R12-dbi 154
Accessing Data From a Subordinate File—Project 13 155
    Problem Definition 155
    The Room Class—R13-room 155
    The DBI—R13-dbi 156
T he File Processors: R13-r-fp and R13-t-fp 158
Room Manager—R13-mgr 158
Summing Up 158
    Project Summary 158
    General Summary 160
Coming Up 160
Assignments 160

Chapter 7

Chapter Introduction

The four-class structure (Manager, UI, Room, and DBI) is a sound, generalized structure that you can look to as a starting point in analyzing many application types. However, there is one flaw in the DBI concept that, when dealing with indexed files, leaves much to be desired. Three examples of this chapter show you how to remove the file processing activities from the DBI and place them in a separate file processing class.

- Room11 illustrates using a file processing class.
- Room12 allows the user to change prices in the object data. The file record is updated from this data.
- Room13 displays room prices that include a special room tax. Access to a second file is required to obtain the tax (thereby requiring two file processors).

Using a File-Processing Class

The Basic Concept

Assume that upon completing the room reservation application, OTC's management decides to design and implement a building security system. Although independent of one another, the two systems must "work together." In particular, both will require a database interface class accessing the room file as illustrated in Figure 7-1.

Now review the DBI of Figure 5-8 (Chapter 5) and you will see that its functions can be considered in to broad categories as illustrated in Figure 7-2.

- Elements specific to the application, such as gathering data for the room object.
- Elements specific to the data file, such as file definition information and record input.

Using this approach for the DBIs illustrated in Figure 7-1, you introduce significant redundancy as both will require the room record definition and methods to access the file (open, close, and read).

Backing off and viewing this from an object-methodology design perspective, you see two distinct class candidates: data interface and file interface. (As a designer, you probably would have recognized this during Phase II of the design, if not during Phase I.) The approach of this chapter revolves around defining a separate file-processor class for each indexed file in a system. The file processor contains the record description entries for the file; thus its object data is the data record

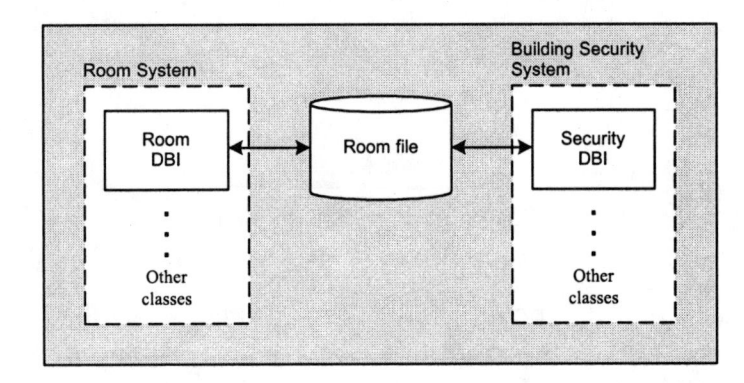

Figure 7-1. Access to the room file.

Figure 7-2. Typical database interface class for accessing an indexed file.

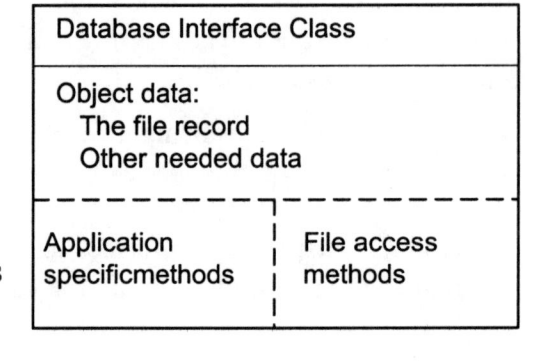

Figure 7-3.
Two file processors.

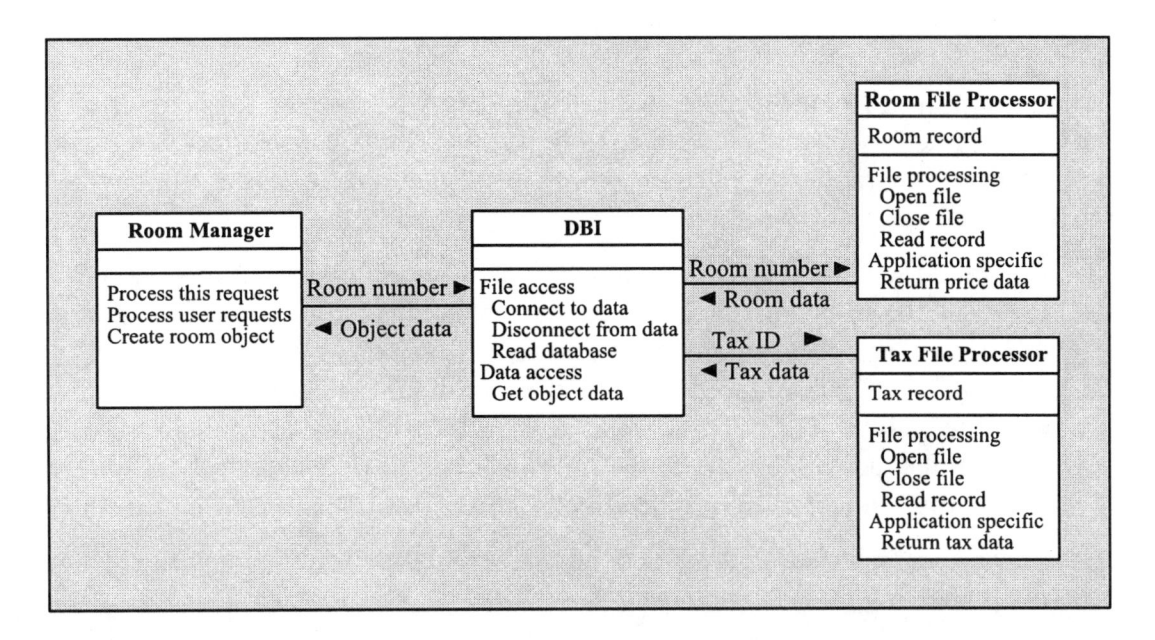

[Diagram: Room Manager (Process this request, Process user requests, Create room object) ↔ DBI (File access: Connect to data, Disconnect from data, Read database; Data access: Get object data) via Room number → and ◄ Object data. DBI connects to Room File Processor (Room record; File processing: Open file, Close file, Read record; Application specific: Return price data) via Room number → and ◄ Room data. DBI connects to Tax File Processor (Tax record; File processing: Open file, Close file, Read record; Application specific: Return tax data) via Tax ID → and ◄ Tax data.]

itself. Its methods fall in two categories: file management (for instance, open, close, and read) and returning data required by DBI for the application. The design example problem statement of Chapter 6 refers to an application in which room prices can include room taxes from a tax file. Figure 7-3 illustrates the way in which the room and tax file processor classes might be incorporated into an application. Notice that the interaction between Room Manager and DBI is identical to their interaction you saw in Room09 of Chapter 5. (Interaction of Room Manager with Room and UI, not shown, is also identical to that of Room09.) Each file processor has the sole responsibility for managing the record: reading a desired record, rewriting a record when values are changed, and making individual fields available to the DBI for object populating.

When other applications requiring access to a given file are planned, the appropriate file processor class can be incorporated with only the addition of application-specific methods to be invoked by that application's DBI. This concept is illustrated in Figure 7-4—compare it to Figure 7-1.

Figure 7-4.
Incorporating the Room File Processor in two applications.

[Diagram: Room System (Room DBI ↔ Room File Processor, Other classes) and Building Security System (Security DBI ↔ Room File Processor, Other classes), both Room File Processors connected to a shared Room file.]

The Room11 Project

Proj0701
Room11

The next project, Room11, incorporates a modified DBI that accesses data from the Room File Processor as illustrated in Figure 7-3 (the Tax File Processor is not included). If you run this application, you will see that it differs from Room09 in two ways.

1. Display of room capacity has been eliminated from the user options in order to reduce the amount of code in the program listings of this book. Deletion of this component does not affect the principles illustrated by this application.
2. A second loop is introduced whereby the user, upon selecting a room, is presented with three options: display room prices, display discounted prices, and exit the display loop. Before examining classes of this application you should run it to get a feel for the affect of this second loop.

This project consists of the following classes—let's examine them to see how the file processing class is implemented

r11-ui	User interface
r11-mgr	Room manager
r11-room	Room Class
r11-dbi	Database interface
r11-r-fp	Room file processor

Driver and the two classes UI and Room are almost identical to their counterparts of Chapter 5's Room09 (code to display room capacity is removed). Let's examine the remaining three classes: Room Manager, DBI, and Room File Processor.

Room Manager—R11-mgr

Room manager for this application, r11-mgr shown in Figure 7-5, differs from r09-mgr (Figure 5-7) only in the process-user-selections method where access to room capacity has been deleted and the inline Perform at lines 123 has been added. The latter allows the user to request other options for the same room. The loop is controlled by the user entry from the following method get-menu-selection taken from the user interface r11-ui.

```
67          Procedure Division Returning ls-menu-choice.
68              Display " "
69              Display "Your options are:"
70              Display " S - Standard prices display"
71              Display " D - Discounted prices display"
72              Display " X - eXit for another room"
73              Display " "
74              Display "Your choice <S/D/X>? "
75                                      no advancing
76              Accept ls-menu-choice
77              Move function upper-case(ls-menu-choice)
78                                      to ls-menu-choice
79                  .
80          End Method get-menu-selection.
```

You can see at lines 124 and 120 in Figure 7-5 that a user entry of X causes termination of this loop.

```cobol
       $set sourceformat "free"
*>*****************************************************
*> Room Rental System
*> W. Price  Dec 13 1999              R11-MGR.CBL
*>
*> RoomManager handles access to the classes of
*> the Room system.
*> Methods:
*>    create-room-object
*>    process-user-requests
*>    process-this-request
*>    process-user-selections
*>*****************************************************

Identification Division.
     Class-ID. RoomManager.

Environment Division.
     Object Section.
         Class-Control.
             RoomManager       is class "r11-mgr"
             UserInterface     is class "r11-ui"
             DatabaseInterface is class "r11-dbi"
             RoomClass         is class "r11-room"
             .
*>======================================================
FACTORY.
   Data Division.
       Object-Storage Section.
           01 theRoomHandle     object reference.

   Procedure Division.
     >*------------------------------------------------
     Method-id. create-room-object.
     >*------------------------------------------------
         Data Division.
             Local-Storage Section.
                 01 lo-room-object-data.
                    10 lo-room-number        pic X(03).
                    10 lo-std-config-price   pic 9(03).
                    10 lo-spec-config-price  pic 9(03).
                    10 lo-room-discount      pic v9(02).

         Procedure Division.
             Invoke DataBaseInterface "get-room-data"
                        Returning lo-room-object-data
             Invoke RoomClass "New"
                        Returning theRoomHandle
             Invoke theRoomHandle
                        "populate-the-room-object"
                        Using lo-room-object-data
         End Method create-room-object.

     >*------------------------------------------------
     Method-id. process-user-requests.
     >*------------------------------------------------
         Data Division.
             Local-Storage Section.
                 01 lo-room-number        pic x(03).
                    88 lo-no-more-room-requests value spaces.
                 01 lo-process-complete-message pic X(40)
                        value "Processing complete".

         Procedure Division.
             Invoke DatabaseInterface "connect-to-data"
             Perform with test after
                   until lo-no-more-room-requests
                Invoke UserInterface
                      "query-for-room-number"
                      Returning lo-room-number
                If lo-no-more-room-requests
                   Continue
                Else
                   Invoke Self "process-this-request"
                     Using lo-room-number
                End-If *>no-more-room-requests
             End-Perform *>with test after
             Invoke DatabaseInterface
                        "disconnect-from-data"
             Invoke UserInterface "display-message"
                        Using lo-process-complete-message
         End Method process-user-requests.

     >*------------------------------------------------
     Method-id. process-this-request.
     >*------------------------------------------------
         Data Division.
             Local-Storage Section.
                 01 lo-record-found-sw       pic X(01).
                    88 lo-record-found       value "Y".
                 01 lo-invalid-room-message  pic X(40)
                        value "Invalid room number".
             Linkage Section.
                 01 ls-room-number           pic X(03).

         Procedure Division Using ls-room-number.
             Invoke DataBaseInterface "read-database"
                        Using ls-room-number
                        Returning lo-record-found-sw
             If lo-record-found
                Invoke Self "create-room-object"
                Invoke Self "process-user-selections"
             Else
                Invoke UserInterface "display-message"
                        Using lo-invalid-room-message
             End-If *>lo-record-found
         End Method process-this-request.

     >*------------------------------------------------
     Method-id. process-user-selections.
     >*------------------------------------------------
         Data Division.
             Local-Storage Section.
                 01 lo-room-prices.
                    10 lo-std-config-price   pic 9(03).
                    10 lo-spec-config-price  pic 9(03).
                 01 lo-menu-choice           pic X(01).
                    88 lo-discounted-prices  value "D".
                    88 lo-standard-prices    value "S".
                    88 lo-exit-option-loop   value "X".

         Procedure Division.
             Perform with test after
                   until lo-exit-option-loop
                Invoke UserInterface
                       "get-menu-selection"
                       Returning lo-menu-choice
                Evaluate TRUE
                   When lo-discounted-prices
                      Invoke theRoomHandle
                         "get-discounted-room-prices"
                         Returning lo-room-prices
                      Invoke UserInterface
                         "display-room-prices"
                         Using lo-room-prices
                   When lo-standard-prices
                      Invoke theRoomHandle "get-room-prices"
                         Returning lo-room-prices
                      Invoke UserInterface
                         "display-room-prices"
                         Using lo-room-prices
                   When other
                      Set lo-exit-option-loop to true
                End-evaluate *>TRUE
             End-Perform *>until lo-exit-option-loop

         End Method process-user-selections.
     >*------------------------------------------------
END FACTORY.
END CLASS RoomManager.
```

Figure 7-5. Room manager—r11-mgr.

Class:	Database Interface (r11-dbi.cbl)
Description:	This class provides the interface between application programs and the room file processor class.
Special note:	Prior to processing, the data source must be made ready by invoking the method connect-to-data. When processing is complete, the data source must be closed by invoking the method disconnect-from-data.

FACTORY		
Public Methods	*Parameters*	*Description*
connect-to-data		Opens required files and or databases required for this application. Collaborator: Room file processor.
disconnect-from-data		Closes all files/databases opened by this class. Collaborator: Room file processor.

get-room-data	Returning:
	  room object data (group item)
	    room number pic x(03)
	    std config price pic 9(03)
	    spec config price pic 9(03)
	    room discount pic v9(02)
		Returns room data required to populate the room object.
		Collaborator: Room file processor.

read-room-file	Using:
	  room number pic X(03)
	Returning
	  record-found switch pic X(01)
	    Y—Record successfully read
	    N—Record not found
		Reads a room record using the input room number as the key. Returned value indicates whether or not record successfully read.
		Collaborator: Room file processor.

Figure 7-6. Documentation for the database interface r11-dbi.

The Database Interface

With the DBI/FP approach of this chapter, the DBI is the interface between the file processor and the project's application class or classes. In general, the DBI is the data accessing "front end" and the file processor, or processors if more than one file, serve as the "back end." In a large installation, one or more programmers may be assigned the tasks of writing and maintaining database interfaces whereas the application programmer sees them from the eyes of a class user.

Let's first look at Figure 7-6's documentation for this example's DBI and compare it to the documentation for the corresponding DBI of Chapter 5 (documented in Figure 6-13). As file processing is removed from this class, the room file record is no longer listed as object data. Comparing the two sets of documentation, you see that methods of the two correspond directly (although two have different names).

Now look at this project's DBI class definition shown in Figure 7-7 and observe the following.

- The file is opened and closed by the connect-to-data and disconnect-from-data methods beginning lines 32 and 40, respectively. Here methods of Room File Processor are invoked to perform the actual open/close operations. (This application uses one file ; the third example of this chapter uses two.)

```cobol
       $set sourceformat "free"
1  *>*************************************************
2  *> Room Rental System
3  *> W. Price  Dec 13, 1999        R11-DBI.CBL
4  *>
5  *> This class definition is the database
6  *> interface between the class user and the
7  *> file processor.
8  *> Factory methods
9  *>    connect-to-data
10 *>    disconnect-from-data
11 *>    get-room-data
12 *>    read-database
13 *>*************************************************
14
15 Identification Division.
16     Class-ID.  RoomDatabaseInterface
17                inherits from BaseClass.
18 Environment Division.
19     Object Section.
20        Class-Control.
21            RoomDatabaseInterface is class "r11-dbi"
22            RoomFileProcessor     is Class "r11-r-fp"
23            BaseClass             is Class "base"
24            .
25 *>===================================================
26 FACTORY.
27
28    Procedure Division.
29 *>..................................................
30 *> ****File Related Methods *******************
31 *>..................................................
32    Method-ID. connect-to-data.
33 *>..................................................
34       Procedure Division.
35          Invoke RoomFileProcessor "open-file"
36          .
37    End Method connect-to-data.
38
39 *>..................................................
40    Method-ID. disconnect-from-data.
41 *>..................................................
42       Procedure Division.
43          Invoke RoomFileProcessor "close-file"
44          .
45    End Method disconnect-from-data.
46
47 *>..................................................
48    Method-ID. read-database.
49 *>..................................................
50       Data Division.
51          Linkage Section.
52          01 ls-room-number          pic x(03).
53          01 ls-record-found-sw      pic X(01).
54             88 ls-record-found          value "Y".
55             88 ls-record-not-found      value "N".
56       Procedure Division Using ls-room-number
57                        Returning ls-record-found-sw.
58          Invoke RoomFileProcessor "read-record"
59                        Using ls-room-number
60                        Returning ls-record-found-sw
61    End Method read-database.
62
63 *>..................................................
64 *> ****Data Access Methods *******************
65 *>..................................................
66    Method-ID. get-room-data.
67 *>..................................................
68       Data Division.
69          Linkage Section.
70          01 ls-room-object-data.
71             10 ls-room-number         pic x(03).
72             10 ls-std-config-price    pic 9(03).
73             10 ls-spec-config-price   pic 9(03).
74             10 ls-room-discount       pic v9(02).
75
76       Procedure Division
77                        Returning ls-room-object-data.
78          Invoke RoomFileProcessor
79                        "get-price-data"
80                        Returning ls-room-object-data
81          .
82    End Method get-room-data.
83 *>..................................................
84 END FACTORY.
85 END CLASS RoomDatabaseInterface.
```

Figure 7-7. The database interface—r11-dbi.

- At line 48 you see the method read-database (in place of read-room-file of Room06's DBI—Figure 4-10) where the file processor is invoked to read the desired record. As in Room06's DBI, the success or failure of the read is returned in the data item ls-record-found-sw.
- At line 66 the get-room-data method invokes the appropriate method of the file processor to extract the desired data from the room record.

The Room File Processor—r11-r-fp

From this example's File Processor documentation in Figure 7-8 you see the room record identified as the class's object data. The methods that you know exist (from your study of the DBI) can be grouped in two categories.

- Methods pertaining to file processing.
    open-file
    close-file
    read-record

Class: Room File Processor (r11-r-fp.cbl)
Description: This class provides random access to records of the room file. A designated record is read and stored as object data of the class.

FACTORY	Object Data:
	Room-file record
	  room number
	  accounting code
	  room type
	  std config price
	  spec config price
	  pricing code
	  room discount
	  room capacity
	  room width
	  room length	

Public Methods	*Parameters*	*Description*
close-file		Close the indexed room file.
open-file		Opens the indexed room file in the input mode.

read-record	Using
	  Room number pic X(03)
	Returning
	  Record-found switch pic X(01)
	    Y—Record found
	    N—Record not found
		Read a record from the indexed file room.

get-price-data	Returning:
	  room object data (group item)
	    room number pic x(03)
	    std config price pic 9(03)
	    spec config price pic 9(03)
	    room discount pic v9(02)
		Returns room data required to populate the room object.

Figure 7-8. Documentation for Room File Processor r11-r-fp.

- Methods pertaining to the application.
  get-price-data

Now look at this project's class definition itself shown in Figure 7-9 where at lines 27-49 you see all the familiar file definition components.

1. The Input-Output Section contains the usual components to designate an indexed file (lines 27-33).
2. The Data Division includes the File Section together with its FD and record description (lines 35-49).
3. All data items of this file/record definition (lines 36-49), including the file name Room-File at line 36, are factory object data and are therefore global to all methods of the factory.
4. For documentation, all record description fields are preceded with a two letter abbreviation indicating the record of which they are components. In this example, the fields at lines 38-46 are prefixed with rr- which identifies them as part of room-record.

> The version of Personal COBOL used in the preparation of this book does not allow file definition information in either the Factory or the Object paragraphs. However, it does allow their inclusion in the Environment Division preceding the Factory paragraph header of line 25 thereby making them global to all methods of the class. For an example, refer to the Personal Cobol version of this example. Note that this is a non-standard implementation.

```cobol
         $set sourceformat "free"
1  *>***********************************************
2  *> Room Rental System
3  *> W. Price   Dec 13, 1999        R11-R-FP.CBL
4  *>
5  *> This class definition is the read file
6  *> processor for the indexed file ROOM.DI. Its
7  *> object data is the room record
8  *> Methods
9  *>    close-file
10 *>    get-price-data
11 *>    open-file
12 *>    read-record
13 *>***********************************************
14
15 Identification Division.
16      Class-ID.  RoomFileProcessor
17                    inherits from BaseClass.
18 Environment Division.
19      Object Section.
20         Class-Control.
21            RoomFileProcessor is class "r11-r-fp"
22            BaseClass         is class "base"
23            .
24 *>=================================================
25 FACTORY.
26     Environment Division.
27        Input-Output Section.
28        File-Control.
29          Select room-file
30                 assign to "c:\eooc2-files\room.di"
31                 organization is indexed
32                 access is random
33                 record key is rr-room-number.
34     Data Division.
35        File Section.
36        FD  Room-File.
37        01   room-record.
38             10  rr-room-number           pic x(03).
39             10  rr-acctg-code            pic x(10).
40             10  rr-room-type             pic x(03).
41             10  rr-std-config-price      pic 9(03).
42             10  rr-spec-config-price     pic 9(03).
43             10  rr-pricing-code          pic 9(01).
44             10  rr-room-discount         pic v9(02).
45             10  rr-room-capacity         pic 9(02).
46             10  rr-room-width            pic 9(02).
47             10  rr-room-length           pic 9(02).
48             10  rr-work-stations         pic 9(02).
49             10  rr-work-station-capacity pic 9(01).
50
51     Procedure Division.
52 *>-------------------------------------------------
53 *> ****File Related Methods ******************
54 *>-------------------------------------------------
55     Method-ID.  open-file.
56 *>-------------------------------------------------
57        Procedure Division.
58           Open Input room-file
59           .
60     End Method open-file.
61
62 *>-------------------------------------------------
63     Method-ID.  close-file.
64 *>-------------------------------------------------
65        Procedure Division.
66           Close room-file
67           .
68     End Method close-file.
69
70 *>-------------------------------------------------
71     Method-ID.  read-record.
72 *>-------------------------------------------------
73        Data Division.
74        Linkage Section.
75         01  ls-room-number              pic x(03).
76         01  ls-action-status            pic X(01).
77             88  ls-record-found           value "Y".
78             88  ls-record-not-found       value "N".
79
80        Procedure Division Using ls-room-number
81                           Returning ls-action-status.
82           Move ls-room-number to rr-room-number
83           Read Room-File
84              Invalid key
85                 Set ls-record-not-found to true
86              Not invalid key
87                 Set ls-record-found to true
88           End-Read *>Room-File
89           .
90     End Method read-record.
91
92 *>-------------------------------------------------
93 *> ****Data Access Related Methods **********
94 *>-------------------------------------------------
95     Method-ID.  get-price-data.
96 *>-------------------------------------------------
97        Data Division.
98        Linkage Section.
99         01  ls-price-data.
100            10  ls-room-number           pic x(03).
101            10  ls-std-config-price      pic 9(03).
102            10  ls-spec-config-price     pic 9(03).
103            10  ls-room-discount         pic v9(02).
104
105        Procedure Division Returning ls-price-data.
106           Move rr-room-number to ls-room-number
107           Move rr-std-config-price
108                             to ls-std-config-price
109           Move rr-spec-config-price
110                             to ls-spec-config-price
111           Move rr-room-discount
112                             to ls-room-discount
113           .
114     End Method get-price-data.
115 *>-------------------------------------------------
116 END FACTORY.
117 END CLASS RoomFileProcessor.
```

Figure 7-9. The room file processor—r11-r-fp.

Notice that the read-record method (lines 71-90) does nothing more than access the requested record thereby "populating" the factory object. You see the key field value moved to the key field of the record description from the linkage section entry ls-room-number (line 82). Output from this method is a data item with a value Y (line 85) or N (line 87) depending upon whether or not the read was successful.

As the room reservation system is expanded or other applications are brought on line requiring data from the room file, the programmer responsible for maintaining this file processor need only add the appropriate methods. The file-accessing methods will not be affected as needed data is accessed from the file record. Also, other application-specific methods will not be affected as each such method is independent of the other.

Updating Records of a File

Some Program Design Considerations

All this book's examples thus far have read and displayed data; let's now look at Room12, an expansion of Room11 that allows the user to update object data. If you run the application, after entering a room number you will see the following menu displayed on your screen.

```
Your options are:
  S - Standard prices display
  D - Discounted prices display
  U - Update prices
  X - eXit for another room

Your choice <S/D/U/X>?
```

Selecting U allows you to change values for either or both the standard configuration price and the special configuration price which are written back to the room object.

Let's step back and consider design aspects of this application from the perspective of the application programmer (responsible for Room and Room Manager) who sees the DBI through the eyes of a class user. Following is a typical scenario.

1. The user enters a room number (assume it's a valid room number).
2. Room Manager invokes a method of DBI which in turn invokes a method of Room File Processor to read the record. Room File Processor possesses the room record as object data.

3. Room Manager creates the room object and populates it with data from Room File Processor (via DBI).
4. The user selects the option to update prices and enter new values.
5. Room Manager invokes an appropriate method of Room to update the object's room prices.

At this point in the cycle, price data stored in the room object (the instantiation of Room) will be different from the data stored in the room record of the Room File Processor. Therefore, at some point in the processing cycle, Room Manager must decide whether or not to return the room object data to Room File Processor (via DBI) to update the file. Knowledge of whether or not a change in the object data has occurred is commonly stored in the form of a switch that can be tested at the appropriate time. A first thought might be to store the switch in Room Manager as Room Manager provides all access to room.

Before jumping to that conclusion, let's back up and consider Room from its design perspective. Specifically, what does Room know about itself? As you are aware, in addition to its number and discount rate, Room knows its prices. So it would seem logical that Room should also know if its prices have been changed during processing. Therefore, defining the "change-switch" as an attribute of Room makes good design sense. There are advantages to this decision. For instance, if at a later date the application is expanded so that multiple instances of Room can exist concurrently, having Room Manager maintain a separate update switch for each instance would be clumsy. Or a future expansion might involve a new class that also can update the object's data. With update capabilities from two or more different classes, it would not be very practical to maintain an update switch in other than the object itself.

This project Room12, to update room prices, consists of the following classes.

r12-ui	User interface
r12-mgr	Room manager
r12-room	Room Class
r12-dbi	Database interface
r12-r-fp	Room file processor

Class: **Room (r12-room.cbl)**
Description: This class contains and manages pricing data for one room. It includes object-data update capability.

OBJECT	Object Data: 　room number 　std config price 　spec config price 　room discount 　object update switch	
Public Methods	*Parameters*	*Description*
`get-discounted-room-prices`	Returning: 　room prices 　　std config price　　pic 9(03) 　　spec config price　pic 9(03)	Computes and returns discounted room prices as a group item.
`get-room-prices`	Returning: 　room prices 　　std config price　　pic 9(03) 　　spec config price　pic 9(03)	Returns room prices as a group item.
`get-object-data`	Using 　room data (O) 　　room number　　　　pic X(03) 　　std config price　　pic 9(03) 　　spec config-price　pic 9(03) 　　room discount　　　pic 9V9(02) 　object update switch (O) pic X(01) 　　Y—object updated 　　N—object not updated	Returns all of the object data. Note that the Using includes two parameters, both output.
`populate-the-room-object`	Using: 　room data 　　room number　　　　pic X(03) 　　std config price　　pic 9(03) 　　spec config-price　pic 9(03) 　　room discount　　　pic 9V9(02)	Populates the room object using data transmitted as a group item. Sets the object-update switch off (value N).
`set-room-prices`	Using: 　room prices 　　std config price　　pic 9(03) 　　spec config price　pic 9(03)	Updates the object's room prices from the input parameter. Also, sets the object-update switch to Y (update has occurred).

Figure 7-10. Summary for Room—r12-room.

Additions to Room and Room Manager—Room12

Let's first examine Room12's Room and Room Manager summaries of Figures 7-10 and 7-11, respectively. New methods, of interest are highlighted.

Room: `get-object-data`. This method returns Room's object data so that the invoking program can check to determine if there has been a change and, if a change has occurred, take appropriate action to update the file.

Class: **Room Manager (r12-mgr.cbl)**
Description: The central class of this application providing query and update capabilities to data of the room object.

FACTORY	Object Data: Room object handle	
Public Methods	*Parameters*	*Description*
process-user-requests		Provides overall process control. Collaborators: Self, UI, DBI
Private Methods	*Parameters*	*Description*
create-room-object		Creates and populates room object. Collaborators: Room, DBI Invoked by: process-this-request
process-this-request	Using: Room number pic X(03)	Handles processing for each room request. Collaborators: Self, UI, DBI Invoked by: process-user-requests
process-user-selections		Evaluates user data request and displays the requested information. Allows user to change prices. Collaborators: Self, UI, Room Invoked by: process-this-request
query-to-update-prices		Accepts user input for new prices. Collaborators: UI, Room Invoked by: process-user-selections
test-for-database-update		Accesses the room object data. If object-update switch on, then sends updated price data to DBI for updating file. Collaborators: DBI, Room Invoked by: process-this-request

Figure 7-11. Summary for Room Manager—r12-mgr.

Room: set-room-prices. This method enters new prices into the room price fields of the room object.

Room Manager: query-to-update-prices. When the user selects the Update option, this method invokes an appropriate method of UI to accept user input. If the user enters a new value, it invokes the set-room-prices method of Room to update the prices.

Room Manager: test-for-database-update. This method invokes the get-object-data method of Room to obtain Room's object data. If the data has been changed, Room Manager invokes a method of DBI to rewrite the record to the file.

The Room Class—R12-room

The room class for this example is listed in Figure 7-12 where you see the following.

- The field object-updated-sw has been added to the class's object data—see line 36. It is initialized when the object is populated—see line 112.
- The new method get-object-data (line 79) returns the object data to the invoking program (Room Manager in this example) for query regarding update status and for sending to DBI for update in the event the data has changed. As two parameters are being returned to the calling program, the method's parameters are listed as Using—refer to lines 92 and 93. (Also, notice that these parameters are identified as output in the class's documentation of Figure 7-10.) Remember, Returning only allows one parameter.
- The new method set-room-prices (line 117) allows Room Manager to update the price fields based on the user's entries. The update switch is also set to true.

Room Manager—R12-mgr

Adding two methods and two relatively minor other code insertions to Room11's Room Manager (Figure 7-5) produces Room Manager for this project—see Figure

```cobol
       $set sourceformat "free"
*>*****************************************************
*> Room Rental System
*> W. Price  Dec 13, 1999           R12-ROOM.CBL
*>
*> This class is an expansion of Room11.
*> It includes the ability to update the objects
*> room prices.
*> Object methods
*>      get-discounted-room-prices
*>      get-object-data
*>      get-room-prices
*>      populate-the-room-object
*>      set-room-prices
*>*****************************************************

Identification Division.
       Class-id. RoomClass
                   inherits from BaseClass
       .
Environment Division.
       Object Section.
           Class-Control.
               RoomClass is class "r12-room"
               BaseClass is class "base"
               .
*>=====================================================

OBJECT.
   Data Division.
       Working-Storage Section.
       01 room-data.
           10  room-number          pic X(03).
           10  std-config-price     pic 9(03).
           10  spec-config-price    pic 9(03).
           10  room-discount        pic v9(02).
       01 object-updated-sw         pic X(1).
           88  object-updated       value "Y".
           88  object-not-updated   value "N".

   Procedure Division.
*>..................................................
   Method-id. get-room-prices.
*>..................................................
       Data Division.
           Linkage Section.
           01 ls-room-prices.
               10  ls-std-config-price    pic 9(03).
               10  ls-spec-config-price   pic 9(03).

       Procedure Division  Returning ls-room-prices.
           Move std-config-price to ls-std-config-price
           Move spec-config-price to ls-spec-config-price
           .
   End Method get-room-prices.

*>..................................................
   Method-id. get-discounted-room-prices.
*>..................................................
       Data Division.
           Local-Storage Section.
           01  lo-price-factor      pic 9(01)v9(02).

           Linkage Section.
           01 ls-room-prices.
               10  ls-std-config-price    pic 9(03).
               10  ls-spec-config-price   pic 9(03).

       Procedure Division Returning ls-room-prices.
           Move std-config-price to ls-std-config-price
           Move spec-config-price to ls-spec-config-price
           Subtract room-discount from 1.0
                           giving lo-price-factor
           Multiply lo-price-factor by ls-std-config-price
           Multiply lo-price-factor by ls-spec-config-price
           .
   End Method get-discounted-room-prices.

*>..................................................
   Method-id. get-object-data.
*>..................................................
       Data Division.
           Linkage Section.
           01 ls-room-data.
               10  ls-room-number        pic X(03).
               10  ls-std-config-price   pic 9(03).
               10  ls-spec-config-price  pic 9(03).
               10  ls-room-discount      pic v9(02).
           01 ls-object-updated-sw       pic X(1).
               88  ls-object-updated       value "Y".
               88  ls-object-not-updated   value "N".

       Procedure Division Using ls-room-data
                                ls-object-updated-sw.
           Move room-data to ls-room-data
           Move object-updated-sw to ls-object-updated-sw
           .
   End Method get-object-data.

*>..................................................
   Method-id. populate-the-room-object.
*>..................................................
       Data Division.
           Linkage Section.
           01 ls-room-data.
               10  ls-room-number        pic X(03).
               10  ls-std-config-price   pic 9(03).
               10  ls-spec-config-price  pic 9(03).
               10  ls-room-discount      pic v9(02).

       Procedure Division  Using ls-room-data.
           Move ls-room-data to room-data
           Set object-not-updated to true
           .
   End Method populate-the-room-object.

*>..................................................
   Method-id. set-room-prices.
*>..................................................
       Data Division.
           Linkage Section.
           01 ls-room-prices.
               10  ls-std-config-price    pic 9(03).
               10  ls-spec-config-price   pic 9(03).

       Procedure Division  Using ls-room-prices.
           Move ls-std-config-price to std-config-price
           Move ls-spec-config-price to spec-config-price
           Set object-updated to true
           .
   End Method set-room-prices.
*>..................................................
END OBJECT.
END CLASS RoomClass.
```

Figure 7-12. The Room class—r12-room.

```cobol
        $set sourceformat "free"
*>****************************************************
*> Room Rental System
*> W. Price  Dec 30, 1999              R12-MGR.CBL
*>
*> RoomManager handles access to the classes of
*> the Room system.
*> Methods:
*>    create-room-object
*>    process-this-request
*>    process-user-requests
*>    process-user-selections
*>    query-to-update-prices
*>    test-for-database-update
*>****************************************************

Identification Division.
    Class-ID. RoomManager.

Environment Division.
    Object Section.
        Class-Control.
            RoomManager        is class "r12-mgr"
            UserInterface      is class "r12-ui"
            DatabaseInterface  is class "r12-dbi"
            RoomClass          is class "r12-room"
            .
*>========================================================
FACTORY.
  Data Division.
    Object-Storage Section.
      01 theRoomHandle   object reference.

  Procedure Division.
*>--------------------------------------------------------
  Method-id. create-room-object.
*>--------------------------------------------------------
    Data Division.
      Local-Storage Section.
        01 lo-room-object-data.
           10 lo-room-number        pic X(03).
           10 lo-std-config-price   pic 9(03).
           10 lo-spec-config-price  pic 9(03).
           10 lo-room-discount      pic v9(02).

    Procedure Division.
        Invoke DataBaseInterface "get-room-data"
                    Returning lo-room-object-data
        Invoke RoomClass "New"
                    Returning theRoomHandle
        Invoke theRoomHandle
                    "populate-the-room-object"
                    Using lo-room-object-data
    End Method create-room-object.

*>--------------------------------------------------------
Method-id. process-user-requests.
*>--------------------------------------------------------
    Data Division.
      Local-Storage Section.
        01 lo-room-number        pic X(03).
           88 lo-no-more-room-requests value spaces.
        01 lo-process-complete-message pic X(40)
                    value "Processing complete".

    Procedure Division.
        Invoke DatabaseInterface "connect-to-data"
        Perform with test after
                until lo-no-more-room-requests
            Invoke UserInterface
                    "query-for-room-number"
                    Returning lo-room-number
            If lo-no-more-room-requests
                Continue
            Else
                Invoke Self "process-this-request"
                    Using lo-room-number
            End-If *>lo-no-more-room-requests
        End-Perform *>with test after
        Invoke DatabaseInterface
                    "disconnect-from-data"
        Invoke UserInterface "display-message"
                    Using lo-process-complete-message
    End Method process-user-requests.
*>--------------------------------------------------------
Method-id. process-this-request.
*>--------------------------------------------------------
    Data Division.
      Local-Storage Section.
        01 lo-record-found-sw      pic X(01).
           88 lo-record-found              value "Y".
        01 lo-invalid-room-message pic X(40)
                    value "Invalid room number".
      Linkage Section.
        01 ls-room-number          pic X(03).

    Procedure Division Using ls-room-number.
        Invoke DataBaseInterface "read-database"
                    Using ls-room-number
                    Returning lo-record-found-sw
        If lo-record-found
            Invoke Self "create-room-object"
            Invoke Self "process-user-selections"
            Invoke Self "test-for-database-update"
        Else
            Invoke UserInterface "display-message"
                    Using lo-invalid-room-message
        End-If *>lo-record-found
        .
    End Method process-this-request.
```

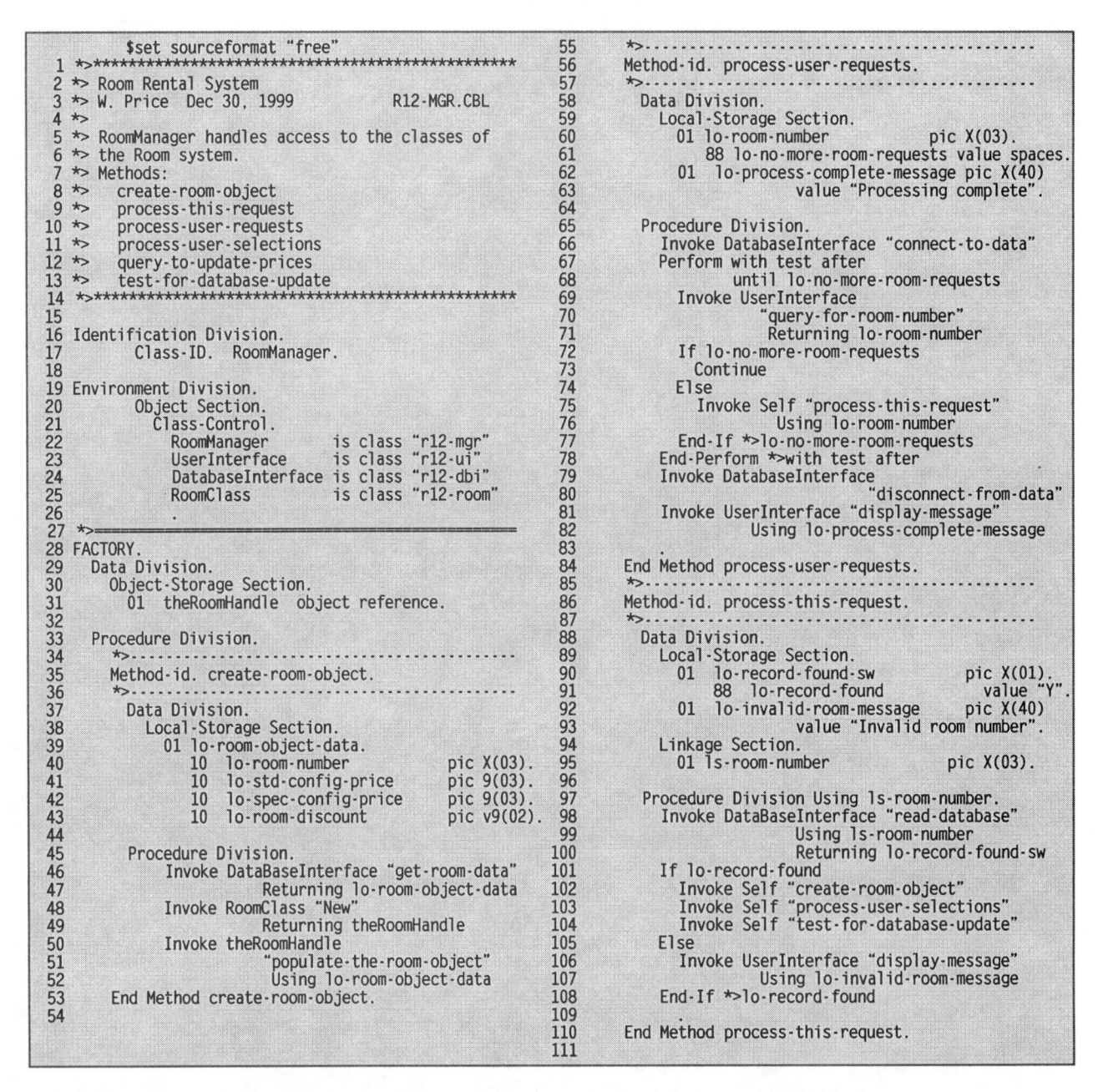

Figure 7-13. The room Manager class—r12-mgr (continued on next page).

7-13. The method query-to-update-prices (beginning line 158), which is invoked by the additional case entry of lines 147 and 148, does the following.

- Accesses the room prices (line 177).
- Allows the user to update the standard configuration price via UI (the Invoke of lines 180-183). If the user does not enter a new price, lo-new-price is returned with a value 0.
- A non-zero value triggers the two statements at line 185 and 186 thereby saving the price and setting the "new-price" switch.

```
112      *>----------------------------------------         174
113      Method-id. process-user-selections.                175       Procedure Division.
114      *>----------------------------------------         176           Set lo-price-not-updated to true
115      Data Division.                                     177           Invoke theRoomHandle "get-room-prices"
116          Local-Storage Section.                         178                       Returning lo-room-prices
117              01 lo-room-prices.                         179           Move 0 to lo-new-price
118                  10 lo-std-config-price   pic 9(03).    180           Invoke UserInterface "query-to-change-price"
119                  10 lo-spec-config-price  pic 9(03).    181                       Using lo-std-config-price-prompt
120              01 lo-menu-choice            pic X(01).    182                             lo-std-config-price
121                  88 lo-discounted-prices    value "D".  183                       Returning lo-new-price
122                  88 lo-standard-prices      value "S".  184           If lo-new-price > 0
123                  88 lo-update-prices        value "U".  185               Set lo-price-updated to true
124                  88 lo-exit-option-loop     value "X".  186               Move lo-new-price to lo-std-config-price
125                                                         187           End-If *> lo-new-price > 0
126      Procedure Division.                                188
127          Perform with test after                        189           Invoke UserInterface "query-to-change-price"
128                  until lo-exit-option-loop              190                       Using lo-spec-config-price-prompt
129              Invoke UserInterface                       191                             lo-spec-config-price
130                      "get-menu-selection"               192                       Returning lo-new-price
131                      Returning lo-menu-choice           193           If lo-new-price > 0
132              Evaluate TRUE                              194               Set lo-price-updated to true
133                  When lo-discounted-prices              195               Move lo-new-price to lo-spec-config-price
134                      Invoke theRoomHandle               196           End-If *> lo-new-price > 0
135                          "get-discounted-room-prices"   197
136                          Returning lo-room-prices       198           If lo-price-updated
137                      Invoke UserInterface               199               Invoke theRoomHandle "set-room-prices"
138                          "display-room-prices"          200                           Using lo-std-config-price
139                          Using lo-room-prices           201                                 lo-spec-config-price
140                  When lo-standard-prices                202           End-If *>lo-price-updated
141                      Invoke theRoomHandle               203           .
142                          "get-room-prices"              204       End Method query-to-update-prices.
143                          Returning lo-room-prices       205
144                      Invoke UserInterface               206       *>----------------------------------------
145                          "display-room-prices"          207       Method-id. test-for-database-update.
146                          Using lo-room-prices           208       *>----------------------------------------
147                  When lo-update-prices                  209       Data Division.
148                      Invoke Self "query-to-update-prices" 210         Local-Storage Section.
149                  When other                             211             01 lo-room-data.
150                      Set lo-exit-option-loop to true    212                 10 lo-room-number        pic X(03).
151              End-evaluate *>TRUE                        213                 10 lo-std-config-price  pic 9(03).
152              Invoke Self "test-for-database-update"     214                 10 lo-spec-config-price pic 9(03).
153          End-Perform *>until lo-exit-option-loop        215                 10 lo-room-discount     pic v9(02).
154          .                                              216             01 lo-object-updated-sw     pic X(1).
155      End Method process-user-selections.                217                 88 lo-object-updated         value "Y".
156                                                         218                 88 lo-object-not-updated     value "N".
157      *>----------------------------------------         219
158      Method-id. query-to-update-prices.                 220       Procedure Division.
159      *>----------------------------------------         221           Invoke theRoomHandle "get-object-data"
160      Data Division.                                     222                       Using lo-room-data, lo-object-updated-sw
161          Local-Storage Section.                         223                       *>Note: Both parameters in the
162              01 lo-new-price              pic 9(03).    224                       *>      above Using return data.
163              01 lo-price-updated-sw       pic X(01).    225           If lo-object-updated
164                  88 lo-price-updated        value "Y".  226               Invoke DatabaseInterface "rewrite-data"
165                  88 lo-price-not-updated    value "N".  227                           Using lo-room-data
166              01 lo-room-prices.                         228           End-If *>lo-object-updated
167                  10 lo-std-config-price   pic 9(03).    229           .
168                  10 lo-spec-config-price  pic 9(03).    230       End Method test-for-database-update.
169              01 lo-user-prompts.                        231       *>----------------------------------------
170                  10 lo-std-config-price-prompt pic X(30) 232     END FACTORY.
171                      value "Standard configuration price: ". 233 END CLASS RoomManager.
172                  10 lo-spec-config-price-prompt pic X(30)
173                      value " Special configuration price: ".
```

Figure 7-13. The room Manager class—r12-mgr (continued from preceding page).

- The process is repeated for the special configuration price at lines 189-196.
- If either price has changed, the object data is updated by the Invoke of line 199.

The method test-for-database-update beginning line 207 (invoked from line 104) is reasonably straightforward. Room's object data is accessed by the Invoke of line 221. If the object's data has changed, DBI is invoked to update the record.

The Room File Processor—R12-r-fp

This file processor differs from its counterpart of Room11 (Figure 7-9) only by the addition of the two methods rewrite-record and set-price-data shown in Figure 7-14. You can see that set-price-data* is exactly the opposite of get-price-data. This method is invoked by DBI which makes updated room data available via the Linkage Section entry ls-price-data.

The method rewrite-record, also invoked by DBI, rewrites the record. Notice that no attempt is made to trap a rewrite failure (see the STOP RUN at line 104). In a production environment, you would have appropriate code to handle this failure, although such a failure should never occur as the record being rewritten is the record that was read.

The DBI—R12-dbi

At line 226 of Room Manager (Figure 7-13) you see the rewrite-data method invoked to update the file's record. This method, shown in Figure 7-15, is the only difference between this project's DBI and that of Room11 (Figure 7-7). As you see, it invokes methods of File Processor to update the room record (line 79) and rewrite the record (line 82).

```
 95      *>............................................
 96      Method-ID. rewrite-record.
 97      *>............................................
 98
 99          Procedure Division.
100              Rewrite room-record
101                  Invalid key
102                      Display "Unable to rewrite record"
103                      Display "Terminating processing"
104                      STOP RUN
105              End-Rewrite *>Room-File
106              .
107      End Method rewrite-record.
108      *>............................................


133      *>............................................
134      Method-ID. set-price-data.
135      *>............................................
136          Data Division.
137              Linkage Section.
138                  01  ls-price-data.
139                      10  ls-room-number       pic x(03).
140                      10  ls-std-config-price  pic 9(03).
141                      10  ls-spec-config-price pic 9(03).
142                      10  ls-room-discount     pic v9(02).
143
144          Procedure Division Using ls-price-data.
145              Move ls-std-config-price
146                      to rr-std-config-price
147              Move ls-spec-config-price
148                      to rr-spec-config-price
149              .
150      End Method set-price-data.
151      *>............................................
```

Figure 7-14.
Room File Processor's new methods.

```
67      *>............................................
68      Method-ID. rewrite-data.
69      *>............................................
70          Data Division.
71              Linkage Section.
72                  01  ls-room-object-data.
73                      10  ls-room-number       pic x(03).
74                      10  ls-std-config-price  pic 9(03).
75                      10  ls-spec-config-price pic 9(03).
76                      10  ls-room-discount     pic v9(02).
77
78          Procedure Division Using ls-room-object-data.
79              Invoke RoomFileProcessor
80                      "set-price-data"
81                      Using ls-room-object-data
82              Invoke RoomFileProcessor
83                      "rewrite-record"
84              .
85      End Method rewrite-data.
86      *>............................................
```

Figure 7-15.
DBI's rewrite-data method.

---

* Although only the prices are required by this method, the other two fields are included for a correspondence to the get method. This is used to illustrate Chapter 10's examples of Cobol's Property clause that simplifies access to an object's data.

Accessing Data From a Subordinate File—Project 13

Problem Definition

For this example, assume that the local county has implemented a special surtax that is solely dependent on the room type. (This example is discussed briefly earlier in this chapter—refer to Figure 7-3.) The room tax file (room-tax.di) includes two fields: the room type and the room tax.

From the user perspective, this application will look exactly like Room11: the user can display the prices for any room in the file. (The project uses the Room11 UI.) However, the displayed prices will include the sum of the room prices (obtained from the room file) and the room tax(obtained from the room-tax file). For simplicity, if no tax entry is found in the tax file, a value of zero is returned. This project consists of the following classes.

r11-ui	User interface
r13-dbi	Database interface
r13-mgr	Room manager
r13-room	Room Class
r13-r-fp	Room file processor
r13-t-fp	Tax file processor

The Room Class—R13-room

Referring to Figure 7-16 you can see that the class Room for this project differs only slightly from r11-room.

- The field room-tax-rate has been added to the object data—refer to line 35. (Also see line 98, necessary to populate the object.)
- The two "get prices" methods include code to perform the appropriate tax computation—refer to lines 58-62 and 79-83.

In Room Manager you see no indication that data is derived from two file processing classes; Room Manager only "knows of" the DBI that it has been referencing in previous examples. Similarly, Room which contains the object data, gives no hint that the object data comes from two different files.

```
        $set sourceformat "free"
1  *>***************************************************
2  *> Room Rental System
3  *> W. Price  Nov 13, 1999         R13-ROOM.CBL
4  *>
5  *> Room-price methods of this version of Room have
6  *> been modified to include the special room tax.
7  *> Room capacity is removed from the object only
8  *> to minimize the amount of code you must look at.
9  *> Object methods
10 *>      get-discounted-room-prices (including tax)
11 *>      get-room-prices            (including tax)
12 *>      populate-the-room-object
13 *>***************************************************
14
15 Identification Division.
16         Class-id. RoomClass
17                 inherits from BaseClass
18                 .
19 Environment Division.
20         Object Section.
21         Class-Control.
22             RoomClass is class "r13-room"
23             BaseClass is class "base"
24             .
25 *>=====================================================
26
27 OBJECT.
28 Data Division.
29     Object-Storage Section.
30     01 room-data.
31        10 room-number       pic X(03).
32        10 std-config-price  pic 9(03).
33        10 spec-config-price pic 9(03).
34        10 room-discount     pic v9(02).
35        10 room-tax-rate     pic V9(03).
36 Procedure Division.
37  *>--------------------------------------------------
38  Method-id. get-discounted-room-prices.
39  *>--------------------------------------------------
40     Data Division.
41     Local-Storage Section.
42        01 lo-price-factor       pic 9(01)v9(03).
43
44     Linkage Section.
45        01 ls-room-prices.
46           10 ls-std-config-price  pic 9(03).
47           10 ls-spec-config-price pic 9(03).
48
49     Procedure Division Returning ls-room-prices.
50        Subtract room-discount from 1.0
51                              giving lo-price-factor
52        Multiply lo-price-factor by std-config-price
53                              giving ls-std-config-price
54        Multiply lo-price-factor
55                              by spec-config-price
56                              giving ls-spec-config-price
57
58        Add 1 to room-tax-rate giving lo-price-factor
59        Multiply lo-price-factor
60                              by ls-std-config-price
61        Multiply lo-price-factor
62                              by ls-spec-config-price
63        .
64 End Method get-discounted-room-prices.
65
66 *>--------------------------------------------------
67 Method-id. get-room-prices.
68 *>--------------------------------------------------
69     Data Division.
70     Working-Storage Section.
71        01 lo-price-factor       pic 9(01)v9(03).
72
73     Linkage Section.
74        01 ls-room-prices.
75           10 ls-std-config-price  pic 9(03).
76           10 ls-spec-config-price pic 9(03).
77
78     Procedure Division Returning ls-room-prices.
79        Add 1 to room-tax-rate giving lo-price-factor
80        Multiply lo-price-factor by std-config-price
81                              giving ls-std-config-price
82        Multiply lo-price-factor by spec-config-price
83                              giving ls-spec-config-price
84        .
85 End Method get-room-prices.
86
87 *>--------------------------------------------------
88 Method-id. populate-the-room-object.
89 *>--------------------------------------------------
90     Data Division.
91     Linkage Section.
92        01 ls-room-data.
93           10 ls-room-number       pic X(03).
94           10 ls-std-config-price  pic 9(03).
95           10 ls-spec-config-price pic 9(03).
96           10 ls-room-discount     pic v9(02).
97           10 ls-room-capacity     pic 9(02).
98           10 ls-room-tax-rate     pic V9(03).
99
100    Procedure Division  Using ls-room-data.
101       Move ls-room-data to room-data
102       .
103 End Method populate-the-room-object.
104 *>--------------------------------------------------
105 END OBJECT.
106 END CLASS RoomClass.
```

Figure 7-16. The Room class—r13-room.

The DBI—R13-dbi

You can see in Figure 7-17's listing of this DBI that it is a minor expansion of Room11's DBI (Figure 7-7). Only the code necessary to accommodate the tax file has been added.

- The connect-to-data and disconnect-from-data now include invokes to open/close the tax file as well as the room file (lines 43 and 52).

```
           $set sourceformat "free"
  1 *>*******************************************
  2 *> Room Rental System
  3 *> W. Price  Dec 13, 1999      R13-DBI.CBL
  4 *>
  5 *> This class definition is the database
  6 *> interface between the class user and the
  7 *> room and tax file processors.
  8 *> Factory methods
  9 *>    connect-to-data
 10 *>    create-room-object
 11 *>    disconnect-from-data
 12 *>    get-room-price-data (private)
 13 *>    get-tax-rate
 14 *>*******************************************
 15
 16 Identification Division.
 17       Class-ID.  RoomDatabaseInterface
 18                  inherits from BaseClass.
 19 Environment Division.
 20       Object Section.
 21         Class-Control.
 22            RoomDatabaseInterface is class "r13-dbi"
 23            RoomFileProcessor     is Class "r13-r-fp"
 24            TaxFileProcessor      is Class "r13-t-fp"
 25            BaseClass             is Class "base"
 26            .
 27 *>======================================
 28 FACTORY.
 29   Data Division.
 30     Object-Storage Section.
 31       01 tax-record-found-sw    pic X(01).
 32          88 tax-record-found       value "Y".
 33          88 tax-record-not-found   value "N".
 34
 35   Procedure Division.
 36 *>--------------------------------------
 37 *> ****File Access Methods ******************
 38 *>--------------------------------------
 39   Method-ID. connect-to-data.
 40 *>--------------------------------------
 41     Procedure Division.
 42       Invoke RoomFileProcessor "open-file"
 43       Invoke TaxFileProcessor  "open-file"
 44       .
 45   End Method connect-to-data.
 46
 47 *>--------------------------------------
 48   Method-ID. disconnect-from-data.
 49 *>--------------------------------------
 50     Procedure Division.
 51       Invoke RoomFileProcessor "close-file"
 52       Invoke TaxFileProcessor  "close-file"
 53       .
 54   End Method disconnect-from-data.
 55
 56 *>--------------------------------------
 57   Method-ID. read-database.
 58 *>--------------------------------------
 59     Data Division.
 60       WLocalStorage Section.
 61         01 lo-room-type          pic X(03).
 62       Linkage Section.
 63         01 ls-room-number        pic X(03).
 64         01 ls-record-found-sw    pic X(01).
 65            88 ls-record-found        value "Y".
 66            88 ls-record-not-found    value "N".
 67     Procedure Division Using ls-room-number
 68                      Returning ls-record-found-sw.
 69       Invoke RoomFileProcessor "read-record"
 70                 Using ls-room-number
 71                 Returning ls-record-found-sw
 72       If ls-record-found
 73          Invoke RoomFileProcessor "get-room-type"
 74                   Returning lo-room-type
 75          Invoke TaxFileProcessor "read-record"
 76                   Using lo-room-type
 77                   Returning tax-record-found-sw
 78       End-If *>ls-record-found
 79       .
 80   End Method read-database.
 81
 82 *>--------------------------------------
 83 *> ****Data Related Methods *****************
 84 *>--------------------------------------
 85   Method-ID. get-room-data.
 86 *>--------------------------------------
 87     Data Division.
 88       Linkage Section.
 89         01 ls-room-object-data.
 90            10 ls-room-price-data.
 91               20 ls-room-number        pic x(03).
 92               20 ls-std-config-price   pic 9(03).
 93               20 ls-spec-config-price  pic 9(03).
 94               20 ls-room-discount      pic v9(02).
 95            10 ls-tax-rate              pic v9(03).
 96
 97     Procedure Division
 98                    Returning ls-room-object-data.
 99       Invoke RoomFileProcessor
100                "get-price-data"
101                Returning ls-room-price-data
102       If tax-record-found
103          Invoke TaxFileProcessor
104                "get-room-tax"
105                Returning ls-tax-rate
106       Else
107          Move 0 to ls-tax-rate
108       End-If *>tax-record-found
109       .
110
111   End Method get-room-data.
112 *>--------------------------------------
```

Figure 7-17. The DBI—r13-dbi.

- In the read-database method, after a room record is successfully read, the room type is obtained from Room File Processor (line 73) and the Tax File Processor is invoked to read the record using lo-room-type as the key field value (line 75).
- The get-room-data, which is invoked by Room Manager, returns the tax rate.

The File Processors: R13-r-fp and R13-t-fp

Both file processors are listed in Figure 7-18. Some of the code is removed from the listings to fit them both on the same page—you can tell by the line number gaps. In Room File Processor (on the left) the file accessing methods, identical to those of r11-r-fp (Figure 7-9), are not shown. In Tax File Processor (on the right) the open and close methods are not shown. Note the following in these two listings.

- In Room File Processor (r13-r-fp.cbl), you see the new method get-room-type. This method is invoked by DBI (line 73 of Figure 7-17) to be used as the key field value sent to Tax File Processor for reading the tax record—see line 76 of Figure 7-17.
- The general structure of Tax File Processor (r13-t-fp.cbl) corresponds closely to that of Room File Processor. The read-record method (beginning line 61) is identical to its counterpart in the Room File Processor. Note that the room type serves as the key field.
- The get-room-tax method (beginning line 85) is invoked by DBI (line 103 of Figure 7-17).

Room Manager—R13-mgr

This project's Room Manager is almost identical to its counterpart of Room11. The only difference is the addition of the tax rate to the data items for populating the room object. If you wish to inspect the program, look at its source file r13-mgr.cbl stored in the folder Proj0703.

Summing Up

Project Summary

Room11 (Proj0701) illustrates moving file processing activities to a separate file processing class. The approach used in this book involves a separate file-processing class for each file in the system. The object data of the class is the file record. Individual methods make data available as required by each application using the file processor.

Room12 (Proj0702) allows the user to change prices in the object data. All record update activity is via the file processor whereby updated data of the room object is returned to the file processor object data from which it is, in turn, written to the file.

Room13 (Proj0703) illustrates the flexibility of the individual file processors as it requires access to a second file containing tax data.

Processing Indexed Files

```
  1 *>************************************************
  2 *> Room Rental System
  3 *> W. Price  Dec 13, 1999        R13-R-FP.CBL
  4 *>
  5 *> This class definition is the read file
  6 *> processor for the indexed file ROOM.DI. It is
  7 *> identical to R11-R-FP but with the insertion
  8 *> of a method to return the room type.
  9 *> Methods
 10 *>    close-file
 11 *>    get-price-data
 12 *>    get-room-type
 13 *>    open-file
 14 *>    read-record
 15 *>************************************************

 26 *>================================================
 27 FACTORY.
 28    Environment Division.
 29    Input-Output Section.
 30    File-Control.
 31       Select room-file
 32             assign to "c:\eooc2-files\room.di"
 33             organization is indexed
 34             access is random
 35             record key is rr-room-number.
 36    Data Division.
 37    File Section.
 38    FD  Room-File.
 39    01  room-record.
 40        10  rr-room-number           pic x(03).
 41        10  rr-acctg-code            pic x(10).
 42        10  rr-room-type             pic x(03).
 43        10  rr-std-config-price      pic 9(03).
 44        10  rr-spec-config-price     pic 9(03).
 45        10  rr-pricing-code          pic 9(01).
 46        10  rr-room-discount         pic v9(02).
 47        10  rr-room-capacity         pic 9(02).
 48        10  rr-room-width            pic 9(02).
 49        10  rr-room-length           pic 9(02).
 50        10  rr-work-stations         pic 9(02).
 51        10  rr-work-station-capacity pic 9(01).
 52
 53    Procedure Division.

 95    *>..............................................
 96    *> ****Data Access Related Methods ***********
 97    *>..............................................
 98    Method-ID. get-price-data.
 99    *>..............................................
100    Data Division.
101    Linkage Section.
102        01  ls-price-data.
103            10  ls-room-number       pic x(03).
104            10  ls-std-config-price  pic 9(03).
105            10  ls-spec-config-price pic 9(03).
106            10  ls-room-discount     pic v9(02).
107
108    Procedure Division Returning ls-price-data.
109        Move rr-room-number to ls-room-number
110        Move rr-std-config-price
111                            to ls-std-config-price
112        Move rr-spec-config-price
113                            to ls-spec-config-price
114        Move rr-room-discount
115                            to ls-room-discount
116        .
117    End Method get-price-data.
118
119    *>..............................................
120    Method-ID. get-room-type.
121    *>..............................................
122    Data Division.
123    Linkage Section.
124        01  ls-room-type             pic X(03).
125
126    Procedure Division Returning ls-room-type.
127        Move rr-room-type to ls-room-type
128        .
129    End Method get-room-type.
130    *>..............................................
131 END FACTORY.
132 END CLASS RoomFileProcessor.
```

```
  1 *>************************************************
  2 *> Room Rental System
  3 *> W. Price  Dec 13, 1999        R13-T-FP.CBL
  4 *>
  5 *> This class definition is the file processor
  6 *> for the indexed file TAX.DI. Its object data is
  7 *> the tax record
  8 *> Methods
  9 *>    close-file
 10 *>    get-price-data
 11 *>    open-file
 12 *>    read-room-record
 13 *>************************************************

 23 *>================================================
 24 FACTORY.
 25    Environment Division.
 26    Input-Output Section.
 27    File-Control.
 28       Select tax-file
 29             assign to "c:\eooc2-files\room-tax.di"
 30             organization is indexed
 31             access is random
 32             record key is tr-room-type.
 33    Data Division.
 34    File Section.
 35    FD  Tax-File.
 36    01  tax-record.
 37        10  tr-room-type           pic X(03).
 38        10  tr-county-tax-code     pic X(11).
 39        10  tr-tax-rate            pic V9(03).
 40    Working-Storage Section.
 41
 42    Procedure Division.
 43    *>..............................................
 44    *> ****File Related Methods ******************
 45    *>..............................................

 60    *>..............................................
 61    Method-ID. read-record.
 62    *>..............................................
 63    Data Division.
 64    Linkage Section.
 65        01  ls-room-type           pic X(03).
 66        01  ls-action-status       pic X(01).
 67            88  ls-record-found        value "Y".
 68            88  ls-record-not-found    value "N".
 69
 70    Procedure Division Using ls-room-type
 71                      Returning ls-action-status.
 72        Move ls-room-type to tr-room-type
 73        Read Tax-File
 74        Invalid key
 75            Set ls-record-not-found to true
 76        Not invalid key
 77            Set ls-record-found to true
 78        End-Read *>Tax-File
 79        .
 80    End Method read-record.
 81
 82    *>..............................................
 83    *> ****Data Access Related Methods ***********
 84    *>..............................................
 85    Method-ID. get-room-tax.
 86    *>..............................................
 87    Data Division.
 88    Linkage Section.
 89        01  ls-tax-rate            pic V9(03).
 90
 91    Procedure Division Returning ls-tax-rate.
 92        Move tr-tax-rate to ls-tax-rate
 93        .
 94    End Method get-room-tax.
 95    *>..............................................
 96 END FACTORY.
 97 END CLASS TaxFileProcessor.
```

Figure 7-18. Room 13's file processors.

General Summary

This chapter illustrates one of the most significant features of object orientation: the independence of objects (classes). Through the three examples of this chapter you've observed the ease with which one or more individual components of a system can be replaced with no affect on the system as a whole.

Coming Up

Chapter 6 briefly addresses inheritance whereby features of a common class are "inherited" by subclasses, a cornerstone of any object-oriented language. The next chapter presents some example programs illustrating how inheritance is implemented in Object-Oriented Cobol.

Assignments

7-1
The program developers at J&B have finally decided to move the file processing code from the DBI to a new file processing class. Make this modification to your assignment of Chapter 5.

7-2
Expand Assignment 7-1 to allow the user to update the number of rolls onhand.

7-3
The marketing department at J&B has decided to add a luxury container (box) to the product line. To that end, the application will require access to two files: the existing dessert file and a new box file with the following format.

File name	BOX.DI
File type	Indexed
Key	Box ID

Field	Format
Box ID	pic X(02)
Box description	pic X(10)
Quantity onhand	pic 9(04)
Price	pic 99V99
Length	pic 9V9
Width	pic 9V9
Height	pic 9V9

You must make the following modifications to your assignment of Chapter 5.

- Move the file processing code from the DBI to a new file processing class.
- Write a file-processing class for the box file.
- Add box data to the dessert object data as needed for this assignment.
- Modify the Inventory-value computation to include:
    Price of box times quantity on hand
- In addition to the inquiry options of Chapter 5's assignment provide the user the option of displaying the Box ID, Box description, and Box quantity onhand.

The dessert record includes a Box ID field identifying the box to be used with the dessert. Use that value as the record key to read the box file.

7-4

The program developers at F&C have finally decided to move the file processing code from the DBI to a new file processing class. Make this modification to your assignment of Chapter 5.

7-5

Expand Assignment 7-4 to allow the user to update the duration field.

7-6

F&B is licensed to position their underwater habitats at several prepared sites throughout the world. The marketing department has decided to provide site information to prospective customers through the online information system. To that end, the application will require access to two files: the existing event file and a new site file with the following format.

File name	SITE.DI
File type	Indexed
Key	Site ID

Field	**Format**
Site ID	pic X(02)
Site location	pic X(20)
Water depth	pic 9(03)
Site surcharge	pic 9V99

You must make the following modifications to your assignment of Chapter 5.

- Move the file processing code from the DBI to a new file processing class.
- Write a file-processing class for the site file.
- In addition to the inquiry options of Chapter 5's assignment provide the user the option of displaying the Site location and the Water depth.
- Modify computation of the Event cost as follows:
    Duration times Daily rate times Site surcharge
- Add site data to the Event object data as needed for this assignment.

Inheritance

Chapter Contents

Two Room Classes—Room14 164
    Problem Definition 164
    The Room Data File 164
    Project Documentation 166
    The Room Classes 166
    The DBI 168
    Room Manager 168
    Overall View of Room14 170
    Redundancy in Room12 170
Classification Structures 170
    Selecting a Pet 170
    Classifying Computers 173
A Simple Example of Inheritance—Room15 173
    Room Classes 173
    A Class and Subclasses 174
    Room Class Documentation 175
    The Room Class Definitions 177
A Variation of the Room Example—Room16 178
    A Sample Dialogue 178
    The Class and Subclasses 180
More About Inheritance 183
    Different Inheritance Scenarios 183
    Inheritance and the Factory Object 185
Summing Up 186
    Project Summary 186
    General Summary 186
Coming Up 186
Assignments 187

Chapter 8

Chapter Introduction

In Chapter 6 you gained an insight to the inheritance structure, a hierarchical structure based on common attributes and procedures between levels of the hierarchy (refer to Figures 6-7 and 6-8). This chapter illustrates implementing inheritance in Cobol. From this chapter, you will learn about the following.

- How to recognize elements of an application that are amenable to implementing using an inheritance hierarchy.
- The Cobol syntax for creating inheritance structures.
- Polymorphism.
- Considerations when populating object data of inheritance hierarchy components.
- Using the Super object identifier in the Invoke statement.

Two Room Classes—Room14

Problem Definition

The programmer for OTC has just learned that OTC wants to treat lecture rooms and laboratory rooms differently. Unfortunately, data requirements for the two are slightly different. That is, the lecture room data includes a room-capacity field where the lab room includes a number-of-work-stations field and a positions-per-work-station field. The lab room capacity is computed as the product of these two fields. Consequently, each room type will require its own class definition.

To minimize code and focus on the new principles, features of this example project are as follows.

Proj0801
Room14

- Room 14's options menu is limited to allowing the user to query for the room capacity and full room prices; the discounted-price option is omitted.
- File access is via the DBI. The file-processor class is omitted only to reduce the number of classes you must look at.
- Two complete room classes are defined: LectureRoom and LabRoom.

The Room Data File

Although you've used the room file in preceding examples, you've seen relatively little focus on the record layout itself. Let's look at it now (refer to Figure 8-1) to ascertain the difference between lecture and lab rooms.

- The third field, rr-room-type, identifies the type of room: LEC for lecture and LAB for lab.
- The last two fields contain the lab room data: number of work stations and individual work-station capacity. For this example, room capacity of lab rooms is to be computed as the product of the number-of-stations and station-capacity fields. The room-capacity field (rr-room-capacity) is ignored.
- The number-of-stations and station-capacity fields are meaningless for lecture rooms and, therefore contain zeroes.

```
01  room-record.
    10  rr-room-number          pic x(03).
    10  rr-acctg-code           pic x(10).
    10  rr-room-type            pic x(03).
    10  rr-std-config-price     pic 9(03).
    10  rr-spec-config-price    pic 9(03).
    10  pricing-code            pic 9(01).
    10  rr-room-discount        pic v9(02).
    10  rr-room-capacity        pic 9(02).
    10  rr-room-width           pic 9(02).
    10  rr-room-length          pic 9(02).
    10  rr-work-stations        pic 9(02).
    10  rr-station-capacity     pic 9(01).
```

Figure 8-1.
Record definition for the room file.

Inheritance

Class: Lecture Room (r14-lec.cbl)
Description: Manages object data for a lecture room.

OBJECT	Object Data: room number standard configuration price special configuration price room capacity	
Public Methods	*Parameters*	*Description*

get-room-prices	Returning:
	room prices
	   std config price pic 9(03)
	   spec config price pic 9(03)
		Returns room prices as a group item.

get-room-capacity	Returning room capacity pic 9(02)	Returns room capacity.

populate-the-room-object	Using:
	room data (group item)
	   room number pic X(03)
	   std config price pic 9(03)
	   spec config-price pic 9(03)
	   room capacity pic 9(02)
		Populates the room object using data transmitted as a group item.

Figure 8-2. Lecture-Room documentation.

Class: Database Interface (r14-dbi.cbl)
Description: This class provides read access to data of the indexed file room.di.

FACTORY	Object Data:
	Room-file record
	   room number pricing code
	   accounting code room discount
	   room type room capacity
	   std config price room width
	   spec config price room length	

Public Methods	*Parameters*	*Description*
close-file		Closes the room file.

get-lab-room-data	Returning:
	room object data (group item)
	   room number pic x(03)
	   std config price pic 9(03)
	   spec config price pic 9(03)
	   number work stations pic 9(02)
	   station capacity pic 9(01)
		Returns lab room data required to populate the room object.

get-lec-room-data	Returning:
	room object data (group item)
	   room number pic x(03)
	   std config price pic 9(03)
	   spec config price pic 9(03)
	   room capacity pic 9(02)
		Returns lecture room data required to populate the room object.

get-room-type	Returning: room type pic x(03)	Returns the room type (lecture or lab).
open-file		Opens the room file.

read-room-file	Using:
	   room number pic X(03)
	Returning
	   record-found switch pic X(01)
	     Y—Record successfully read
	     N—Record not found
		Reads a room record using the input room number as the key. Returned value indicates whether or not record successfully read.

Figure 8-3. DBI documentation.

As you might anticipate, DBI reads the desired room record as before. However, the value stored in rr-room-type determines whether the room capacity or the work-station data is returned to an invoking program.

Project Documentation

Before considering the programs, let's look at the class documentation on the preceding page. The lecture-room class (see Figure 8-2) is little changed from earlier room classes. The lab-room class is similar except the object data includes number-of-work stations and station-capacity.

DBI, described in Figure 8-3, is substantially different from previous versions as indicated by the highlighted method descriptions. For instance, you see two different methods for access to the room data: one for a lab room and the other for a lecture room. The method get-room-type makes the room type available so that Room Manager will know which of the room data access methods to invoke.

Room Manager, described in Figure 8-4, includes separate methods for instantiating the room object. One for the Lecture Room class and the other for the Lab Room class.

Documentation for the UI class is not included here as the changes from previous versions of UI are relatively minor.

Class: Room Manager (r14-mgr.cbl)
Description: The general control class that handles access to other classes of the room system.

FACTORY	Object Data: Room object handle	
Public Methods	*Parameters*	*Description*
process-user-requests		Provides overall process control. Collaborators: Self, UI, DBI
Private Methods	*Parameters*	*Description*
create-lab-room-object		Creates a lab room object and populates it. Collaborators: Lab Room, DBI Invoked by: process-this-request
create-lec-room-object		Creates a lecture room object and populates it Collaborators: Lecture Room, DBI Invoked by: process-this-request
process-this-request	Using: Room number pic X(03)	Handles processing for each room request. Collaborators: Self, DBI, UI Invoked by: process-user-requests
process-user-selections		Evaluates user data request and displays the requested information. Collaborators: UI, Room object Invoked by: process-this-request

Figure 8-4. Room-Manager documentation.

Inheritance

```cobol
           $set sourceformat "free"
 1 *>****************************************
 2 *> Room Rental System
 3 *> W. Price  Feb 3, 2000              R14-LEC.CBL
 4 *> This class is same as R06-ROOM except the
 5 *> method get-discounted-room-prices is removed.
 6 *> Methods.
 7 *>    get-room-capacity
 8 *>    get-room-prices
 9 *>    populate-the-room-object
10 *>****************************************
11
12 Identification Division.
13        Class-id.   LecRoomClass
14                    inherits from BaseClass
15                    .
16 Environment Division.
17        Object Section.
18          Class-Control.
19             LecRoomClass is class "r14-lec"
20             BaseClass    is class "base"
21             .
22 *>=======================================
23 OBJECT.
24   Data Division.
25     Object-Storage Section.
26     01  room-data.
27         10   room-number      pic X(03).
28         10   std-config-price pic 9(03).
29         10   spec-config-price pic 9(03).
30         10   room-capacity    pic 9(02).
31
32   Procedure Division.
33     *>--------------------------------------
34     Method-id. get-room-prices.
35     *>--------------------------------------
36       Data Division.
37         Linkage Section.
38         01  ls-room-prices.
39             10  ls-std-config-price   pic 9(03).
40             10  ls-spec-config-price  pic 9(03).
41
42       Procedure Division  Returning ls-room-prices.
43         Move std-config-price to ls-std-config-price
44         Move spec-config-price to ls-spec-config-price
45         .
46     End Method get-room-prices.
47
48     *>--------------------------------------
49     Method-id. get-room-capacity.
50     *>--------------------------------------
51       Data Division.
52         Linkage Section.
53         01  ls-room-capacity        pic 9(02).
54
55       Procedure Division  Returning ls-room-capacity.
56         Move room-capacity to ls-room-capacity
57         .
58     End Method get-room-capacity.
59
60
61     *>--------------------------------------
62     Method-id. populate-the-room-object.
63     *>--------------------------------------
64       Data Division.
65         Linkage Section.
66         01  ls-room-data.
67             10  ls-room-number       pic X(03).
68             10  ls-std-config-price  pic 9(03).
69             10  ls-spec-config-price pic 9(03).
70             10  ls-room-capacity     pic 9(02).
71
72
73       Procedure Division  Using ls-room-data.
74         Move ls-room-data to room-data
75         .
76     End Method populate-the-room-object.
77     *>--------------------------------------
78 END OBJECT.
79 END CLASS LecRoomClass.
```

```cobol
           $set sourceformat "free"
 1 *>****************************************
 2 *> Room Rental System
 3 *> W. Price  Feb 3, 2000              R14-LAB.CBL
 4 *>
 5 *> This class is the lab-room version of R14-LEC.
 6 *> Methods.
 7 *>    get-room-capacity
 8 *>    get-room-prices
 9 *>    populate-the-room-object
10 *>****************************************
11
12 Identification Division.
13        Class-id.   LabRoomClass
14                    inherits from BaseClass
15                    .
16 Environment Division.
17        Object Section.
18          Class-Control.
19             LabRoomClass is class "r14-lab"
20             BaseClass    is class "base"
21             .
22 *>=======================================
23 OBJECT.
24   Data Division.
25     Working-Storage Section.
26     01  room-data.
27         10   room-number       pic X(03).
28         10   std-config-price  pic 9(03).
29         10   spec-config-price pic 9(03).
30         10   work-stations     pic 9(02).
31         10   station-capacity  pic 9(01).
32   Procedure Division.
33     *>--------------------------------------
34     Method-id. get-room-prices.
35     *>--------------------------------------
36       Data Division.
37         Linkage Section.
38         01  ls-room-prices.
39             10  ls-std-config-price   pic 9(03).
40             10  ls-spec-config-price  pic 9(03).
41
42       Procedure Division  Returning ls-room-prices.
43         Move std-config-price to ls-std-config-price
44         Move spec-config-price to ls-spec-config-price
45         .
46     End Method get-room-prices.
47
48     *>--------------------------------------
49     Method-id. get-room-capacity.
50     *>--------------------------------------
51       Data Division.
52         Linkage Section.
53         01  ls-room-capacity        pic 9(02).
54
55       Procedure Division  Returning ls-room-capacity.
56         Move work-stations to ls-room-capacity
57         Multiply station-capacity by ls-room-capacity
58         .
59     End Method get-room-capacity.
60
61     *>--------------------------------------
62     Method-id. populate-the-room-object.
63     *>--------------------------------------
64       Data Division.
65         Linkage Section.
66         01  ls-room-data.
67             10  ls-room-number       pic X(03).
68             10  ls-std-config-price  pic 9(03).
69             10  ls-spec-config-price pic 9(03).
70             10  ls-work-stations     pic 9(02).
71             10  ls-station-capacity  pic 9(01).
72
73       Procedure Division  Using ls-room-data.
74         Move ls-room-data to room-data
75         .
76     End Method populate-the-room-object.
77     *>--------------------------------------
78 END OBJECT.
79 END CLASS LabRoomClass.
```

Figure 8-5. The lecture and lab room classes.

The Room Classes

You can see by inspecting Figure 8-5 (on the preceding page) that the two class definitions are almost identical. Lines 27-29 contain object data that is common to both programs. Line 30 in r14-lec and lines 30 and 31 in r14-lab contain object data that is unique to each room type.

Notice that corresponding object methods use the same names. In fact, the entire method get-room-prices is identical in the two programs. The other two methods differ slightly consistent with the requirements of the individual room type.

The DBI

DBI's new code (documented in Figure 8-3) is shown in the partial listing of Figure 8-6. The method get-room-type provides the invoking program the needed room type necessary to determine whether to invoke either get-lab-room-data or get-lec-room-data.

```
36      Data Division.
37          File Section.
38          FD  Room-File.
39          01  room-record.
40              10  rr-room-number            pic x(03).
41              10  rr-acctg-code             pic x(10).
42              10  rr-room-type              pic x(03).
43              10  rr-std-config-price       pic 9(03).
44              10  rr-spec-config-price      pic 9(03).
45              10  rr-pricing-code           pic 9(01).
46              10  rr-room-discount          pic v9(02).
47              10  rr-room-capacity          pic 9(02).
48              10  rr-room-width             pic 9(02).
49              10  rr-room-length            pic 9(02).
50              10  rr-work-stations          pic 9(02).
51              10  rr-station-capacity       pic 9(01).
52          Working-Storage Section.

63      *>............................................
64      Method-ID. get-lab-room-data.
65      *>............................................
66          Data Division.
67              Linkage Section.
68              01  ls-room-object-data.
69                  10  ls-room-number        pic x(03).
70                  10  ls-std-config-price   pic 9(03).
71                  10  ls-spec-config-price  pic 9(03).
72                  10  ls-work-stations      pic 9(02).
73                  10  ls-station-capacity   pic 9(01).
74
75          Procedure Division
76                      Returning ls-room-object-data.
77              Move rr-room-number to ls-room-number
78              Move rr-std-config-price
79                      to ls-std-config-price
80              Move rr-spec-config-price
81                      to ls-spec-config-price
82              Move rr-work-stations
83                      to ls-work-stations
84              Move rr-station-capacity
85                      to ls-station-capacity
86              .
87      End Method get-lab-room-data.

88
89      *>............................................
90      Method-ID. get-lec-room-data.
91      *>............................................
92          Data Division.
93              Linkage Section.
94              01  ls-room-object-data.
95                  10  ls-room-number        pic x(03).
96                  10  ls-std-config-price   pic 9(03).
97                  10  ls-spec-config-price  pic 9(03).
98                  10  ls-room-capacity      pic 9(02).
99
100         Procedure Division
101                     Returning ls-room-object-data.
102             Move rr-room-number to ls-room-number
103             Move rr-std-config-price
104                     to ls-std-config-price
105             Move rr-spec-config-price
106                     to ls-spec-config-price
107             Move rr-room-capacity
108                     to ls-room-capacity
109             .
110     End Method get-lec-room-data.
111
112     *>............................................
113     Method-ID. get-room-type.
114     *>............................................
115         Data Division.
116             Linkage Section.
117             01  ls-room-type              pic X(03).
118
119         Procedure Division Returning ls-room-type.
120             Move rr-room-type to ls-room-type
121             .
122     End Method get-room-type.
```

Figure 8-6. Selected code from DBI.

Room Manager

Room Manager's listing of Figure 8-7 is complete except for the omitted process-user-requests method (lines 82-108)—it is identical to those of preceding examples. Let's step through the method process-this-request.

1. DBI is invoked at line 124 to access the desired record—assume the requested record is found.
2. DBI is invoked at line 128 to obtain the room type.
3. Either a lecture room object or a lab room object is created depending on the room type—refer to the If statement at lines 130-134.
4. The appropriate class is instantiated and populated at lines 47-54 or lines 69-76. It is significant that the same handle (theRoomHandle) is used for both room types.
5. Control is transferred to the process-user-selections method by the Invoke of line 135.
6. Within the process-user-selections method the room capacity is accessed (line 166) and displayed (line 169) without regard to the room type.

Overall View of Room14

By using the same method names in the two class programs for methods performing the same function, Room Manager can invoke methods without concern for the type of object it is referencing. For instance, consider the following statement (lines 166-168 of Figure 8-7).

```
Invoke theRoomHandle
    "get-room-capacity"
    Returning lo-room-capacity
```

You cannot tell by looking at this statement the type of room object: it could be either lecture or lab. However, the runtime system "knows" and will invoke the proper get-room-capacity method: either that of the LectureRoom class or that of LabRoom class. Although the method names are the same, the method procedures are different. This is another example of polymorphism. That is, the same message to different receivers produces actions.

Redundancy in Room12

As you see, the two room classes contain considerable redundancy. In fact, the method get-room-type of LectureRoom is identical to that of LabRoom. This duplication is highly undesirable. For instance, if the procedure for obtaining the room type were changed, then code in both classes would require changing. Object technology gets around this problem through inheritance, the next topic in this chapter.

```cobol
         $set sourceformat "free"
*>*******************************************
*> Room Rental System
*> W. Price  Jan 24, 2000            R14-MGR.CBL
*>
*> RoomManager handles access to the classes of
*> the Room system.
*> Methods:
*>    create-room-object
*>    process-user-requests
*>    process-this-request
*>    process-user-selections
*>*******************************************

Identification Division.
      Class-ID. RoomManager.

Environment Division.
      Object Section.
         Class-Control.
            UserInterface       is class "r14-ui"
            DatabaseInterface   is class "r14-dbi"
            LabRoomClass        is class "r14-lab"
            LecRoomClass        is class "r14-lec"
            RoomManager         is class "r14-mgr"
            .
*>===========================================
FACTORY.
   Data Division.
      Object-Storage Section.
         01 theRoomHandle    object reference.
         01 room-type        pic X(03).

   Procedure Division.
      *>---------------------------------------
      Method-id. create-lab-room-object.
      *>---------------------------------------
         Data Division.
            Local-Storage Section.
               01 lo-room-object-data.
                  10 lo-room-number        pic X(03).
                  10 lo-std-config-price   pic 9(03).
                  10 lo-spec-config-price  pic 9(03).
                  10 lo-work-stations      pic 9(02).
                  10 lo-station-capacity   pic 9(01).

         Procedure Division.
            Invoke DataBaseInterface
                    "get-lab-room-data"
                       Returning lo-room-object-data
            Invoke LabRoomClass "New"
                       Returning theRoomHandle
            Invoke theRoomHandle
                    "populate-the-room-object"
                       Using lo-room-object-data
         End Method create-lab-room-object.

      *>---------------------------------------
      Method-id. create-lec-room-object.
      *>---------------------------------------
         Data Division.
            Local-Storage Section.
               01 lo-room-object-data.
                  10 lo-room-number        pic X(03).
                  10 lo-std-config-price   pic 9(03).
                  10 lo-spec-config-price  pic 9(03).
                  10 lo-room-capacity      pic 9(02).

         Procedure Division.
            Invoke DataBaseInterface
                    "get-lec-room-data"
                       Returning lo-room-object-data
            Invoke LecRoomClass "New"
                       Returning theRoomHandle
            Invoke theRoomHandle
                    "populate-the-room-object"
                       Using lo-room-object-data
         End Method create-lec-room-object.

      *>---------------------------------------
      Method-id. process-user-requests.
      *>---------------------------------------

      End Method process-user-requests.

      *>---------------------------------------
      Method-id. process-this-request.
      *>---------------------------------------
         Data Division.
            Local-Storage Section.
               01 lo-record-found-sw       pic X(01).
                  88 lo-record-found             value "Y".
               01 lo-invalid-room-message  pic X(40)
                          value "Invalid room number".
            Linkage Section.
               01 ls-room-number           pic X(03).

         Procedure Division Using ls-room-number.
            Invoke DataBaseInterface "read-room-file"
                       Using ls-room-number
                       Returning lo-record-found-sw
            If lo-record-found
               Invoke DataBaseInterface "get-room-type"
                          Returning room-type
               If room-type = "LEC"
                  Invoke Self "create-lec-room-object"
               Else
                  Invoke Self "create-lab-room-object"
               End-If *>room-type = "LEC"
               Invoke Self "process-user-selections"
            Else
               Invoke UserInterface "display-message"
                          Using lo-invalid-room-message
            End-If *>lo-record-found
         End Method process-this-request.

      *>---------------------------------------
      Method-id. process-user-selections.
      *>---------------------------------------
         Data Division.
            Local-Storage Section.
               01 lo-room-prices.
                  10 lo-std-config-price   pic 9(03).
                  10 lo-spec-config-price  pic 9(03).
               01 lo-room-capacity         pic 9(02).
               01 lo-menu-choice           pic X(01).
                  88 lo-standard-prices          value "S".

         Procedure Division.
            Invoke UserInterface
                    "get-menu-selection"
                       Returning lo-menu-choice
            Evaluate TRUE
               When lo-standard-prices
                  Invoke theRoomHandle "get-room-prices"
                             Returning lo-room-prices
                  Invoke UserInterface
                          "display-room-prices"
                             Using lo-room-prices
               When other
                  Invoke theRoomHandle
                          "get-room-capacity"
                             Returning lo-room-capacity
                  Invoke UserInterface
                          "display-room-capacity"
                             Using lo-room-capacity
            End-evaluate *>TRUE
            .
         End Method process-user-selections.
      *>---------------------------------------
END FACTORY.
END CLASS RoomManager.
```

Figure 8-7. Room Manager.

Inheritance

[Figure 8-8: (a) A simple classification structure showing Pet with subcategories Dog, Snake, Bird. (b) Another level of classification adding Beagle, Terrier under Dog; Garter, Coral under Snake; Parrot, Canary under Bird.]

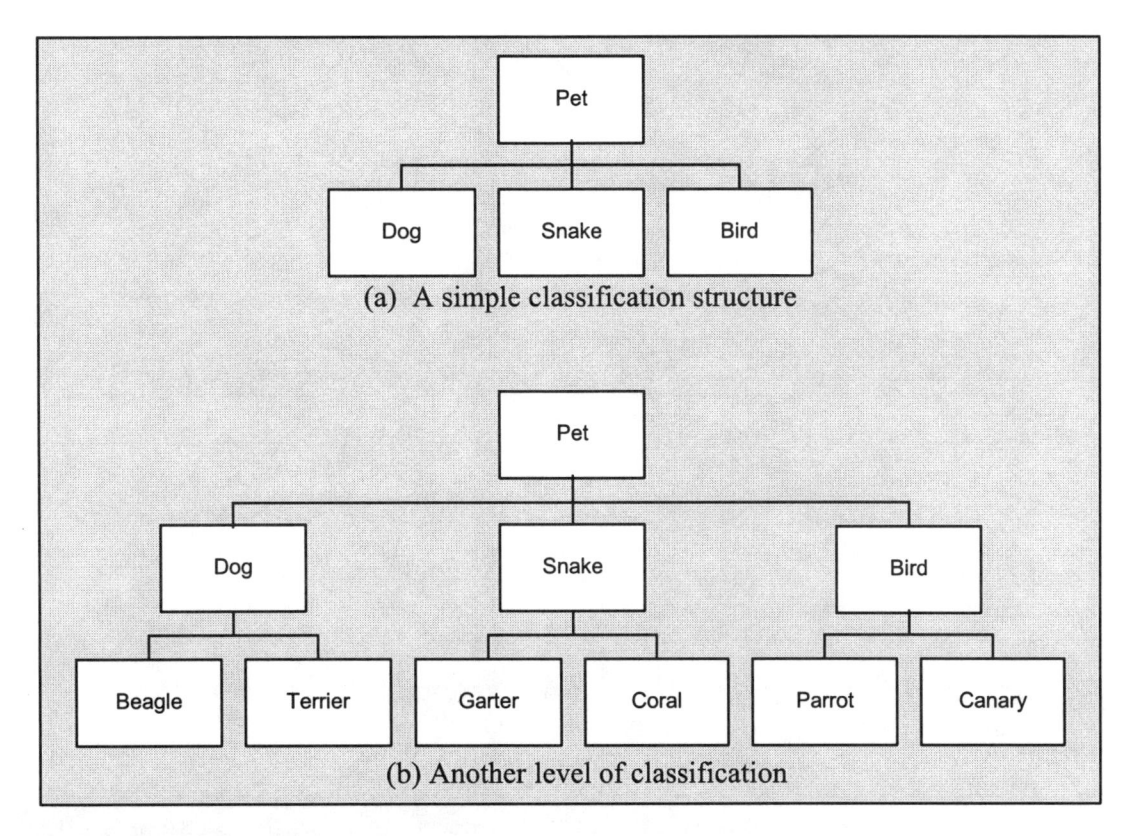

Figure 8-8. Classification structures.

Classification Structures

Selecting a Pet

Before beginning your study of inheritance in OOCobol, let's consider how, as human beings, we employ structure in studying the real world. For a non-data processing example, consider the action of a father in directing the selection of a family pet. Assume that members of the family have expressed their desires and the species candidates are a dog (very conventional), a snake, and a bird. Being a programmer, Father cannot resist introducing object orientation into the evaluation of the candidates. To that end, he constructs the chart of Figure 8-8(a) which illustrates the general category pet and subcategories *dog*, *snake*, and *bird*. Then as would any good programmer, he proceeds to expand upon this hierarchy by introducing another level as shown in Figure 8-8(b).

Let's look at his handiwork. This chart progresses from a *generalization* at the top to *specialization* at the bottom. Each member at a given level is a member of each level above it. For instance, a dog is a pet and a bird is a pet. Furthermore, the beagle is not only a dog, but it is also a pet. This chart classifies pets into meaningful categories. It is commonly called a **classification structure** or a **classification hierarchy**; it is also called a **generalization-specialization** (or **gen-spec**) **hierarchy**. You will commonly hear it referred to as an **is-a** structure taken from the notion that a lower-level category *is a* subset of any higher-level category. For instance, a bird *is a* pet.

```
┌─────────────────────────────────────────────────────────┐
│                    ┌─────────────────────┐              │
│                    │ Pet                 │              │
│                    ├─────────────────────┤              │
│                    │ Attribute: Name     │              │
│                    ├─────────────────────┤              │
│                    │ Service: Provide    │              │
│                    │ pleasure to the     │              │
│                    │ family.             │              │
│                    └─────────▲───────────┘              │
│         ┌────────────────────┼────────────────────┐     │
│  ┌──────┴──────┐      ┌──────┴──────┐      ┌──────┴──────┐
│  │ Dog         │      │ Snake       │      │ Bird        │
│  ├─────────────┤      ├─────────────┤      ├─────────────┤
│  │Attribute:   │      │Attribute:   │      │Attribute:   │
│  │Weight       │      │Length       │      │Height       │
│  ├─────────────┤      ├─────────────┤      ├─────────────┤
│  │Service:Bark │      │Service:     │      │Service:     │
│  │at intruders │      │Startle      │      │Sing/talk    │
│  │             │      │friends      │      │             │
│  └─────────────┘      └─────────────┘      └─────────────┘
└─────────────────────────────────────────────────────────┘
```

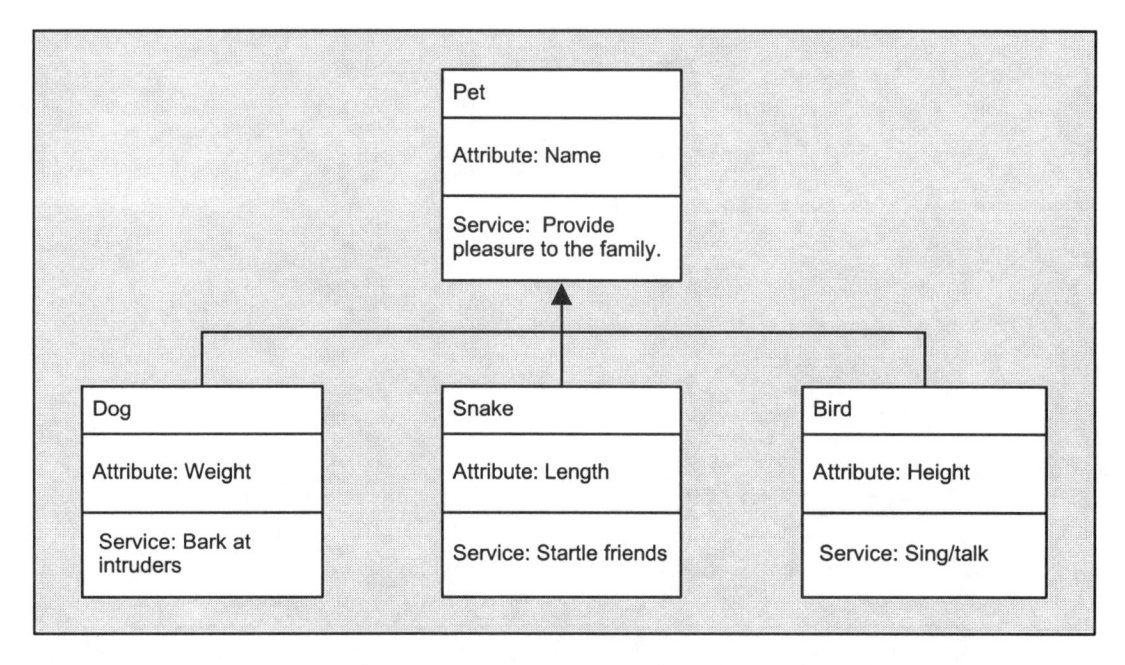

Figure 8-9. Classification structure showing attributes and services.

At this point, Father can't help himself and his analysis/design background begins to overshadow the activity of choosing a pet. To that end, he expands upon Figure 8-8(a) by showing attributes and services in Figure 8-9. You see that an attribute of a pet is the pet's name. The "service" provided by a pet is giving pleasure to the family. Although displayed in the pet box, this attribute and service are common to *any* pet lower in the hierarchy.

Now look at individual pet candidates, for instance, the dog. Its attribute is its weight. (Father considers the weight important as he is not interested in feeding a 40 pound dog.) The dog provides the service of barking at strangers thereby functioning as a watch dog.

Contrast this attribute and service to those of the snake and the bird. They are distinctly different. For example, the dog's service of barking at strangers is unique to the dog. It is unlikely that a snake or bird will bark at strangers (although the bird might chirp).

Let's summarize what we see here for Dog.

Pet
    Attribute: Name
    Service: Provide family pleasure

Dog
    Attribute: Weight
    Service: Bark at intruders

Dog has the attribute weight, which is unique to Dog *and* the attribute name which is derived from the general category pet. Similarly, Dog provides a service unique to Dog (bark) and the general service of providing pleasure, derived from Pet. You see generalized attributes and services common to all pets and specialized attributes and services unique to each pet. In object-oriented terms, Dog is said to **inherit** the properties of Pet giving the following.

> Dog
>> Attributes:
>>> Name (inherited from Pet)
>>> Weight
>>
>> Services:
>>> Provide family pleasure (inherited from Pet)
>>> Bark at intruders

If we consider Dog, Snake, and Bird as *subcategories* of Pet, then Pet is the *supercategory* of Dog, Snake, and Bird.

Classifying Computers

We classify things in all aspects of life in order to simplify. For instance, read any computer magazine and you will see personal computers classified by numerous criteria. One classification is by make:

> Personal computer
>> IBM compatible
>> MacIntosh compatible

Another classification is by style:

> Personal computer
>> Desktop computer
>> Tower computer
>>> Minitower computer
>>> Fulltower computer
>>> Maxitower computer
>>
>> Laptop computer

Classification is a method we use in every aspect of our lives in understanding complex things.

A Simple Example of Inheritance—Room15

Room Classes

Like pets, rooms (the focus of this book) can be classified according to room type. Specifically, Room14 introduced you to two categories of rooms: lecture rooms and laboratory rooms. You saw that certain data is common to both room types and other data is unique to each type. In terms of classes, we have a generalization-specialization grouping as follows.

>Room
>>Room number
>>Standard configuration price
>>Special configuration price
>
>Lecture Room
>>Capacity
>
>Lab Room
>>Number of work stations
>>Positions per work station

Limiting to the above object data, the data and services can be represented as shown in Figure 8-10. (You can see that the representations here are identical to those of Figure 8-9 for pets.) The Lab Room class and Lecture Room class are said to be a **subclasses** of the Room Class. Correspondingly, the Room Class is said to be a **superclass** of these corresponding subclasses.

A Class and Subclasses

Ideally, we want to deal with either a Lecture Room or a Lab Room class and have access to the services of the individual class *and* the superclass Room. As users of either of the two subclasses, we should not need to identify both the subclass and the superclass. This separation should be transparent to us as class users. Cobol's inheritance feature of object orientation provides exactly this capability.

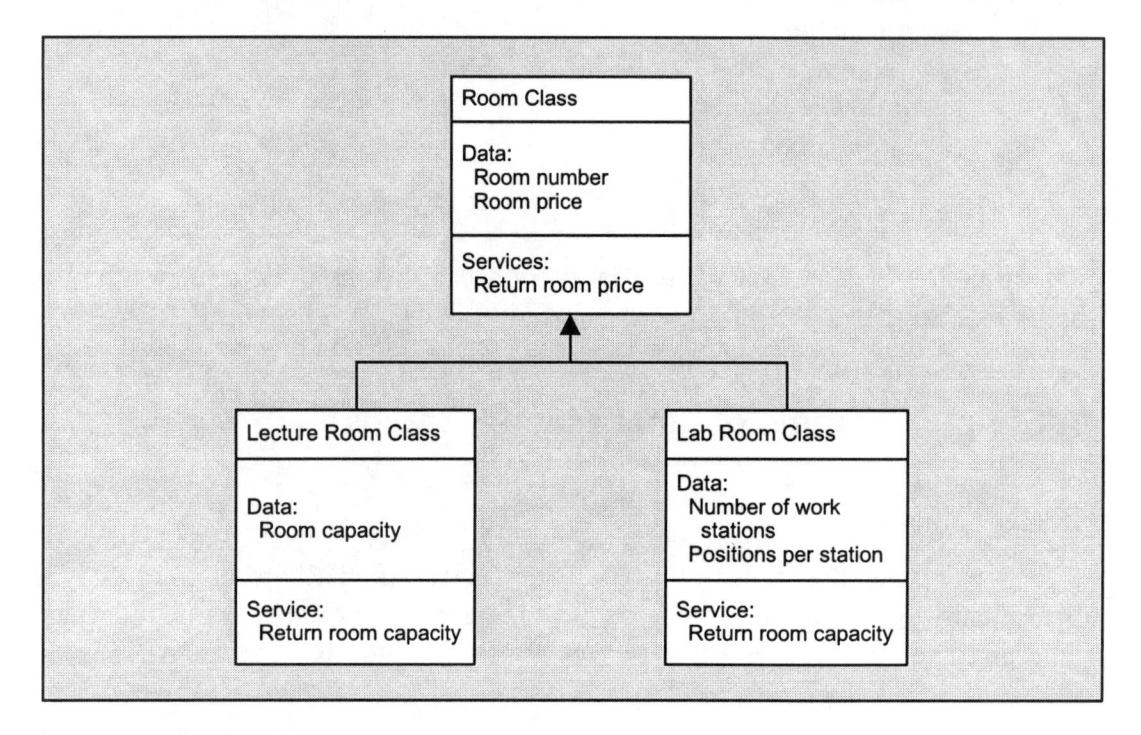

Figure 8-10. A room classification hierarchy.

Inheritance

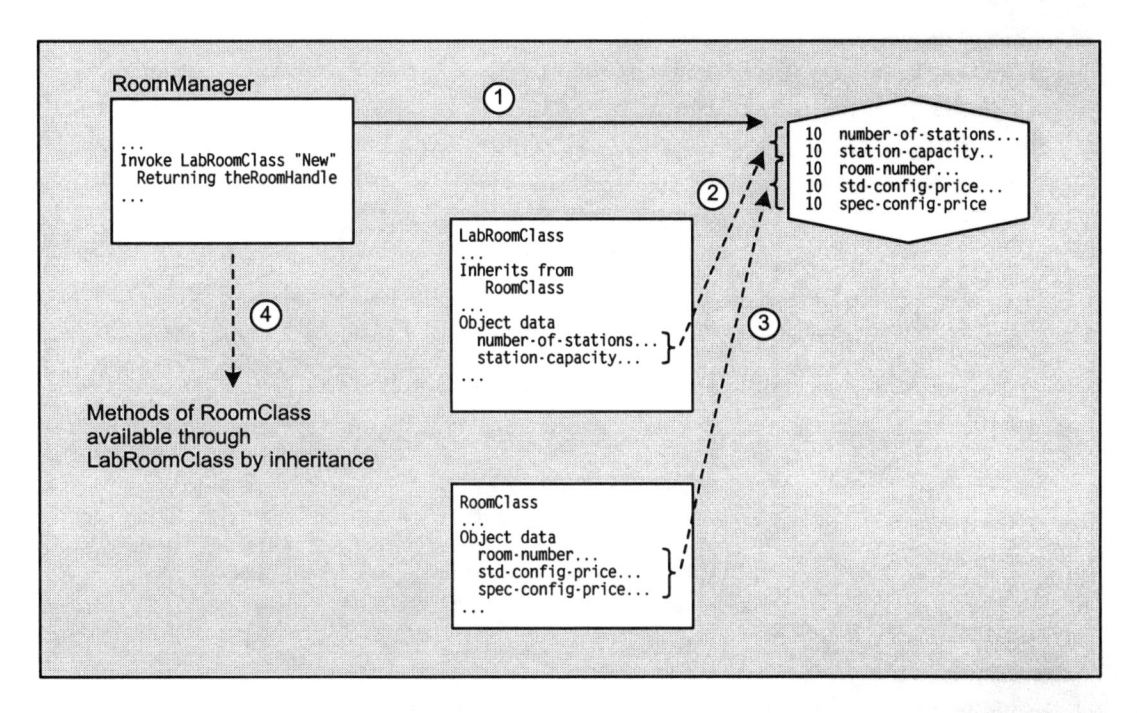

Figure 8-11. Constructing an object from its class and its superclass.

Look at Figure 8-11 for an insight to how instantiating the Lab Room class can make available to the instantiating program the methods and object data of the Room superclass. Invoking the method New causes the following to occur.

1. Establish an object memory area for replication of the class's object data and assign the designated object handle as a "pointer" to that area.
2. Replicate the object data definitions from the designated class (LabRoom in this case) into the object memory area.
3. From the `inherits from RoomClass` clause, locate the class definition for RoomClass and replicate its object data definitions into the object memory area.
4. Make available to the invoking program (via the object handle) the methods of both classes.

Thus all the object data and methods of RoomClass are available to any invoking program through LabRoomClass. You do *not* instantiate RoomClass nor make any reference to it in the processing methods.

Assume that the room class definitions are part of a general room class library and you are using them solely as a class user. You've never examined the code itself because you've never had a need. From this perspective, you would see the lab room class as a single entity with no hint that the component you are using actually consists of two classes, one inheriting from the other. In this case, inheritance is transparent to you. You would probably never use the room class by itself; it would normally be available only through inheritance. A class such as this for which you do not explicitly create an instance is called an **abstract class**.

Class:	Lab Room (r15-lab.cbl)	
Superclass:	Room (r15-room.cbl)	
Description:	Manages that portion of the object data that is unique to lab rooms.	

OBJECT	Object Data: number of work stations station capacity	
Public Methods	*Parameters*	*Description*
get-room-capacity	Returning 　room capacity　　　　pic 9(02)	Calculates room capacity as product of work-stations and station-capacity. Returns room capacity.
populate-the-room-object	Using: 　room data (group item) 　　room number　　　pic X(03) 　　std config price　　pic 9(03) 　　spec config-price　　pic 9(03) 　　work stations　　　pic 9(02) 　　station capacity　　pic 9(01)	Populates the lab room subclass object using data transmitted as a group item. Invokes a method of the super class to populate the super class object.

Class:	Lecture Room (r15-lec.cbl)	
Superclass:	Room (r15-room.cbl)	
Description:	Manages that portion of the object data that is unique to lecture rooms.	

OBJECT	Object Data: room capacity	
Public Methods	*Parameters*	*Description*
get-room-capacity	Returning 　room capacity　　　　pic 9(02)	Returns room capacity.
populate-the-room-object	Using: 　room data (group item) 　　room number　　　pic X(03) 　　std config price　　pic 9(03) 　　spec config-price　　pic 9(03) 　　room capacity　　　pic 9(02)	Populates the lecture room subclass object using data transmitted as a group item. Invokes a method of the super class to populate the room super class object.

Figure 8-12. Documentation for room subclasses.

Room Class Documentation

Proj0802 Room15

This project is identical to Room14 except that the room inheritance hierarchy of Figure 8-10 is implemented. If you looked at Room Manager (r15-mgr), you would not see any difference from r14-mgr.cbl (except for external references in the Class Control paragraph). Specifically, you would see the following If statement that gives you no hint the lecture and lab room classes are part of an inheritance hierarchy.

Class:	Room (r15-room.cbl)—abstract class
Subclasses:	Lab Room (r15-lab.cbl) and Lecture Room (r15-lec.cbl)
Description:	Manages object data common to both lab rooms and lecture rooms.

OBJECT	Object Data: room number standard configuration price special configuration price	
Public Method	*Parameters*	*Description*

get-room-prices	Returning:
	room prices
	  std config price pic 9(03)
	  spec config price pic 9(03)
		Returns room prices as a group item.

Private Method	*Parameters*	*Description*

populate-the-room-object	Using:
	room data (group item)
	  room number pic X(03)
	  std config price pic 9(03)
	  spec config-price pic 9(03)
		Invoked by the subclass. Populates the room object using data transmitted as a group item from the subclass.

Figure 8-13. Documentation for the room superclass.

```
If room-type = "LEC"
  Invoke Self "create-lec-room-object"
Else
  Invoke Self "create-lab-room-object"
End-If *>room-type = "LEC"
```

Now look at the documentation in Figure 8-12 for the two subclasses and notice the following.

- Each includes the get-room-capacity method. These are identical to the corresponding methods of the room classes in Room14.
- In both cases, the parameters of the method populate-the-room-object include data items required for the subclass (work-stations and station-capacity for lab room and room-capacity for room). They also include the room number and prices—data items required by the superclass.
- In addition to populating its own object, the method populate-the-room-object must invoke an appropriate method of the superclass to populate the superclass object data.

The room class documentation of Figure 8-13 includes the method get-room-prices, the common method identified from Room14. It also includes a populate-the-room-object method to populate its "share" of the object.

The Room Class Definitions

Figure 8-14 includes two class definitions. The class program r15-room (RoomClass) on the left contains data that is common to both types of rooms. It also contains the method get-room-prices which provides access to the room-price object data. There is nothing here you have not seen in many previous examples.

Correspondingly, r15-lab (LabRoomClass) on the right contains object data unique to lab rooms and the method necessary to compute and return the room capacity. (Be aware that the Lecture Room class is essentially the same except its object data consists only of the room capacity.) Notice the establishment of the inheritance hierarchy at lines 16 and 17 of LabRoomClass:

```
Class-ID.  LabRoomClass
           Inherits from RoomClass
```

In turn, RoomClass inherits from BaseClass, as in all preceding examples.

Remember that the lab room object created by RoomManager contains object data items from both LabRoomClass and RoomClass (see Figure 8-11). Remember also that object data is available only through methods of the class from which that object was created. Therefore, each of the two classes must include a method to populate its portion of the object. The following steps illustrate creating and populating the object.

1. RoomManager instantiates the LabRoomClass thereby creating an object consisting of both lab room and room object data.
2. RoomManager invokes a LabRoomClass method to populate the object. The data for both components of the object is transmitted. Refer to the method beginning line 49 of the lab room definition in Figure 8-14.
3. The LabRoomClass method moves the lab room specific data into the LabRoomClass object at lines 67-69.
4. Because the LabRoomClass does not have direct access to the Room object data, it invokes a RoomClass method to populate room's portion of the object data.

The following Invoke (from lines 72 and 73) shows how you invoke a method of a superclass.

```
Invoke Super "populate-the-room-object"
       Using lo-price-data
```

That is, use the reserved word Super as the object identifier in the Invoke statement. This causes the program to look to the next higher level in the inheritance hierarchy for the designated method. Remember, RoomClass has not been explicitly instantiated and therefore has no handle of its own.

Notice that both class definitions use the same method name to populate their respective object data components—this is another example of polymorphism.

A Variation of the Room Example—Room16

Proj0803 Room16

A Sample Dialogue

Preceding examples of this chapter compute room capacity of lab rooms as number of workstations times workstation capacity. The room capacity field (from the data

```
        $set sourceformat "free"
 1 *>*****************************************
 2 *> Room Rental System
 3 *> W. Price  Jan 24, 2000          R15-ROOM.CBL
 4 *>
 5 *> Room class (inherited by Lab & Lecture Rooms)
 6 *> Object data is:
 7 *>    room-number
 8 *>    std-config-price
 9 *>    spec-config-price
10 *> Methods are:
11 *>    get-room-prices
12 *>    populate-the-room-object
13 *>*****************************************
14
15 Identification Division.
16       Class-id.   RoomClass
17                   inherits from BaseClass
18                   .
19 Environment Division.
20       Object Section.
21       Class-Control.
22          RoomClass is class "r15-room"
23          BaseClass    is class "base"
24          .
25 *>========================================
26 OBJECT.
27   Data Division.
28     Object-Storage Section.   *> OBJECT DATA
29     01 room-price-data.
30        10 room-number       pic X(03).
31        10 std-config-price  pic 9(03).
32        10 spec-config-price pic 9(03).
33
34   Procedure Division.
35     *>----------------------------------------
36     Method-id. get-room-prices.
37     *>----------------------------------------
38       Data Division.
39         Linkage Section.
40         01 ls-room-prices.
41            10 ls-std-config-price   pic 9(03).
42            10 ls-spec-config-price  pic 9(03).
43
44       Procedure Division  Returning ls-room-prices.
45         Move std-config-price to ls-std-config-price
46         Move spec-config-price to ls-spec-config-price
47         .
48     End Method get-room-prices.
49
50     *>----------------------------------------
51     Method-id. populate-the-room-object.
52     *>----------------------------------------
53       Data Division.
54         Linkage Section.
55         01 ls-price-data.
56            10 ls-room-number        pic X(03).
57            10 ls-std-config-price   pic 9(03).
58            10 ls-spec-config-price  pic 9(03).
59
60       Procedure Division Using ls-price-data.
61         Move ls-room-number to room-number
62         Move ls-std-config-price
63                                to std-config-price
64         Move ls-spec-config-price
65                                to spec-config-price
66         .
67     End Method populate-the-room-object.
68     *>----------------------------------------
69 END OBJECT.
70 END CLASS RoomClass.
```

```
        $set sourceformat "free"
 1 *>*****************************************
 2 *> Room Rental System
 3 *> W. Price  Jan 24, 2000          R15-LAB.CBL
 4 *>
 5 *> This class is the
 6 *> lab-room subclass to Room.
 7 *> Object data:
 8 *>    work-stations
 9 *>    station-capacity
10 *> Methods.
11 *>    get-room-prices
12 *>    populate-the-room-object
13 *>*****************************************
14
15 Identification Division.
16       Class-id.   LabRoomClass
17                   inherits from RoomClass
18                   .
19 Environment Division.
20       Object Section.
21       Class-Control.
22          LabRoomClass is class "r15-lab"
23          RoomClass    is class "r15-room"
24          .
25 *>========================================
26 OBJECT.
27   Data Division.
28     Object-Storage Section.
29     01 room-data.
30        10 work-stations     pic 9(02).
31        10 station-capacity  pic 9(01).
32
33   Procedure Division.
34
35     *>----------------------------------------
36     Method-id. get-room-capacity.
37     *>----------------------------------------
38       Data Division.
39         Linkage Section.
40         01 ls-room-capacity      pic 9(02).
41
42       Procedure Division  Returning ls-room-capacity.
43         Move work-stations to ls-room-capacity
44         Multiply station-capacity by ls-room-capacity
45         .
46     End Method get-room-capacity.
47
48     *>----------------------------------------
49     Method-id. populate-the-room-object.
50     *>----------------------------------------
51       Data Division.
52         Local-Storage Section.
53         01 lo-price-data.
54            10 lo-room-number       pic X(03).
55            10 lo-std-config-price  pic 9(03).
56            10 lo-spec-config-price pic 9(03).
57         Linkage Section.
58         01 ls-room-data.
59            10 ls-room-number       pic X(03).
60            10 ls-std-config-price  pic 9(03).
61            10 ls-spec-config-price pic 9(03).
62            10 ls-work-stations     pic 9(02).
63            10 ls-station-capacity  pic 9(01).
64
65       Procedure Division  Using ls-room-data.
66         *> First populate the Lab room object
67         Move ls-work-stations to work-stations
68         Move ls-station-capacity
69                                to station-capacity
70         *> Next populate the room object
71         Move ls-room-data to lo-price-data
72         Invoke Super "populate-the-room-object"
73                                Using lo-price-data
74         .
75     End Method populate-the-room-object.
76     *>----------------------------------------
77 END OBJECT.
78 END CLASS LabRoomClass.
```

Figure 8-14. The Room class and Lab Room class definitions.

```
Room number (Blank if finished) 100

The options are:
   C - Room capacity (default)
   S - Standard room prices

Your choice <C,S>? C

Number of work stations: 12
    Work station capacity: 3
           Room capacity: 42

Room number (Blank if finished) 101

The options are:
   C - Room capacity (default)
   S - Standard room prices

Your choice <C,S>? C

Room capacity: 40
```

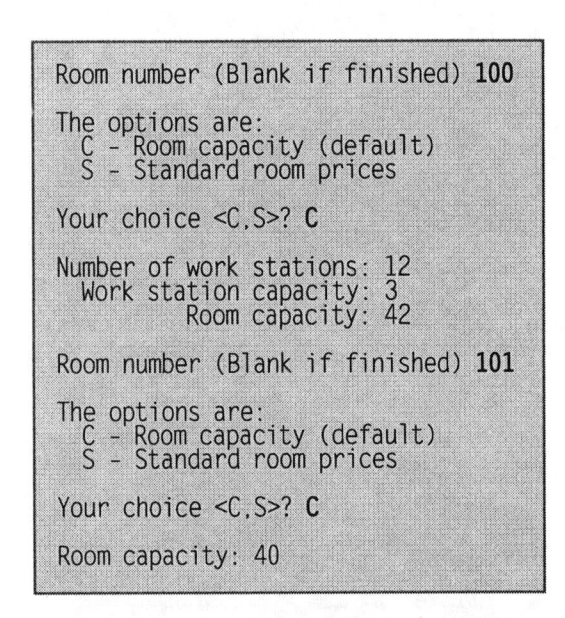

Figure 8-15.
Typical inquiry dialogue—Room16.

file) is ignored. However, if you look at the data file listing (refer to Appendix D) you will see that lab rooms contain an entry for room capacity, the value that you've seen in earlier examples that make no distinction between lab and lecture rooms. Room16 assumes that each lab room is used for both lab workshops and for lectures. When used for a lab workshop, its capacity is computed as number of workstations times station capacity; when used as a lecture room its capacity is obtained directly from the file (as in earlier examples).

If you run Room16 you will see a screen dialogue that looks something like Figure 8-15. As room 100 is a lab room, you see three data items displayed: number of workstations, station capacity, and room capacity. On the other hand, room 101 is a lecture room so you see only the room capacity. As room capacity is now common to both the lab and lecture room classes, it should reasonably become an attribute of the super class room. Correspondingly, the room class must also include a method to access this data item. Let's look at how this is implemented.

The Class and Subclasses

Room class, shown in Figure 8-16, is identical to the room class of the preceding example except for the addition of the room-capacity attribute and the method get-room-capacity.

Now look at the method get-lab-room-capacity in the lab room subclass in Figure 8-17.

- Lines 42 and 43 access work station data for return to the invoking program.

Inheritance

```cobol
            $set sourceformat "free"
  1 *>*********************************************
  2 *> Room Rental System
  3 *> W. Price  Feb 1, 2000              R16-ROOM.CBL
  4 *>
  5 *> Room class (inherited by Lab & Lecture Rooms)
  6 *> Object data is:
  7 *>      room-number
  8 *>      std-config-price
  9 *>      spec-config-price
 10 *>      room-capacity
 11 *> Methods are:
 12 *>      get-room-capacity
 13 *>      get-room-prices
 14 *>      populate-the-room-object
 15 *>*********************************************
 16
 17 Identification Division.
 18       Class-id.  RoomClass
 19                  inherits from Base
 20          .
 21 Environment Division.
 22       Object Section.
 23          Class-Control.
 24              RoomClass is class "r16-room"
 25              Base      is class "base"
 26          .
 27 *>=============================================
 28 OBJECT.
 29    Data Division.
 30       ObjectStorage Section.    *> OBJECT DATA
 31       01 room-price-data.
 32          10  room-number         pic X(03).
 33          10  std-config-price    pic 9(03).
 34          10  spec-config-price   pic 9(03).
 35          10  room-capacity       pic 9(02).
 36
 37    Procedure Division.
 38       *>-------------------------------------
 39       Method-id. get-room-capacity.
 40       *>-------------------------------------
 41       Data Division.
 42          Linkage Section.
 43          01  ls-room-capacity        pic 9(02).
 44
 45          Procedure Division  Returning ls-room-capacity.
 46             Move room-capacity to ls-room-capacity
 47          .
 48       End Method get-room-capacity.
 49
 50       *>-------------------------------------
 51       Method-id. get-room-prices.
 52       *>-------------------------------------
 53       Data Division.
 54          Linkage Section.
 55          01 ls-room-prices.
 56             10  ls-std-config-price   pic 9(03).
 57             10  ls-spec-config-price  pic 9(03).
 58
 59          Procedure Division  Returning ls-room-prices.
 60             Move std-config-price to ls-std-config-price
 61             Move spec-config-price to ls-spec-config-price
 62          .
 63       End Method get-room-prices.
 64
 65       *>-------------------------------------
 66       Method-id. populate-the-room-object.
 67       *>-------------------------------------
 68       Data Division.
 69          Linkage Section.
 70          01 ls-price-data.
 71             10  ls-room-number       pic X(03).
 72             10  ls-std-config-price  pic 9(03).
 73             10  ls-spec-config-price pic 9(03).
 74             10  ls-room-capacity     pic 9(02).
 75
 76          Procedure Division Using ls-price-data.
 77             Move ls-room-number to room-number
 78             Move ls-std-config-price
 79                                to std-config-price
 80             Move ls-spec-config-price
 81                                to spec-config-price
 82             Move ls-room-capacity
 83                                to room-capacity
 84          .
 85       End Method populate-the-room-object.
 86       *>-------------------------------------
 87 END OBJECT.
 88 END CLASS RoomClass.
```

Figure 8-16. The Room superclass—r16-room.

- Lines 44 and 45 invoke the get-room-capacity method of the superclass to access the room capacity.

The method get-lec-room-capacity in the lecture room subclass simply accesses the room capacity from the superclass.

The calling sequence from Room Manager to access room data is shown in Figure 8-18 where you see the appropriate method invoked (line 171 or line 178).

```
                $set sourceformat "free"
1  *>****************************************************
2  *> Room Rental System
3  *> W. Price  Feb 2, 2000                    R16-LAB.CBL
4  *>
5  *> This class is the
6  *> lab-room subclass to Room.
7  *> Object data:
8  *>    work-stations
9  *>    station-capacity
10 *> Methods.
11 *>    get-room-prices
12 *>    populate-the-room-object
13 *>****************************************************
14 Identification Division.
15     Class-id.  LabRoomClass
16                inherits from RoomClass
17         .
18 Environment Division.
19     Object Section.
20     Class-Control.
21         LabRoomClass is class "r16-lab"
22         RoomClass    is class "r16-room"
23         .
24 *>=================================================
25 OBJECT.
26   Data Division.
27     Object-Storage Section.
28     01 room-data.
29        10  work-stations      pic 9(02).
30        10  station-capacity   pic 9(01).
31   Procedure Division.
32   *>--------------------------------------------------
33   Method-id. get-lab-room-capacity.
34   *>--------------------------------------------------
35     Data Division.
36       Linkage Section.
37       01 ls-capacity-data.
38          10  ls-room-capacity    pic 9(02).
39          10  ls-work-stations    pic 9(02).
40          10  ls-station-capacity pic 9(01).
41     Procedure Division Returning ls-capacity-data.
42       Move work-stations to ls-work-stations
43       Move station-capacity to ls-station-capacity
44       Invoke Super "get-room-capacity"
45                    Returning ls-capacity-data
46       .
47   End Method get-lab-room-capacity.
48   *>--------------------------------------------------
49   Method-id. populate-the-room-object.
50   *>--------------------------------------------------
51     Data Division.
52       Local-Storage Section.
53       01 lo-price-data.
54          10  lo-room-number      pic X(03).
55          10  lo-std-config-price pic 9(03).
56          10  lo-spec-config-price pic 9(03).
57          10  lo-room-capacity    pic 9(02).
58       Linkage Section.
59       01 ls-room-data.
60          10  ls-room-number      pic X(03).
61          10  ls-std-config-price pic 9(03).
62          10  ls-spec-config-price pic 9(03).
63          10  ls-room-capacity    pic 9(02).
64          10  ls-work-stations    pic 9(02).
65          10  ls-station-capacity pic 9(01).
66     Procedure Division Using ls-room-data.
67     *> First populate the Lab room object
68       Move ls-work-stations to work-stations
69       Move ls-station-capacity
70                            to station-capacity
71     *> Next populate the room object
72       Move ls-room-data to lo-price-data
73       Invoke Super "populate-the-room-object"
74                    Using lo-price-data
75       .
76   End Method populate-the-room-object.
77   *>--------------------------------------------------
78 END OBJECT.
79 END CLASS LabRoomClass.
```

```
                $set sourceformat "free"
1  *>****************************************************
2  *> Room Rental System
3  *> W. Price  Feb 2, 2000                    R16-LEC.CBL
4  *>
5  *> This class is the
6  *> lecture-room subclass to Room.
7  *> Object data:
8  *>    room-capacity
9  *> Methods.
10 *>    get-room-capacity
11 *>    populate-the-room-object
12 *>****************************************************
13
14 Identification Division.
15     Class-id.  LecRoomClass
16                inherits from RoomClass
17         .
18 Environment Division.
19     Object Section.
20     Class-Control.
21         LecRoomClass is class "r16-lec"
22         RoomClass    is class "r16-room"
23         .
24 *>=================================================
25 OBJECT.
26   Procedure Division.
27   *>--------------------------------------------------
28   Method-id. get-lec-room-capacity.
29   *>--------------------------------------------------
30     Data Division.
31       Linkage Section.
32       01 ls-room-capacity       pic 9(02).
33
34     Procedure Division Returning ls-room-capacity.
35       Invoke Super "get-room-capacity"
36                    Returning ls-room-capacity
37       .
38   End Method get-lec-room-capacity.
39
40   *>--------------------------------------------------
41   Method-id. populate-the-room-object.
42   *>--------------------------------------------------
43     Data Division.
44       Linkage Section.
45       01 ls-room-data.
46          10  ls-room-number      pic X(03).
47          10  ls-std-config-price pic 9(03).
48          10  ls-spec-config-price pic 9(03).
49          10  ls-room-capacity    pic 9(02).
50
51     Procedure Division Using ls-room-data.
52     *> Pass all data on to the superclass
53       Invoke Super "populate-the-room-object"
54                    Using ls-room-data
55       .
56   End Method populate-the-room-object.
57   *>--------------------------------------------------
58 END OBJECT.
59 END CLASS LecRoomClass.
```

Figure 8-17. The Lab room and Lecture room subclasses—r16-lab and r16-lec.

```
143      *>................................................
144      Method-id. process-user-selections.
145      *>................................................
146          Data Division.
147              Local-Storage Section.
148                  01 lo-room-prices.
149                      10 lo-std-config-price    pic 9(03).
150                      10 lo-spec-config-price   pic 9(03).
151                  01 lo-capacity-data.
152                      10 lo-room-capacity       pic 9(02).
153                      10 lo-work-stations       pic 9(02).
154                      10 lo-station-capacity    pic 9(01).
155                  01 lo-menu-choice             pic X(01).
156                      88 lo-standard-prices     value "S".
157
158          Procedure Division.
159              Invoke UserInterface
160                          "get-menu-selection"
161                          Returning lo-menu-choice
162              Evaluate TRUE
163                  When lo-standard-prices
164                      Invoke theRoomHandle "get-room-prices"
165                              Returning lo-room-prices
166                      Invoke UserInterface
167                              "display-room-prices"
168                              Using lo-room-prices
169                  When other
170                      If room-type = "LEC"
171                          Invoke theRoomHandle
172                              "get-lec-room-capacity"
173                              Returning lo-room-capacity
174                          Invoke UserInterface
175                              "display-lec-room-capacity"
176                              Using lo-room-capacity
177                      Else
178                          Invoke theRoomHandle
179                              "get-lab-room-capacity"
180                              Returning lo-capacity-data
181                          Invoke UserInterface
182                              "display-lab-room-capacity"
183                              Using lo-capacity-data
184                      End-If *>room-type = "LEC"
185              End-evaluate *>TRUE
186              .
187      End Method process-user-selections.
188      *>................................................
```

Figure 8-18. The process-user-selections method from Room Manager.

As you might expect, the UI class contains a new method to display work station data.

Before reading on, look at this code and determine what would happen if the Invoke of lines 171-173 were changed as follows.

```
170          If room-type = "LEC"
171              Invoke theRoomHandle
172                  "get-room-capacity"
173                  Returning lo-room-capacity
```

The answer is that the application would function correctly. As there is no method get-room-capacity in the lecture room subclass, the execution moves to the superclass, thereby returning the desired value. With this technique, the method get-lec-room-capacity can be removed from the lecture room subclass. Which technique is the better in this case, this approach or that illustrated in Room16? It's probably debatable. Personally, I prefer the approach illustrated in the example as it maintains "parallel" construction of the two subclasses.

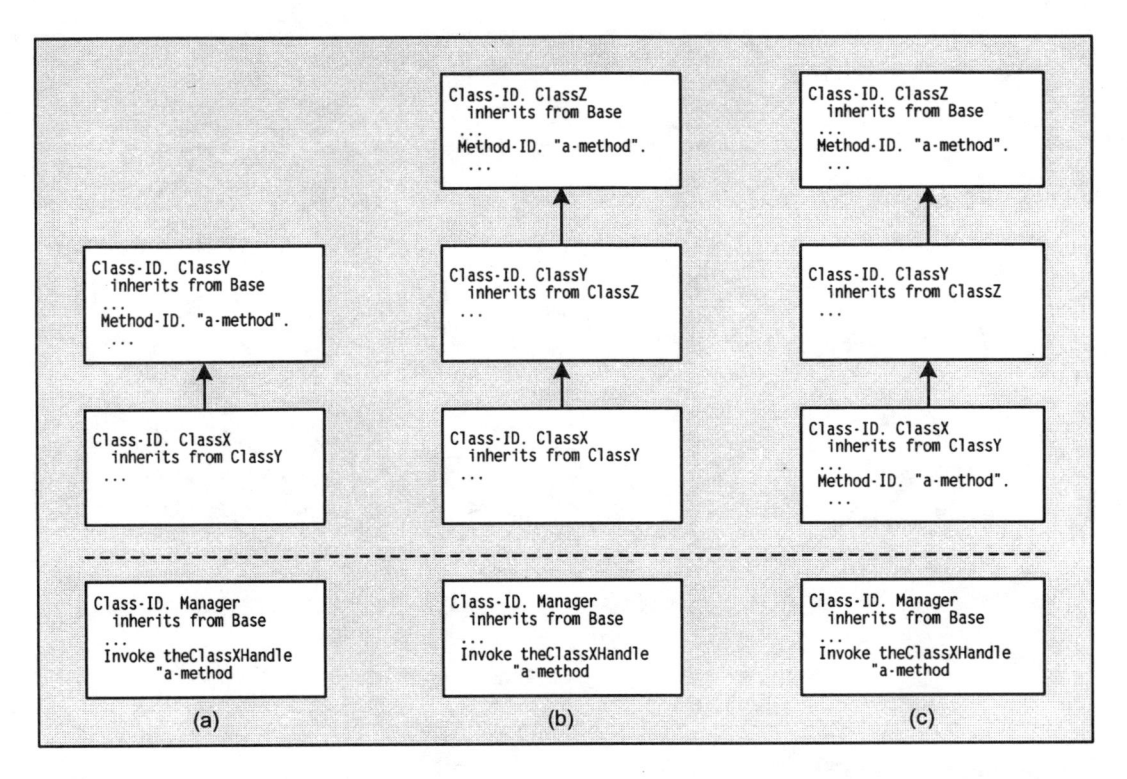

Figure 8-19. Illustrating inheritance.

More About Inheritance

Different Inheritance Scenarios

Let's consider inheritance in a broader sense than the preceding examples. Figure 8-19(a) illustrates the basic structure of the preceding examples of this chapter in which, for instance, the lab room class inherits from the room class. In this skeleton, assume that classes are properly declared and that ClassX has been instantiated by Manager. You know that a-method in ClassY is available to Manager through ClassX by inheritance. Therefore, the Invoke in Manager is valid.

The skeletons of Figure 8-19(b) include another class in the inheritance chain. This makes no difference because of the defined inheritance sequence of ClassX to ClassY to ClassZ. Basically, a-method is every bit as available to Manager as if it were defined in ClassX. In fact, it's unlikely that a class user would even be aware of the levels of inheritance in a prewritten class library.

However, as a class writer, you must be fully aware of this inheritance framework. For instance, consider Figure 8-19(c) in which ClassX also contains a method named a-method. Note that neither the compiler nor the runtime system considers this an error—it is perfectly valid. At execution the system searches up the hierarchy chain for the method name designated in the Invoke statement. The first one encountered is the one that is invoked. In this example, a-method of ClassX is invoked. Be aware that there is no way to "skip" an inheritance level, ClassX in this case, and force execution to a-method of ClassZ.

Inheritance

Let's consider some other scenarios that you might encounter relating to Figure 8-19(c) and invoking a-method from other than Manager.

1. To invoke a-method of ClassZ from ClassX use:
   Invoke Super "a-method" ...
   Forces execution up the hierarchy chain to a-method in ClassZ. Ignores a-method in the invoking ClassX.
2. To invoke a-method of ClassZ from ClassY use:
   Invoke Super "a-method" ...
   Forces execution up the hierarchy chain to a-method in ClassZ.
3. To invoke a-method of ClassX from ClassX use:
   Invoke Self "a-method" ...
   ClassX contains a method named a-method so it is the one invoked.
4. Consider the following Invoke from within ClassY.
   Invoke Self "a-method" ...
   Notice that ClassY does not contain the method a-method. According to the new standard, when the object identifier is Self, the search is *down* the hierarchy chain. Therefore, a-method of ClassX will be invoked.

Inheritance and the Factory Object

All of the inheritance characteristics you have studied in this chapter have pertained to instance objects. However, exactly the same principles apply to factory objects. But remember, the factory and instance objects are completely independent of one another.

Now you can understand what takes place when you instantiate a class using method new of the class Base. In Figure 8-20 the Invoke statement of RoomManager says to invoke the LabRoomClass's factory method new. (That new is a factory method is implied by the class name as the object identifier.) The following takes place.

1. The LabRoomClass definition does not have a Factory, let alone a factory method named new so the search continues up the inheritance chain to RoomClass.
2. RoomClass does not have a method new so the search continues up to Base.
3. Through inheritance, the system finds the designated method in the Base class and executes the method thereby creating the requested object and returning the object handle.

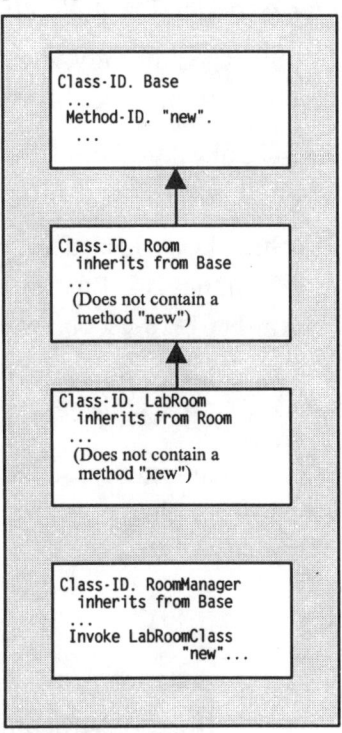

Figure 8-20.
Inheriting the method new from the base class.

Summing Up

Project Summary

Room14 (Proj0801) uses two totally independent room classes: one for lecture rooms and one for lab rooms. The resulting redundancy sets the stage for the room/lecture-room/lab-room inheritance structure.

Room15 (Proj0802) illustrates the inheritance structure whereby the superclass Room contains data and methods common to be subclasses Lecture Room and Lab Room. The inheritance structure is transparent to the class user who sees what appears to be two separate classes: Lecture Room and Lab Room.

Room16 (Proj0803) is a variation on Room16 in which lab rooms serve a dual purpose functioning either for lab or lecture activities.

General Summary

In everyday life, one way we place things in perspective is by classification: we classify and sub-classify. For instance, the general example of this book uses Pet as the general classification, and Dog, Snake, and Bird as subclassifications. In terms of this book's case study, Room is identified as the general classification, and Lecture Room and Lab Room as the subclassifications. Several terms are used to identify this type of structure: *classification hierarchy*, *generalization-specialization hierarchy*, and *is-a* hierarchy.

In object technology, the classification hierarchy forms the basis for inheritance, a means by which methods of one class are directly available to a subclass.

In OOCobol, you implement inheritance as follows (assume SubClass inherits from MainClass).

1. SubClass must include the clause
    ```
    inherits from MainClass
    ```
    in its Class-ID paragraph.
2. SubClass must be instantiated (MainClass must not be instantiated)
3. All methods of SubClass and MainClass are available to in invoking program.

A class that is accessed indirectly (through inheritance), such as MainClass, is called an *abstract* class.

Coming Up

The classification structure is one way we use to view things. Another is to break an item down into component parts: an aggregate structure. Chapter 9 incorporates a reservation calendar into the room class. Room and its calendar are treated as an aggregate structure.

Assignments

8-1

J&B has begun marketing a packaged product called Delight which is sold by the package (rather than by the foot as is Dessert). The information system must be modified to provide for both products—this sets the stage for inheritance. You must modify the application of Assignment 7-1 as follows.

Class   Dessert
Description   This is the superclass containing data common to both subclasses.
Object data
    Dessert Id
    Flavor description
    Dessert type
Class methods
As required by the subclasses.

Class   RopeDessert: inherits from Dessert.
Description   This is a subclass containing data unique to the Rope product.
Object data
    Roll length
    Rolls onhand
    Per inch cost
Class methods
    Return the Flavor description and the Inventory value as in previous assignments.
    Other methods as required by the application.

Class   DelightDessert: inherits from Dessert.
Description   This is a subclass containing data unique to the Delight product.
Object data
    Packages onhand
    Unit cost
Class methods
    Return the Flavor description and the Inventory value which is calculated as:
       Packages onhand times Unit cost
    Other methods as required by the application.

User options
Upon entering a dessert ID, the user must be allowed to select either of the following display options.

1. Flavor description and dessert type
2. Flavor description and the Inventory value.

```
01  dessert-record.
    10  dr-dessert-id          pic X(03).  ⎫
    10  dr-flavor-description  pic X(10).  ⎬ Common to both
    10  dr-dessert-type        pic X(04).  ⎭ dessert types
    10  dr-roll-length         pic 9(02).  ⎫
    10  dr-rolls-onhand        pic 9(03).  ⎬ Pertains only to
    10  dr-per-inch-cost       pic 9V99.   ⎭ rope dessert type
    10  dr-box-id              pic X(02).  ⎫
    10  dr-packages-onhand     pic 9(04).  ⎬ Pertains only to
    10  dr-unit-cost           pic 99V99.  ⎭ delight dessert type
```

Figure 8-21. The Dessert record.

The Dessert file

Until now you've used the Dessert file dessert.di as containing only Rope desserts. To minimize the number of classes you must work with thereby allowing your primary focus to be on inheritance, the Dessert file contains both Rope and Delight records with data items allocated as shown in Figure 8-21. In determining whether you must create a rope object or a delight object, you must inspect the field dr-dessert-type which can contain either of the following entries.

ROPE   Indicates this record must be treated as a Rope dessert and that fields designated for Delight must be ignored.

DELI   Indicates this record must be treated as a Delight dessert and that fields designated for Rope must be ignored.

8-2

Following their highly successful "ocean events" F&B has contracted with a private satellite company to provide "space events" in newly-launched luxury space habitats. To this end, the information system must be modified to provide access to both ocean event and space event information—a perfect inheritance structure. You must modify the application of Assignment 7-2 as follows.

Class   Event
Description   This is the superclass containing data common to both subclasses.
Object data
    Event ID
    Event description
    Facility
    Duration
Class methods
As required by the subclasses.

Class OceanEvent: inherits from Event.
Description This is a subclass containing data unique to the Ocean event.
Object data
  Daily rate
Class methods
  Return the Event cost which is calculated as:
    Daily rate times Duration (from superclass)
  Other methods as required by the application.

Class SpaceEvent: inherits from Event.
Description This is a subclass containing data unique to the Space event.
Object data
  Accommodation charge
  Launch fee
Class method
  Return the Event cost which is calculated as:
  Accommodation charge plus Launch fee
  Other methods as required by the application.

User options
User display options must be identical to those of Assignment 7-1 with the addition of the Event type in each of the two displays.

The Event file

Until now you've used the Event file EVENT.DI as containing only Ocean events. To minimize the number of classes you must work with thereby allowing your primary focus to be on inheritance, the Event file contains both Ocean and Space records with data items allocated as shown in Figure 8-22. In determining whether you must create a ocean object or a space object, you must inspect the field er-event-type which can contain either of the following entries.

  0   Indicates this record must be treated as an Ocean event and that fields designated for Space must be ignored.
  S   Indicates this record must be treated as a Space event and that fields designated for Ocean must be ignored.

Figure 8-22. The Event record.

```
01  event-record.
    10  er-event-id              pic X(04).  ⎤
    10  er-event-description     pic X(20).  ⎬ Common to both
    10  er-event-type            pic X(01).  ⎨ event types
    10  er-facility              pic X(07).  ⎪
    10  er-duration              pic 9(02).  ⎦
    10  er-site-id               pic X(02).  ⎱ Pertains only to
    10  er-daily-rate            pic 9(04).  ⎰ ocean event
    10  er-accommodation-charge  pic 9(04).  ⎱ Pertains only to
    10  er-launch-fee            pic 9(04).  ⎰ space event
```

Aggregate Structures in Object-Oriented Cobol

Chapter Contents

The Aggregation Structure 192
    Reviewing the Classification Hierarchy 192
    Simple Examples of Aggregation Structures 192
    A Combination Structure 193
    About Inheritance 193
    A Road Map to this Chapter's Examples 193
    The Client Manager Class 195
Room17's Aggregate Structure 196
    Documentation 196
    Instantiating a Class from the Class's Factory 198
    The Client Class 198
Features of the Database Interface 201
    Input Data Files 201
    Database Interface Documentation 201
    The Company File Processor 204
Adding a Calendar Class to the Aggregate Structure 207
About Room18 207
Company 207
The Case for a Calendar Class 208
The Client Manager Class 209
The Calendar Class—Room18 212
    Data Definition 212
    Searching the Calendar Table 212
Other Components of Room18 214
    The Client Class 214
    The Calendar File 216
Calendar Database Access 216
Summing Up 218
    Project Summary 218
    General Summary 218
Coming Up 218
Assignments 219

Chapter 9

Chapter Introduction

The classification structure of Chapter 8 is one method we use for organizing things to better understand complexity. Another is the aggregation structure whereby an entity is broken down into component parts. This chapter focuses on using the aggregation structure in Cobol by inspecting the room rental system from another perspective: that of the client. From the chapter you will learn about the following.

- Basic characteristics of the aggregate structure.
- Distinction between the aggregate structure and the inheritance structure.
- Defining a client (customer) class that is itself composed of aggregate components.
- A technique for including a room reservation calendar as an aggregate component of a client class.

The Aggregation Structure

Reviewing the Classification Hierarchy

Classification hierarchies of Chapter 8 (the basis of inheritance) allow us to categorize things by proceeding from the general to the specific. For instance, one of Chapter 8's examples involves the categorization of the personal computer as follows.

>   Personal computer system
>   Desktop computer
>   Tower computer
>   Mini-tower
>   Full-tower computer
>   Maxi-tower computer
>   Laptop computer

Recall that this is commonly called an *is-a* structure because any item at a lower level *is a* item of a higher level. For instance, a mini-tower computer is a tower computer; also, it is a personal computer. The classification hierarchy is a powerful tool that helps us understand things, define things, and communicate about things to others. It forms a cornerstone of object orientation.

Simple Examples of Aggregation Structures

Breaking a complex item into component parts is another means of simplifying and understanding. In fact, structured methodology is based on repeatedly breaking a large problem into simple elemental parts, each of which is readily understood. The end result is commonly a structure chart that shows the hierarchical relationship of the whole and its parts. Such a structure is commonly called a **whole-part hierarchy**; it is also called an **aggregation structure**.

To illustrate, consider how a salesperson might represent the components of a personal computer to a prospective customer.

>   Personal computer
>   Main unit
>   Disk drive
>   Memory
>   Monitor
>   Keyboard
>   Printer

Notice that this structure has the same *form* as the classification structure. However, it has an entirely different meaning. It is often called a **has-a** structure taken from the notion that a Personal computer has a Main unit, a Personal computer has a Keyboard, and so on. Similarly, a Main unit has a Disk drive; also, a Personal computer has a Disk drive.

A Combination Structure

Sometimes it's easy to become confused with such structures. For instance, consider the following breakdown of the Personal computer.

> Personal computer
> > Main unit
> > Monitor
> > Keyboard
> > Disk drive
> > > Floppy drive
> > > Hard drive
> > > CD drive
> >
> > Printer

At a glance, this appears to be a slight variation of the previous aggregation structure. But is it? For the answer, apply the *has-a* test. Certainly a Personal computer has a Disk drive. However, look at the subcategories under Disk drive. You cannot say that a Disk drive has a Floppy drive. The relationship here is *is-a*; a Floppy drive is a Disk drive. If you are unsure of a particular relationship, applying the *is-a* or *has-a* test will usually clear up any confusion.

About Inheritance

Where inheritance is an important element of classification structures, it is not applicable to aggregation structures. For instance, a Keyboard does not inherit properties of the Personal computer. In programming, you may find instances in which you could use inheritance to make methods available to subordinate aggregate classes. However, that is an incorrect application of inheritance and should be avoided.

A Road Map to this Chapter's Examples

The focus thus far in this book has revolved around the room pricing structure—a relatively narrow perspective of a room rental system but one well suited to exploring the principles of OOCobol. This chapter's examples shift the focus from Object Training Center's rooms to its clients (customers). The first example, Room17, accesses and displays information regarding the client: name, address, and sales representative. The client class consists of two components. First the client's company class containing data and methods pertaining to the company, and the sales representative class containing data and methods pertaining to the OTC sales representative assigned to the client. In this example's class diagram of Figure 9-1 you see the aggregate class Client with object handles to the aggregate components as its object data.

Proj0901
Room17

Run this application, stored in the folder Proj0901, and you will see output such as that of Figure 9-2. (For your test runs, use client number values 1001 through 1010.) In Figure 9-2 the user has entered a client number 1001 where you see the results for both the "Client information" option and the "Client's sales-rep information" option.

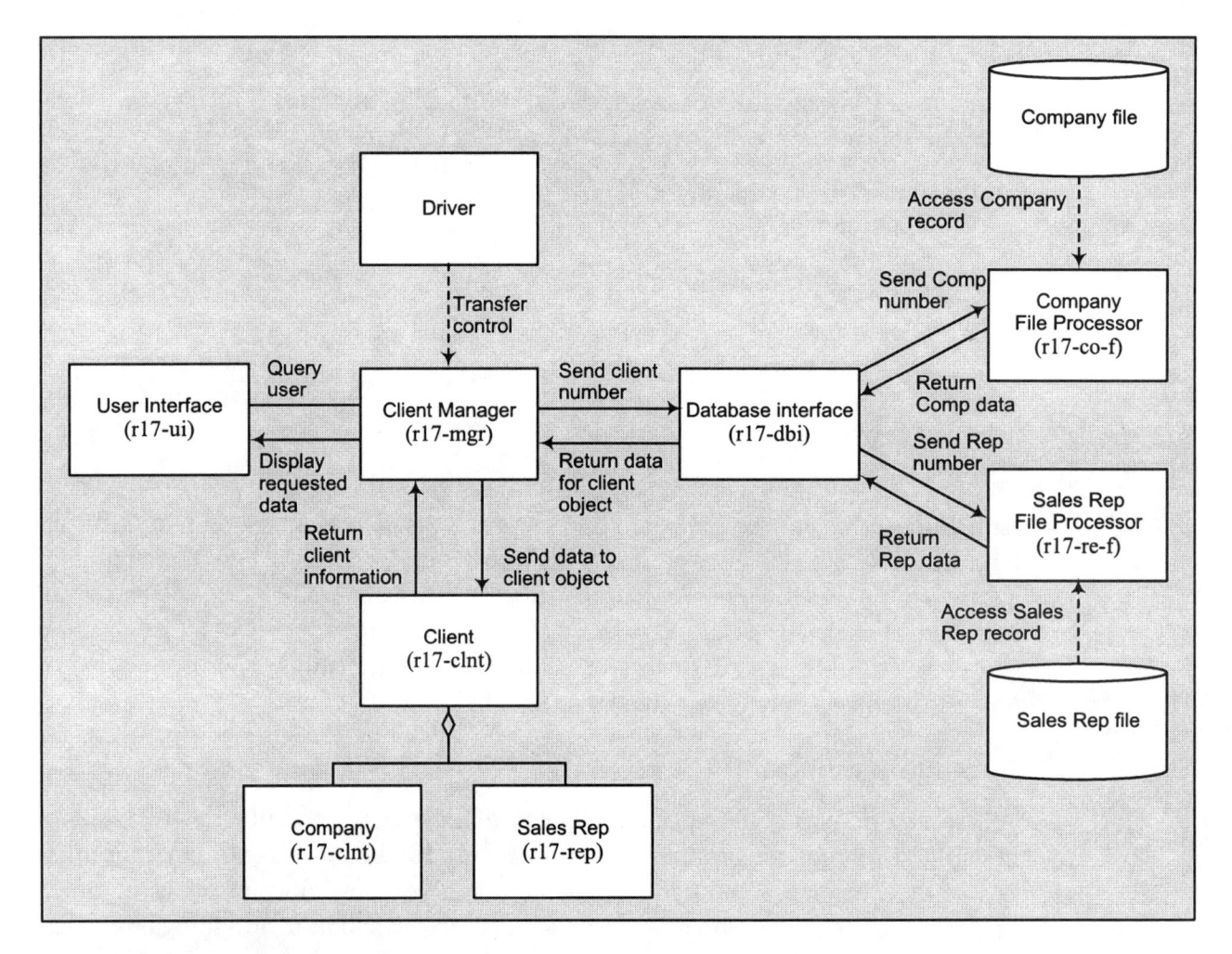

Figure 9-1. Class diagram for Room17.

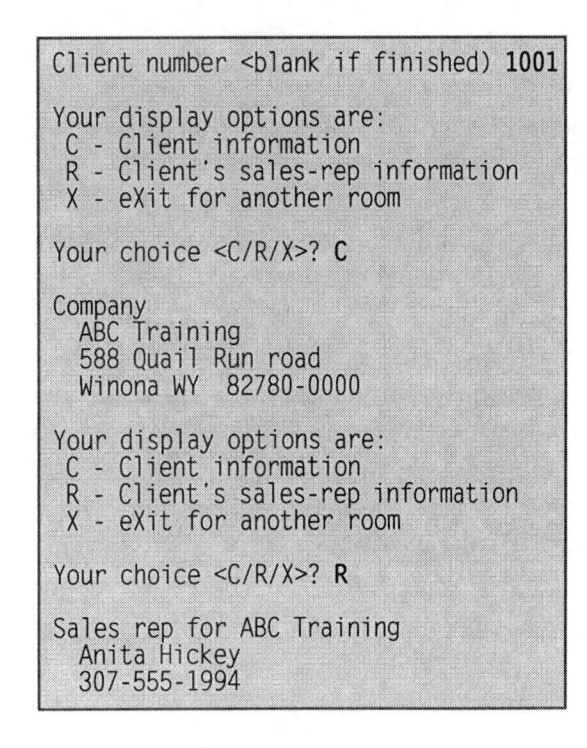

```
Client number <blank if finished) 1001

Your display options are:
 C - Client information
 R - Client's sales-rep information
 X - eXit for another room

Your choice <C/R/X>? C

Company
  ABC Training
  588 Quail Run road
  Winona WY  82780-0000

Your display options are:
 C - Client information
 R - Client's sales-rep information
 X - eXit for another room

Your choice <C/R/X>? R

Sales rep for ABC Training
  Anita Hickey
  307-555-1994
```

Figure 9-2.
Sample dialogue with the client system.

The Client Manager Class

Based on the sample dialogue of Figure 9-2, you probably guess that the overall structure of this application is identical to that of preceding room managers you've studied. In fact, the class's documentation of Figure 9-3 looks much like the documentation of, for instance, Room09—see Figure 6-10 in Chapter 6.

Notice that in the following code, taken from the create-client-object method of Client Manager (r17-mgr.cbl), you see no indication that the Client class is the superclass of an aggregate structure.

```
Invoke DataBaseInterface "get-client-data"
        Returning lo-client-object-data
Invoke ClientClass "New"
        Returning theClientHandle
Invoke theClientHandle
        "populate-the-client-object"
        Using lo-client-object-data
```

In fact, this code corresponds exactly to that of previous Room Manager classes—for instance, refer to lines 44-50 of Figure 7-5.

Similarly, the method process-user-selections contains code to access data from the client class with no indication of that class's structure.

```
Evaluate TRUE
   When lo-company-data-option
      Invoke theClientHandle "get-company-data"
              Returning lo-company-data
      Invoke UserInterface "display-company-data"
              Using lo-company-data
   When lo-rep-data-option
      Invoke theClientHandle "get-rep-data"
              Returning lo-rep-data
      Invoke UserInterface "display-rep-data"
              Using lo-rep-data
```

Class: Client Manager (r17-mgr.cbl)
Description: The general control class that handles access to other classes of the client information component of the room system.

FACTORY	Object Data: Client object handle	
Public Methods	*Parameters*	*Description*
process-user-requests		Provides overall process control. Collaborators: Self, UI, DBI
Private Methods	*Parameters*	*Description*
create-client-object		Creates and populates client object. Collaborators: Client, DBI Invoked by: process-this-request
process-this-request	Using: Client number pic X(04)	Handles processing for each room request. Collaborators: Self, DBI, UI Invoked by: process-user-requests
process-user-selections		Evaluates user data request and displays the requested information. Collaborators: UI, Room Invoked by: process-this-request

Figure 9-3. Documentation for the Client Manager class.

Class: Client (r17-clnt.cbl)
Subclasses: Company (r17-comp.cbl)
             Sales Rep (r17-rep.cbl)
Description: The superclass for the client aggregate structure.

FACTORY	Object Data: None	
Public Methods	*Parameters*	*Description*
new	Returning: client object handle	Invokes base to create an instance of this class's Object. Then instantiates the aggregate components of the class.

OBJECT	**Object Data:**
	  company object handle
	  sales rep object handle	

Public Methods	*Parameters*	*Description*

get-company-data	Returning:
	  company data
	    client name pic X(20)
	    street address pic X(20)
	    city pic X(12)
	    state pic X(02)
	    zip pic X(10)
		Returns basic company address data.

get-rep-data	Returning:
	  sales representative data
	    client-name pic X(20)
	    rep-name pic X(15)
	    rep-phone-number pic X(12)
		Returns sales representative name and phone number and the name of the client to whom this rep is assigned.

populate-the-client-object	Using:
	  client data
	    client name pic X(20)
	    street address pic X(20)
	    city pic X(12)
	    state pic X(02)
	    zip pic X(10)
	    sales representative pic X(15)
	    rep phone number pic X(12)
		Invokes appropriate methods of the aggregate components to populate them.

Private Methods	*Parameters*	*Description*
put-company-handle	Using: company object handle	Saves the object handle of the company aggregate component as object data of this object.
put-rep-handle	Using: sales rep object handle	Saves the object handle of the sales rep aggregate component as object data of this object.

Figure 9-4. Documentation for the Client superclass.

Room17's Aggregate Structure

Documentation

Two elements of this example that introduce new concepts are the aggregate structure of the client class and the database interface together with its associated file

Aggregate Structures in Object-Oriented Cobol

processors. Let's first consider documentation for the aggregate structure's client superclass Client (r17-clnt) shown in Figure 9-4.

- This class consists of both a Factory paragraph and an Object paragraph.
- The Factory includes one method: new. Recall that to instantiate a class, you invoke a method of this name. As you see in the documentation, this method creates instances of the aggregate components of this class. You will see this in the code.
- Public methods of the Object paragraph are exactly as you would expect, providing access to data of the object and populating the object.
- Private methods make available to the client superclass of this aggregate structure the object handles of the aggregate component classes.

You should be aware that Figures 9-3 and 9-4 document the system for class writers as it describes features needed for the maintenance activities. In contrast, documentation for class users (programmers incorporating this class as an element of an application) would likely consist only of the public methods so identified in Figure 9-4.

Figure 9-5's documentation for the Company component of this aggregate shows that this element of the structure is relatively straightforward, consisting of a method to return customer data and a method to populate this component's object.

Class: Company (r17-comp.cbl)
Superclass: Client.
Description: Manages object data for the company aggregate component of the client class.

OBJECT	Object Data: client name street address city state zip	
Public Methods	*Parameters*	*Description*

get-company-data	Returning:
	company data
	  client name pic X(20)
	  street address pic X(20)
	  city pic X(12)
	  state pic X(02)
	  zip pic X(10)
		Returns company name and address data.

populate-the-company-object	Using:
	company data
	  client name pic X(20)
	  street address pic X(20)
	  city pic X(12)
	  state pic X(02)
	  zip pic X(10)
		Populates the company object using data transmitted as a group item.

Figure 9-5. Documentation for the Company aggregate component.

Instantiating a Class from the Class's Factory

Remember, designating a class name as the object identifier causes the system to search for the designated method in the class's factory or in the factory of the class from which it inherits. In Figure 9-6 you see the typical scenario of all examples of previous chapters: since the invoked class does not include a method new (or a factory for that matter), the system finds the method in the base class. This instantiates the referenced class.

In contrast, the Room17 application requires that the client class together with its aggregate components be instantiated. Furthermore, you want this done in a way that is transparent to the class user—for instance, by an Invoke statement such as the following.

```
Invoke ClientClass "new"
               Returning theClientHandle
```

One solution is to include a method new in the Client class factory that does the following.

1. Creates an instance of its own object (Client).
2. Instantiates the Customer aggregate component.
3. Instantiates the Rep aggregate component.
4. Passes the handles of the two aggregate components to the client object.

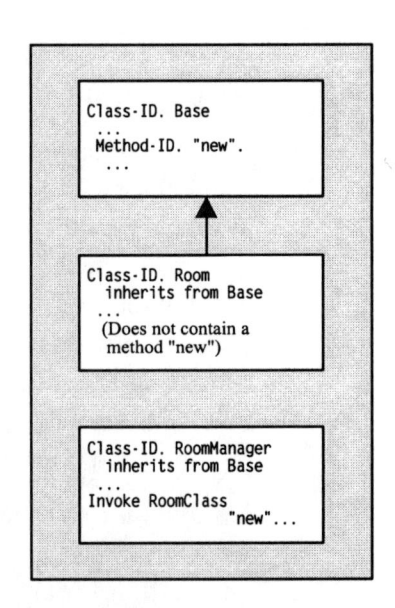

Figure 9-6.
Invoking the method new.

The Client Class

First, look at the Factory of the Client class in Figure 9-7. The Invoke of line 38 uses Super as its object identifier. From Chapter 8 you know that the identifier Super causes the system to move up one level in the hierarchy chain to begin the search. This is illustrated in Figure 9-8.

Then at lines 44 and 48 the program instantiates Company and Rep. Lines 46 and 50 invoke methods to move the object handles into the instance object's Object-Storage Section (lines 61 and 62) via the put methods (beginning lines 142 and 153). In studying this portion of the class definition, remember that the Factory and the Instance Object are independent entities at execution. Although elements of the same source module, the Factory does not have direct access to data of the Object except through methods of the object definitions.

Next, look at the OBJECT paragraph beginning line 57 where you see as object data, the object handles of the company and sales rep objects (refer to lines 61 and 62). As object data, these handles are available to all instance methods of this class. For example, the method get-company-data accesses company data from the company object using theCompanyHandle as its object identifier. Let's see what takes place when this method is invoked.

Aggregate Structures in Object-Oriented Cobol

```cobol
          $set sourceformat "free"
  1 *>*********************************************
  2 *> Room Rental System
  3 *> W. Price   Mar 12, 2000              R17-CLNT.CBL
  4 *>
  5 *> This is a client aggregate class containing
  6 *> handles to the following two component classes:
  7 *>     Company
  8 *>     Rep
  9 *> These aggregate components are instantiated
 10 *> in this class's Factory.
 11 *>*********************************************
 12
 13 Identification Division.
 14        Class-id.  ClientClass
 15                   inherits from Base.
 16
 17 Environment Division.
 18        Object Section.
 19        Class-Control.
 20            ClientClass      is class "r17-clnt"
 21            CompanyClass     is class "r17-comp"
 22            RepClass         is class "r17-rep"
 23            BaseClass        is class "base"
 24            .
 25 *>=============================================
 26 FACTORY.
 27
 28   Method-ID. new.
 29   Data Division.
 30     Local-Storage Section.
 31        01 theCompanyHandle  object reference.
 32        01 theRepHandle      object reference.
 33     Linkage Section.
 34        01 ls-clientHandle        object reference.
 35
 36   Procedure Division Returning ls-clientHandle.
 37     *> Create instance of this object.
 38     Invoke Super "New"
 39                  Returning ls-clientHandle
 40     *> Create instances of the aggregate components
 41     *> This is the client factory object. The
 42     *> client instance object must have access to
 43     *> the company and rep objects.
 44     Invoke CompanyClass "New"
 45                  Returning theCompanyHandle
 46     Invoke ls-clientHandle "put-company-handle"
 47                  Using theCompanyHandle
 48     Invoke RepClass "New"
 49                  Returning theRepHandle
 50     Invoke ls-clientHandle "put-rep-handle"
 51                  Using theRepHandle
 52     .
 53   End Method new.
 54
 55 END FACTORY.
 56 *>=============================================
 57 OBJECT.
 58
 59   Data Division.
 60     Object-Storage Section.
 61        01 theCompanyHandle  object reference.
 62        01 theRepHandle      object reference.
 63
 64   Procedure Division.
 65
 66 *>-----------------------------------------
 67   Method-id. get-company-data.
 68 *>-----------------------------------------
 69   Data Division.
 70     Linkage Section.
 71        01 ls-company-data.
 72           10 ls-client-name      pic X(20).
 73           10 ls-street-address   pic X(20).
 74           10 ls-city             pic X(12).
 75           10 ls-state            pic X(02).
 76           10 ls-zip              pic X(10).
 77
 78   Procedure Division Returning ls-company-data.
 79     Invoke theCompanyHandle "get-company-data"
 80                  Returning ls-company-data
 81     .
 82   End method get-company-data.
 83 *>-----------------------------------------
 84   Method-id. get-rep-data.
 85 *>-----------------------------------------
 86   Data Division.
 87     Local-Storage Section.
 88        01 lo-company-data.
 89           10 lo-client-name      pic X(20).
 90           10 lo-street-address   pic X(20).
 91           10 lo-city             pic X(12).
 92           10 lo-state            pic X(02).
 93           10 lo-zip              pic X(10).
 94        01 lo-rep-data.
 95           10 lo-rep-name         pic X(15).
 96           10 lo-rep-phone-number pic X(12).
 97     Linkage Section.
 98        01 ls-rep-data.
 99           10 ls-client-name      pic X(20).
100           10 ls-rep-name         pic X(15).
101           10 ls-rep-phone-number pic X(12).
102
103   Procedure Division
104                  Returning ls-rep-data.
105     Invoke theCompanyHandle
106                  "get-company-data"
107                  Returning lo-company-data
108     Invoke theRepHandle "get-rep-data"
109                  Returning lo-rep-data
110     Move lo-client-name to ls-client-name
111     Move lo-rep-name to ls-rep-name
112     Move lo-rep-phone-number
113                        to ls-rep-phone-number
114     .
115   End method get-rep-data.
116
117 *>-----------------------------------------
118   Method-id. populate-the-client-object.
119 *>-----------------------------------------
120   Data Division.
121     Linkage Section.
122        01 ls-client-data.
123           10 ls-company-data.
124              20 ls-client-name      pic X(20).
125              20 ls-street-address   pic X(20).
126              20 ls-city             pic X(12).
127              20 ls-state            pic X(02).
128              20 ls-zip              pic X(10).
129           10 ls-rep-data.
130              20 ls-rep-person      pic X(15).
131              20 ls-rep-phone-number pic X(12).
132
133   Procedure Division  Using ls-client-data.
134     Invoke theCompanyHandle
135                  "populate-the-company-object"
136                  Using ls-company-data
137     Invoke theRepHandle
138                  "populate-the-rep-object"
139                  Using ls-rep-data
140     .
141   End Method populate-the-client-object.
142 *>-----------------------------------------
143   Method-id. put-company-handle.
144 *>-----------------------------------------
145   Data Division.
146     Linkage Section.
147        01 ls-theCompanyHandle object reference.
148
149   Procedure Division Using ls-theCompanyHandle.
150     Set theCompanyHandle to ls-theCompanyHandle
151     .
152   End method put-company-handle.
153 *>-----------------------------------------
154   Method-id. put-rep-handle.
155 *>-----------------------------------------
156   Data Division.
157     Linkage Section.
158        01 ls-theRepHandle object reference.
159
160   Procedure Division Using ls-theRepHandle.
161     Set theRepHandle to ls-theRepHandle
162     .
163   End method put-rep-handle.
164 *>-----------------------------------------
165 END OBJECT.
166 END CLASS ClientClass.
```

Figure 9-7. The Client class—Room 17.

1. From Client Manager (not shown here) the following Invoke is executed.

   ```
   Invoke theClientHandle "get-company-data"
          Returning lo-company-data
   ```

   Notice that the object reference is the client handle.

2. You see the designated method beginning line 66 (Figure 9-7). In turn, the following Invoke (from line 78) is executed

   ```
   Invoke theCompanyHandle "get-company-data"
          Returning ls-company-data
   ```

   Although the same name (get-company-data) is used in both classes, there is no ambiguity as the object identifier specifies the appropriate object.

3. In the Company class of Figure 9-9 the method get-company-data accesses the desired object data.

In a nutshell, Client Manager (or any other class) "asks" Client for the company data. In turn, Client asks Customer for the data. Customer returns the data to Client which passes it on to Client manager.

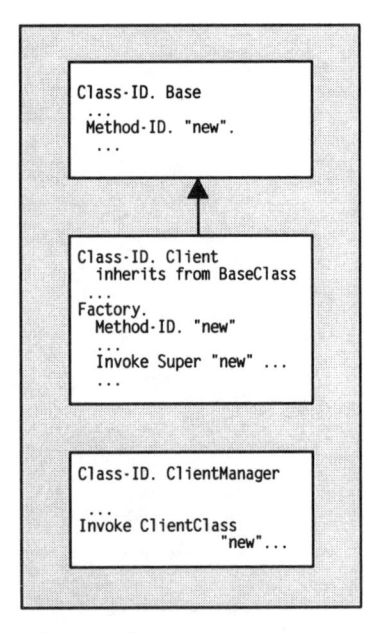

Figure 9-8.
Using Super as an object identifier.

```
        $set sourceformat "free"
 1 *>*********************************************
 2 *> Room Rental System
 3 *> W. Price  Mar 12, 2000        R17-COMP.CBL
 4 *>
 5 *> This is a client aggregate class containing
 6 *> handles to the following two component classes:
 7 *>    Company
 8 *>    Rep
 9 *> These aggregate components are instantiated
10 *> in this class's Factory.
11 *>*********************************************
12
13 Identification Division.
14     Class-id.  CompanyClass
15                inherits from Base.
16
17 Environment Division.
18     Object Section.
19     Class-Control.
20         CompanyClass     is class "r17-comp"
21         BaseClass        is class "base"
22         .
23 *>_____
24 OBJECT.
25
26 Data Division.
27     Object-Storage Section.
28     01 company-data.
29         10 client-name      pic X(20).
30         10 street-address   pic X(20).
31         10 city             pic X(12).
32         10 state            pic X(02).
33         10 zip              pic X(10).
34
35 Procedure Division.
36 *>...........................................
37 Method-id. get-company-data.
38 *>...........................................
39 Data Division.
40     Linkage Section.
41     01 ls-company-data.
42         10 ls-client-name     pic X(20).
43         10 ls-street-address  pic X(20).
44         10 ls-city            pic X(12).
45         10 ls-state           pic X(02).
46         10 ls-zip             pic X(10).
47
48 Procedure Division Returning ls-company-data.
49     Move company-data to ls-company-data
50
51 End method get-company-data.
52
53 *>*>.........................................
54 Method-id. populate-the-company-object.
55 *>*>.........................................
56 Data Division.
57     Linkage Section.
58     01 ls-company-data.
59         10 ls-client-name     pic X(20).
60         10 ls-street-address  pic X(20).
61         10 ls-city            pic X(12).
62         10 ls-state           pic X(02).
63         10 ls-zip             pic X(10).
64
65 Procedure Division Using ls-company-data.
66     Move ls-company-data to company-data
67
68 End Method populate-the-company-object.
69 *>*>.........................................
70 END OBJECT.
71 END CLASS CompanyClass.
```

Figure 9-9. The Company aggregate component class.

The action of populating Client essentially involves the reverse process—that is, the following occurs.

1. Client Manager executes the following:

   ```
   Invoke theClientHandle
           "populate-the-client-object"
           Using Io-client-object-data
   ```

2. You see this method beginning line 117 of Figure 9-7 where data transmitted (defined at lines 121-130) consists of both company and sales representative data. At line 133, the appropriate method of Company is invoked to pass its portion of the data on. At line 136, the appropriate method of Rep is invoked for the remainder of the data.

Features of the Database Interface

Although the database interface for this application does not utilize techniques specific to aggregate structures, it does illustrate approaches that you will find useful in dealing with applications requiring access to multiple files.

Input Data Files

Database input for this application is derived from two indexed files: client and rep having the following record layout.

Client File		*Rep File*	
Client number	pic X(04)	Representative ID	pic X(05)
Company name	pic X(20)	Assignment-code	pic X(01)
Street address	pic X(20)	Representative name	pic X(15)
City	pic X(12)	Rep phone-number	pic X(12)
State	pic X(02)		
Zip	pic X(10)		
not used	pic X(10)		
Representative ID	pic X(05)		

Client number is the key field for the client file and Representative ID is the key field for the rep file. Accessing data for a selected client involves:

1. Read the desired client record using a designated key field value (for instance, client 1004).
2. Access the Representative ID value from the input client record.
3. Using that value, read the required record from the rep file.

Database Interface Documentation

The client file processor documented in Figure 9-10 is relatively straightforward. It includes the usual file open and close methods and a method to read a designated record (read-record). It also includes to methods for access to data of the object.

Class: Client File Processor (r17-cl-f.cbl)
Description: This class provides random access to records of the client file. A designated record is read and stored as object data of the class.

FACTORY	Object Data:
	Room-file record
	  client name pic X(20)
	  street address pic X(20)
	  city pic X(12)
	  state pic X(02)
	  zip pic X(10)
	  sales rep id pic X(05)	

Public Methods	*Parameters*	*Description*
`close-file`		Close the indexed client file.
`open-file`		Opens the indexed client file for input.

`read-record`	Using
	  Client number pic X(04)
	Returning
	  Record-found switch pic X(01)
	    Y—Record found
	    N—Record not found
		Read a record from the indexed company file.

`get-company-data`	Returning:
	  company data (group item)
	    company name pic X(20)
	    street address pic X(20)
	    city pic X(12)
	    state pic X(02)
	    zip pic X(10)
		Returns company data required to populate the company object.

`get-rep-id`	Returning: sales rep ID pic X(05)	Returns sales rep ID needed to access sales rep record from sales rep file.

Figure 9-10. Documentation for the client file processor.

The first of these, `get-company-data`, is much like corresponding methods of the room system returning company data required by the invoking program. The final method, `get-rep-id`, returns the sales representative ID value necessary for subsequently reading the sales rep record. Compare this documentation to that of Room11 in Chapter 7's Figure 7-8 and you will see that they are identical in structure except for the addition of the `get-rep-id` method.

Neither the documentation nor the program listing for the sales representative file processor are shown here as they closely parallel that of the company file processor.

DBI's documentation in Figure 9-11 suggests a rather substantial class. But as with the file processor, you will find a close parallel with the Room11 database interface—see Chapter 7's Figure 7-6 for the corresponding documentation. The components of the Room 11's DBI are:

- Database connect and disconnect (`connect-to-data` and `disconnect-from-data`).
- Read a record (`read-room-file`)
- Access data from the record (`get-room-data`)

Aggregate Structures in Object-Oriented Cobol

Class: **Client Database Interface (r17-dbi.cbl)**
Description: This class provides the data interface between client application programs and the customer system file processor classes.
Special note: Prior to processing, the data source must be made ready by invoking the method `connect-to-data`. When processing is complete, the data source must be closed by invoking the method `disconnect-from-data`.

FACTORY		
Public Methods	*Parameters*	*Description*
connect-to-data		Opens required files and or databases required for this application. Collaborators: Company file processor and Sales Rep file processor.
disconnect-from-data		Closes all files/databases. Collaborators: Company file processor and Sales Rep file processor.

get-client-data	Returning:
	  client data
	    client name pic X(20)
	    street address pic X(20)
	    city pic X(12)
	    state pic X(02)
	    zip pic X(10)
	    sales rep id pic X(05)
	    sales rep name pic X(15)
	    rep phone number pic X(12)
		Returns client data required to populate the client object. Collaborator: Self.

get-company-data	Returning:
	  company data
	    client name pic X(20)
	    street address pic X(20)
	    city pic X(12)
	    state pic X(02)
	    zip pic X(10)
		Returns company data accessed from the company file. Collaborator: Company file processor.

get-rep-data	Returning:
	  sales rep data
	    sales rep id pic X(05)
	    sales rep name pic X(15)
	    rep phone number pic X(12)
		Returns sales representative data accessed from the sales rep personnel file. Collaborator: Sales rep file processor.

read-client-database	Using:
	  client number pic X(04)
	Returning
	  record-found switch pic X(01)
	    Y—Record successfully read
	    N—Record not found
		Reads a company record using the input client number as the key. If the record is found, reads the sales-rep file using the sales-rep ID field from the company record as the key. Returned value indicates whether or not both records successfully read. Collaborators: Self, Company file processor.

read-company-file	Using:
	  client number pic X(04)
	Returning
	  record-found switch pic X(01)
	    Y—Record successfully read
	    N—Record not found
		Reads a company record using the input client number as the key. Returned value indicates whether or not record successfully read. Collaborator: Company file processor.

read-rep-file	Using:
	  sales rep number pic X(05)
	Returning
	  record-found switch pic X(01)
	    Y—Record successfully read
	    N—Record not found
		Reads a sales rep record using the input client number as the key. Returned value indicates whether or not record successfully read. Collaborator: Sales rep file processor.

Figure 9-11. Documentation for the client database interface.

For this application, the class user sees the same interfaces to the client database interface as with previous examples.

- Database connect and disconnect (connect-to-data and disconnect-from-data).
- Read a "record" (read-client-database)
- Access data from the "record" (get-client-data)

The difference of course is that data access is to two files. The method read-client-database invokes two other methods of this class, read-company-file and read-rep-file to read the desired records—study the description entry in Figure 9-11's documentation. Similarly, access to the data is achieved in the method get-client-data by invoking the two methods of this class get-company-data and get-rep-data.

Perhaps you are wondering why the four methods read-company-file, read-rep-file, get-company-data and get-rep-data are not designated as private methods as they are invoked from other methods of this class. The reason is that they are relatively independent methods that could be invoked from other classes as the scope of this application is broadened.

The Company File Processor

Code of the company file processor (see Figure 9-12) is reasonably straightforward. Consistent with the documentation, it differs from, for instance, Room11's file processor (refer to Figure 7-9) only by the additional method to access the sales representative number (get-rep-id).

DBI's code of Figure 9-13 follows directly from the documentation of Figure 9-11. First, look at the method get-client-data (beginning line 113), the method invoked by the class user to obtain data necessary to populate the client object.

- Line 130 invokes the method get-company-data (see line 137) to obtain needed data from the company record.
- Line 132 invokes the method get-rep-data (see line 157) to obtain needed data from the sales representative record.

Next, look at the procedural code of read-client-database, lines 66-75 to access data for populating the client object; its sequence is as follows.

1. Line 66 invokes the method read-company-file (line 79 of this class).
2. Control is transferred to that method which invokes the file processor method read-record (Figure 9-12's line 68) returning an indication of the read status (ls-action-status).
3. At line 69, the read-status switch is tested. If the company record was successfully read, the sales representative ID is accessed (line 70) and used as the input parameter to access sales representative data (line 72).

Aggregate Structures in Object-Oriented Cobol

```cobol
       $set sourceformat "free"
1  *>***********************************************
2  *> Company Rental System
3  *> W. Price  Mar 10, 2000       R17-CO-F.CBL
4  *>
5  *> This class definition is the read file
6  *> processor for the indexed file COMPANY.DI.
7  *> Its object data is the company record
8  *> Methods
9  *>    close-file
10 *>    get-contact-data
11 *>    get-company-data
12 *>    open-file
13 *>    read-record
14 *>***********************************************
15
16 Identification Division.
17      Class-ID.  CompanyFileProcessor
18                 inherits from BaseClass.
19 Environment Division.
20      Object Section.
21        Class-Control.
22          CompanyFileProcessor is class "r17-co-f"
23          BaseClass            is class "base"
24          .
25 *>==================================================
26   FACTORY.
27     Environment Division.
28       Input-Output Section.
29       File-Control.
30         Select company-file
31             assign to "c:\Eooc2\eData\company.di"
32             organization is indexed
33             access is random
34             record key is co-client-number.
35     Data Division.
36       File Section.
37       FD Company-File.
38       01 co-company-record.
39           10  co-client-number      pic X(04).
40           10  co-company-name       pic X(20).
41           10  co-street-address     pic X(20).
42           10  co-city               pic X(12).
43           10  co-state              pic X(02).
44           10  co-zip                pic X(10).
45           10                        pic X(10).
46           10  co-rep-id             pic X(05).
47
48     Procedure Division.
49 *>..................................................
50 *> ****File Related Methods ******************
51 *>..................................................
52     Method-ID. open-file.
53 *>..................................................
54        Procedure Division.
55           Open Input company-file
56           .
57        End Method open-file.
58
59 *>..................................................
60     Method-ID. close-file.
61 *>..................................................
62        Procedure Division.
63           Close company-file
64           .
65        End Method close-file.
66
67 *>..................................................
68     Method-ID. read-record.
69 *>..................................................
70        Data Division.
71          Linkage Section.
72          01 ls-client-number         pic x(04).
73          01 ls-action-status         pic X(01).
74             88 ls-record-found       value "Y".
75             88 ls-record-not-found   value "N".
76
77        Procedure Division Using ls-client-number
78                     Returning ls-action-status.
79           Move ls-client-number to co-client-number
80           Read Company-File
81             Invalid key
82               Set ls-record-not-found to true
83             Not invalid key
84               Set ls-record-found to true
85           End-Read *>Company-File
86           .
87        End Method read-record.
88
89 *>..................................................
90 *> ****Data Access Related Methods ***********
91 *>..................................................
92     Method-ID. get-company-data.
93 *>..................................................
94        Data Division.
95          Linkage Section.
96          01 ls-company-data.
97             10  ls-company-name      pic X(20).
98             10  ls-street-address    pic X(20).
99             10  ls-city              pic X(12).
100            10  ls-state             pic X(02).
101            10  ls-zip               pic X(10).
102
103       Procedure Division Returning ls-company-data.
104          Move co-company-name    to ls-company-name
105          Move co-street-address  to ls-street-address
106          Move co-city            to ls-city
107          Move co-state           to ls-state
108          Move co-zip             to ls-zip
109          .
110       End Method get-company-data.
111 *>..................................................
112    Method-ID. get-rep-id.
113 *>..................................................
114       Data Division.
115         Linkage Section.
116         01 ls-rep-id            pic X(05).
117
118       Procedure Division Returning ls-rep-id.
119          Move co-rep-id to ls-rep-id
120          .
121       End Method get-rep-id.
122 *>..................................................
123 END FACTORY.
124 END CLASS CompanyFileProcessor.
```

Figure 9-12. The client file processor—r17-cl-f.cbl.

```cobol
       $set sourceformat "free"
 1  *>**********************************************
 2  *> Room Rental System
 3  *> W. Price   Mar 12                    R17-DBI.CBL
 4  *>
 5  *> This class definition is the database
 6  *> interface between the class user and the
 7  *> company file processor.
 8  *> Factory methods
 9  *>     connect-to-data
10  *>     disconnect-from-data
11  *>     get-client-data
12  *>     get-company-data
13  *>     get-rep-data
14  *>     read-client-database
15  *>     read-company-file
16  *>     read-rep-file
17  *>**********************************************
18
19  Identification Division.
20       Class-ID.   RoomDatabaseInterface
21                       inherits from BaseClass.
22  Environment Division.
23       Object Section.
24         Class-Control.
25            RoomDatabaseInterface is class "r17-dbi"
26            CompanyFileProcessor  is class "r17-co-f"
27            RepFileProcessor      is class "r17-re-f"
28            BaseClass             is class "base"
29            .
30  *>==============================================
31  FACTORY.
32     Procedure Division.
33  *>----------------------------------------------
34  *> ****File Related Methods ********************
35  *>----------------------------------------------
36     Method-ID. connect-to-data.
37  *>----------------------------------------------
38       Procedure Division.
39          Invoke CompanyFileProcessor "open-file"
40          Invoke RepFileProcessor "open-file"
41          .
42     End Method connect-to-data.
43
44  *>----------------------------------------------
45     Method-ID. disconnect-from-data.
46  *>----------------------------------------------
47       Procedure Division.
48          Invoke CompanyFileProcessor "close-file"
49          Invoke RepFileProcessor "close-file"
50          .
51     End Method disconnect-from-data.
52
53  *>----------------------------------------------
54     Method-ID. read-client-database.
55  *>----------------------------------------------
56       Data Division.
57         Local-Storage Section.
58           01 lo-rep-ID             pic X(05).
59         Linkage Section.
60           01 ls-client-number      pic x(04).
61           01 ls-record-found-sw    pic X(01).
62              88 ls-record-found         value "Y".
63              88 ls-record-not-found     value "N".
64         Procedure Division Using ls-client-number
65                       Returning ls-record-found-sw.
66            Invoke Self "read-company-file"
67                Using ls-client-number
68                Returning ls-record-found-sw
69            If ls-record-found
70              Invoke CompanyFileProcessor"get-rep-ID"
71                Returning lo-rep-ID
72              Invoke Self "read-rep-file"
73                Using lo-rep-ID
74                Returning ls-record-found-sw
75            End-If *>ls-record-found
76     End Method read-client-database.
77
78  *>----------------------------------------------
79     Method-ID. read-company-file.
80  *>----------------------------------------------
81       Data Division.
82         Linkage Section.
83           01 ls-client-number      pic x(04).
84           01 ls-record-found-sw    pic X(01).
85              88 ls-record-found         value "Y".
86              88 ls-record-not-found     value "N".
87         Procedure Division Using ls-client-number
88                       Returning ls-record-found-sw.
89            Invoke CompanyFileProcessor "read-record"
90                Using ls-client-number
91                Returning ls-record-found-sw
92     End Method read-company-file.
93
94  *>----------------------------------------------
95     Method-ID. read-rep-file.
96  *>----------------------------------------------
97       Data Division.
98         Linkage Section.
99           01 ls-rep-id             pic x(05).
100          01 ls-record-found-sw    pic X(01).
101             88 ls-record-found         value "Y".
102             88 ls-record-not-found     value "N".
103        Procedure Division Using ls-rep-id
104                      Returning ls-record-found-sw.
105           Invoke RepFileProcessor "read-record"
106               Using ls-rep-id
107               Returning ls-record-found-sw
108    End Method read-rep-file.
109
110 *>----------------------------------------------
111 *> ****Data Access Methods *********************
112 *>----------------------------------------------
113    Method-ID. get-client-data.
114 *>----------------------------------------------
115      Data Division.
116        Linkage Section.
117          01 ls-client-data.
118             10 ls-company-data.
119                20 ls-company-name     pic X(20).
120                20 ls-street-address   pic X(20).
121                20 ls-city             pic X(12).
122                20 ls-state            pic X(02).
123                20 ls-zip              pic X(10).
124             10 ls-rep-data.
125                20 ls-rep-name         pic X(15).
126                20 ls-rep-phone-number pic X(12).
127        Procedure Division
128                      Returning ls-client-data.
129           Invoke Self "get-company-data"
130               Returning ls-company-data
131           Invoke Self "get-rep-data"
132               Returning ls-rep-data
133
134    End Method get-client-data.
135 *>----------------------------------------------
136    Method-ID. get-company-data.
137 *>----------------------------------------------
138      Data Division.
139        Linkage Section.
140          01 ls-company-data.
141             10 ls-company-name        pic X(20).
142             10 ls-street-address      pic X(20).
143             10 ls-city-state-zip      pic X(26).
144             10 ls-city                pic X(12).
145             10 ls-state               pic X(02).
146             10 ls-zip                 pic X(10).
147
148        Procedure Division
149                      Returning ls-company-data.
150           Invoke CompanyFileProcessor
151                      "get-company-data"
152                      Returning ls-company-data
153           .
154    End Method get-company-data.
155 *>----------------------------------------------
156    Method-ID. get-rep-data.
157 *>----------------------------------------------
158      Data Division.
159        Linkage Section.
160          01 ls-rep-data.
161             10 ls-rep-name            pic X(15).
162             10 ls-rep-phone-number    pic X(12).
163
164        Procedure Division
165                      Returning ls-rep-data.
166           Invoke RepFileProcessor
167                      "get-rep-data"
168                      Returning ls-rep-data
169           .
170    End Method get-rep-data.
171 *>----------------------------------------------
172 END FACTORY.
173 END CLASS RoomDatabaseInterface.
```

Figure 9-13. The database interface—r17-dbi.cbl

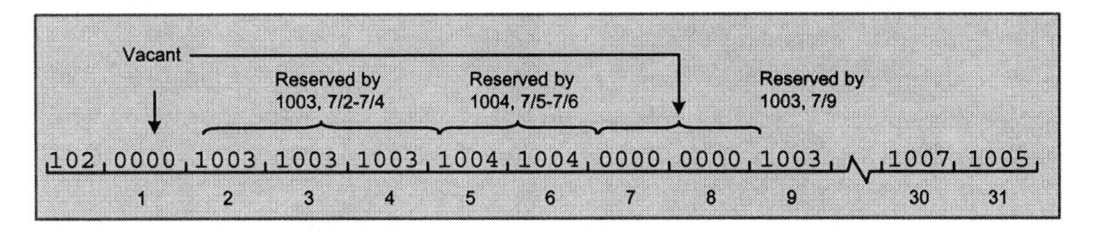

```
         Vacant
              ┌─ Reserved by ──┬─ Reserved by ──┐      Reserved by
              │  1003, 7/2-7/4 │  1004, 7/5-7/6 │      1003, 7/9
              ↓                                 ↓
|102|0000|1003|1003|1003|1004|1004|0000|0000|1003| ~ |1007|1005|
   1    2    3    4    5    6    7    8    9         30   31
```

Figure 9-14. Calendar record for room 102.

Adding a Calendar Class to the Aggregate Structure

About Room18

The next example, Room18 stored in the Proj0902 folder, expands on Room17 with the addition of room reservation data available from a room calendar file. To simplify file and calendar data access (and maintain our focus on object techniques), the calendar file is limited to a single month: July. The record layout, depicting data for room 102, is illustrated in Figure 9-14. Notice that the first three positions contain the room number. The remainder of the record consists of four-position fields, one for each of the 31 days in July. Each of them contains either the client number of the client renting the room for that day or zeros if the room is not rented. From this record, you see that room 102 is not rented on July 1 but client 1003 has reserved the room 102 for July 2-4 (and also July 9).

Proj0902 / Room18

Data from this file will be used in Room18 to display customer information in the form illustrated by a sample output of Figure 9-15. Inspection of the output (data from each room) gives you a hint regarding the nature of the calendar class required for this application.

For an insight to the processing needs of this example, consider Figures 9-14 and 9-15.

- Input required to produce the output of Figure 9-15 is the client number, 1003 in this example.
- For the Company portion of the output, the client number is the key field to access the company file. This requirement is identical to that of Room17.
- The list of reservation dates is obtained by searching the repeating elements (client-number entries) of each room calendar record for the input client number, for instance, refer to Figure 9-14.

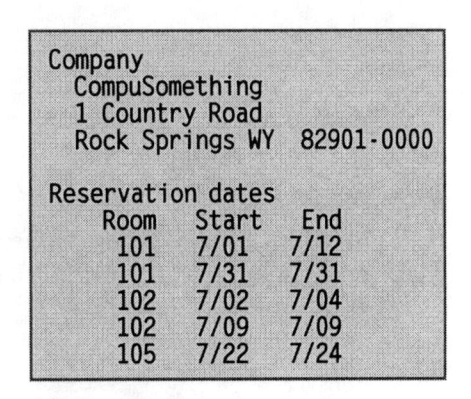

```
Company
   CompuSomething
   1 Country Road
   Rock Springs WY  82901-0000

Reservation dates
   Room    Start    End
    101    7/01    7/12
    101    7/31    7/31
    102    7/02    7/04
    102    7/09    7/09
    105    7/22    7/24
```

Figure 9-15.
Sample output from Room18.

The Case for a Calendar Class

A reasonable approach to this new element would be to expand the aggregate structure of the client class to include a reservation class containing room numbers and dates displayed in the example output of Figure 9-15. The structure of the Client would then be as shown in Figure 9-16. Then DBI would access the calendar file, extract the data required by Reservation, and pass it to RoomManager to be assembled with other Client object data.

However, before simply "plugging in" another component, the program designer is wise to step back and assess the application's overall needs. This component is part of a room reservation system in which access to the reservation calendar will include not only accessing data but also updating (for instance, recording a new room reservation for a client). To that end, it makes sense to incorporate a separate calendar class (containing data for all rooms) into the system for the purpose of providing full access to calendar data.

In Figure 9-17 you see the addition of the following elements to the class diagram of Figure 9-1.

- A calendar file processing class (Calendar File Processor) providing access to the calendar file.
- A Calendar class to handle all calendar processing needs. Like Client Manager and other classes (and in contrast to Client and its components), there will be a single instance of this class for the duration of a run. Therefore, this component is defined as a Factory object.
- A Reservation aggregate component to the client class designed specifically to store reservation data pertaining to this client.

Addition of these three classes requires appropriate modification to code all of the other classes (with the exception of Sales Rep, Company File Processor, and Sales Rep File Processor).

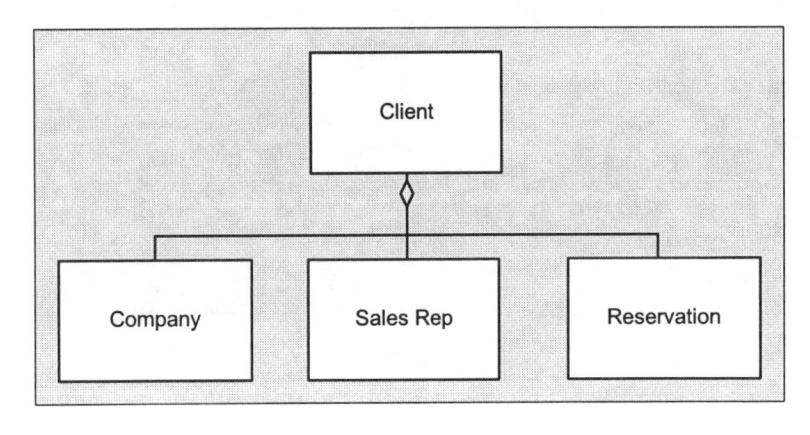

Figure 9-16.
The aggregate structure with reservation data.

Aggregate Structures in Object-Oriented Cobol   209

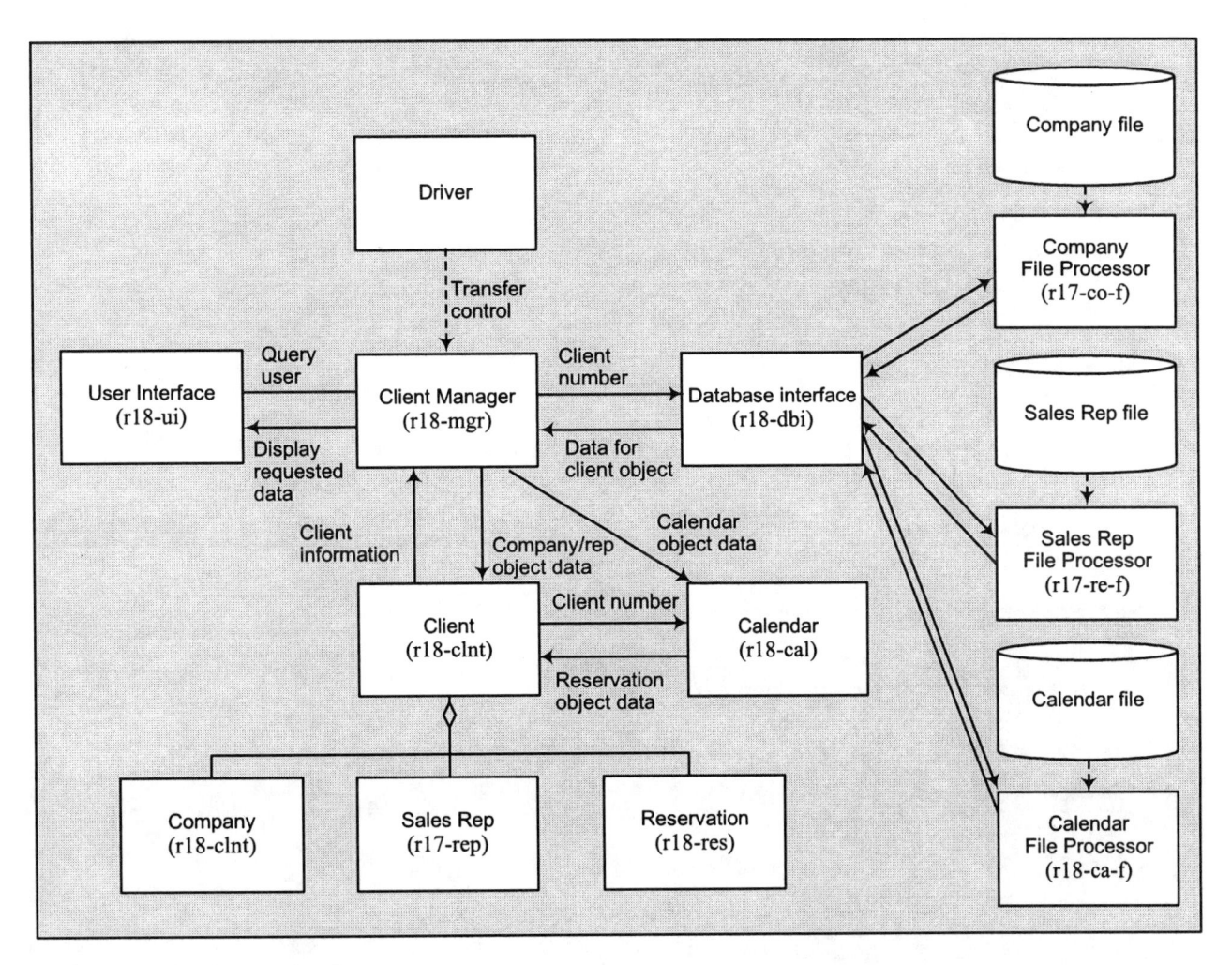

Figure 9-17. Class diagram—Room18.

Notice the positioning of Calendar in Figure 9-17. As you will see in the code, Client Manager provides data from DBI to populate Calendar's factory object data. During the processing cycle, Client accesses Calendar to obtain reservation data necessary to populate its aggregate component Reservation. This is in contrast to Company and Sales Rep data that is provided Client by Client Manager.

The Client Manager Class

Let's begin by inspecting Client Manager listed in Figure 9-18. Although it differs only slightly from the corresponding manager of Room17, those differences are significant.

```cobol
       $set sourceformat "free"
 1 *>****************************************
 2 *> Client Rental System
 3 *> W. Price   May 17, 2000         R18-MGR.CBL
 4 *>
 5 *> ClientManager handles access to the classes of
 6 *> the Client component of the Room system.
 7 *> Methods:
 8 *>    create-client-object
 9 *>    process-this-request
10 *>    process-user-requests
11 *>    process-user-selections
12 *>    set-up-for-processing
13 *>****************************************
14
15 Identification Division.
16      Class-ID.  ClientManager.
17
18 Environment Division.
19      Object Section.
20      Class-Control.
21          ClientManager     is class "r18-mgr"
22          UserInterface     is class "r18-ui"
23          DatabaseInterface is class "r18-dbi"
24          ClientClass       is class "r18-clnt"
25          CalendarClass     is class "r18-cal"
26          .
27 *>================================================
28 FACTORY.
29   Data Division.
30     Object-Storage Section.
31       01 theClientHandle   object reference.
32       01 client-number     pic x(04).
33
34   Procedure Division.
35     *>--------------------------------------------
36     Method-id. set-up-for-processing.
37     *>--------------------------------------------
38       Data Division.
39         Local-Storage Section.
40           01 lo-room-calendar-table.
41             10 lo-calendar-record
42                                  occurs 10 times.
43               20 lo-room-number      pic X(03).
44               20 lo-customer-number  pic X(04)
45                                  occurs 31 times.
46       Procedure Division.
47         Invoke DatabaseInterface "connect-to-data"
48         Invoke DatabaseInterface "get-calendar-data"
49                 Returning lo-room-calendar-table
50         Invoke CalendarClass
51                 "populate-the-calendar-object"
52                 Using lo-room-calendar-table
53         .
54     End Method set-up-for-processing.
55
56     *>--------------------------------------------
57     Method-id. process-user-requests.
58     *>--------------------------------------------
59       Procedure Division.
60         Perform with test after
61                 until client-number = spaces
62           Invoke UserInterface
63                 "query-for-client-number"
64                 Returning client-number
65           If  client-number = spaces
66             Continue
67           Else
68             Invoke Self "process-this-request"
69                 Using client-number
70           End-If *> client-number = spaces
71         End-Perform *>until client-number = spaces
72         Invoke DatabaseInterface
73                 "disconnect-from-data"
74         Invoke UserInterface "display-message"
75                 Using "Processing complete"
76         .
77     End Method process-user-requests.
78
79     *>--------------------------------------------
80     Method-id. process-this-request.
81     *>--------------------------------------------
82       Data Division.
83         Local-Storage Section.
84           01 lo-record-found-sw         pic X(01).
85             88 lo-record-found          value "Y".
86           01 lo-invalid-client-message  pic X(40)
87                   value "Invalid client number".
88         Linkage Section.
89           01 ls-client-number           pic X(03).
90
91       Procedure Division Using ls-client-number.
92         Invoke DataBaseInterface
93                 "read-client-database"
94                 Using ls-client-number
95                 Returning lo-record-found-sw
96         If lo-record-found
97           Invoke Self "create-client-object"
98           Invoke Self "process-user-selections"
99                 Using ls-client-number
100        Else
101          Invoke UserInterface "display-message"
102                 Using lo-invalid-client-message
103        End-If *>lo-record-found
104        .
105    End Method process-this-request.
106
```

Figure 9-18. The Client Manager class (continued next page).

- The initialization method of lines 36-54 serves two purposes. First, it directs DBI to prepare access to the data base—open the three needed files, in this case. Second, it accesses calendar data from DBI and passes it to Calendar in order to populate its factory object data. Remember, this data is static for the duration of the run. If you look at Driver, you will see the following two Invoke statements.

```
Invoke ClientManager "set-up-for-processing"
Invoke ClientManager "process-user-requests"
```

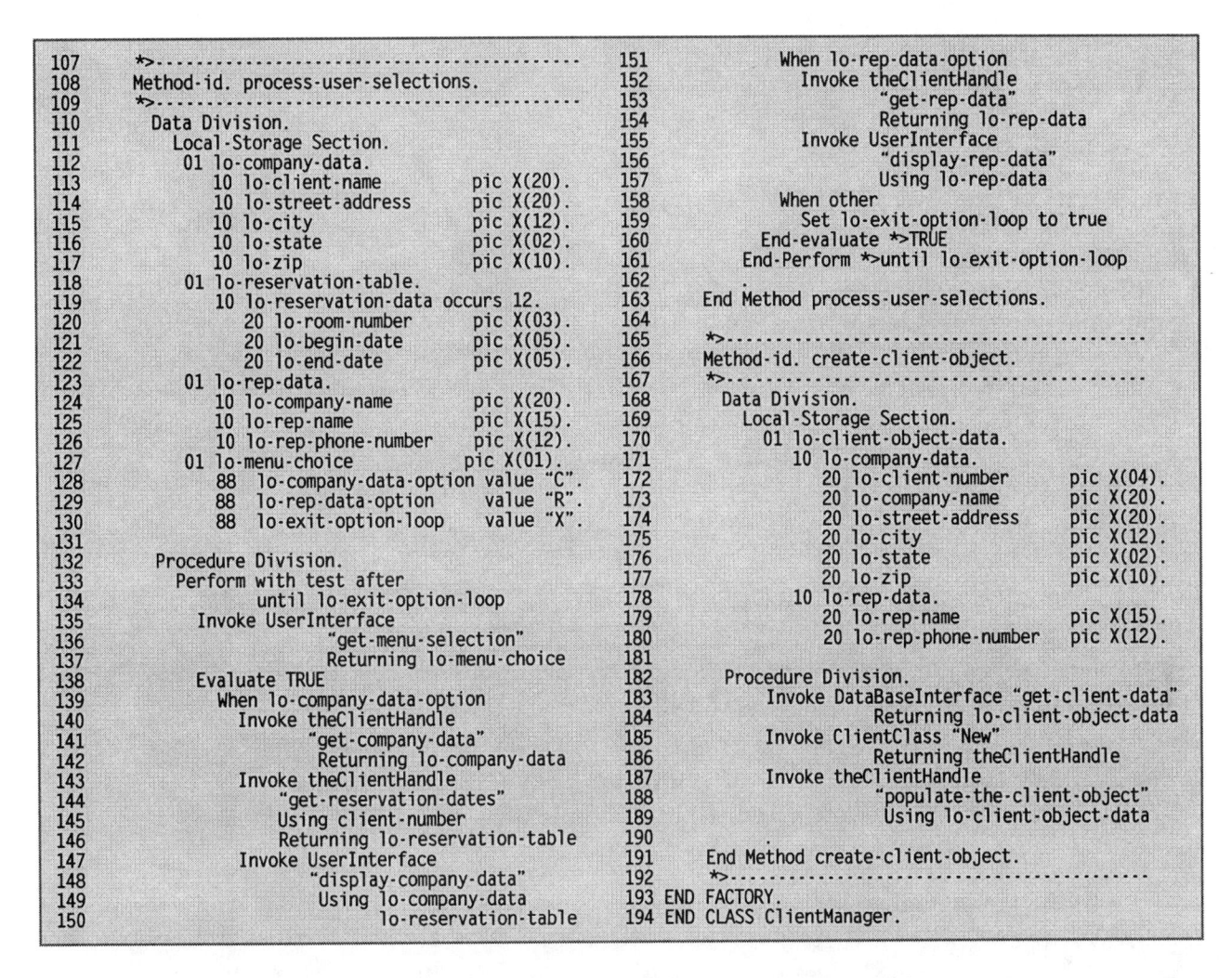

```
107      *>-------------------------------------------
108      Method-id. process-user-selections.
109      *>-------------------------------------------
110      Data Division.
111        Local-Storage Section.
112          01 lo-company-data.
113             10 lo-client-name          pic X(20).
114             10 lo-street-address       pic X(20).
115             10 lo-city                 pic X(12).
116             10 lo-state                pic X(02).
117             10 lo-zip                  pic X(10).
118          01 lo-reservation-table.
119             10 lo-reservation-data occurs 12.
120                20 lo-room-number      pic X(03).
121                20 lo-begin-date       pic X(05).
122                20 lo-end-date         pic X(05).
123          01 lo-rep-data.
124             10 lo-company-name        pic X(20).
125             10 lo-rep-name            pic X(15).
126             10 lo-rep-phone-number    pic X(12).
127          01 lo-menu-choice            pic X(01).
128             88 lo-company-data-option value "C".
129             88 lo-rep-data-option     value "R".
130             88 lo-exit-option-loop    value "X".
131
132      Procedure Division.
133        Perform with test after
134              until lo-exit-option-loop
135          Invoke UserInterface
136                    "get-menu-selection"
137                    Returning lo-menu-choice
138          Evaluate TRUE
139            When lo-company-data-option
140              Invoke theClientHandle
141                      "get-company-data"
142                      Returning lo-company-data
143              Invoke theClientHandle
144                      "get-reservation-dates"
145                      Using client-number
146                      Returning lo-reservation-table
147              Invoke UserInterface
148                      "display-company-data"
149                      Using lo-company-data
150                            lo-reservation-table
151            When lo-rep-data-option
152              Invoke theClientHandle
153                      "get-rep-data"
154                      Returning lo-rep-data
155              Invoke UserInterface
156                      "display-rep-data"
157                      Using lo-rep-data
158            When other
159              Set lo-exit-option-loop to true
160          End-evaluate *>TRUE
161        End-Perform *>until lo-exit-option-loop
162      .
163      End Method process-user-selections.
164
165      *>-------------------------------------------
166      Method-id. create-client-object.
167      *>-------------------------------------------
168      Data Division.
169        Local-Storage Section.
170          01 lo-client-object-data.
171             10 lo-company-data.
172                20 lo-client-number    pic X(04).
173                20 lo-company-name     pic X(20).
174                20 lo-street-address   pic X(20).
175                20 lo-city             pic X(12).
176                20 lo-state            pic X(02).
177                20 lo-zip              pic X(10).
178             10 lo-rep-data.
179                20 lo-rep-name         pic X(15).
180                20 lo-rep-phone-number pic X(12).
181
182      Procedure Division.
183          Invoke DataBaseInterface "get-client-data"
184                      Returning lo-client-object-data
185          Invoke ClientClass "New"
186                      Returning theClientHandle
187          Invoke theClientHandle
188                      "populate-the-client-object"
189                      Using lo-client-object-data
190      .
191      End Method create-client-object.
192      *>-------------------------------------------
193 END FACTORY.
194 END CLASS ClientManager.
```

Figure 9-18. The Client Manager class (continued from preceding page).

- The method process-user-selections (lines 108-163) now includes an additional component to return reservation data for this room—refer to the Invoke at line 143 and the corresponding data entries at lines 118-122.
- Notice that the method create-client-object (lines 166-191) does not pass reservation data (see the parameter lo-client-object-data beginning line 170). As you will see, Client accesses that data from Calendar. For that, it needs the client number, which is included with the company data—see line 172.

The Calendar Class—Room18

Data Definition

To focus on basics of object methodology, the Calendar class of Figure 9-19 includes the following simplifications.

- The database includes exactly 10 rooms (consistent with all preceding examples).
- Calendar processing is limited to the month of July. (There's no need to get into the complexities of real calendar processing when the objective here is to illustrate OO principles.)
- Indexes are defined for these tables to permit using the Search verb for scanning the table.
- No customer will have more than 12 room reservations for the month.

First, look at the class's object data in lines 29-35 where you see its following features.

- The data item room-calendar-entry is an array with a dimension of 10, one for each room—see the occurs clause at line 30.
- This room-calendar record includes room-number and the array client-number with a dimension of 31, one for each of the days of July—see the occurs clause at line 34. Compare this record description to the illustration in Figure 9-14.

At line 105 you see the relatively basic method populate-the-calendar-object. It is invoked from Client Manager (see Figure 9-18's line 50) which had obtained it from DBI (see Figure 9-18's line 48). Both of these are executed as part of the application start up process.

Calendar's method get-reservation-dates, beginning line 39, is invoked by Client Manager to access the table of room-number/dates for the display of Figure 9-15. The Local-Storage Section entries at lines 44-47 provide a setup area for formatting dates—refer to the sample output in Figure 9-15. (Remember, this simple illustration is limited to the month of July.)

The Linkage-Section, beginning line 51, includes the client number as input and a reservation table, corresponding to the list of dates in Figure 9-15, as output.

Searching the Calendar Table

Let's take a quick look at the search code of this method, although it is not the intent of this book to cover details of table searching. Assume that a user has entered a request for reservation information of client 1003 (ls-client-number contains 1003). The Perform at line 63 repeats the code that follows for each of the 10 rooms. To understand how the nested search (Search verbs at lines 70 and 84), consider the sample object data for room 102 shown in Figure 9-20 (repeated from Figure 9-15).

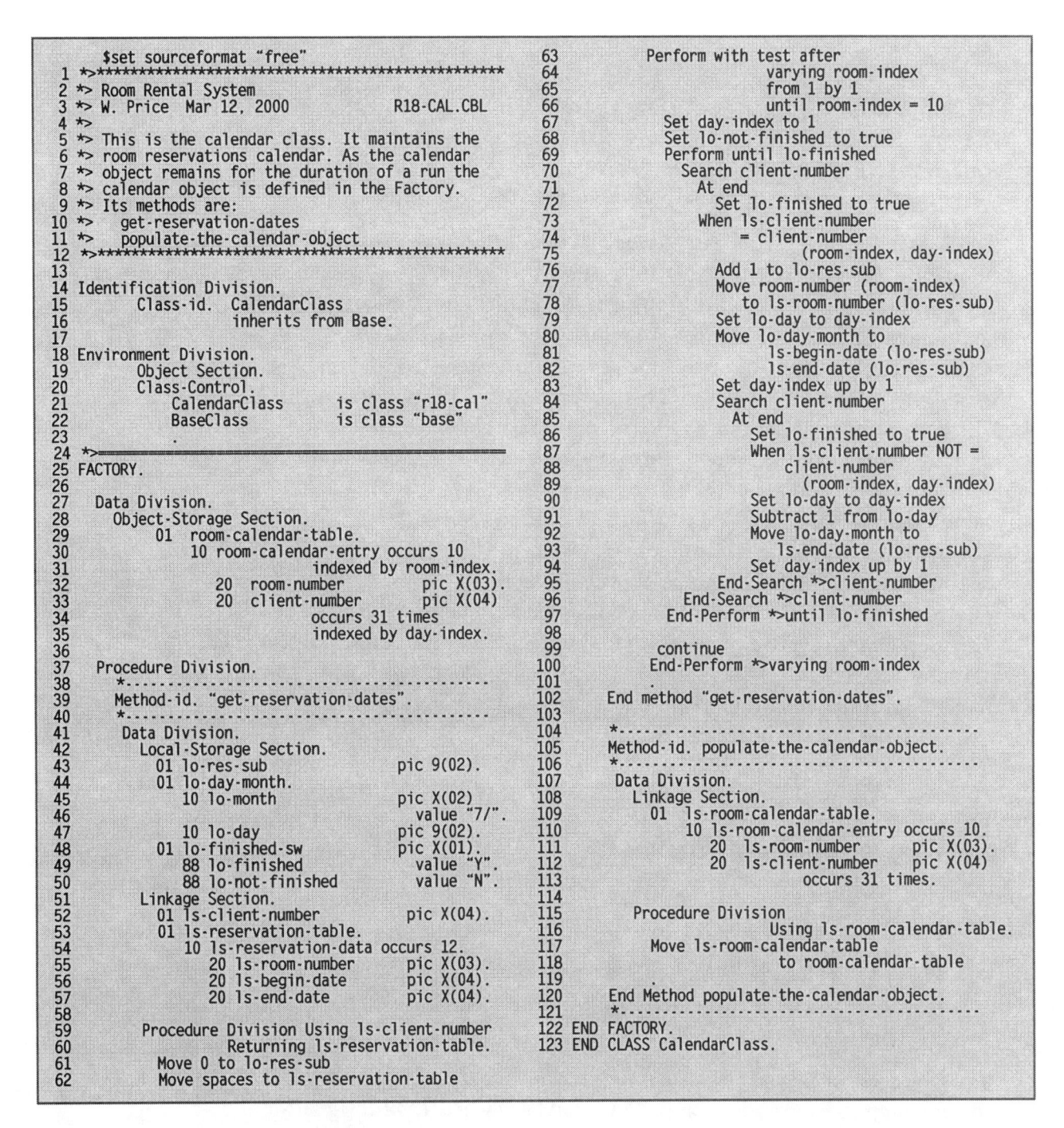

Aggregate Structures in Object-Oriented Cobol

```cobol
        $set sourceformat "free"
 1 *>*****************************************
 2 *> Room Rental System
 3 *> W. Price  Mar 12, 2000           R18-CAL.CBL
 4 *>
 5 *> This is the calendar class. It maintains the
 6 *> room reservations calendar. As the calendar
 7 *> object remains for the duration of a run the
 8 *> calendar object is defined in the Factory.
 9 *> Its methods are:
10 *>    get-reservation-dates
11 *>    populate-the-calendar-object
12 *>*****************************************
13
14 Identification Division.
15     Class-id. CalendarClass
16              inherits from Base.
17
18 Environment Division.
19     Object Section.
20     Class-Control.
21         CalendarClass        is class "r18-cal"
22         BaseClass            is class "base"
23         .
24 *>
25 FACTORY.
26
27     Data Division.
28         Object-Storage Section.
29         01 room-calendar-table.
30             10 room-calendar-entry occurs 10
31                    indexed by room-index.
32                 20 room-number       pic X(03).
33                 20 client-number     pic X(04)
34                    occurs 31 times
35                    indexed by day-index.
36
37     Procedure Division.
38     *---------------------------------------
39     Method-id. "get-reservation-dates".
40     *---------------------------------------
41     Data Division.
42         Local-Storage Section.
43         01 lo-res-sub            pic 9(02).
44         01 lo-day-month.
45             10 lo-month          pic X(02)
46                                  value "7/".
47             10 lo-day            pic 9(02).
48         01 lo-finished-sw        pic X(01).
49             88 lo-finished       value "Y".
50             88 lo-not-finished   value "N".
51         Linkage Section.
52         01 ls-client-number      pic X(04).
53         01 ls-reservation-table.
54             10 ls-reservation-data occurs 12.
55                 20 ls-room-number    pic X(03).
56                 20 ls-begin-date     pic X(04).
57                 20 ls-end-date       pic X(04).
58
59     Procedure Division Using ls-client-number
60              Returning ls-reservation-table.
61         Move 0 to lo-res-sub
62         Move spaces to ls-reservation-table
63         Perform with test after
64                  varying room-index
65                  from 1 by 1
66                  until room-index = 10
67             Set day-index to 1
68             Set lo-not-finished to true
69             Perform until lo-finished
70                 Search client-number
71                     At end
72                         Set lo-finished to true
73                     When ls-client-number
74                           = client-number
75                             (room-index, day-index)
76                         Add 1 to lo-res-sub
77                         Move room-number (room-index)
78                             to ls-room-number (lo-res-sub)
79                         Set lo-day to day-index
80                         Move lo-day-month to
81                             ls-begin-date (lo-res-sub)
82                             ls-end-date (lo-res-sub)
83                         Set day-index up by 1
84                         Search client-number
85                             At end
86                                 Set lo-finished to true
87                             When ls-client-number NOT =
88                                   client-number
89                                     (room-index, day-index)
90                                 Set lo-day to day-index
91                                 Subtract 1 from lo-day
92                                 Move lo-day-month to
93                                     ls-end-date (lo-res-sub)
94                                 Set day-index up by 1
95                         End-Search *>client-number
96                 End-Search *>client-number
97             End-Perform *>until lo-finished
98
99             continue
100         End-Perform *>varying room-index
101         .
102     End method "get-reservation-dates".
103
104     *---------------------------------------
105     Method-id. populate-the-calendar-object.
106     *---------------------------------------
107     Data Division.
108         Linkage Section.
109         01 ls-room-calendar-table.
110             10 ls-room-calendar-entry occurs 10.
111                 20 ls-room-number    pic X(03).
112                 20 ls-client-number  pic X(04)
113                    occurs 31 times.
114
115     Procedure Division
116              Using ls-room-calendar-table.
117         Move ls-room-calendar-table
118              to room-calendar-table
119         .
120     End Method populate-the-calendar-object.
121     *---------------------------------------
122 END FACTORY.
123 END CLASS CalendarClass.
```

Figure 9-19. The Calendar class.

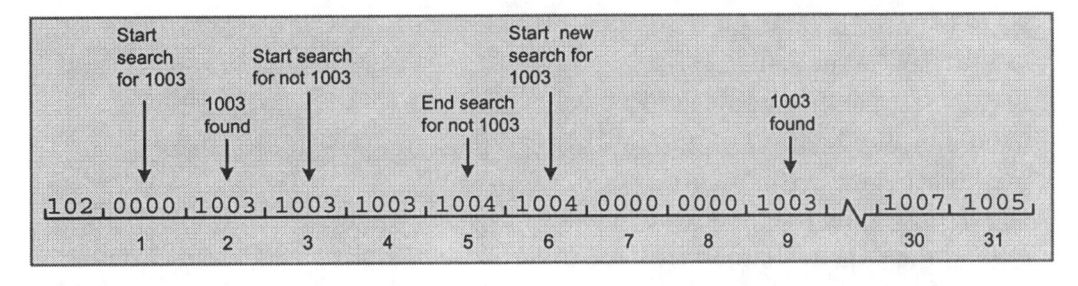

Figure 9-20. Searching the room 102 portion of the calendar object.

Remember:

- The input to the method (ls-client-number) is 1003.
- The array contains client numbers of clients renting room 102.
- Referring to Figure 9-20, client 1003 has reserved this room for 7/2-7/4 and for 7/9.

1. The search begins at table entry 1 (day 1) which contains the value 0000 indicating the room is not rented for that day.
2. The Perform at line 69 controls repeated searching across the entire room component of this table component (days 1 through 31).
3. The Search verb (line 70) begins the search with element 1 and ends when the condition of lines 73-75 is met. This occurs at day 2 (Figure 9-20).
4. The code at lines 76-82 moves the room number and date (day 2) to corresponding entries of the output ls-reservation-table. Notice that the day number is moved to the ending date as well as the beginning date. This accommodates a single-day reservation.
5. The Search verb at line 84 resumes the search looking for an entry not equal to 1003 (lines 87-89). The search terminates at day 5.
6. The code of lines 91-93 moves the ending date to the reservation table.
7. The loop beginning line 69 is repeated thus searching for the next occurrence of client 1003.
8. Execution of the outer loop (Perform at line 63) is terminated when the table end is reached by the Search at either line 70 or 84—refer to lines 71/72 and 85/86.

Other Components of Room18

The Client Class

If you compare selected code segments from Room 18's Client (Figure 9-21) you will see that this class is the expected expansion of Room17's Client (Figure 9-7). Notice its following features.

- The Class-Control paragraph now includes declarations for ReservationClass (designating the aggregate component) and CalendarClass (designating the source from which reservation data will be obtained)—see lines 24 and 25.
- ReservationClass is instantiated and the handle saved (lines 56-60).
- Reservation data is made available through the method get-reservation-dates (beginning line 121).
- Populating the Company and Rep aggregate components (lines 166-171) is handled as in Room17—look at Client Manager's create-client-object method (beginning line 166, Figure 9-18). Object data is obtained from DBI and is passed on to Client by Manager's Invoke of line 187 (Figure 9-18). In Client, the data available in the Linkage Section (lines 153-163 of Figure 9-21) where it is passed on to the Company and Rep aggregate objects (refer to lines 166 and 169).

Aggregate Structures in Object-Oriented Cobol

- In contrast, Client accesses data for the Reservation object through the Invoke of line 172 then passes it on to the Reservation aggregate component through the Invoke of line 175.

```cobol
        $set sourceformat "free"
1   *>*********************************************
2   *> Room Rental System
3   *> W. Price  Mar 12, 2000                 R18-CLNT.CBL
4   *>
5   *> This is a client aggregate class containing
6   *> handles to the following three component classes:
7   *>      Company
8   *>      Rep
9   *>      Reservation
10  *> These aggregate components are instantiated
11  *> in this class's Factory.
12  *>*********************************************
13
14  Identification Division.
15      Class-id.  ClientClass
16                  inherits from Base.
17
18  Environment Division.
19      Object Section.
20      Class-Control.
21          ClientClass         is class "r18-clnt"
22          CompanyClass        is class "r18-comp"
23          RepClass            is class "r17-rep"
24          ReservationClass    is class "r18-res"
25          CalendarClass       is class "r18-cal"
26          BaseClass           is class "base"
27              .
28  *>==============================================
29  FACTORY.
30
31  Method-ID. New.
32  Data Division.
33      Local-Storage Section.
34          01 lo-theCompanyHandle       object reference.
35          01 lo-theRepHandle           object reference.
36          01 lo-theReservationHandle   object reference.
37      Linkage Section.
38          01 ls-clientHandle           object reference.
39
40  Procedure Division Returning ls-clientHandle.
41      *> Create instance of this object.
42      Invoke Super "New"
43                  Returning ls-clientHandle
44      *> Create instances of the aggregate components
45      *> This is the client factory object. The
46      *> client instance object must have access to
47      *> the company, rep, and calendar objects.
48      Invoke CompanyClass "New"
49                  Returning lo-theCompanyHandle
50      Invoke ls-clientHandle "put-company-handle"
51                  Using lo-theCompanyHandle
52      Invoke RepClass "New"
53                  Returning lo-theRepHandle
54      Invoke ls-clientHandle "put-rep-handle"
55                  Using lo-theRepHandle
56      Invoke ReservationClass "New"
57                  Returning lo-theReservationHandle
58      Invoke ls-clientHandle
59                  "put-reservation-handle"
60                  Using lo-theReservationHandle
61          .
62  End Method New.
63
64  END FACTORY.
65  *>==============================================
66  OBJECT.
67
68  Data Division.
69      Object-Storage Section.
70          01 theCompanyHandle       object reference.
71          01 theRepHandle           object reference.
72          01 theReservationHandle   object reference.

120
121 Method-id. get-reservation-dates.
122 *>---------------------------------------------
123 Data Division.
124     Linkage Section.
125         01 ls-client-number          pic X(04).
126         01 ls-reservation-table.
127             10 ls-reservation-data occurs 12.
128                 20 ls-room-number    pic X(03).
129                 20 ls-begin-date     pic X(04).
130                 20 ls-end-date       pic X(04).
131
132     Procedure Division Using ls-client-number
133                 Returning ls-reservation-table.
134         Invoke theReservationHandle
135             "get-reservation-dates"
136             Using ls-client-number
137             Returning ls-reservation-table
138         .
139 End method get-reservation-dates.
140
141 *>---------------------------------------------
142 Method-id. populate-the-client-object.
143 *>---------------------------------------------
144 Data Division.
145     Local-Storage Section.
146         01 lo-reservation-table.
147             10 lo-reservation-data occurs 12.
148                 20 lo-room-number    pic X(03).
149                 20 lo-begin-date     pic X(04).
150                 20 lo-end-date       pic X(04).
151
152     Linkage Section.
153         01 ls-client-data.
154             10 ls-company-data.
155                 20 ls-client-number    pic X(04).
156                 20 ls-client-name      pic X(20).
157                 20 ls-street-address   pic X(20).
158                 20 ls-city             pic X(12).
159                 20 ls-state            pic X(02).
160                 20 ls-zip              pic X(10).
161             10 ls-rep-data.
162                 20 ls-rep-person       pic X(15).
163                 20 ls-rep-phone-number pic X(12).
164
165     Procedure Division  Using ls-client-data.
166         Invoke theCompanyHandle
167             "populate-the-company-object"
168             Using ls-company-data
169         Invoke theRepHandle
170             "populate-the-rep-object"
171             Using ls-rep-data
172         Invoke CalendarClass "get-reservation-dates"
173             Using ls-client-number
174             Returning lo-reservation-table
175         Invoke theReservationHandle
176             "populate-the-reservation-object"
177             Using lo-reservation-table
178         .
179 End Method populate-the-client-object.

216 END OBJECT.
217 END CLASS ClientClass.
```

Figure 9-21. Code segments from Client.

The Calendar File

The indexed calendar file includes one record for each room; each of these records contains the following.

> Room number
> Daily room reservation data
> > Required room configuration code
> > Client number of client renting the room.

The daily room reservation data is repeated 31 time, once for each day of the month. You will see the exact format in the calendar file processor.

Calendar Database Access

File processing in preceding examples have involved a two-step approach: (1) read the selected record and store it as object data of the class's object and (2) access data from the record object as needed. This application differs in that the calendar object consists of data from all records of the calendar file.

First look at Client DBI in Figure 9-22 which "collects" data from the Client File Processor and organizes it into a form needed to populate the Calendar object.

- The Linkage-Section entry (line 128) is formatted to correspond to the object data definition in Calendar—see Figure 9-20.
- The procedural code beginning line 137 utilizes the common "priming read" concept in that the first record is read prior to the read loop.
- Reaching the end of the file is indicated by the calendar data parameter (lo-calendar-record) containing spaces—refer to line 142.

Finally, look at the listing of the client file processor class Figure 9-23 where you see the format of the calendar file defined at lines 38-42. Consecutive records of this file are read by the code of the read-next-record method.

```
 20 Identification Division.
 21      Class-ID.  ClientDBI
 22             inherits from BaseClass.

117      *>
118      Method-ID. get-calendar-data.
119      *>
120          Data Division.
121          Local-Storage Section.
122          01 lo-calendar-record.
123             10 lo-room-number         pic X(03).
124             10 lo-customer-number     pic X(04)
125                          occurs 31 times.
126          01 lo-counter                pic 9(02).
127          Linkage Section.
128          01 ls-room-calendar-table.
129             10 ls-calendar-record
130                          occurs 10 times.
131                20 ls-room-number      pic X(03).
132                20 ls-customer-number  pic X(04)
133                          occurs 31 times.

134          Procedure Division
135                        Returning ls-room-calendar-table.
136          *> Get first record
137          Invoke CalendarFileProcessor
138                        "read-next-record"
139                        Returning lo-calendar-record
140          Perform with test after
141                   varying lo-counter from 1 by 1
142                   until lo-calendar-record = spaces
143
144             Move lo-calendar-record to
145                   ls-calendar-record (lo-counter)
146          *> Get subsequent records
147             Invoke CalendarFileProcessor
148                        "read-next-record"
149                        Returning lo-calendar-record
150          End-Perform *> with test after
151          End Method get-calendar-data.
152          *>
221 END FACTORY.
222 END CLASS ClientDBI.
```

Figure 9-22. The get-calendar-data method of the Client DBI.

- For each instantiation of Client, a new reservation object is created. Don't assume that data of the calendar component will be static for the duration of the run as, in a multi-user environment, data in the calendar file would be in a constant state of update.
- This indexed file will be read sequentially because every record of the file is needed to build the calendar object.
- To understand the code of this method, remember that two circumstances exist under which this file is read: (1) a new client is to be processed so the first record of the file must be read, and (2) subsequent records of the file must be read to complete input for the calendar object. These two scenarios are controlled by the program switch lo-another-client-sw (line 71).

```cobol
          $set sourceformat "free"
1  *>*************************************************
2  *> Calendar Rental System
3  *> W. Price   Mar 10, 2000        R18-CA-F.CBL
4  *>
5  *> This file processor class definition provides
6  *> sequential read to the indexed file CALENDAR.DI.
7  *> Its object data is the calendar record
8  *> Methods
9  *>    close-file
10 *>    open-file
11 *>    read-next-record
12 *>*************************************************
13
14 Identification Division.
15      Class-ID.   CalendarFileProcessor
16                  inherits from BaseClass.
17 Environment Division.
18      Object Section.
19      Class-Control.
20          CalendarFileProcessor
21                      is class "w"
22          BaseClass   is class "base"
23              .
24 *>==================================================
25 FACTORY.
26 Environment Division.
27      Input-Output Section.
28      File-Control.
29          Select calendar-file
30              assign to "c:\Eooc2\eData\calendar.di"
31              organization is indexed
32              access is dynamic
33              record key is cr-room-number
34
35 Data Division.
36   File Section.
37   FD calendar-File.
38   01 cr-calendar-record.
39        10 cr-room-number           pic X(03).
40        10 cr-reservation-data occurs 31 times.
41            20 cr-configuration-code pic X(01).
42            20 cr-client-number      pic X(04).
43
44 Procedure Division.
45  *>---------------------------------------------
46  *> ****File Related Methods ******************
47  *>---------------------------------------------
48 Method-ID. open-file.
49  *>---------------------------------------------
50    Procedure Division.
51        Open Input calendar-file
52        .
53 End Method open-file.
54
55 *>---------------------------------------------
56 Method-ID. close-file.
57 *>---------------------------------------------
58    Procedure Division.
59        Close calendar-file
60        .
61 End Method close-file.
62
63 *>---------------------------------------------
64 *> ****Data Access Related Methods ***********
65 *>---------------------------------------------
66 Method-ID. read-next-record.
67 *>---------------------------------------------
68    Data Division.
69      Local-Storage Section.
70      01 lo-day-sub              pic 9(02).
71      01 lo-another-client-sw    pic X(01)
72                                 value "Y".
73         88 lo-another-client    value "Y".
74         88 lo-current-client    value "N".
75      Linkage Section.
76      01 ls-calendar-record.
77          10 ls-room-number      pic X(03).
78          10 ls-client-number    pic X(04)
79                                 occurs 31 times.
80    Procedure Division
81                Returning ls-calendar-record.
82      If lo-another-client
83      *> Position to first record of file for
84      *> another client
85          Move "100" to cr-room-number
86          Start calendar-file
87          Set lo-current-client to true
88      End-If *>lo-anothor-client
89      Read Calendar-File next
90        at end
91          Move spaces to ls-calendar-record
92          Set lo-another-client to true
93        not at end
94          Move cr-room-number to ls-room-number
95          Perform varying lo-day-sub
96                  from 1 by 1
97                  until lo-day-sub > 31
98            Move cr-client-number (lo-day-sub)
99              to ls-client-number (lo-day-sub)
100         End-Perform *>varying lo-day-sub
101       End-Read *>Calendar-File
102
103 End Method read-next-record.
104 *>---------------------------------------------
105 END FACTORY.
106 END CLASS CalendarFileProcessor.
```

Figure 9-23. The Calendar File Processor class definition.

- The If statement of lines 82-88 initializes the file pointer and sets lo-current-client to true. This prevents this conditional code of the If from being executed during succeeding executions of this method for the selected client.
- After each successful read, file data is moved to the linkage section parameter components—see lines 94-100.
- Upon detecting the end-of-file, spaces are moved to the method's parameter and the lo-another-client is set to true thereby initializing for the next sequence requiring creation of calendar object.

Summing Up

Project Summary

Room17, Proj0901 illustrates the aggregate structure of a Client class composed of the two aggregate subclasses Customer and Calendar. Object data of the Client class consists only of the Customer and Client object handles. Figure 9-1 is a class diagram for this application.

Room18, Proj0902 expands upon Room17 with the addition of a calendar class aggregate component of Client. Implementation of this class differs from that of the other components as Calendar is defined in the Factory—it contains, as its object data, the complete calendar (for all rooms).

General Summary

From Chapter 8 and this chapter, you've learned about two structure types used to help us understand complexity: classification and aggregation.

An aggregation structure is a representation of something broken down into its component parts. These structures are often called *whole-part* structures.

Sometimes you might find it confusing in determining whether you are dealing with a classification structure or an aggregation structure. For this, use the has-a or the is-a approach. See which fits: "X is a Y" or "Y has an X."

Aggregation follows structured practices we have used for years—break a complex item down into its component parts.

Implement aggregation in Cobol by including the object handle of the "part" object as an object data item in the "whole" class definition.

Coming Up

Chapter 10 treats you to some "goodies"—a few of OOCobol's features that make programming a little easier. Topics include a feature for automatic creation of methods to access an object's data and the inline invoke.

Assignments

9-1

The simple cardboard box of Assignment 7-3 is now history. J&B has come up with a phenomenal dessert material that allows them to make an edible (in fact, delectable) box in which personalized dessert rolls are packaged. In fact, the box has been so successful, that it has become a product in its own right. (It is not an unusual sight to see riders of public transportation eating J&B boxes during commute hours. One rider was seen throwing away the rolls and eating the box.)

The J&B systems group wants you to reprogram much of the application (use the system of Assignment 7-1 as your starting point) to include a Box aggregate component of the Dessert class as illustrated in Figure 9-24.

For a selected product (based on the Desert ID field) the user must have a minimum of the following two display options (you may include other options if you so desire).

1. Dessert description
   Box description
2. Inventory value of dessert (assume all desserts in the file are Rope desserts)
   Inventory value of the box.
   Total inventory value (dessert plus box)

The box file has the following format.

File name	BOX.DI
File type	Indexed
Key	Box ID

Field	Format
Box ID	pic X(02)
Box description	pic X(10)
Quantity onhand	pic 9(04)
Price	pic 99V99
Length	pic 9V9
Width	pic 9V9
Height	pic 9V9

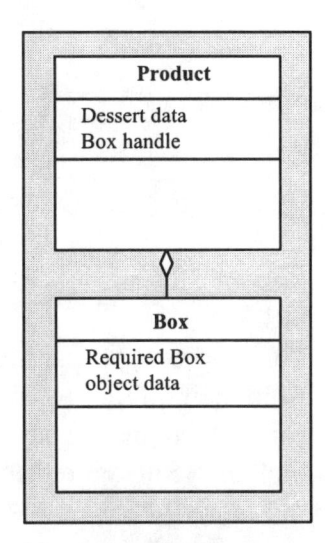

Figure 9-24.
Aggregate structure for Assignment 9-1.

9-2

The systems analyst has decided to expand the definition of Assignment 9-1 to include a Product class as illustrated in Figure 9-25. As you see, the Product class's object data is comprised of:

- Product ID (use the Dessert ID as the identification field for the dessert-box combination).
- Object handle of the Dessert aggregate object component.
- Object handle of the Box aggregate object component.

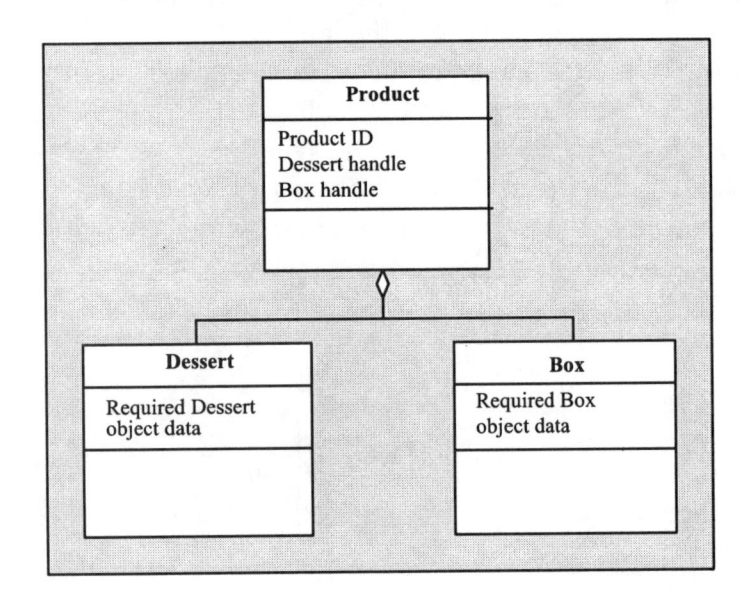

Figure 9-25.
Aggregate structure for Assignment 9-2.

9-3

The marketing department of F&C wants site information available from their online system. So you are to reprogram much of the application (use the system of Assignment 7-2 as your starting point) to include a Site aggregate component of the Event class as illustrated in Figure 9-26.

For a selected event the user must have a minimum of the following three display options (you may include other options if you so desire).

1. Event ID
   Event description
   Facility
   Duration
2. Event ID
   Event description
   Event cost
      Calculate the Event cost as follows
         Duration times Daily rate times Site surcharge factor

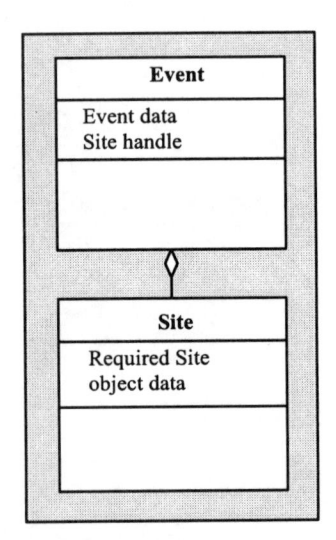

Figure 9-26.
Aggregate structure for Assignment 9-3.

3. Event description
   Site description
   Water depth

Site data is available from the site file which has the following format.
(Note: The Site ID field of each event record contains the key-field value of the desired Site record.)

File name	SITE.DI
File type	Indexed
Key	Site ID

Field	**Format**
Site ID	pic X(02)
Site location	pic X(20)
Water depth	pic 9(03)
Site surcharge factor	pic 9V99

9-4

The system analyst has decided to expand the definition of Assignment 9-3 to include the Event class with the aggregate components illustrated by Figure 9-27. The EventDetails object will contain data previously store in the Event object. As you see, the Event class's object data is comprised of:

- Event ID.
- Object handle of the EventDetail aggregate object component.
- Object handle of the Site aggregate object component.

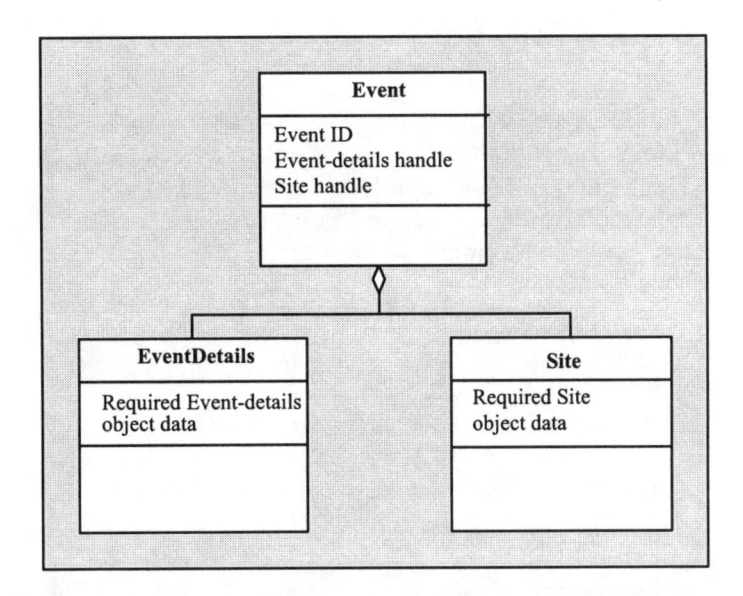

Figure 9-27. Aggregate structure for Assignment 9-4.

Other OOCobol Goodies

Chapter Contents

ISO2000 Features 224
Interface Definitions 225
   Restricting Access to Methods of a Class 225
   Interface Definition General Form 226
   An Interface Example—Documentation 226
   The Client Interface 227
   Room Manager 229
Inline Invoke 229
Property Clause 232
   Data Name Qualification 232
   Qualification to an Object 232
   Get and Set Methods and the Property Clause 234
   The RDF File 235
Summing Up 236
   Project Summary 236
   General Summary 236
Coming Up 236

Chapter 10

Chapter Introduction

Merant Micro Focus Cobol compilers all include capabilities for designating a variety of Cobol dialects (for instance, Cobol-85, IBM, and so on). Net Express includes the dialect ISO2000 which is based on features of the new standard. (Merant Micro Focus compilers conform reasonably well to the standard except, as with most vendors, extensions are included as deemed useful by the vendor.) Object-oriented capabilities are especially susceptible since, as of the date of the publication of this book, the standard was not completely finalized. Some of the examples in this chapter will compile with Net Express 3.0 and others will not. However, those that do compile (and those that will be functional under future releases) require the ISO2000 dialect.

From this chapter you will learn about the following topics. Each has its valuable place in the programmer's "toolbox."

- Interface definitions that can be use to restrict access to methods of a class.
- The inline Invoke that allows you to imbed implicit invokes within other Cobol statements.
- The Property clause that provides simplified access to data elements of an object.

ISO2000 Features

All examples of this book use free format by including the compiler directive:

    $set sourceformat free"

Both Personal Cobol and Net Express allow you to specify the Cobol dialect through the dialect directive. In particular, Net Express includes the directive

    $set dialect(iso2000)

which allows you to tell the compiler you are using ISO2000 dialect. Actually, the differences introduced to examples of this book by this directive are relatively few (but very significant)—see Figure 10-1. Notice that in both cases the name of the class is `RoomManager`.

Net Express Dialect	**ISO2000 Dialect**
The class name (`RoomManager`) is linked to the external file name (`r09-mgr`) in the `Class-control` paragraph of the `Environment Division`.	The class name (`RoomManager`) is linked to the external file name (`r09-mgr`) in the `Class-ID` paragraph of the `Identification Division` by the as phrase.
The `Environment Division` includes an `Object Section` which in turn includes a `Class-control` paragraph identifying all classes referenced by this class.	The `Environment Division` includes a `Repository` paragraph under the `Configuration Section` paragraph identifying all classes referenced by this class
The internal class names are associated with their external names with the is phrase, for instance: `RoomManager is class "r09-mgr"`	The internal class names are associated with their external names with the as phrase, for instance: class `class RoomManager as "r09-mgr"`

```
        $set sourceformat "free"              $set dialect(iso2000)
                                              $set sourceformat "free"
Identification Division.              Identification Division.
    Class-ID.  RoomManager.               Class-ID.  RoomManager
                                                     as "r09-mgr".

Environment Division.                 Environment Division.
    Object Section.                       Configuration Section.
      Class-control.                        Repository.
        RoomManager       is class "r09-mgr"     class UserInterface       as "r08-ui"
        UserInterface     is class "r08-ui"      class DatabaseInterface   as "r06-dbi"
        DatabaseInterface is class "r06-dbi"     class RoomClass           as "r06-room"
        RoomClass         is class "r06-room"    .

 (a)  Net Express dialect (default)    (b)  ISO2000 dialect
```

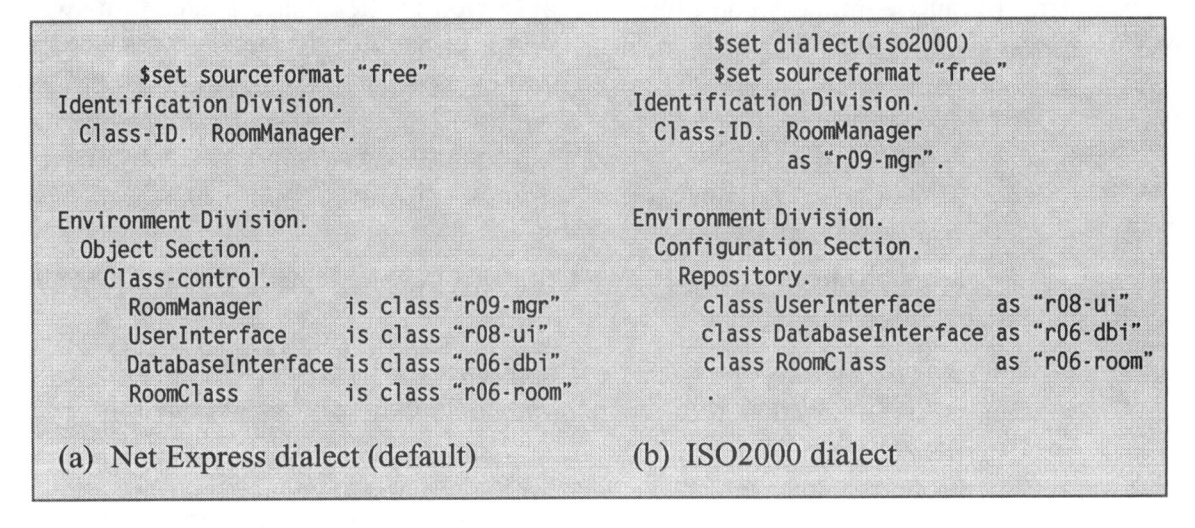

Figure 10-1. Comparison of Merant Micro Focus and ISO2000 dialects.

Be aware that if you use the ISO2000 directive without adhering to syntax of the new standard your program will produce compiler errors. For instance, all examples of preceding chapter will result in compiler errors.

Interface Definitions

Restricting Access to Methods of a Class

In previous chapters you have seen methods of a class categorized as:

- Public—methods that are intended to be invoke from other programs/classes and must be "visible" to the class user.
- Private—methods that are intended for use within the class in which they are defined and should not be "visible" to the class user.

Unfortunately, OOCobol has no provisions for declaring methods within a class definition as public or private—in essence, all methods are public and are therefore accessible to the class user. However, OOCobol includes a feature call an **interface definition** that you can use to restrict access to methods of a class. That is, methods of a class are accessible through an interface as illustrated in the representation of Figure 10-2 in which the class user is provided access to only the public methods of the class. Documentation available to the user describes access only via the interface (to the public methods). If the class is available only in compiled form (as a dll) then for all practical purposes the user will have no knowledge of the method names and will therefore be unable to invoke them. (If you are familiar with relational database concepts then you will recognize an interface used in this way as akin to a database view.)

Similarly, in the depiction of Figure 10-3 an interface provides access to methods from two different classes. Notice that the method names used in the interface need not be the same as those used in the classes.

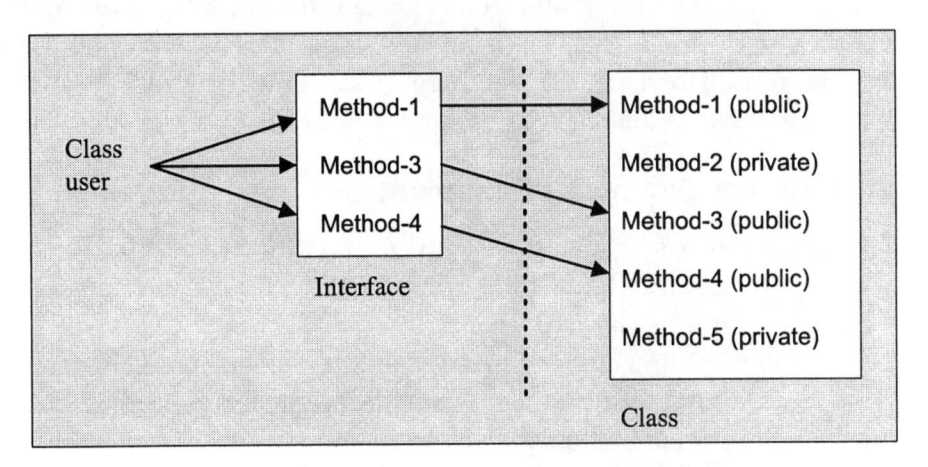

Figure 10-2. Interface limiting access to methods of a class.

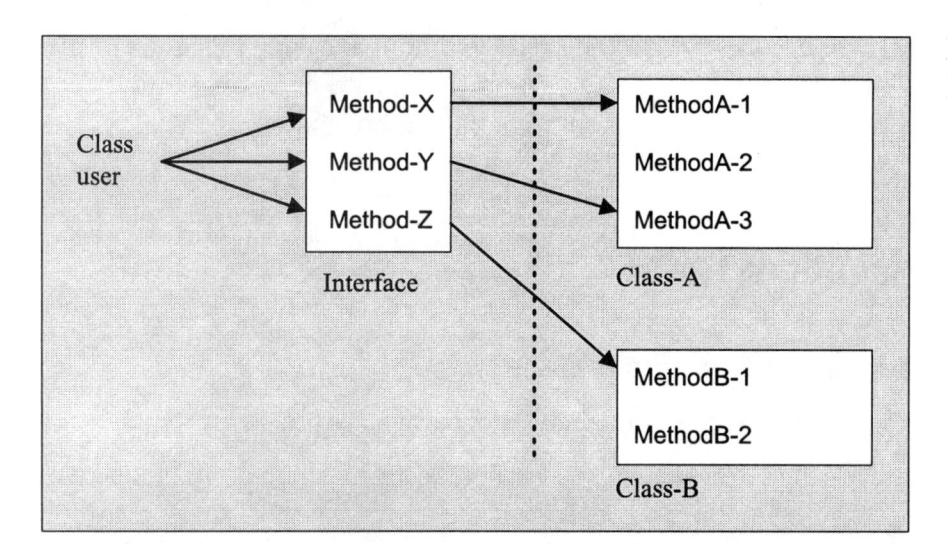

Figure 10-3.
Interface providing access to two classes.

Interface Definition General Form

Before looking at this example's interface definition, you should be aware of the allowable components of an interface definition as shown by the following general form.

>   [IDENTIFICATION DIVISION]
>   INTERFACE-ID. interface-name-1 [AS literal-1]
>   [INHERITS FROM {interface-name-2 ...}
>   [USING [parameter-name-1 ...}.
>   [options-paragraph]
>   [environment-division]
>   [procedure-division]
>   END INTERFACE interface-name-1.

Notice that this is considerably different than the allowable format for the class definition. As the function of an interface is to provide access to methods of a class, the factory/object distinction is irrelevant (consequently, you see no Factory or Object paragraphs). Furthermore, object data is meaningless to an interface so you see no provisions for a Data Division following the environment-division entry in the general form. However, the procedure-division entry provides for method definition, as you will see in the client example.

An Interface Example—Documentation

The client class of Chapter 9's Room17 serves as the basis for illustrating use of an interface definition. Refer to Figure 9-4 for the class-writer documentation and to Figure 9-7 for the class definition.

Interface documentation, intended for the class user, is shown here in Figure 10-4. Notice that only the public methods from the corresponding client class definition (Figure 9-4) are included—those that must be visible to the class user.

Interface: Client (r19-cln.cbl)
Description: Provides access to client information.

Methods	Parameters	Description
new	Returning: client object handle	Invokes base to create an instance of the client class. .

get-company-data	Using:
	  client object handle
	Returning:
	  company data
	    client name pic X(20)
	    street address pic X(20)
	    city pic X(12)
	    state pic X(02)
	    zip pic X(10)
		Returns basic company address data.

get-rep-data	Using:
	  client object handle
	Returning:
	  sales representative data
	    client-name pic X(20)
	    rep-name pic X(15)
	    rep-phone-number pic X(12)
		Returns sales representative name and phone number and the name of the client to whom this rep is assigned.

populate-the-client-object	Using:
	  client object handle
	  client data
	    client name pic X(20)
	    street address pic X(20)
	    city pic X(12)
	    state pic X(02)
	    zip pic X(10)
	    sales representative pic X(15)
	    rep phone number pic X(12)
		Invokes appropriate methods of the client class to populate object data.

Figure 10-4. Documentation for client interface.

The Client Interface

Source code for this example is stored in the folder Proj1001 as Room19. Be aware that one component of this application contains an element not yet supported by Net Express Version 3 (or a preliminary copy of Version 3.1). So a compiler error makes it impossible to run the application. Therefore, *the interface definition has not been tested*. Hopefully, later versions of Net Express will provide needed support for you to test and run this application.

Notice the following features of the complete ISO2000 compliant interface definition of the client interface listed in Figure 10-5.

- Line 15 includes an Interface-ID paragraph identifying this as an interface definition (as opposed to the Class-ID paragraph identifying a class definition).
- The as phrase identifies the external name of the file (r17-cln).
- As indicated by the general form, the interface does not include separate Factory and Object paragraphs nor does it include object data.

Proj1001 Room19

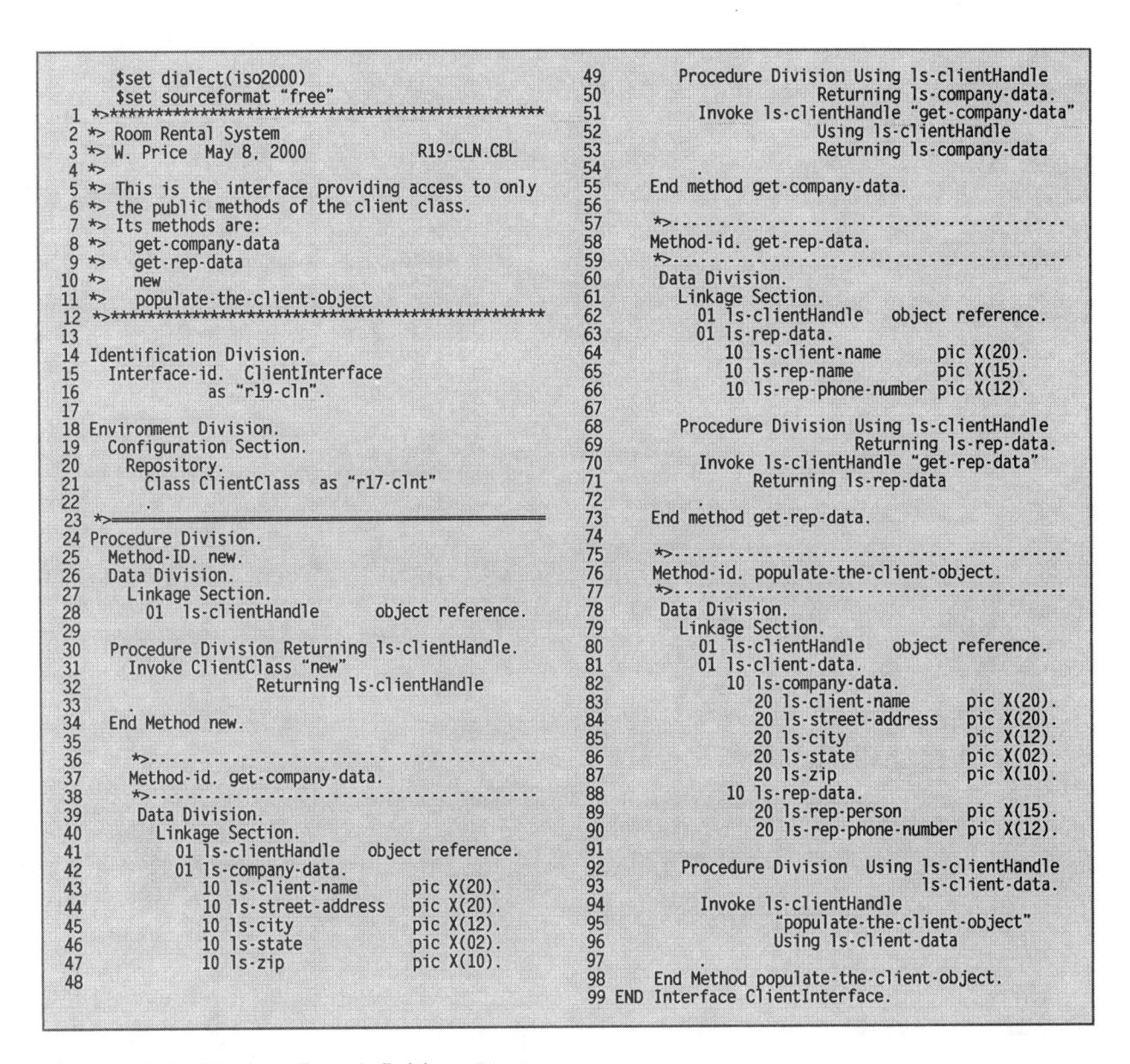

```cobol
       $set dialect(iso2000)
       $set sourceformat "free"
 1 *>***********************************************
 2 *> Room Rental System
 3 *> W. Price  May 8, 2000              R19-CLN.CBL
 4 *>
 5 *> This is the interface providing access to only
 6 *> the public methods of the client class.
 7 *> Its methods are:
 8 *>    get-company-data
 9 *>    get-rep-data
10 *>    new
11 *>    populate-the-client-object
12 *>***********************************************
13
14 Identification Division.
15   Interface-id. ClientInterface
16          as "r19-cln".
17
18 Environment Division.
19   Configuration Section.
20     Repository.
21       Class ClientClass as "r17-clnt"
22       .
23 *>=================================================
24 Procedure Division.
25   Method-ID. new.
26   Data Division.
27     Linkage Section.
28       01 ls-clientHandle       object reference.
29
30   Procedure Division Returning ls-clientHandle.
31     Invoke ClientClass "new"
32              Returning ls-clientHandle
33       .
34   End Method new.
35
36 *>-------------------------------------------------
37   Method-id. get-company-data.
38 *>-------------------------------------------------
39   Data Division.
40     Linkage Section.
41       01 ls-clientHandle       object reference.
42       01 ls-company-data.
43         10 ls-client-name      pic X(20).
44         10 ls-street-address   pic X(20).
45         10 ls-city             pic X(12).
46         10 ls-state            pic X(02).
47         10 ls-zip              pic X(10).
48
49   Procedure Division Using ls-clientHandle
50                  Returning ls-company-data.
51     Invoke ls-clientHandle "get-company-data"
52              Using ls-clientHandle
53              Returning ls-company-data
54       .
55   End method get-company-data.
56
57 *>-------------------------------------------------
58   Method-id. get-rep-data.
59 *>-------------------------------------------------
60   Data Division.
61     Linkage Section.
62       01 ls-clientHandle       object reference.
63       01 ls-rep-data.
64         10 ls-client-name      pic X(20).
65         10 ls-rep-name         pic X(15).
66         10 ls-rep-phone-number pic X(12).
67
68   Procedure Division Using ls-clientHandle
69                  Returning ls-rep-data.
70     Invoke ls-clientHandle "get-rep-data"
71              Returning ls-rep-data
72       .
73   End method get-rep-data.
74
75 *>-------------------------------------------------
76   Method-id. populate-the-client-object.
77 *>-------------------------------------------------
78   Data Division.
79     Linkage Section.
80       01 ls-clientHandle       object reference.
81       01 ls-client-data.
82         10 ls-company-data.
83           20 ls-client-name      pic X(20).
84           20 ls-street-address   pic X(20).
85           20 ls-city             pic X(12).
86           20 ls-state            pic X(02).
87           20 ls-zip              pic X(10).
88         10 ls-rep-data.
89           20 ls-rep-person       pic X(15).
90           20 ls-rep-phone-number pic X(12).
91
92   Procedure Division  Using ls-clientHandle
93                             ls-client-data.
94     Invoke ls-clientHandle
95              "populate-the-client-object"
96              Using ls-client-data
97       .
98   End Method populate-the-client-object.
99 END Interface ClientInterface.
```

Figure 10-5. The interface definition r19-cln.

- Since it must provide the class programmer all the functionality of the client class, the interface includes a method new (lines 25-34). New instantiates Client and returns the handle to the invoking program (via the linkage item ls-clientHandle).
- With the exception of one data item, the call parameters of each method correspond exactly to the corresponding parameters of Client's method invoked by the interface method. For instance, compare the parameter definition of lines 81-90 to the corresponding definitions in lines 121-130 of Figure 9-7.

As the interface has no object data, it has no capabilities for storing data that would be global to all methods of the interface—basically, the interface knows nothing. Specifically, the object handle of the Client object created by the new method is not directly available to the other methods of this interface. Therefore, it must be passed as a parameter for each method of this class. For instance, at line 68 you see the phrase Using ls-clientHandle and at line 70 you see it used as the object reference of the Invoke statement.

Room Manager

Room Manager listed in Figure 10-6 contains most of the same components as Chapter 9's r17-mgr.

- At line 24 you see the interface identified with the Interface phrase in exactly the same way classes are identified with the Class phrase. (As of the publication date of this book, Net Express did not support the needed Interface phrase required at line 24 with the result that the compiler does not recognize ClientInterface.)
- The interface ClientInterface invokes the interface method new which, as you know from Figure 10-5, instantiates the Client class. The object handle theClientHandle is stored as object data of this class and is therefore available to all methods of this class. This technique is common to many of the preceding managers classes.
- At line 57-60 the client object is populated via the populate-the-client-object method of the interface. Note that one of the parameters passed is the client object handle (line 59).
- Inspect the remainder of this class and you will see that it is identical to its counterpart r17-mgr except for inclusion of the client object handle as a parameter for all invokes to methods of the interface.

Inline Invoke

Object-oriented Cobol provides a shorthand technique for invoking methods called **inline invocation** allowing you to imbed an implicit invoke within a Cobol statement. (Note: Inline invocation is not implemented in Net Express, Version 3.) To illustrate, assume you've an application in which you must work with the data item lo-room-capacity that you obtain by adding 5 to the room's capacity. Your code sequence might look like the following

```
01 lo-room-capacity    pic 99.
01 lo-max-capacity     pic 99.
...
    Invoke theRoomHandle "get-room-capacity" Returning lo-room-capacity
    Add 5 to lo-room-capacity giving lo-max-capacity.
```

Inline invocation allows you to extract the object reference and the method name from the Invoke and insert them directly within the Add statement as follows.

```
01 lo-max-capacity     pic 99.
...
    Add 5 to theRoomHandle :: "get-room-capacity" giving lo-max-capacity
```

Notice that the data item lo-room-capacity of the first example is replace by the object reference (theRoomHandle) and the method name ("get-room-capacity") separated by a pair of colons. You need not define a separate data item to hold the value returned by the method (lo-room-capacity in the first example) as the compiler automatically generates a temporary work area to hold the returned value. Obviously, the method you specify in an inline invoke must include a Returning phrase specifying a data item for inclusion in the statement action.

You can use an inline invoke in anywhere the general form designates an identifier so long as that identifier is not a receiving item. Following are two additional examples.

Conventional Invoke with work-variable.

```
01 lo-room-capacity     pic 99.
...
Invoke theRoomHandle "get-room-capacity" Returning lo-room-capacity
If lo-room-capacity > 30
...
```

Equivalent form using inline invoke

```
If theRoomHandle :: "get-room-capacity" > 30
...
```

Valid and invalid Move examples

```
01 lo-room-capacity-save    pic 99.
...
*> Valid action—moves returned value to save data item.
Move theRoomHandle :: "get-room-capacity" to lo-room-capacity-save

*> Invalid action—not used as a receiving item.
Move lo-room-capacity-save to theRoomHandle :: "get-room-capacity"
```

Although not illustrated by the preceding examples, the inline invoke can also involve input parameters, that is, the Using phrase. Look at the following minor variation of code taken from RoomManager (Figure 10-6, lines 107-111).

```
Invoke DataBaseInterface
        "read-client-database"
        Using ls-client-number
        Returning lo-record-found-sw
If lo-record-found-sw = "Y"
...
```

The Using data item is incorporated into the inline invoke by enclosing the parameter (or list of parameters) enclosed within parentheses as follows.

```
If DataBaseInterface :: "read-client-database" (ls-client-number) = "Y"
...
```

```cobol
        $set dialect(iso2000)
        $set sourceformat "free"
  1 *>***********************************************
  2 *> Client Rental System
  3 *> W. Price   May 8              R19-MGR.CBL
  4 *>
  5 *> ClientManager handles access to the classes of
  6 *> the Client component of the Room system. It is
  7 *> identical R17-MGR except access to the client
  8 *> class is though the interface class
  9 *>   ClientInterface.
 10 *> Methods:
 11 *>    create-client-object
 12 *>    process-user-requests
 13 *>    process-this-request
 14 *>    process-user-selections
 15 *>***********************************************
 16
 17 Identification Division.
 18   Class-ID.  ClientManager
 19             as "r19-mgr".
 20
 21 Environment Division.
 22   Configuration Section.
 23   Repository.
 24       Interface ClientInterface as "r19-cln"
 25       Class UserInterface       as "r17-ui"
 26       Class DatabaseInterface   as "r17-dbi"
 27       .
 28 *>=================================================
 29 FACTORY.
 30   Data Division.
 31     Working-Storage Section.
 32       01 theClientHandle    object reference.
 33
 34   Procedure Division.
 35     *>------------------------------------------
 36     Method-id. create-client-object.
 37     *>------------------------------------------
 38       Data Division.
 39         Working-Storage Section.
 40           01 ws-client-object-data.
 41              10 ws-company-data .
 42                 20 ws-company-name    pic X(20).
 43                 20 ws-street-address  pic X(20).
 44                 20 ws-city-state-zip  pic X(26).
 45                 20 ws-city            pic X(12).
 46                 20 ws-state           pic X(02).
 47                 20 ws-zip             pic X(10).
 48              10 ws-rep-data.
 49                 20 ws-rep-name        pic X(15).
 50                 20 ws-rep-phone-number pic X(12).
 51
 52       Procedure Division.
 53         Invoke DataBaseInterface "get-client-data"
 54                    Returning ws-client-object-data
 55         Invoke ClientInterface "new"
 56                    Returning theClientHandle
 57         Invoke ClientInterface
 58                    "populate-the-client-object"
 59                    Using theClientHandle
 60                          ws-client-object-data
 61       End Method create-client-object.
 62
 63     *>------------------------------------------
 64     Method-id. process-user-requests.
 65     *>------------------------------------------
 66       Data Division.
 67         Working-Storage Section.
 68           01 ws-client-number       pic x(04).
 69              88 ws-no-more-client-requests value spaces.
 70           01 ws-process-complete-message pic X(40)
 71                    value "Processing complete".
 72
 73       Procedure Division.
 74         Invoke DatabaseInterface "connect-to-data"
 75         Perform with test after
 76                 until ws-no-more-client-requests
 77            Invoke UserInterface
 78                    "query-for-client-number"
 79                    Returning ws-client-number
 80            If ws-no-more-client-requests
 81               Continue
 82            Else
 83               Invoke Self "process-this-request"
 84                    Using ws-client-number
 85            End-If *>no-more-client-requests
 86         End-Perform *>with test after
 87         Invoke DatabaseInterface
 88                    "disconnect-from-data"
 89         Invoke UserInterface "display-message"
 90                    Using ws-process-complete-message
 91
 92       End Method process-user-requests.
 93
 94     *>------------------------------------------
 95     Method-id. process-this-request.
 96     *>------------------------------------------
 97       Data Division.
 98         Working-Storage Section.
 99           01 ws-record-found-sw      pic X(01).
100              88 ws-record-found         value "Y".
101           01 ws-invalid-client-message pic X(40)
102                    value "Database error - Data not found".
103         Linkage Section.
104           01 ls-client-number        pic X(04).
105
106       Procedure Division Using ls-client-number.
107         Invoke DataBaseInterface
108                    "read-client-database"
109                    Using ls-client-number
110                    Returning ws-record-found-sw
111         If ws-record-found
112            Invoke Self "create-client-object"
113            Invoke Self "process-user-selections"
114         Else
115            Invoke UserInterface "display-message"
116                    Using ws-invalid-client-message
117         End-If *>ws-record-found
118       End Method process-this-request.
119
120     *>------------------------------------------
121     Method-id. process-user-selections.
122     *>------------------------------------------
123       Data Division.
124         Working-Storage Section.
125           01 ws-company-data.
126              10 ws-client-name      pic X(20).
127              10 ws-street-address   pic X(20).
128              10 ws-city             pic X(12).
129              10 ws-state            pic X(02).
130              10 ws-zip              pic X(10).
131           01 ws-rep-data.
132              10 ws-company-name     pic X(20).
133              10 ws-rep-name         pic X(15).
134              10 ws-rep-phone-number pic X(12).
135           01 ws-menu-choice         pic X(01).
136              88  ws-company-data-option  value "C".
137              88  ws-rep-data-option      value "R".
138              88  ws-exit-option-loop     value "X".
139
140       Procedure Division.
141         Perform with test after
142                 until ws-exit-option-loop
143            Invoke UserInterface
144                    "get-menu-selection"
145                    Returning ws-menu-choice
146            Evaluate TRUE
147            When ws-company-data-option
148               Invoke ClientInterface "get-company-data"
149                    Using theClientHandle
150                    Returning ws-company-data
151               Invoke UserInterface "display-company-data"
152                    Using ws-company-data
153            When ws-rep-data-option
154               Invoke ClientInterface "get-rep-data"
155                    Using theClientHandle
156                    Returning ws-rep-data
157               Invoke UserInterface "display-rep-data"
158                    Using ws-rep-data
159            When other
160               Set ws-exit-option-loop to true
161            End-evaluate *>TRUE
162         End-Perform *>until ws-exit-option-loop
163         .
164       End Method process-user-selections.
165     *>------------------------------------------
166 END FACTORY.
167 END CLASS ClientManager.
```

Figure 10-6. Room Manager with an Interface class

Property Clause

Data Name Qualification

By now you realize that you have access (both read or write) to data of an object through methods of the class from which the object was created. However, there is a second mechanism by which you have access to data of an object: through the **Property clause**. For an idea of how this technique works, let's diverge for a moment and consider qualification of data names, a familiar Cobol concept.

In the following code you see the data item field-3 defined in both first-record and second-record. However, reference to field-3 in the Move statement is not ambiguous because the operand includes the qualifier of second-record.

```
Working-Storage Section.
01   first-record.
     10   field-1      pic X(10).
     10   field-2      pic X(32).
     10   field-3      pic 99V99.
01   second-record.
     10   ssn          pic X(11).
     10   field-3      pic X(16).

Procedure Division.
     Move spaces to field-3 of second-record
```

Qualification to an Object

Proj1002
Room20

The final example of this chapter, Room20, provides access to an object's data by, in a sense, using qualification to reference individual data items. This example includes two modules: a driver and a room class. Driver performs three actions: instantiates Room, populates the room object (moves data to the object), and accesses the room capacity (obtains data from the object).

First, look at Driver's Move statement (lines 38 and 39) in Figure 10-7 and you see that the second operand contains a qualifier.

```
room-record of theRoomHandle
```

Here the data item room-record is qualified as pertaining to the room object created at line 34. Thus data of the-room-data is "moved" to the field room-record of the room object. Similarly, the Display of line 45 accesses room-capacity of the room object through identical qualification.

However, as both of these data items are external to the current program, some means is required to designate them as an external references. Object-oriented Cobol accomplishes this with the Property phrase—see lines 17 and 18.

Other Cobol Goodies

```cobol
          $set dialect(iso2000)
          $set sourceformat "free"
 1 *>*****************************************
 2 *> Room Rental System
 3 *> W. Price  May 12, 2000        R20-DRVR.CBL
 4 *>
 5 *> This example illustrates using the Property
 6 *> to access data from an object.
 7 *>*****************************************
 8
 9 Identification Division.
10     Program-ID.  Room20Driver
11              as "r20-drvr"
12              .
13 Environment Division.
14     Configuration Section.
15     Repository.
16         Class RoomClass as "r20-room"
17         Property room-capacity
18         Property room-record
19         .
20 Data Division.
21
22     Working-Storage Section.
23
24     01 theRoomHandle    object reference RoomClass.
25     01 the-room-data.
26        10 room-number         pic X(03) value "100".
27        10 std-config-price    pic 9(03) value 225.
28        10 spec-config-price   pic 9(03) value 385.
29        10 room-discount       pic v9(02) value .05.
30        10 the-capacity        pic 9(02) value 38.
31
32 Procedure Division.
33
34     Invoke RoomClass "New" returning theRoomHandle
35
36     *> Populate room object through data item
37     *> defined with Property clause
38     Move the-room-data to
39          room-record of theRoomHandle
40
41     Display "Room capacity from Property is "
42                         with no advancing
43
44     *>Get the room capacity through Property
45     Display room-capacity of theRoomHandle
46     Stop run
47     .
```

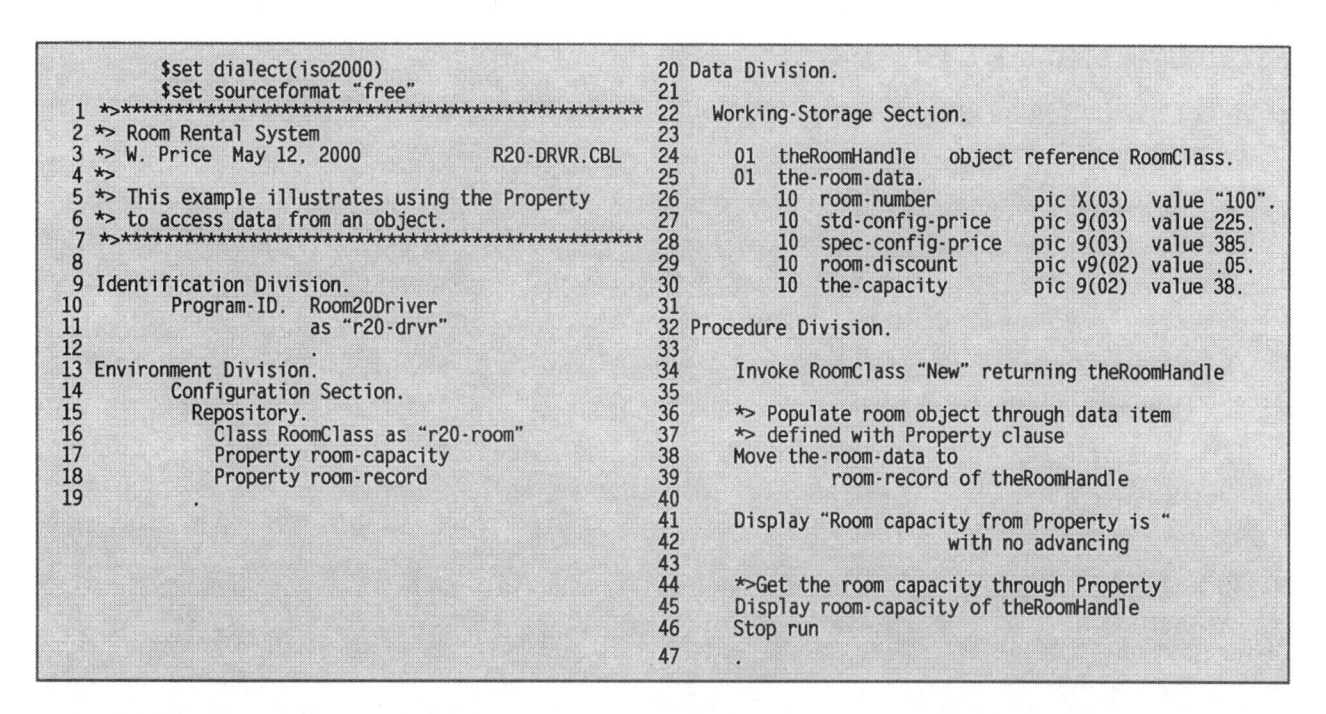

Figure 10-7. Access to an object using Property—r20-drvr.

- The Property phrase is a Repository entry.
- Each Property phrase can list only one property reference.
- Whenever the property reference is an object handle (as in these examples), then the Usage clause defining that handle must include the class name—see line 24 and refer to the following description.

All object handles you've seen created in preceding examples use untyped object handles. For example, DBI has always included

    01 theRoomHandle object reference

and used it as the reference to its instantiation of RoomClass. But, if the logic of the application so required under certain conditions, code of DBI could use that handle to instantiate some other class. However, if you **type** an object handle then that handle can be used only for objects of the designated type. For example, if you included the following in a class definition, then theRoomHandle could be used only to create instances of RoomClass (or its subclasses).

    01 theRoomHandle object reference RoomClass

Get and Set Methods and the Property Clause

Room's class definition (r20-room) shown in Figure 10-8 includes the following methods.

- A programmer written method (return-room-prices) to return the room prices to the invoking program.
- A pair of **Get** and **Set** methods included by Net Express to return and update, respectively, the room-capacity.
- A pair of **Get** and **Set** methods included by Net Express to return and update, respectively, room's object data

First look at line 31 in which the definition for the data item room-capacity contains a property clause. It is this designation that allows you to reference the data

```
            $set dialect(iso2000)
            $set sourceformat "free"
            >>Repository update on
 1  *>***********************************************
 2  *> Room Rental System
 3  *> W. Price May 12, 2000                R20-ROOM.CBL
 4  *>
 5  *> Illustrating the Property clause
 6  *>***********************************************
 7
 8  Identification Division.
 9      Class-id. RoomClass as "r20-room"
10                inherits from BaseClass.
11
12  Environment Division.
13    Configuration Section.
14      Repository.
15        Class BaseClass as "base"
16          .
17  *>─────────────
18  FACTORY.
19    Working-Storage Section.
20  END FACTORY.
21
22  OBJECT.
23
24    Data Division.
25      Working-Storage Section.
26        01  room-data.
27            10  room-number       pic X(03).
28            10  std-config-price  pic 9(03).
29            10  spec-config-price pic 9(03).
30            10  room-discount     pic v9(02).
31            10  room-capacity     pic 9(02) property.
32        01  room-record redefines room-data pic X(13)
33                                            property.
34
35    Procedure Division.
36      Method-ID. return-room-prices.
37        Data Division.
38          Linkage Section.
39            01  ls-room-prices.
40                10  ls-std-config-price pic 9(03).
41                10  ls-spec-config-price pic 9(03).
42        Procedure Division.
43          Move std-config-price to ls-std-config-price
44          Move spec-config-price to ls-spec-config-price
45          .
46      End Method return-room-prices.
47
48  *>
49      METHOD-ID. GET PROPERTY ROOM-CAPACITY.
50      DATA DIVISION.
51      LINKAGE SECTION.
52      01 LS1 PICTURE 9(2).
53      PROCEDURE DIVISION RETURNING LS1.
54          MOVE ROOM-CAPACITY TO LS1
55          EXIT METHOD.
56      END METHOD.
57  *>
58  *>
59      METHOD-ID. SET PROPERTY ROOM-CAPACITY.
60      DATA DIVISION.
61      LINKAGE SECTION.
62      01 LS1 PICTURE 9(2).
63      PROCEDURE DIVISION USING LS1.
64          MOVE LS1 TO ROOM-CAPACITY
65          EXIT METHOD.
66      END METHOD.
67  *>
68  *>
69      METHOD-ID. GET PROPERTY ROOM-RECORD.
70      DATA DIVISION.
71      LINKAGE SECTION.
72      01 LS1 PICTURE X(13).
73      PROCEDURE DIVISION RETURNING LS1.
74          MOVE ROOM-RECORD TO LS1
75          EXIT METHOD.
76      END METHOD.
77  *>
78  *>
79      METHOD-ID. SET PROPERTY ROOM-RECORD.
80      DATA DIVISION.
81      LINKAGE SECTION.
82      01 LS1 PICTURE X(13).
83      PROCEDURE DIVISION USING LS1.
84          MOVE LS1 TO ROOM-RECORD
85          EXIT METHOD.
86      END METHOD.
87  *>
88  *>
89  END OBJECT.
90  END CLASS RoomClass.
```

Figure 10-8. Get and Set methods—r20-room.

item externally through qualification, for instance, in the Display of line 45 of Figure 10-7.

```
Display room-capacity of theRoomHandle
```

It also causes Net Express to insert Get and Set methods into the class definition—see lines 49-56 and 59-66. When the above Display is executed, Net Express automatically invokes the Get method. If Driver included a statement such as

```
Move 44 to room-capacity of theRoomHandle
```

Net Express would automatically Invoke the Set method for room-capacity.

Similarly, the Property clause on room-record (lines 32 and 33) cause Net Express to generate the Get and Set pair of lines 69-76 and 79-86. The Set method is automatically invoked by execution of Driver's Move statement at lines 38 and 39 (Figure 10-8). Be aware that you will not see these methods in your original source code as they are only inserted under direct control of Net Express.

Perhaps you wondered why the Property clause is not assigned to room-data rather than room-record, the result of a redefines. The answer is that syntax rules do not permit the Property clause to be used with a group item.

Frequently when using Property, you do not want both Get and Set methods inserted for a given object data item. For instance, you may want property read access to room-capacity, but not write access because during normal processing changing the room capacity is not permitted. You prevent inclusion of the Set property as follows.

```
10 room-capacity  pic 9(02) property no set
```

Similarly, you can prevent inclusion of the Get property with the no get phrase.

Special note:
The following two problems exist with the original release of Net Express 3.0. Presumably these are corrected in WebSync and/or later releases.

1. Inclusion of either the no set and no get produces a compiler error.
2. Any class that includes a Property clause must be compiled before any other program that refers to that property. For instance, r20-room must be compiled before r20-drvr as the external references (for room-capacity and room-record) must be established before they are referenced.

The RDF File

The final key to using the Property clause is the following compiler directive from the third line of r20-room (Figure 10-8).

```
>>Repository update on
```

This directive instructs the compiler to create an RDF file (check the project directory and you will see r20-room.rdf). It is used by the compiler when checking other classes or a driver that refers to that class in some way.

Summing Up

Project Summary

Room19 Proj1001 incorporates an interface to limit access to only public methods of Room17's Client class (from Chapter 9).

Room20 Proj1002 is a minimum application consisting only of a driver and a room class. It utilizes the Property phrase and illustrates automatic generation of Get and Set methods for access to object data items.

General Summary

Although Cobol does not include the capability to designate methods of a class as private (thereby restricting access from other classes), an interface can be used to serve that purpose.

An interface definition contains neither object data nor the Factory/Object distinction. It is composed primarily of methods that provide access to methods of one or more objects

The inline Invoke allows you to replace a "receiving" item of a conventional Cobol statement with an object reference and a method name—this is called an **implicit invoke**. The invoked method must include a Returning phrase.

Including a Property clause in the definition of any object data item causes the compiler to generate Get and Set methods (within the class) thereby providing read and write access to that data item.

Coming Up

One of the features of object-oriented languages is the notion of code reusability. That is, you can write generalized classes, place them in libraries, and have them available to all applications. The next chapter is devoted to a particular type of class library: collection classes. You will see different types of collection classes. When you begin studying them, some will have a familiar ring, for example, the array and the dictionary. Others will be new to you and, perhaps, appear a little strange such as the bag.

Collection Classes

Chapter Contents

The Concept of the Collection Class 240
    The Table as a Container 240
    Simplifying Examples 241
Micro Focus Collection Classes 242
    About Collection Classes 242
    Collection Class Types 242
    Method Name Conventions 244
    Collection Class Constructor Methods 244
    Collection Class Instance Methods 245
    About Parameters 245
The Bag Collection Class 246
    About Bags 246
    About Room21 246
    The Room Class—r21-room 248
    Creating and Using a Bag—r21-drvr 248
Using an Iterator on a Bag 251
    Principles of the Callback 251
    Iterating the Callback Method 252
The Select Iterator—Room22 252
    Sample Display 252
    Room's Select Callback Method 253
    Invoking the Select Method—r22-drvr 253
Returning Results From an Iterator 254
    Creating an Intrinsic Data Class 254
    Callback with Optional Parameters 256
    About Room23 257
    Using an Optional Parameter in the Callback—r23-drvr 258
    The Callback Method compute-capacity from r23-tran 259
Preview of Next Three Examples 260
Using the Array Collection Class—Room24 260
    About Room24 260
    Driver—Room24 261
Searching an Array for a Desired Block—Room25 263
    About Room25 263
    The Calendar Class 264
Using a Dictionary—Room26 266
    About Cobol Tables 266
    About the Dictionary Collection Class 267
    Multiple Room Calendars—Room26 267
    Creating a Dictionary 268
    Loading the Dictionary 270
    Accessing a Dictionary 271
    Room Manager—r26-mgr 272
More About Collection Classes 272
    Features of the Micro Focus Collection Classes 272
    Some Other Typical Collection Class Instance Methods 274
Summing Up 275
    Project Summary 275
    General Summary 276
Assignments 276

Chapter 11

Chapter Introduction

This chapter is devoted to collection classes, a mechanism that provides means for grouping and operating on data and objects. The Cobol table (array as more commonly called in computing) is a simple such mechanism. To set the stage for investigating some of OOCobol's collection class features, two table processing examples involving the room calendar are presented. Both examples are expanded to illustrate a particular type of OOCobol collection class. From this chapter you will learn about the following

- The general characteristics of collection classes.
- How to use the Bag, Array, and Dictionary collection classes.
- Creating intrinsic classes.
- Using associations.
- Using callbacks with iterator methods.

The Concept of the Collection Class

The Table as a Container

Let's step back for a moment and consider the nature of the Cobol table, or array as it is more commonly called in computing. A table, such as that defined by the following statement taken from Calendar (refer to Figure 9-19), is a device for storing a set of data values.

```
01  room-calendar-table.
    10  room-calendar-entry occurs 10
                indexed by room-index.
        20  room-number       pic X(03).
        20  client-number     pic X(04)
                occurs 31 times
                indexed by day-index.
```

Characteristics of this table are:

1. There are 10 entries for `room-calendar-entry` (as designated by the occurs 10 clause).
2. Each of the 10 `room-calendar-entry` entries consists of two elements: `room-number` defined by the pic X(03) and `client-number` which itself includes 31 entries—each pic X(04).
3. Each room-calendar "row" as well as each room number is accessible by its data name and the index `room-index`.
4. Each client-number entry is accessible by the pair of indexes `room-index` and `day-index`.
5. The entire table is accessible by the table name `room-calendar-table`.

In a broad sense, you can think of a table as a **container** that can hold a **collection** of data—see Figure 11-1. Associated with this type of container is a special verb, Search, that you can use for searching the table. Furthermore, some 1989 intrinsic functions operate on tables to determine such things as the mean, the smallest entry, and so on. In a nutshell, you have "something" and procedures associated with that something.

As you learned in Chapter 4, you are not limited to "conventional" data (pic X and pic 9) when creating tables. For instance, the driver r06-drv3.cbl (Figure 4-14) uses the following definition to create five concurrently existing object handles.

```
01  theRoomHandle object reference
                occurs 5 times.
```

Object reference data items are internal address references and are fixed in size as determined by the implementor—we as programmers have no control over this. Therefore, you do not need a pic when defining the array (see the above and Figure 11-2).

Summarizing, tables, we have (1) a "container" and (2) "procedures" that operate on elements in that container. In a broad sense of the term, you have a primitive container or **collection class** that provides means for storing and operating on multiple data entities.

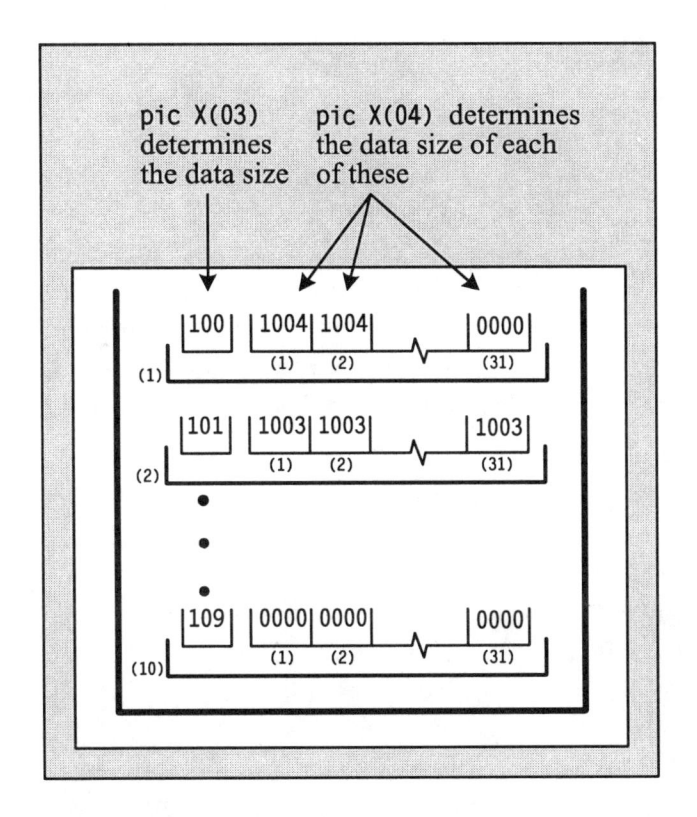

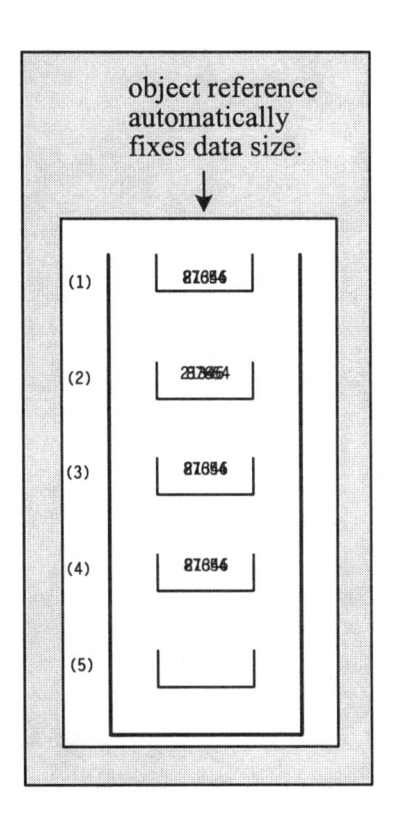

Figure 11-1.
A multi-dimension array.

Figure 11-2.
An array of objects handles.

Although we can group objects using conventional table syntax, we would be using a relatively mundane grouping tool (tables) for a very elegant structure (objects). As you have learned from this book, objects denote not only physical entities (data) but also behavior (methods of the class). Therefore, it would seem logical that an object-oriented language would implement a grouping structure that itself has behavior: that structure is called a **collection**. Collections, of which there are several types, are essentially "smart" containers for objects.

Simplifying Examples

As you will discover, the collection classes topic is probably the most difficult of any presented in this book. With that in mind, I've taken great care to present the concepts using the simplest possible examples. As a consequence, you will find the applications somewhat contrived and perhaps a bit simple-minded. Furthermore, to reduce the number of components you must look at, I've minimized the number of classes for each example. To that end, you will find most of the code representing collection class concepts in the driver program (contrary to previous "full" applications that center around a manager class). Keep in mind that this is done solely to place the focus on the topic at hand—using collection classes.

Micro Focus Collection Classes

About Collection Classes

Collection classes allow you to create objects to hold a group of related and sometimes unrelated items (conventional Cobol data or other objects). They are similar to the conventional Cobol table but are vastly superior: for instance, they can grow or shrink in size, they include functionality you would otherwise need to program yourself, and they include iterative techniques unavailable with conventional Cobol. The Micro Focus collection classes can be classified according to the following characteristics.

- **Indexed or non-indexed.** Depending on the particular class, you can specifiy a desired element by its position or by its index value (much like accessing elements of a conventional Cobol table).
- **Automatically or manually growable.** All Micro Focus collection sizes can increase or decrease in size dynamically (during execution). For most, the size increases automatically as the collection object becomes full. For two of them, the programmer must designate the increase or decrease in size.
- **Duplicates allowed or not allowed.** Most allow duplicate elements; one does not. You can think of the latter as corresponding to an indexed file with an alternate record key. By default you cannot enter two or more records with the same alternate key field (duplicate entries). However, you can specifiy `with duplicates` in the `alternate record` clause thereby permitting such duplication.

Collection Class Types

The collection classes implemented in both Personal COBOL for Windows and Net Express are listed by their hierarchy in Figure 11-3 where public classes (those you will instantiate) are shown in boldface. The name of each is followed by class program's filename enclosed in parentheses. [You will find the source code for these classes in NetExpress\Base\Source\Basecl (Net Express) and PCOBWIN\Classlib (Personal COBOL).] Three of the classes are identified as abstract, meaning that they are not themselves instantiated but contain methods inherited by subordinate classes. One is identified as private, a Micro Focus designation meaning that it is not accessed directly by the class user but by other classes.

Most collection classes can contain either **intrinsic data** (data items defined by a picture clause) or objects. Following is a brief description of each type.

Bag—Properties: Non-indexed, automatically growable, duplicates permitted. As you might guess from the name, a Bag is completely unordered collection of data elements. It is as if you simply "toss" entities into a bag now and worry about them later. For instance, you may want to capture transaction data (each transaction an object) from a multiuser system by the simplest means possible then process the data at a later time. Or you may need to bundle data values (objects) and send them

Figure 11-3.
Micro Focus
collection classes.

```
Collection (collectn)—abstract
    Bag (bag.cbl)
        SequencedCollection (sequence)—private
            ArrayedCollection (arrayed)—abstract
                Array (array)
                    CharacterArray (carray.cbl)
                DynamicArrayedCollection (dynarray)—abstract
                    OrderedCollection (ordrdcll.cbl)
                    SortedCollection (srtdclln.cbl)
        ValueSet (valueset.cbl)
            IdentitySet (iset.cbl)
        Dictionary (dictinry.cbl)
            IdentityDictionary (idictnry.cbl)
```

to a remote site for processing. Creating a bag object and storing other objects in the bag is a versatile means for doing these operations.

Array—Properties: Indexed, manually growable, duplicates permitted. An Array allows you to store either intrinsic data or objects in the same way you store data in a conventional Cobol table. Entries are accessible by their index (essentially a subscript).

CharacterArray—Properties: Indexed, manually growable, duplicates permitted. The CharacterArray collection class is designed to provide common functions one encounters in string processing plus many more functions generally associated with collection classes. This collection class may contain only **intrinsic data** (conventional Cobol pic X). All other collection classes may contain either intrinsic data or objects.

OrderedCollection—Properties: Indexed, automatically growable, duplicates permitted. An OrderedCollection manages the storage of elements in the order in which they were added to the collection. One of the main advantages of OrderedCollections over Arrays is that they can grow dynamically as more elements are added. You can use OrderedCollections to implement stacks and queues.

SortedCollection—Properties: Indexed, automatically growable, duplicates permitted. A SortedCollection provides indexed storage of elements. Elements are stored in an order determined by a sort method. By default, elements are stored in ascending order.

ValueSet—Properties: Indexed, automatically growable, duplicates permitted. A ValueSet stores non-ordered objects or intrinsics in a collection.

IdentitySet—Properties: Indexed, automatically growable, duplicates permitted. ValueSet and IdentitySet only differ in the way they determine duplicate elements. ValueSets compare the values of elements and disallows duplicate values; IdentitySets compare object references, and disallow storing the same object more than once.

Dictionary—Properties: Indexed by key entry, automatically growable, duplicates permitted. Dictionary and is a special type of collection that stores key/data pairs. You will see an example of a Dictionary in this chapter. They determine duplicate keys in the same way that ValueSet and IdentitySet determine duplicate elements.

IdentityDictionary—Properties: Indexed key entry, automatically growable, duplicates permitted. An IdentityDictionary is more specific than a Dictionary as it compares object references instead of values.

Illustrating all the collection classes and demonstrating their methods is beyond the scope of this book. (That task alone could easily require a book of its own.) However, the classes Bag, Array, and Dictionary are used in this chapter to give you a brief insight to collection classes and how you use them.

Method Name Conventions

As you know, data item naming conventions of this book include the following.

- Object method names: All lowercase with words separated by a hyphen, for instance, populate-room-object.
- Object handles: Camelback (first letter lowercase, other first letter of word uppercase) with no hyphens, for instance, theRoomHandle.
- Class names: First letter of each word comprising the name is uppercase with no hyphens, for instance, RoomClass.

In contrast, Micro Focus uses camelback for class library method names. For instance, the character array class includes the method lessThanOrEqual. Using all lowercase (the convention of this book) gives lessthanorequal, in which the individual words do not stand out. Therefore, in this chapter, to improve readability and avoid conflict with Micro Focus class libraries their method naming convention is used.

Collection Class Constructor Methods

To use a conventional table in a program, you must define it as intrinsic data in the Data Division. The compiler reserves memory and the table is ready to use. Collection classes are much more dynamic. To implement a collection class, you must:

1. Instantiate the class (a runtime action) thereby creating an instance of the class (a collection object).
2. Invoke methods of the class.

You can create a collection to store either objects (a collection of **references**) or intrinsic data (a collection of values). A collection of references can contain more than one type of object, whereas a collection of values is initialized for storing data of a particular type and length. The collection classes include several methods for creating their instances. Two **constructor methods** you will examine in this book are the following.

OfReferences—instantiates a collection class for holding objects.
OfValues—instantiates a collection class for holding intrinsic data.

Collection Class Instance Methods

Each of the collection classes includes many instance methods. For example, the class Array has 65 (including those inherited from its superclasses). Collection class methods may be divided into the following nine basic categories based on their function.

- Adding—Add elements to a collection.
- Changing—Change the size (capacity) of a collection.
- Converting—Convert from one type of collection to another.
- Copying—Make copies of all or part of a collection.
- Inquiring—Inquire about the condition of a collection.
- Iterating—Perform a predefined or user-defined action on each element in the collection.
- Removing—Remove elements from the collection or destroy the collection.
- Retrieving—Retrieve elements from the collection.
- Testing—Test for conditions of the collection: for instance, presence of an element, emptiness of the collection, or the number of occurrence of an element.

About Parameters

Assume that you have written a class whose object data is a table of numeric data. One of your methods returns the sum of elements between two designated points of the table. The Invoke statement might look something like:

```
Invoke theObject "sum-elements"
              Using beginning-element, ending-element
              Returning the-total
```

What about the nature of the data items serving as parameters? Normally we think of these parameters as being the same data type and size as the corresponding parameters in the invoked Procedure Division's header. Interestingly, the Standard says that the correspondence between parameters of the Invoke (or Call) and the invoked (called) Procedure Division header is established on a positional basis. However, it says nothing about respective lengths and data types of the corresponding parameters. For the purpose of ensuring uniformity throughout their class library, Micro Focus uses two special data types that produce four-byte binary items. They are illustrated by the following examples.

```
01  a-pic-x-sample    pic X(04) comp-5.
01  a-pic-9-sample    pic S9(09) comp-5.
```

The comp-5 usage is a Micro Focus variation of the Standard comp (binary) usage. When used with a pic X definition (as in the first example) it generates a binary data item with a length in bytes equal to the number of "X"s in the pic—four in the preceding example. Being in binary, the data item can hold an unsigned number of up to nine digits. When used with pic 9 (as in the second example), the compiler reserves sufficient storage to hold, in binary, the number of decimal digits indicated by the number of "9"s in the pic. A provision is made for the sign if the pic so indicates. In the second example, pic S9(09) generates a four-byte data item. If you inspect the class library source code, you will find that some methods use the pic X form and others use the pic 9 form. Micro Focus technical support has indicated (via email to me) that they can be used interchangeably and suggested using the `pic X` form. In descriptions of this book, the term "four-byte `comp-5`" is used. It refers to either of these two forms.

Some collection-class methods return true-false (Boolean) values. For these, the standard usage is as illustrated in the following example.

```
01  true-false-data-item   pic X comp-5.
    88  true-false-value      value 1
                              false 0.
```

As you can see, a true result is indicated by numeric 1 and a false value by a numeric 0.

The Bag Collection Class

About Bags

The first collection class you will learn about in this book is the bag, the most general type of collection. As you might guess from the name, a **bag** is completely unordered collection of data elements. Think of an array without subscripts with which you have provisions for inserting new elements but no means for addressing an individual element. It is as if you simply "toss" entities into a bag now and worry about them later. For instance, you may want to capture transaction data (each transaction an object) from a multiuser system by the simplest means possible then process the data at a later time. Or you may need to bundle data values (objects) and send them to a remote site for processing. Creating a bag object and storing other objects in the bag is a versatile means for doing these operations.

The first of three bag projects is a simple demonstration of basic bag methods. It also illustrates iterator methods, a powerful technique whereby an operation can be executed acting on all objects of a collection.

About Room21

The bag examples of this chapter utilize the simplest possible framework to illustrate principles of collection classes. To that end, each of these three examples utilize the structure of Figure 11-4's "conceptual" class diagram. In this example, processing normally associated with UI and manager classes is all contained within Driver. Furthermore, in place of an input data file and a file processor, all data is accessed from `Data` statements within DBI.

Proj1101
Room21

The sequence of actions performed by Driver of Room21, under keyboard control, is as follows.

1. Access data for a user requested room and create a room object. Place the room object in a bag. Save the room object handle.
2. Repeat Step 1 one or more times, except don't save the object handle.
3. Ask the bag how many objects it contains; display this value.
4. Remove the first object placed in the bag then check the size again.
5. Execute an iterative method to display the bag contents.

Collection Classes 247

Figure 11-4.
A "conceptual" class diagram for Room21.

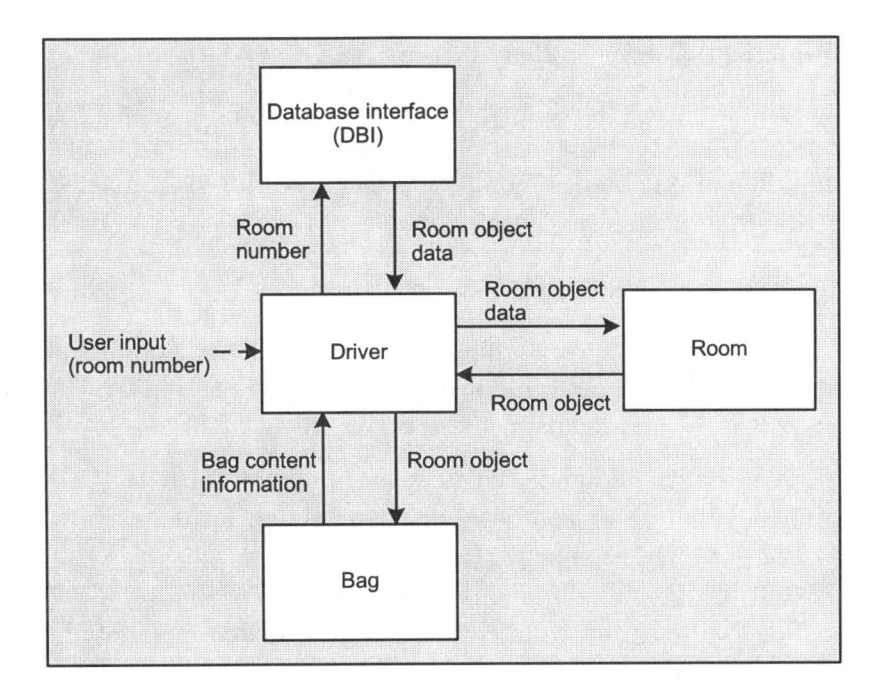

Output from a typical run are annotated in Figure 11-5—following is a description of each annotated segment.

```
Enter the room number> 105
Room capacity 47
Enter the room number (blank to end)> 103
Room capacity 43
Enter the room number (blank to end)> 106
Room capacity 49
Enter the room number (blank to end)> 104
Room capacity 43
Enter the room number (blank to end)>

Number of rooms you accessed: 04

+0000000004 objects in bag.

First bag entry has been removed
+0000000003 objects now in bag.

       Reg   Spec
Room  Price Price Capacity
103    280   465     43
106    350   610     49
104    305   505     43
```

1. The user is prompted to enter a room number (user entries are shown in boldface). Driver creates a room object, displays the room capacity, and stores the object in the Bag object.
2. After the user terminates input, Driver displays the value of a counter indicating the number of rooms processed.
3. Driver queries Bag for the number of objects stored in Bag and displays the count.
4. Driver then directs Bag to remove the first object stored, then queries Bag for the current number of objects stored and displays the count.
5. Bag iterates a method to display data from each stored room object.

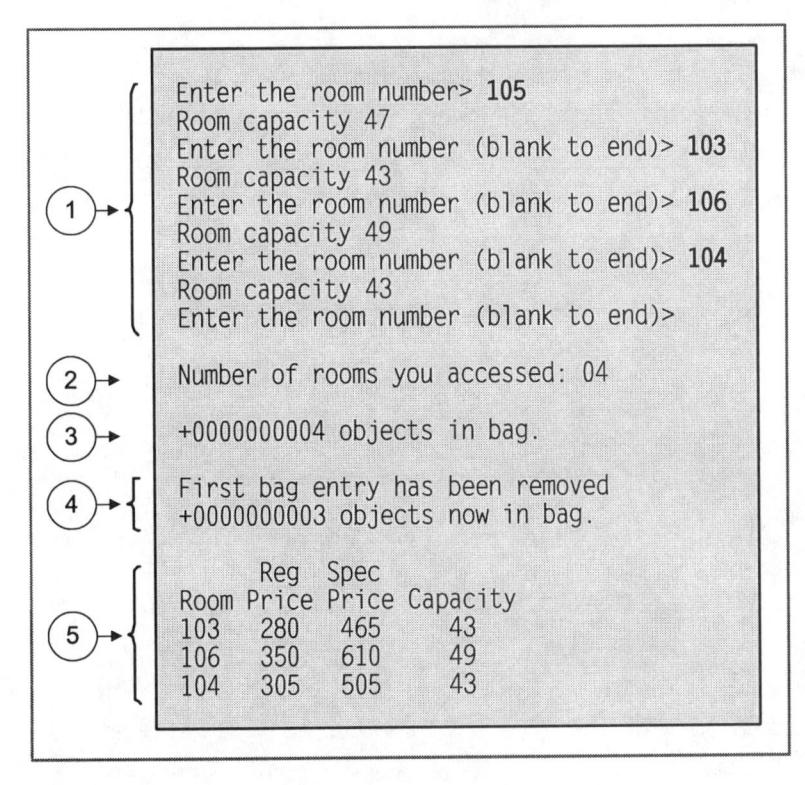

Figure 10-5. Typical Room21 output.

The primary focus for this example is code of Driver. But first, let's take a quick look at Room.

The Room Class—r21-room

In Figure 11-6 you see that the object data and the two methods get-room-capacity and populate-the-room-object are identical to corresponding code of many earlier examples of this book. The method display-room-data makes available the output identified as Item 5 in Figure 11-5.

Creating and Using a Bag—r21-drvr

The driver program, containing all of the bag related code, is shown in Figure 11-7. First, look at the overall input-processing code of lines 69-106 where repetition is controlled by user input—refer to the Perform Until at line 72.

- The first room number entry is accepted at line 70.
- The data item ws-rooms-accessed, a counter for the number of rooms accessed, is initialized at line 71.
- DBI is invoked at line 73 for the requested room.
- For a valid room request, Room is instantiated, populated, and counted at lines 83-89.

```
 1       $set sourceformat "free"
 1      *>*********************************************
 2      *> Room Rental System
 3      *> W. Price   April 9, 2000           R21-ROOM.CBL
 4      *>
 5      *> This class is a simplified version of earlier
 6      *> room classes. Its purpose is to illustrate a
 7      *> bag and using an iterator method in
 8      *> conjunction with the bag.
 9      *> It's methods are:
10      *>    display-room-data
11      *>    get-room-capacity
12      *>    populate-the-room-object
13      *>*********************************************
14
15      Identification Division.
16          Class-id.  RoomClass
17                     inherits from BaseClass.
18
19      Environment Division.
20          Object Section.
21          Class-Control.
22              RoomClass    is class "r21-room"
23              BaseClass    is class "base"
24              .
25      *>==============================================
26      OBJECT.
27
28      Data Division.
29          Object-Storage Section.    *> OBJECT DATA
30          01  room-data.
31              10  room-number          pic x(03).
32              10  std-config-price     pic 9(03).
33              10  spec-config-price    pic 9(03).
34              10  room-discount        pic v9(02).
35              10  room-capacity        pic 9(02).
36

37      Procedure Division.
38      *>..............................................
39      Method-id. display-room-data.
40      *>..............................................
41          Procedure Division.
42              Display room-number,       "  "
43                      std-config-price,  "  "
44                      spec-config-price, "  "
45                      room-capacity
46              .
47      End Method display-room-data.
48
49      *>..............................................
50      Method-id. get-room-capacity.
51      *>..............................................
52          Data Division.
53          Linkage Section.
54              01  ls-room-number        pic 9(03).
55              01  ls-room-capacity      pic 9(02).
56
57          Procedure Division Returning ls-room-capacity.
58              Move room-capacity to ls-room-capacity
59              .
60      End Method get-room-capacity.
61
62      *>..............................................
63      Method-id. populate-the-room-object.
64      *>..............................................
65          Data Division.
66          Linkage Section.
67              01  ls-room-data.
68                  10  ls-room-number       pic x(03).
69                  10  ls-std-config-price  pic 9(03).
70                  10  ls-spec-config-price pic 9(03).
71                  10  ls-room-discount     pic v9(02).
72                  10  ls-room-capacity     pic 9(02).
73
74          Procedure Division Using ls-room-data.
75              Move ls-room-data to room-data
76              .
77      End Method populate-the-room-object.
78      *>..............................................
79      END OBJECT.
80      END CLASS RoomClass.
```

Figure 11-6. The Room Class—r21-room.

- The room capacity is accessed and displayed (so you can see what is taking place in the example) at lines 90-92.
- The room object is placed in the bag at line 94.
- The handle for the first room processed is saved and the programmed switch is "turned off" so that subsequent handles will not be saved (lines 96-99). This sequence is solely for the purpose of illustrating a feature of bags.

```
            $set sourceformat "free"
1  *>*****************************************
2  *> Room Rental System
3  *> W. Price  March 5, 2000          R21-DRVR.CBL
4  *>
5  *> This projects illustrates two concepts:
6  *     Using a bag and using a callback.
7  *> Room objects are added to a bag via a program
8  *> loop. After loop completion, the number of
9  *> objects in the bag is displayed, the first
10 *> is deleted, and the object count is again
11 *> displayed.
12 *> A callback is invoked using the "do". The
13 *> iterated callback method displays each
14 *> element of the bag.
15 *> This project includes the following classes:
16 *>    R21-ROOM    RoomClass
17 *>    R21-DBI     DatabaseInterface
18 *>*****************************************
19
20 Identification Division.
21     Program-ID. R21Driver.
22
23 Environment Division.
24     Object Section.
25     Class-Control.
26         RoomClass          is class "r21-room"
27         DatabaseInterface  is class "r21-dbi"
28         Bag                is class "bag"
29         CallBack           is class "callback"
30         .
31 Data Division.
32
33     Working-Storage Section.
34     01 ws-room-data.
35        10  ws-room-number          pic X(03).
36        10  ws-std-config-price     pic 9(03).
37        10  ws-spec-config-price    pic 9(03).
38        10  ws-room-discount        pic v9(02).
39        10  ws-room-capacity        pic 9(02).
40
41     01 ws-rooms-accessed           pic 9(02).
42
43     01 ws-library-parameter-fields.
44        10  ws-bag-size      pic s9(9) comp-5.
45        10  ws-bag-contents  pic s9(9) comp-5.
46
47     01 ws-first-time-sw   pic x(1) value "T".
48        88 ws-first-time      value "T"
49                              false "F".
50
51     01 aRoomHandle          object reference.
52     01 userInterfaceHandle  object reference.
53     01 theBagHandle         object reference.
54     01 saveHandle           object reference.
55     01 theMethodName        object reference.
56
57     01 ws-messages.
58        10  ws-invalid-room-message   pic x(40)
59                value "Invalid room number".
60
61 Procedure Division.
62
63  *> Create the bag
64  Move 1 to ws-bag-size *>Make bag size small
65  Invoke Bag "OfReferences" Using ws-bag-size
66                      Returning theBagHandle
67
68  *> Query for first room number (or terminate)
69  Display "Enter the room number> " no advancing
70  Accept ws-room-number
71  Move 0 to ws-rooms-accessed
72  Perform Until ws-room-number = spaces
73     Invoke DatabaseInterface "read-room-record"
74                   Using ws-room-number
75                   Returning ws-room-data
76
77     *> If record was not found, the parameter
78     *> contains spaces.
79     Evaluate ws-room-data
80       When spaces
81          Display "No such room number"
82       When other
83          Invoke RoomClass "New"
84                   Returning aRoomHandle
85          Invoke aRoomHandle
86                   "populate-the-room-object"
87                   Using ws-room-data
88
89          Add 1 to ws-rooms-accessed
90          Invoke aRoomHandle "get-room-capacity"
91                   Returning ws-room-capacity
92          Display "Room capacity " ws-room-capacity
93          *> Add instance to bag
94          Invoke theBagHandle "Add" Using aRoomHandle
95
96          If ws-first-time
97             Set saveHandle to aRoomHandle
98             Set ws-first-time to false
99          End-if
100
101    End-evaluate *> aRoomHandle
102    *> Query for next room number (or terminate)
103    Display "Enter room number (blank to end> "
104                     with no advancing
105    Accept ws-room-number
106 End-Perform *> Until ws-room-number = spaces
107 Display " "
108 Display "Number of rooms you accessed: "
109          ws-rooms-accessed
110 Display " "
111
112 *> See how many I have
113 Invoke theBagHandle "Size"
114             Returning ws-bag-contents
115 Display ws-bag-contents " objects in bag."
116
117 Invoke theBagHandle "Remove" Using saveHandle
118 Display " "
119 Display "First bag entry has been removed"
120
121 *> Now see how many I have
122 Invoke theBagHandle "Size"
123             Returning ws-bag-contents
124 Display ws-bag-contents " objects now in bag."
125 Display " "
126
127 *> Now invoke the Display-room-number method
128 *> for every object in the bag.
129
130 Invoke CallBack "New" Using aRoomHandle
131                "display-room-data"
132                Returning theMethodName
133 Display "    Reg  Spec"
134 Display "Room Price Price Capacity"
135 Invoke theBagHandle "Do" Using theMethodName
136
137 Stop run
138   .
```

Figure 11-7. Driver—r21-drvr.

In our programming roles as both class writers and class users, for this example we must write two class definitions (Room and DBI) and use two classes from the Micro Focus class library. As you might expect, these must be designated in the Class-Control paragraph—at lines 28 and 29 you see Bag and Callback.

Remember from an earlier description that you are working with collection *classes* that must be instantiated thereby producing a collection *object* capable of holding other elements. For many of the collection classes, you will create the collection object with an Invoke consisting of:

- The name of the class, Bag for this first example.
- The name of the class's method to create the desired object. Remember, a collection object can be created to contain other objects (method name "ofReferences") or intrinsic data (method name "ofValues").
- An input parameter indicating the initial size of the collection object (the number of entries it can store).
- An output parameter with the object handle of the collection object.

To those ends, look at the following code taken from lines 64-66:

```
Move 1 to ws-bag-size *>Make bag size small
Invoke Bag "OfReferences" Using ws-bag-size
                    Returning theBagHandle
```

Notice that at line 44 the data item ws-bag-size is defined using the required comp-5 form. At line 64 this data item is set to 1, not a reasonable size to contain a "collection" of objects. The reason here is to illustrate a characteristic of the bag: its capacity grows automatically as it becomes full. Normally, you will define the initial size as some reasonable value that you anticipate will be required. As there is considerable overhead in increasing the size of a collection object, it is a good idea to use your best estimate in setting the initial size of any collection object.

The program places the current room object in the bag by the following statement using the bag's object method add (line 94).

```
Invoke theBagHandle "add" Using aRoomHandle
```

The Using parameter is the object handle of the object to be added to the bag.

The purpose of the sequence in lines 96-99 is to save the handle of the first instance added to the bag so the program can delete it later. Upon breaking out of the loop (the End-Perform at line 106), the Invoke of line 113 uses the method Size to determine how many objects are contained in the bag.

```
Invoke theBagHandle "size" Returning bag-contents
```

The single Returning parameter is a four-byte comp-5 data item into which the bag size is returned. That value is displayed by line 115—refer to the sample output Item 3 in Figure 10-5.

The following Invoke from line 117 removes the first element stored in the bag using the remove method.

```
Invoke theBagHandle "remove" Using saveHandle
```

The single Using parameter is the object handle of the particular object to be removed.

Remember, the only way you can directly reference an object in a bag is through its handle.

The Invoke at line 122 obtains the size again for output via the Display at line 124 (refer to Figure 10-5, output Item 4).

Using an Iterator on a Bag

Principles of the Callback

The functionality of collection classes by themselves is further extended when used in conjunction with callbacks. A **callback*** is nothing more than the name of a method that can be invoked on all elements of a collection. When you invoke a callback it sends each item of a collection object to the method named in the callback. For instance, the three lines of data output of Item 5 in Figure 11-5 were displayed by execution of a single Invoke. Let's see how that was done.

To create a Callback object, you must invoke the "new" method of the Callback class by supplying it with:

1. the identity of the object containing the method you want written into the Callback,
2. the name of the method, and
3. an object reference data item into which the method new returns the newly created Callback object handle.

The Callback object for this example is created by the following Invoke (from Figure 11-7's lines 130-132).

```
Invoke Callback "New" Using aRoomHandle
                          "display-room-data"
                Returning theMethodName
```

Following is the method (refer to lines 39-47 of Figure 11-6) identified in this Callback creation. This Callback example uses a literal to designate the method name ("display-room-data"); it can be a pic X data item containing the method name. The method itself can be defined in the same class from which the object was created or it can be defined in another class. If the object reference in the Using is a class name, then the method must be Factory method; if the reference is an object handle, then the method must be an instance Object method.

```
*>--------------------------------
Method-id. "display-room-data".
*>--------------------------------
    Procedure Division.
        Display room-number, "   "
                std-config-price, "   "
                spec-config-price, "   "
                room-capacity
        .
End Method "display-room-data".
```

* My good friend and respected colleague Gene Webb of Dallas, Texas was a terrific resource in providing me insight to some of the subtleties of callbacks as well as object methodology in general. I suggest you visit his Web site www.objectz.com/tutorial/.

Iterating the Callback Method

Once you've defined the callback, you can use it in conjuction with the Do iterator of the Bag class as follows (refer to Figure 11-7's line 135).

    Invoke theBagHandle "Do" Using theMethodName

This statement is almost self-explanatory: the Do sends the message contained in theMethodName to every element contained in the designated bag. The method display-room-data is executed for each object in the bag, as illustrated in Figure 11-8, thereby displaying the room prices and capacity.

The Select Iterator—Room22

Sample Display

Where the Do iterator "visits" each element in a bag and does something, the Select iterator visits each element and applies a program-defined criterion for adding the element to a new collection. Its use is illustrated in Room22 to create a new bag containing all room objects for which the room capacity is 44 or less. Like Room21, this application accepts room numbers from a user, accesses data from a simulated DBI, creates a room object, then stores that room object in a bag. Upon completing this loop, the new bag is created. In the sample run of Figure 11-9 you see that four of the six room selections have room capacities not exceeding 44 (the third has a capacity of 49 and the fourth a capacity 47). Correspondingly, the new bag is identified as containing four objects.

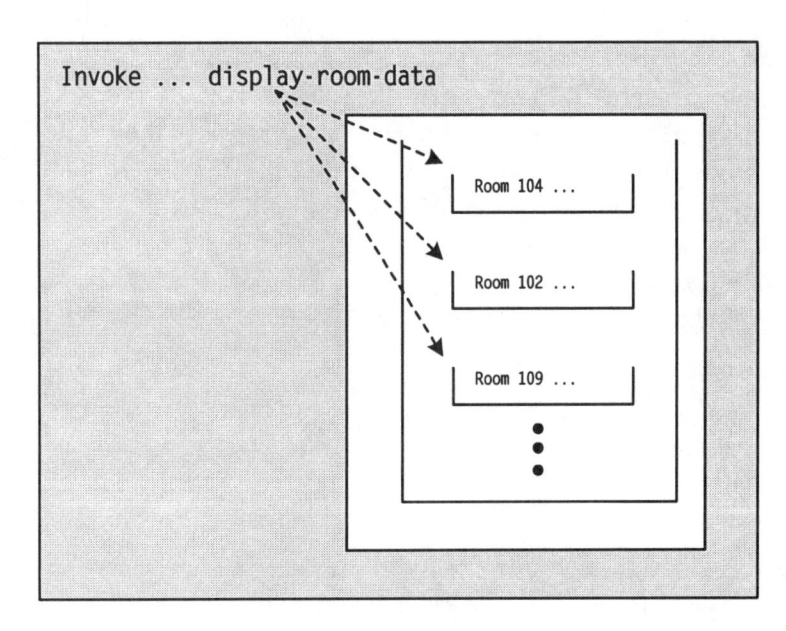

Figure 11-8.
Iterating a method on each object in a bag.

Figure 11-9.
Sample display for Room22.

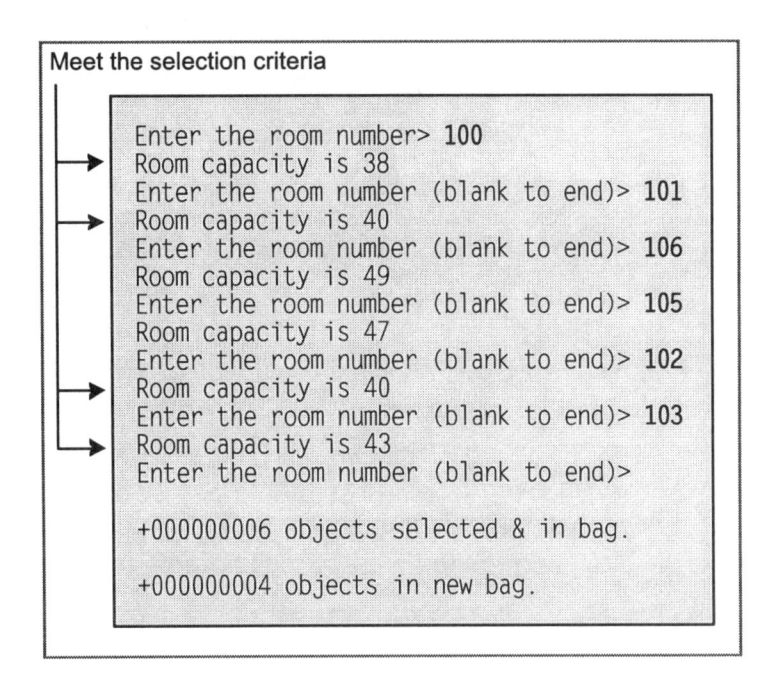

```
Meet the selection criteria

  Enter the room number> 100
  Room capacity is 38
  Enter the room number (blank to end)> 101
  Room capacity is 40
  Enter the room number (blank to end)> 106
  Room capacity is 49
  Enter the room number (blank to end)> 105
  Room capacity is 47
  Enter the room number (blank to end)> 102
  Room capacity is 40
  Enter the room number (blank to end)> 103
  Room capacity is 43
  Enter the room number (blank to end)>

  +000000006 objects selected & in bag.

  +000000004 objects in new bag.
```

Room's Select Callback Method

The Room class for this project is identical to that of Room21 except for the callback method which is shown here in Figure 11-10. When used with the Select iterator, the method must return a single true-false parameter defined as `pic X comp-5: ls-true-false` in this example. Code of the method must set this parameter to either true or false (1 or 0) according to the requirements of the application. The Select iterator invokes this method on each object in the bag. If the returned true-false parameter is true, that object is added to a new bag; otherwise that object is ignored. In either case, the original bag is unchanged.

Invoking the Select Method—r22-drvr

Inspect Driver in Figure 11-11 and you will see that it uses much the same code as the preceding example driver. However, that the Callback at lines 102-104 designates the method name (message) select-room-objects. Then at line105 bag's method "select" (the Select iterator) is implemented. This callback then (1) creates a new

```
65   *>------------------------------------------------
66        Method-id. select-room-objects.
67   *>------------------------------------------------
68        Data Division.
69          Linkage Section.
70            01 ls-true-false            pic X comp-5.
71              88 ls-is-true                 value 1
72                                            false 0.
73        Procedure Division Returning ls-true-false.
74          Evaluate room-capacity
75            When 1 through 44
76              Set ls-is-true to true
77            When 45 through 99
78              Set ls-is-true to false
79          End-Evaluate *>room-capacity
80          .
81        End Method select-room-objects.
82   *>------------------------------------------------
```

Figure 11-10.
Room's Select Callback method.

bag (identified by the handle `theNewBagHandle`) and (2) populates it with selected objects from the original bag..

> Notice that the object reference at line 102 is `nullObject` (defined at line 47) rather than `aRoomHandle`, the object containing the subject method. As the compiler initializes all object references to null and this program does not set a value to `nullObject`, it contains null at execution of line 102's Invoke. This is the technique used with Personal COBOL. On the other hand, Net Express is intended to allow use of the object handle of the class containing the designated method. Unfortunately, the application did not function properly using `aRoomHandle`. The only way I could make this work was by using `nullObject` as shown here. Unfortunately this restricts the callback method to a method of the class from which the object was created. Hopefully, this will be repaired in a future WebSync update.

Returning Results From an Iterator

Creating an Intrinsic Data Class

The ability to store and manipulate intrinsic data in object-oriented ways is useful when working with collection classes. To that end, the class library includes a set of classes corresponding to some of Cobol's intrinsic data types; objects from these classes correspond to Cobol data items.[*] The supplied intrinsic classes are only capable of storing data of preset length. If you want to use them for intrinsic data of any other length, you must first clone the class, creating a new class for the length of data you require. The three Cobol data types supported by the class library are:

```
PIC X(n)
PIC X(n) COMP-X
PIC X(n) COMP-5
```

Collection classes defined for intrinsic data require that the size of the data be explicitly designated. For instance, the next example uses a 5-position accumulator that must be treated as an object—appropriate code from that driver is shown in Figure 11-12 (you will look at the complete program later).

- At lines 81 and 82 the method `newclass` of the `CompX` class is invoked with the following parameters:
  - `Using` that designates a `comp-5` data item containing the pic size of the new class to be created—in this case, a `pic X(5)` class.
  - `Returning` that lists the the object handle identifying the name of the new class, `ItemSizeClass`, in the case.
- The Invoke at lines 83 and 84 then instantiates the newly created class thereby creating an intrinsic data object (`totalCapacityObject`) capable of storing a single 5-position data item.

---

[*] Net Express Help includes some reasonably good descriptions on this subject. Under Help Topics enter "intrinsic data objects."

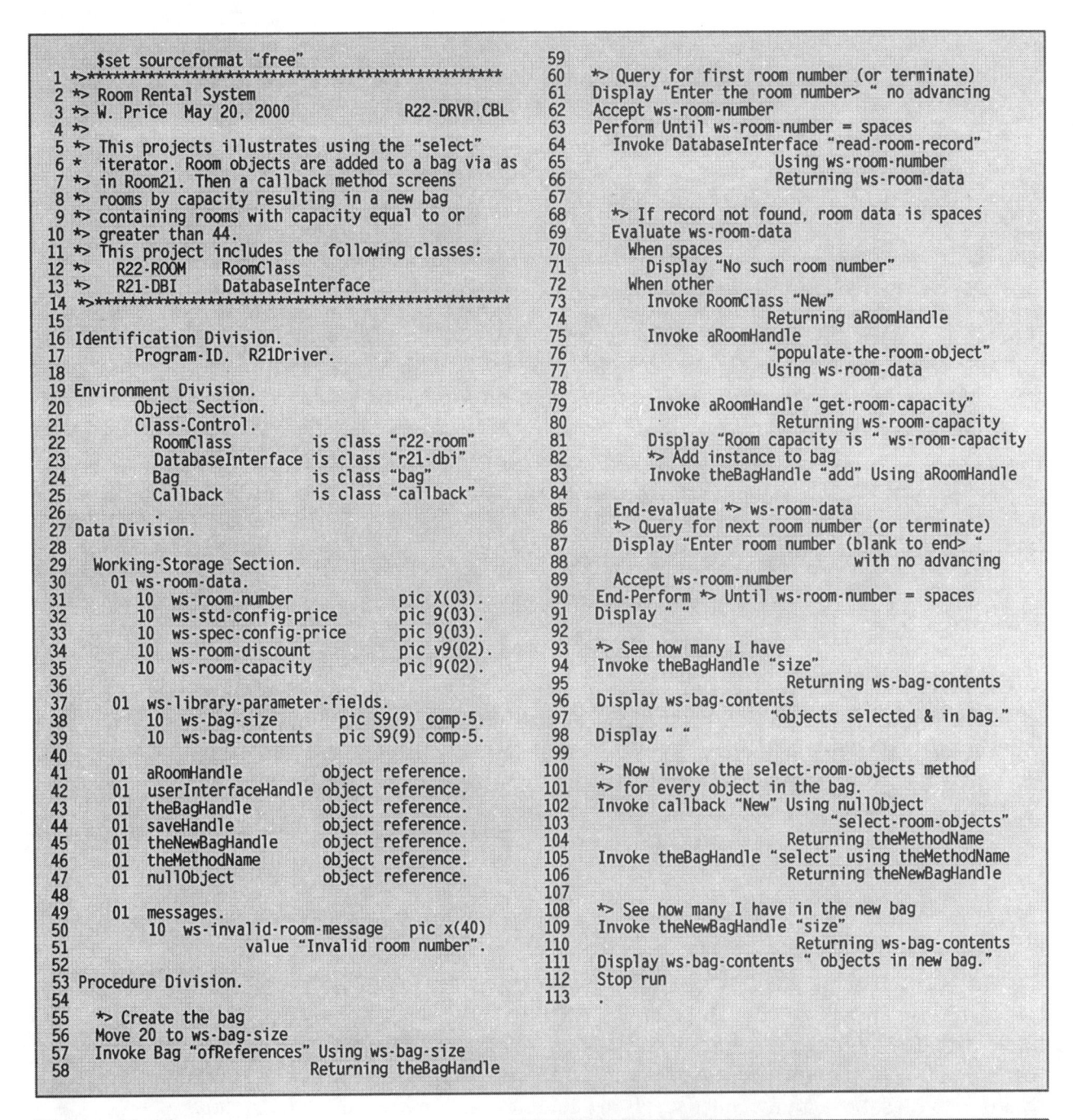

Collection Classes

```cobol
     $set sourceformat "free"
1  *>************************************************
2  *> Room Rental System
3  *> W. Price  May 20, 2000              R22-DRVR.CBL
4  *>
5  *> This projects illustrates using the "select"
6  *  iterator. Room objects are added to a bag via as
7  *> in Room21. Then a callback method screens
8  *> rooms by capacity resulting in a new bag
9  *> containing rooms with capacity equal to or
10 *> greater than 44.
11 *> This project includes the following classes:
12 *>   R22-ROOM      RoomClass
13 *>   R21-DBI       DatabaseInterface
14 *>************************************************
15
16 Identification Division.
17      Program-ID. R21Driver.
18
19 Environment Division.
20      Object Section.
21      Class-Control.
22          RoomClass         is class "r22-room"
23          DatabaseInterface is class "r21-dbi"
24          Bag               is class "bag"
25          Callback          is class "callback"
26          .
27 Data Division.
28
29      Working-Storage Section.
30      01 ws-room-data.
31         10 ws-room-number           pic X(03).
32         10 ws-std-config-price      pic 9(03).
33         10 ws-spec-config-price     pic 9(03).
34         10 ws-room-discount         pic v9(02).
35         10 ws-room-capacity         pic 9(02).
36
37      01 ws-library-parameter-fields.
38         10 ws-bag-size       pic S9(9) comp-5.
39         10 ws-bag-contents   pic S9(9) comp-5.
40
41      01 aRoomHandle          object reference.
42      01 userInterfaceHandle  object reference.
43      01 theBagHandle         object reference.
44      01 saveHandle           object reference.
45      01 theNewBagHandle      object reference.
46      01 theMethodName        object reference.
47      01 nullObject           object reference.
48
49      01 messages.
50         10 ws-invalid-room-message   pic x(40)
51                value "Invalid room number".
52
53 Procedure Division.
54
55   *> Create the bag
56   Move 20 to ws-bag-size
57   Invoke Bag "ofReferences" Using ws-bag-size
58                             Returning theBagHandle
59
60   *> Query for first room number (or terminate)
61   Display "Enter the room number> " no advancing
62   Accept ws-room-number
63   Perform Until ws-room-number = spaces
64      Invoke DatabaseInterface "read-room-record"
65                            Using ws-room-number
66                            Returning ws-room-data
67
68      *> If record not found, room data is spaces
69      Evaluate ws-room-data
70        When spaces
71          Display "No such room number"
72        When other
73          Invoke RoomClass "New"
74                              Returning aRoomHandle
75          Invoke aRoomHandle
76                     "populate-the-room-object"
77                     Using ws-room-data
78
79          Invoke aRoomHandle "get-room-capacity"
80                           Returning ws-room-capacity
81          Display "Room capacity is " ws-room-capacity
82          *> Add instance to bag
83          Invoke theBagHandle "add" Using aRoomHandle
84
85      End-evaluate *> ws-room-data
86      *> Query for next room number (or terminate)
87      Display "Enter room number (blank to end> "
88                               with no advancing
89      Accept ws-room-number
90   End-Perform *> Until ws-room-number = spaces
91   Display " "
92
93   *> See how many I have
94   Invoke theBagHandle "size"
95                            Returning ws-bag-contents
96   Display ws-bag-contents
97                     "objects selected & in bag."
98   Display " "
99
100  *> Now invoke the select-room-objects method
101  *> for every object in the bag.
102  Invoke callback "New" Using nullObject
103                           "select-room-objects"
104                           Returning theMethodName
105  Invoke theBagHandle "select" using theMethodName
106                           Returning theNewBagHandle
107
108  *> See how many I have in the new bag
109  Invoke theNewBagHandle "size"
110                           Returning ws-bag-contents
111  Display ws-bag-contents " objects in new bag."
112  Stop run
113  .
```

Figure 11-11.
Invoking the Select method—r22-drvr.

```cobol
31  Working-Storage Section.

38    01 ws-total-capacity-size     pic X(04) comp-5.
39    01 ws-bag-size                pic S9(9) comp-5.
40    01 ws-total-capacity          pic 9(05).
41
42    01 ItemSizeClass          object reference.
43    01 totalCapacityObject    object reference.

78    *> Create a pic X(5) data class to hold the
79    *> room capacity (required by callback)
80    Move 5 to ws-total-capacity-size *>Length of data item
81    Invoke CompX "newclass" Using ws-total-capacity-size
82                            Returning ItemSizeClass
83    Invoke ItemSizeClass "new"
84                     Returning totalCapacityObject
85    Move 0 to ws-total-capacity
86    Invoke totalCapacityObject "SetValue"
87                     Using ws-total-capacity
```

Figure 11-12.
Creating and instantiating a pic X class.

- The subject data item is to serve as an accumulator therefore requiring initialization to 0. Line 85 moves 0 to a 5-position numeric (display) field.
- At lines 86 and 87 the SetValue method of this class is invoked which effectively moves the intrinsic data item (ws-total-capacity in this example) into the intrinsic data object—refer to Figure 11-13. (Note: For lack of a better term, I'm inclined to refer to this action as *"objectifying"* the data item.)

Callback with Optional Parameters

Room22 illustrates the Do iterator operating with a relatively simple method that displays data from the bag's objects. Perhaps you wondered how data (or objects) can be returned from execution of an iterator. The answer is that Callback allows you to include optional parameters for this purpose when you create the callback. As you've learned, Callback stores a method name for later invocation. It also stores optional parameters for communicating data. For instance, consider the following Invoke.

```
Invoke callback "new" Using nullObject
                       "a-method"
                       object-ref-param-1
                       object-ref-param-2
               Returning theMethodName
```

This is the same as the callback of r22-drvr except for the additional parameters object-ref-param-1 and object-ref-param-2. (Note that these parameters must be object reference.) They will correspond to two parameters listed in the Procedure Division header of the method a-method. For instance, consider the following.

```
Method-id. "a-method".
    ...
    Procedure Division Using one-object-ref-item, another-object-ref-item.
```

The correspondence is object-ref-param-1 to one-object-ref-item and object-ref-param-2 to another-object-ref-item. Obviously, both one-object-ref-item and another-object-ref-item must be object reference. (You can create callbacks using one to six optional parameters.) This provides the capability for the invoking program to both pass data to the iterator method and receive data from it. Although all examples of this book have returned results via the Returning parameter, the Using works exactly as with subprograms. Since the Using default is "by reference" a change to a Using parameter in the invoked program changes the value of the corresponding parameter in the invoking program.

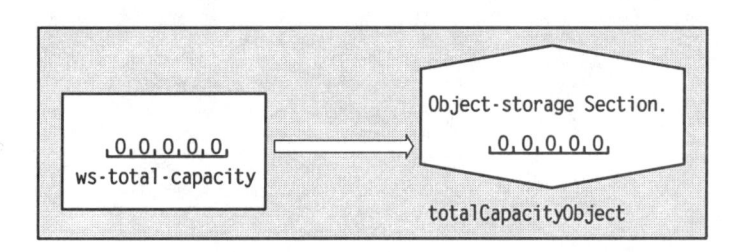

Figure 11-13.
Populating an intrinsic data object.

About Room23

Assume that one component of the room reservation system creates a transaction object containing the following data.

> room reservation date
> room number
> room capacity

When the transaction activity is completed, the transaction object is stored in a bag. At the end of a run cycle, data in the bag is processed. You can probably imagine an environment in which a bag of such data might be passed to two or more different departments, each with its own processing requirements. For this simple illustration, let's consider the task of determining the total room capacity for all transactions stored in the bag. Thus the iterator method will require an accumulator data item into which it can add the capacity from each object. Furthermore, that data item must to be returned to the invoking program.

Room23 includes a driver (r23-drvr), a room transaction class (r23-tran), and a transaction data class (r23-data) interrelated to each other exactly as corresponding classes of Room21 (see Figure 11-4). The purpose of the transaction data class is to provide transaction records for use as room transaction object data, thereby simulating an actual transaction application. The room transaction class contains the iterator method `compute-capacity`.

Figure 11-14 shows the output from this example where individual room data (stored as objects in a bag) is displayed exactly as in the two preceding examples. The total capacity requires using an optional parameter.

```
              The following transaction data is extracted from the bag.

              Date        Room  Capacity
              05/26/2000  100   38
              05/28/2000  102   40
              05/29/2000  108   45
              05/29/2000  109   50
              05/31/2000  108   45
              06/02/2000  106   49
              06/02/2000  103   43
              06/02/2000  101   40
              06/02/2000  106   49
              05/26/2000  109   50

              Capacity of all rooms processed is 00449
```

Using the Do iterator, each of these is extracted from the bag, displayed, and its Capacity entry added to the Capacity accumulator.

The Capacity accumulator is returned as an optional parameter of the Do and displayed by Driver.

Figure 11-14. Room23 output.

```
        $set sourceformat "free"
 1 *>****************************************************
 2 *> Room Rental System
 3 *> W. Price   10/18/96                      R23-DRVR.CBL
 4 *>
 5 *> Bag processing example.
 6 *> This driver simulates room transaction
 7 *> processing in which each transaction is placed
 8 *> in a bag. Then the "do" iterator is used to
 9 *> process each transaction object in the bag.
10 *> including accumulating the room capacity item.
11 *> The latter is returned via an optional parameter.
12 *> Following classes are included in the project:
13 *>    R23-TRAN   RoomTransaction
14 *>    R23-DATA   TransactionData
15 *>****************************************************
16
17 Identification Division.
18       Program-ID.  Room23Driver.
19
20 Environment Division.
21       Object Section.
22       Class-Control.
23            RoomTransaction   is class "r23-tran"
24            TransactionData   is class "r23-data"
25            Compx             is class "compx"
26            Bag               is class "bag"
27            Callback          is class "callback"
28            .
29 Data Division.
30
31    Working-Storage Section.
32
33    01 ws-transaction-record.
34       10 ws-trans-date       pic X(12).
35       10 ws-room-number      pic X(03).
36       10 ws-room-capacity    pic 9(02).
37
38    01 ws-total-capacity-size pic X(04) comp-5.
39    01 ws-bag-size            pic S9(9) comp-5.
40    01 ws-total-capacity      pic 9(05).
41
42    01 ItemSizeClass          object reference.
43    01 totalCapacityObject    object reference.
44    01 theTransactionHandle   object reference.
45    01 theDataHandle          object reference.
46    01 theBagHandle           object reference.
47    01 theMethodName          object reference.
48    01 nullObject             object reference.
49
50 Procedure Division.
51
52    Set nullObject to null
53    *> Create the bag
54    Move 10 to ws-bag-size
55    Invoke Bag "ofReferences" Using ws-bag-size
56                              Returning theBagHandle
57
58    Invoke TransactionData "read-trans-record"
59                     Returning ws-transaction-record
60 *>The following loop accesses each transaction
61 *>from a data table (simulating processing) from
62 *>table and creates an object for it. The room
63 *>transaction class stores each record in the bag.
64 *>The preceding Invoke serves as a "priming" read
65    Perform until ws-transaction-record = spaces
66       Invoke RoomTransaction "New"
67                     Returning theTransactionHandle
68       Invoke theTransactionHandle
69            "populate-the-transaction-object"
70            Using ws-transaction-record
71       Invoke theBagHandle "add"
72                     Using theTransactionHandle
73       *> Access next record
74       Invoke TransactionData "read-trans-record"
75                     Returning ws-transaction-record
76    End-Perform *>until ws-transaction-record = spaces
77
78    *> Create a pic X(5) data class to hold the
79    *> room capacity (required by callback)
80    Move 5 to ws-total-capacity-size *>Length of data item
81    Invoke CompX "newclass" Using ws-total-capacity-size
82                     Returning ItemSizeClass
83    Invoke ItemSizeClass "new"
84                     Returning totalCapacityObject
85    Move 0 to ws-total-capacity
86    Invoke totalCapacityObject "SetValue"
87                     Using ws-total-capacity
88
89    *>Create the callback and iterate the method
90    Invoke callback "New" Using nullObject
91                          "compute-capacity "
92                          totalCapacityObject
93                     Returning theMethodName
94
95    Display "The following transaction data is"
96                     with no advancing
97    Display " extracted from the bag."
98    Display " "
99    Display " Date      Room Capacity"
100   Invoke theBagHandle "Do" using theMethodName
101   *> Convert the "objectified" accumulator to pic 9.
102   Invoke totalCapacityObject "GetValue"
103                   Returning ws-total-capacity
104   Display " "
105   Display "Capacity of all rooms processed is "
106                   ws-total-capacity
107   Stop run
108   .
```

Figure 11-15. The Driver r23-drvr.

Using an Optional Parameter in the Callback—r23-drvr

In Driver's listing of Figure 11-15 you see the basic processing sequence and loop to access transaction objects and store them in the bag (lines 54-76). At lines 80-87 you see code (described in a preceding section) for creating an intrinsic data class, instantiating that class, them populating the resulting intrinsic data object.

The callback is defined by the Invoke of lines 90-93 which differs from that of Room22 by the inclusion of the optional parameter at line 92. This is the intrinsic data object created and initialized by lines 80-87 (refer to Figure 11-13). At line 100 the method compute-capacity (specified in the callback at line 91) is iterated via the Do method. The GetValue method invoke at lines 102 and 103 returns the value stored in the object to the data item ws-total-capacity. Note that this method performs the reverse action of the SetValue method at line 86 and described in Figures 11-12 and 11-13).

The Callback Method compute-capacity from r23-tran

The callback method from r23-tran is listed in Figure 11-16 where you see the the local work data item lo-total-capacity (which is an intrinsic data item, not the object version) defined at line 36. At execution of this sequence, the following takes place.

1. The total capacity is accessed from the object ls-total-capacity into the local data item lo-total-capacity by the Invoke of lines 43-44.
2. The current room's capacity room-capacity (an object data item) is added to the local data item lo-total-capacity at line 49.
3. The value of the local data item lo-total-capacity is returned to object data item ls-total-capacity by the Invoke of lines 52 and 53.

As the callback is iterated for each transaction object in the bag, the corresponding individual room capacity will be added—see line 49.

If you have in mind to use lo-total-capacity as the accumulator, forget it. Remember that data items defined in the Local-Storage Section are not persistent, that is, they are initialized with each invocation of the method.

```
31      *>..............................................
32      Method-id. compute-capacity.
33      *>..............................................
34         Data Division.
35            Local-Storage Section.
36               01 lo-total-capacity  pic 9(05).
37            Linkage Section.
38               01 ls-total-capacity object reference.
39
40         Procedure Division using ls-total-capacity.
41            *> Access the total capacity object data
42            *> item into lo-total-capacity.
43            Invoke ls-total-capacity "getvalue"
44                    Returning lo-total-capacity
45            *>Display each room from the bag
46            Display transaction-date no advancing
47            Display "  " room-number no advancing
48            Display "   " room-capacity
49            Add room-capacity to lo-total-capacity
50            *> Store the lo-total-capacity back to
51            *>  intrinsic data object.
52            Invoke ls-total-capacity "setvalue"
53                    Using lo-total-capacity
54            .
55      End Method compute-capacity.
```

Figure 11-16.
The compute-capacity method.

Preview of Next Three Examples

In Chapter 9 you studied aggregate structures via a room reservation calendar. The next three examples of this chapter use that calendar data to illustrate the array and dictionary collection classes. Each accepts a user-request room number, creates an array collection object (for that room) from data in the calendar file, and searches the calendar object to determine room availability.

In Room24 the user enters an acceptable date range for a single-day request. The application searches the selected object to determine the earliest day the room is available during the designated time period.

Room25 is similar except the user enters the desired number of days and the earliest acceptable day. The application searches the calendar object for the earliest date the room is available for the requested number of days.

Room26 is identical to Room25 except the calendar file is loaded into a dictionary composed of the room number and calendar array objects. (This is roughly equivalent to the object data of Chapter 9's Room18 calendar aggregate component's.) With each user request, the calendar object for the requested room is accessed from the dictionary and searched as in Room25.

Using the Array Collection Class—Room24

About Room24

Proj1104
Room24

Room24 consists of the following three components.

- A user interface class containing methods to (1) display an announcement screen, (2) accept a room number from the user, and (3) accept a date range.
- A file processor class that accesses calendar data from the calendar file. This class is basically the file processor class of Room18 to which a method has been added for accessing calendar data for a selected room.
- A driver containing all the array collection class processing code.

Code of Driver accesses reservation data for a selected room and places it into an array collection object. Figure 11-17 illustrates the contents of the array for room 100. Recall from Chapter 9 that each day's entry is either the client number who has reserved the room or 0000 indicating the room is available.

1004	1004	1004	1004	1004	0000	0000	1001	1001	1001	
1	2	3	4	5	6	7	8	9	10	
	1002	0000	0000	0000	1004	1004	1004	0000	0000	0000
	11	12	13	14	15	16	17	18	19	20
	0000	0000	1002	1002	1002	1002	1002	1002	0000	0000	1010
	21	22	23	24	25	26	27	28	29	30	31

Figure 11-17. Reservation array for Room 100.

Figure 11-18.
Sample session—Room24.

```
This application determines single-day
availability of a selected room.
Input can be a selected day or a range
of days.

Enter room number (blank to end) 100

Beginning day (2 digits) 01
    Ending day (2 digits) 05

Room not available

Enter room number (blank to end) 100

Beginning day (2 digits) 10
    Ending day (2 digits) 15

Room available on day 12
```

In the typical user session shown in Figure 11-18 you see that the user is informed that the room is not available during the period days 1-5. However, as indicated by the second request for the day 10-15 request, it is available on day 12. You can confirm this by inspecting the calendar of Figure 11-17. That is, the room is full scheduled in the day range 1-5; the first free day in the range 10-15 is indeed day 12.

Driver—Room24

There are four primary items of interest in Figure 11-19's Driver listing.

- Environment and Data Division entries.
- The collection classes used in this example, are equated to their external filenames in the Class-Control paragraph. Whenever you use a class from the library, you must designate it as you do any other class.
- Creation of the array object.
- Loading and searching the array object.

At lines 25 and 26 you see the designation of two collection classes required by this application library: Array and CompX. Lines 39-45 define the variety of comp-5 data items required by the parameters of these class's methods.

In the Procedure Division you see the array collection class instantiated by invoking the OfValues class method of the class Array with the following statement (lines 107-109).

```
Invoke Array "OfValues" Using picX4Class
                              ws-array-size
                    Returning calendarArrayCollection
```

Notice the input and output parameters of the OfValues method.

- Using requires two parameters.
  The first is an object reference, the name of the 4-byte pic X class
  (the size of the array element to contain the 4-byte client number), created at lines 100-104.

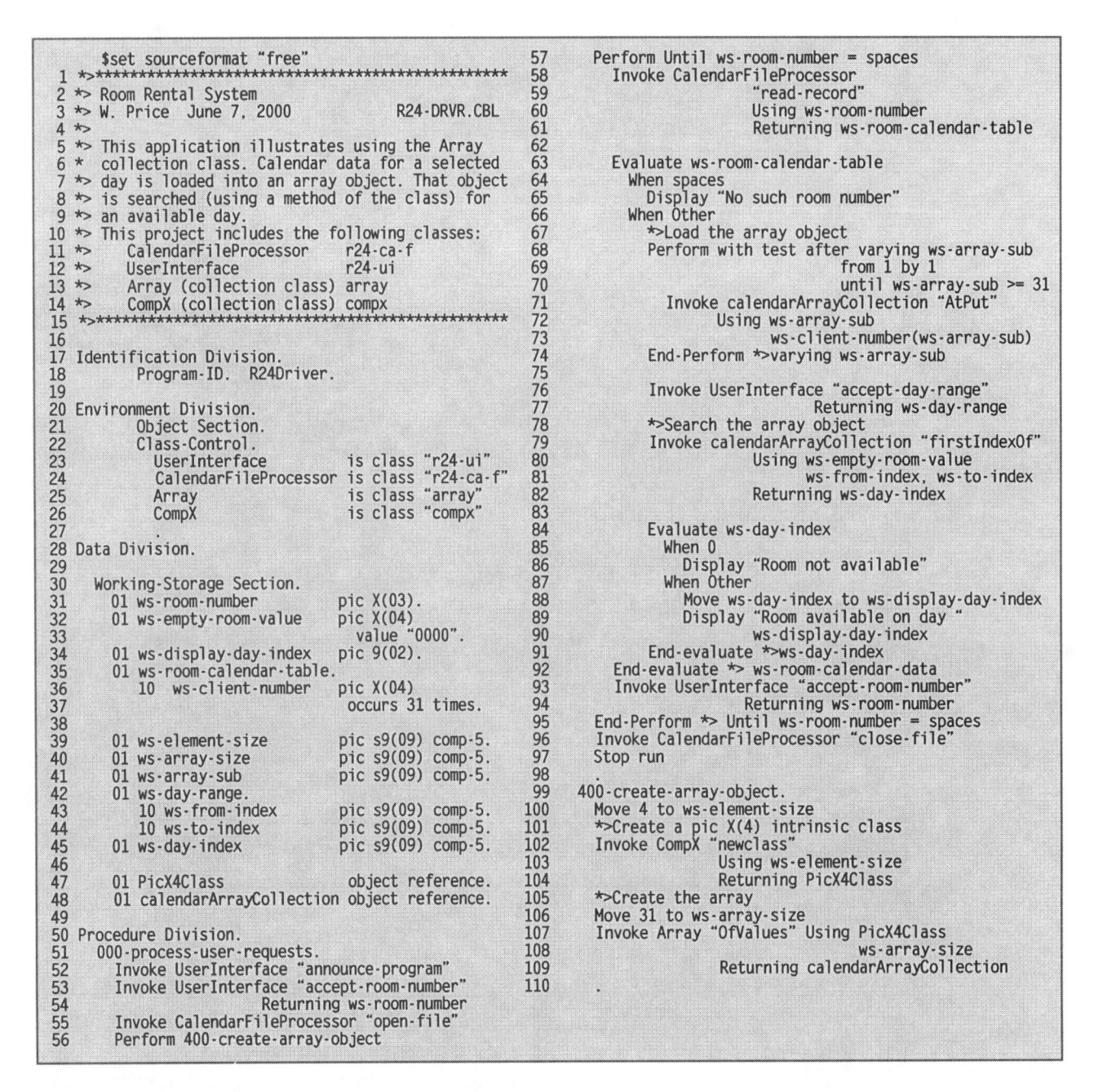

```cobol
       $set sourceformat "free"
  1 *>***********************************************
  2 *> Room Rental System
  3 *> W. Price  June 7, 2000              R24-DRVR.CBL
  4 *>
  5 *> This application illustrates using the Array
  6 *  collection class. Calendar data for a selected
  7 *> day is loaded into an array object. That object
  8 *> is searched (using a method of the class) for
  9 *> an available day.
 10 *> This project includes the following classes:
 11 *>    CalendarFileProcessor   r24-ca-f
 12 *>    UserInterface           r24-ui
 13 *>    Array (collection class) array
 14 *>    CompX (collection class) compx
 15 *>***********************************************
 16
 17 Identification Division.
 18     Program-ID.  R24Driver.
 19
 20 Environment Division.
 21     Object Section.
 22     Class-Control.
 23         UserInterface          is class "r24-ui"
 24         CalendarFileProcessor  is class "r24-ca-f"
 25         Array                  is class "array"
 26         CompX                  is class "compx"
 27         .
 28 Data Division.
 29
 30     Working-Storage Section.
 31     01 ws-room-number          pic X(03).
 32     01 ws-empty-room-value     pic X(04)
 33                                value "0000".
 34     01 ws-display-day-index    pic 9(02).
 35     01 ws-room-calendar-table.
 36         10 ws-client-number    pic X(04)
 37                                occurs 31 times.
 38
 39     01 ws-element-size         pic s9(09) comp-5.
 40     01 ws-array-size           pic s9(09) comp-5.
 41     01 ws-array-sub            pic s9(09) comp-5.
 42     01 ws-day-range.
 43         10 ws-from-index       pic s9(09) comp-5.
 44         10 ws-to-index         pic s9(09) comp-5.
 45     01 ws-day-index            pic s9(09) comp-5.
 46
 47     01 PicX4Class              object reference.
 48     01 calendarArrayCollection object reference.
 49
 50 Procedure Division.
 51  000-process-user-requests.
 52     Invoke UserInterface "announce-program"
 53     Invoke UserInterface "accept-room-number"
 54                          Returning ws-room-number
 55     Invoke CalendarFileProcessor "open-file"
 56     Perform 400-create-array-object
 57     Perform Until ws-room-number = spaces
 58        Invoke CalendarFileProcessor
 59                          "read-record"
 60                          Using ws-room-number
 61                          Returning ws-room-calendar-table
 62
 63        Evaluate ws-room-calendar-table
 64        When spaces
 65            Display "No such room number"
 66        When Other
 67            *>Load the array object
 68            Perform with test after varying ws-array-sub
 69                               from 1 by 1
 70                               until ws-array-sub >= 31
 71               Invoke calendarArrayCollection "AtPut"
 72                  Using ws-array-sub
 73                        ws-client-number(ws-array-sub)
 74            End-Perform *>varying ws-array-sub
 75
 76            Invoke UserInterface "accept-day-range"
 77                               Returning ws-day-range
 78            *>Search the array object
 79            Invoke calendarArrayCollection "firstIndexOf"
 80                  Using ws-empty-room-value
 81                        ws-from-index, ws-to-index
 82                  Returning ws-day-index
 83
 84            Evaluate ws-day-index
 85            When 0
 86                Display "Room not available"
 87            When Other
 88                Move ws-day-index to ws-display-day-index
 89                Display "Room available on day "
 90                        ws-display-day-index
 91            End-evaluate *>ws-day-index
 92        End-evaluate *> ws-room-calendar-data
 93        Invoke UserInterface "accept-room-number"
 94                          Returning ws-room-number
 95     End-Perform *> Until ws-room-number = spaces
 96     Invoke CalendarFileProcessor "close-file"
 97     Stop run
 98
 99  400-create-array-object.
100     Move 4 to ws-element-size
101     *>Create a pic X(4) intrinsic class
102     Invoke CompX "newclass"
103                          Using ws-element-size
104                          Returning PicX4Class
105     *>Create the array
106     Move 31 to ws-array-size
107     Invoke Array "OfValues" Using PicX4Class
108                                   ws-array-size
109                          Returning calendarArrayCollection
110     .
```

Figure 11-19. Room24's Driver

The second is comp-5 data item containing the number of elements in the array (the array size).

- Returning requires one parameter: an object reference data item to be used as the handle to the instantiated array object.

The desired room reservation record is accessed from the room file processor by the Invoke at line 58. Then data from the table is loaded into the array object within the loop of lines 68-74 by the following Invoke.

```
Invoke calendarArrayCollection "AtPut"
    Using ws-array-sub
          ws-client-number(ws-array-sub)
```

The array instance method AtPut requires two parameters in the Using clause. The first designates the array element number into which the data value is to be loaded. The second designates the data value itself. The size (number of bytes) of the data element must be consistent with the declared element size when the object was created (PicX4Class obtained from ws-element-size).

The array is searched by following Invoke of the array method FirstIndexOf—refer to lines 79-82.

```
Invoke calendarArrayCollection "FirstIndexOf"
    Using ws-empty-room-value
          ws-from-index, ws-to-index
    Returning ws-day-index
```

This method searches all or part of an array object for a designated data value. It requires the following parameters.

- Using requires three parameters.
  The first parameter (ws-empty-room-value defined at lines 32 and 33 in this example) must be an intrinsic data item of the same size as the array elements. It must contain the designated data value for the search comparison. Remember, the entry 0000 means the room is available.
  The second and third parameters must be four-byte comp-5 items containing the element numbers at which the array search is to begin and end. Here the entries are ws-from-index and ws-to-index whose values are obtained from user input by the Invoke of lines 76 and 77—also refer to lines 43 and 44.
- Returning requires one parameter (ws-day-index); it will contain the number of the first element found equal to the value of the first parameter of the Using. If none is found, the method returns a value of zero. This parameter must be a four-byte comp-5 data item.

As you review this example, it may occur to you that using the array collection class for this example is considerably more complex than simply searching the conventional Cobol table of line 35. Keep in mind that the purpose of this example is to illustrate using the array collection class.

Searching an Array for a Desired Block—Room25

About Room25

For an insight to the nature of this application, look at the sample dialogue of Figure 11-20. The first user request is for a block of five days no earlier than day 20. The system responds that no such block is available from day 20 to the end of the month. The second request designates day 11 as the beginning point. The system responds that such a block is available beginning day 18.

Proj1105 Room25

```
This application determines multi-day
availability of a selected room.
Input is a search-start date and the
number of consecutive days required.
Output is the day number of the first
day of the consecutive day block.

Enter room number (blank to end) 100

        Number of days (2 digits) 5
Earliest beginning day (2 digits) 20

Room not available

Enter room number (blank to end) 100

        Number of days (2 digits) 5
Earliest beginning day (2 digits) 11

Room available for 04 days beginning day 18
```

Figure 11-20.
Sample dialogue—Room25.

The illustration of Figure 11-21 gives you an idea of what takes place. Remember that a room open date is indicated by 0000 stored as the client number. The five-element day block with each element containing 0000 serves as a comparison template. The search begins with the designated day entry (11) and continues across the array object until a group of five days is found matching the template.

The Calendar Class

The preceding is implemented through relatively minor variation of Room 24's Driver (Figure 11-22).

1. The user-requested number of days is returned from UI in the data item `ws-number-of-days`—refer to lines 87-89 and 43-45.
2. The method `CopyEmptyWithSize` designated by the `Invoke` of lines 92-95 creates an empty array of size 5 (from the `Using` data item `ws-number-of-days`) with the object handle `emptyArrayTemplate`.

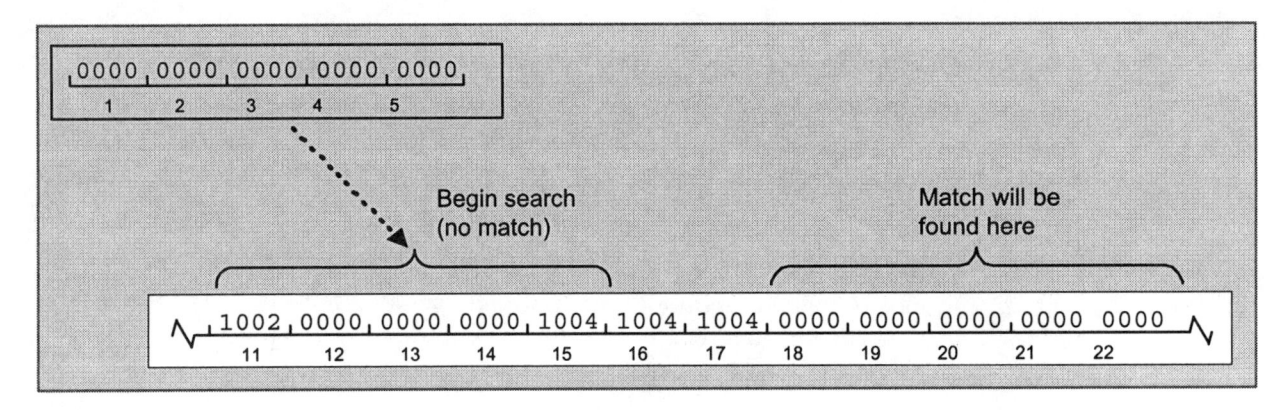

Figure 11-21. Searching the array for a block of entries.

Collection Classes

```cobol
       $set sourceformat "free"
1  *>*********************************************
2  *> Room Rental System
3  *> W. Price  June 7, 2000            R25-DRVR.CBL
4  *>
5  *> This application illustrates using the Array
6  *  collection class. Calendar data for a selected
7  *> room is loaded into an array object. That
8  *> object is searched (using a method of the class)
9  *> for an available day.
10 *> This project includes the following classes:
11 *>    CalendarFileProcessor       r24-ca-f
12 *>    UserInterface               r25-ui
13 *>    Array (collection class)    array
14 *>    CompX (collection class)    compx
15 *>*********************************************
16
17 Identification Division.
18     Program-ID. R25Driver.
19
20 Environment Division.
21     Object Section.
22     Class-Control.
23         CalendarFileProcessor is class "r24-ca-f"
24         UserInterface         is class "r25-ui"
25         Array                 is class "array"
26         CompX                 is class "compx"
27         .
28 Data Division.
29
30   Working-Storage Section.
31     01 ws-room-number         pic X(03).
32     01 ws-room-calendar-table.
33        10 ws-client-number    pic X(04)
34                               occurs 31 times.
35     01 ws-empty-room-value pic X(04)
36                               value "0000".
37     01 ws-display-2-byte-numeric  pic 9(02).
38
39     01 ws-comp-5-data-items.
40        10 ws-element-size     pic s9(09) comp-5.
41        10 ws-array-size       pic s9(09) comp-5.
42        10 ws-array-sub        pic s9(09) comp-5.
43        10 ws-day-info.
44           20 ws-number-of-days pic s9(09) comp-5.
45           20 ws-from-index    pic s9(09) comp-5.
46        10 ws-day-index        pic s9(09) comp-5.
47
48     01 PicX4Class                  object reference.
49     01 calendarArrayCollection     object reference.
50     01 emptyArrayTemplate          object reference.
51
52 Procedure Division.
53   000-process-user-requests.
54     Invoke UserInterface "announce-program"
55     Invoke UserInterface "accept-room-number"
56                         Returning ws-room-number
57     Invoke CalendarFileProcessor "open-file"
58     Perform 400-create-array-object
59     Perform Until ws-room-number = spaces
60        Invoke CalendarFileProcessor
61                    "read-record"
62                    Using ws-room-number
63                    Returning ws-room-calendar-table
64
65        Evaluate ws-room-calendar-table
66          When spaces
67             Display "No such room number"
68          When Other
69             Perform 200-process-room-request
70        End-evaluate *> ws-room-calendar-data
71        Invoke UserInterface "accept-room-number"
72                            Returning ws-room-number
73     End-Perform *> Until ws-room-number = spaces
74     Invoke CalendarFileProcessor "close-file"
75     Stop run
76     .
77  200-process-room-request.
78     *>Load the array object
79     Perform with test after varying ws-array-sub
80                                 from 1 by 1
81                                 until ws-array-sub >= 31
82         Invoke calendarArrayCollection "AtPut"
83              Using ws-array-sub
84                    ws-client-number(ws-array-sub)
85     End-Perform *>varying ws-array-sub
86
87     Invoke UserInterface
88                  "accept-day-request-info"
89                  Returning ws-day-info
90     *>First create a subarray of the
91     *>desired block of days.
92     Invoke calendarArrayCollection
93           "CopyEmptyWithSize"
94           using ws-number-of-days
95           returning emptyArrayTemplate
96     Invoke emptyArrayTemplate "AtAllPut"
97           Using ws-empty-room-value
98
99     *>Now search calendar for subarray
100    Invoke calendarArrayCollection
101          "IndexOfSubcollection"
102          Using emptyArrayTemplate
103                ws-from-index
104          Returning ws-day-index
105    Evaluate ws-day-index
106       When 0
107          Display "Room not available"
108       When Other
109          Move ws-number-of-days
110                 to ws-display-2-byte-numeric
111          Display "Room available for "
112                 ws-display-2-byte-numeric
113                 with no advancing
114          Move ws-day-index
115                 to ws-display-2-byte-numeric
116          Display " days beginning day "
117                 ws-display-2-byte-numeric
118    End-evaluate *>ws-day-index
119    .
120  400-create-array-object.
121    Move 4 to ws-element-size
122    *>Create a pic X(4) intrinsic class
123    Invoke CompX "newclass"
124                 Using ws-element-size
125                 Returning PicX4Class
126    *>Create the array
127    Move 31 to ws-array-size
128    Invoke Array "OfValues" Using PicX4Class
129                            ws-array-size
130                 Returning calendarArrayCollection
131    .
```

Figure 11-22. Room25's Driver.

3. The method AtPutAll designated by the Invoke of lines 96 and 97 loads 0000 (from the data item ws-empty-room-value defined at lines 35 and 36) into each of the five elements of the array.

4. The IndexOfSubcollection method invoked beginning line 100 searches the array.

```
            Invoke calendarArrayCollection
                   "IndexOfSubCollection"
                   Using emptyArrayTemplate
                         ws-from-index
                   Returning ws-day-index
```

This method's parameters are as follows.

- Using requires two parameters.

  The first parameter (emptyArrayTemplate) is usage object reference that identifies the comparison array.

  The second parameter (ws-from-index) must be a four-byte comp-5 data item containing the element number at which the array search is to start.

- Returning requires one parameter (ws-day-index) that will contain the number of the first element of the block found to be identical to the comparison block of the Using. If none is found, the method returns a value of zero. This parameter must be a four-byte comp-5 data item.

Using a Dictionary—Room26

The next "agenda item" is the dictionary collection class, a convenient device for storing calendars for many rooms. However, before jumping into that topic, let's review a common use of ordinary Cobol tables. This will provide you an insight to the dictionary.

About Cobol Tables

Assume J&B (of the programming assignments) has assigned product IDs as follows.

Product ID	Description
110	Mello Blue
300	X-Tacey
320	Strawberry
120	Superb
200	Stretch

For much of the processing, the product number is to be replaced by a product description taken from the preceding table. To illustrate how you would use this table, assume you want the description for product 120. You scan the left column searching for the entry equal to 120. Upon finding it, you read across and access the description Superb. In mathematical terminology, the left column contains the *table arguments* and the right column contains the *table functions*. Setting up such a table in Cobol is relatively simple:

```
01  product-table.
    10   product-table-entries      occurs 20 times
                                    indexed by product-index.
         20   product-ID            pic X(03).
         20   product-description   pic X(12).
```

The Search verb provides a convenient means for performing the above described search; assuming you want the description for product 120, the statement takes the following form.

```
Search product-table
  at end
    Move spaces to product-description
  When product-ID (product-index) = "120"
    Move product-description (product-index)
              to product-description
End-Search *> product-table
```

A table used this way is sometimes called a **keyed table** because the first entry is serves as the key field of the table. In such a table, the key field must be unique. Consider the application: it would be erroneous to have two different products with the same product number. However, Cobol does not prohibit such duplication in a simple table like this.

About the Dictionary Collection Class

An OOCobol dictionary is a lot like the table of the preceding section (except you do not have access to data by the entry number). Each entry consists of two components: a **key** and a **data element**. The dictionary is a keyed collection class that does not allow duplicate keys. A dictionary can contain objects as well as intrinsic data with the flexibility shown by the table of Figure 11-23.

Multiple Room Calendars—Room26

Room24 and Room25 illustrate using the array class for storage and access to the calendar for a single room where the room-calendar array is created for each room request. However, another way to handle this is to create and load a dictionary object with calendars for all rooms—something similar to the product table. Components of the dictionary will be:

- Key: The room number (intrinsic data)
- Data element: The room's calendar object

The next example, Room26, uses the dictionary to perform exactly the same function as the preceding Room25. You see the components of this application in Figure 11-24.

- The application is expanded to full object orientation by the inclusion of a manager class.

Key	Data Element
intrinsic data	intrinsic data
intrinsic data	object
object	intrinsic data
object	object

Figure 11-23 Dictionary types.

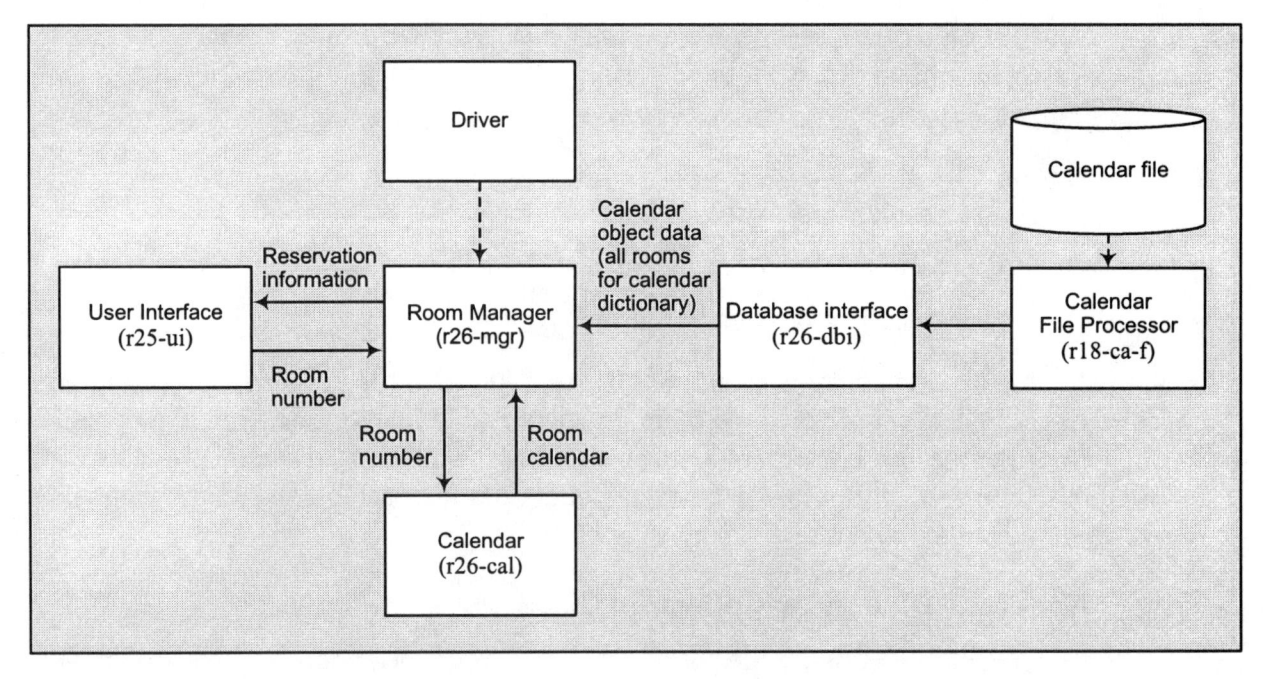

[Figure: Class diagram showing Driver, User Interface (r25-ui), Room Manager (r26-mgr), Calendar (r26-cal), Database interface (r26-dbi), Calendar File Processor (r18-ca-f), and Calendar file, with data flows labeled: Reservation information, Room number, Room number, Room calendar, Calendar object data (all rooms for calendar dictionary)]

Figure 11-24. Class diagram for Room26.

- Separate database and file handling classes are included for access to the calendar file. The File Processor is taken from Room18, the file processor used in Chapter 9 illustrating aggregate structures.
- A Calendar class contains the calendar dictionary as object data.
- The UI is taken from Room25, the preceding application.

In the Calendar class listing of Figure 11-25 you will be focusing on three basic dictionary functions: creating, loading, and accessing. You will find the first two activities in `create-calendar-dictionary` method and the third in the `get-room-calendar-object` method.

Creating a Dictionary

Creating a dictionary object is slightly more complicated than creating an array.

1. Either component of the dictionary (key or data element) or both of them can be intrinsic. If intrinsic data, you must create an intrinsic class designating the size of that component.
2. You must define the type of dictionary you want to create (refer to Figure 11-23) using a method of the class Association that produces a **dictionary template**.
3. Using the dictionary template, you must instantiate the dictionary class thereby creating a dictionary object.

These three actions are performed at lines 74-89 of Calendar. Since the key of the room dictionary is to be intrinsic data, the room number's length is returned in

Collection Classes

```cobol
        $set sourceformat "free"
*>*******************************************
*> Room Rental System
*> W. Price  Jun 9, 2000          R26-CAL.CBL
*>
*> This class contains the room-calendar dictionary
*> as object data.
*> It provides an invoking program an array object
*> consisting of 31-day reservation status for
*> a requested room.
*>*******************************************

Identification Division.
      Class-id.  CalendarClass
                 inherits from Base.

Environment Division.
      Object Section.
      Class-Control.
            CalendarClass      is class "r26-cal"
            Association        is class "associtn"
            Array              is class "array"
            Dictionary         is class "dictinry"
            CompX              is class "compx"
            Base               is class "base"
                 .
*>=============================================
FACTORY.

   Data Division.
      Object-Storage Section.
         01 roomCalendarDictionary  object reference.

   Procedure Division.
*>-------------------------------------------
   Method-id. create-calendar-dictionary.
*>-------------------------------------------
      Data Division.
         Working-Storage Section.

         01 collection-class-params.
            *>These used to create the dictionary
            10 ws-key-length       pic S9(9) comp-5
                                   value 3.
            10 ws-dict-capacity    pic S9(9) comp-5
                                   value 10.
            10 KeyTemplate         object reference.
            10 DataTemplate        object reference.
            10 DictionaryTemplate  object reference.

            *>These are used to create the arrays
            *>that are loaded into the dictionary.
            10 ws-array-size       pic S9(9) comp-5
                                   value 31.
            10 ws-element-size     pic S9(9) comp-5
                                   value 4.
            10 ws-day-sub          pic S9(9) comp-5.
            10 ws-room-sub         pic 9(02).

            10 elementTemplate     object reference.
            10 reservationArray    object reference.

         Linkage Section.
            01 ls-room-calendar-table.
               10 ls-calendar-record
                                   occurs 10 times.
                  20 ls-room-number   pic X(03).
                  20 ls-client-number pic X(04)
                                   occurs 31 times.

      Procedure Division
                  Using ls-room-calendar-table.
      *>Create pic X class to define the key.
      *>    (room number is 3 bytes)
         Invoke CompX "NewClass"
             Using ws-key-length
             Returning KeyTemplate

      *>Set DataTemplate to null which tells
      *>NewClass that data part is an object
      *>Then create the dictionary template
         Set DataTemplate to null
         Invoke Association "NewClass"
             Using KeyTemplate, DataTemplate
             Returning DictionaryTemplate

      *>Now create the dictionary
         Invoke Dictionary "OfValues"
             Using DictionaryTemplate, ws-dict-capacity
             Returning roomCalendarDictionary

      *>The next step is to load the two tables
      *>defined above into array objects then
      *>load each into the dictionary
         Invoke CompX "NewClass"
             Using ws-element-size
             Returning elementTemplate

         Perform with test after varying ws-room-sub
                 from 1 by 1
                     until ws-room-sub = 10
         *>Create the array
         Invoke Array "OfValues"
                     Using elementTemplate
                        ws-array-size
                     Returning reservationArray
         *>Load the array object
         Perform with test after varying ws-day-sub
                 from 1 by 1
                     until ws-day-sub >= 31
             Invoke reservationArray "AtPut"
                 Using ws-day-sub
                     ls-client-number(ws-room-sub,
                                      ws-day-sub)
         End-Perform *>varying ws-day-sub
         *>The array is loaded so put the room
         *>number and the array in the dictionary
         Invoke roomCalendarDictionary "AtPut"
                 Using ls-room-number(ws-room-sub)
                     reservationArray
         End-Perform *>varying ws-room-sub

   End Method create-calendar-dictionary.
*>-------------------------------------------
   Method-ID. get-room-calendar-object.
*>-------------------------------------------
      Data Division.
         Working-Storage Section.
            01 ws-room-switch-bool      pic X comp-5.
               88 ws-invalid-room-number   value 0.
               88 ws-valid-room-number     value 1.

         Linkage Section.
            01 ls-room-number           pic X(03).
            01 ls-roomCalendarObject    object reference.

      Procedure Division Using ls-room-number
                         Returning ls-roomCalendarObject.
      *> Check to ensure room is in the dictionary
         Invoke roomCalendarDictionary "IncludesKey"
                 Using ls-room-number
                     Returning ws-room-switch-bool
         Evaluate TRUE
            When ws-invalid-room-number
               Set ls-roomCalendarObject to null
            When ws-valid-room-number
               Invoke roomCalendarDictionary "At"
                   Using ls-room-number
                       Returning ls-roomCalendarObject
         End-Evaluate *>TRUE
   End Method get-room-calendar-object.
*>-------------------------------------------
END FACTORY.
END CLASS CalendarClass.
```

Figure 11-25. The Calendar class—r26-cal.

KeyTemplate (line 46) by the Invoke of line 74. You are familiar with this technique from previous examples.

Next, the dictionary's template is created by the NewClass method of the Association class (see lines 82-84).

```
Invoke Association "NewClass"
        Using KeyTemplate, DataTemplate
        Returning DictionaryTemplate
```

This method's parameters are as follows.

- Using requires two parameters.
  The first parameter (KeyTemplate) designates the key. In this case, it is the key size class created at line 74.
  The second parameter (DataTemplate) is an object reference data item set to null (see line 81).
- Returning requires one parameter (DictionaryTemplate); it is an object reference data item that identifies the dictionary template.

Note that the NewClass method determines which type of dictionary to create (refer to Figure 11-23) by inspecting the two objects listed as Using parameters. A value of null indicates an object; any non-null is treated as an intrinsic definition.

The dictionary is then instantiated by the Dictionary class's OfValues method (lines 87-89).

```
Invoke Dictionary "OfValues"
        Using DictionaryTemplate, ws-dict-capacity
        Returning roomCalendarDictionary
```

This method's parameters are as follows.

- Using requires two parameters.
  The first parameter (DictionaryTemplate) designates the dictionary template created by the Association class.
  The second parameter (ws-dict-capacity) is a four-byte comp-5 data item designating the size of the dictionary (the number of entries). Its value is defined at line 45).
- Returning requires one parameter (roomCalendarDictionary); it is an object reference data item that will serve as the object handle to the newly created dictionary. Note that roomCalendarDictionary is Calendar class's object data (line 31).

Loading the Dictionary

Once you create the dictionary object, you can load it. Remember, the dictionary object itself contains objects (calendar arrays) as well as intrinsic data (room numbers) as illustrated in Figure 11-26. So in the process of loading the dictionary, you must first create a calendar object then place the calendar data in that object. The code of lines 98-114 in Figure 11-25 does this.

The newly created array object is placed in the dictionary using the dictionary object method AtPut (see lines 117-119).

```
Invoke ls-dictionary "AtPut"
          Using ls-room-number(ws-room-sub)
                reservationArray
```

This method's parameters are as follows.

- Using requires two parameters.
  The first parameter [the subscripted item ls-room-number(ws-room-sub)] designates the key. If the key is intrinsic data, this parameter must be the same size and type as the key. Notice that this is a data value and *not* an index or subscript value as with conventional Cobol tables.
  The second parameter (reservationArray) designates the data element.

Since duplication of the key value is not allowed in a dictionary, the AtPut replaces the previous entry if a current entry is found with the same key value. If this is a concern in an application, you must check for existence of the key value using the Dictionary's IncludesKey method. You will see it used in the get-room-calendar-object method.

Accessing a Dictionary

If there is no dictionary entry with the input key value when you access a dictionary, an error occurs and terminates the program unless trapped. So prior to attempting an entry access the room number is validated by the following Invoke (from lines 139-141).

```
Invoke room-dict "IncludesKey"
          Using ls-room-number
          Returning ls-room-switch-bool
```

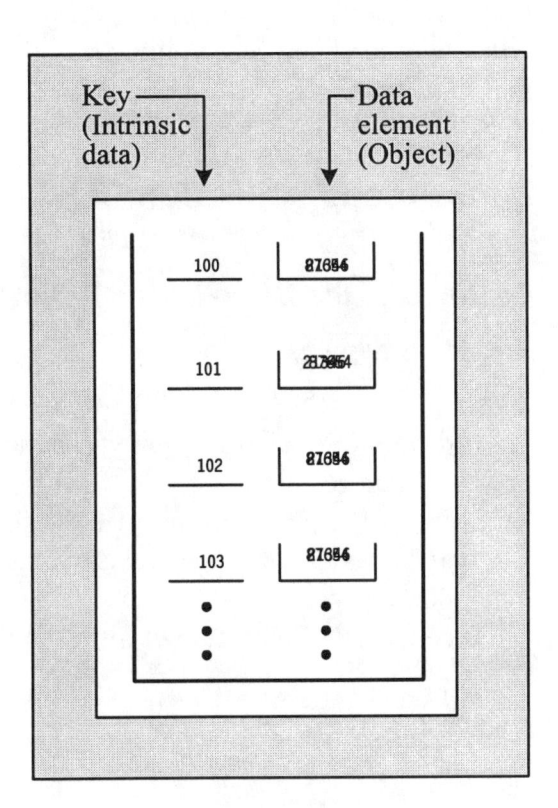

Figure 11-26.
The dictionary: an object containing other objects.

This method's parameters are as follows.
- Using requires one parameter (ls-room-number), a data item that designates the key value for which the dictionary is to be checked. It must be the same data type as the dictionary's key.
- Returning requires one parameter (ws-room-switch-bool), a pic X comp-5 data item. A value 1 (true) is returned if there is an entry in the dictionary with its key value the same as the input key value. If not, it returns a value 0 (false).

Accessing the desired dictionary entry is accomplished by the At method of lines 146-148.

```
Invoke roomCalendarDictionary "At"
    Using ls-room-number
    Returning ls-roomCalendarObject
```

This method's parameters are as follows.
- Using requires one parameter (ls-room-number), a data item that designates the key value for which the dictionary is to be searched. It must be the same data type as the dictionary's key.
- Returning requires one parameter (roomCalendarObject), a data item to contain the returned data element. Its type must correspond to that of the dictionary's data element.

Room Manager—r26-mgr

Room Manager, listed in Figure 11-27 involves no new collection class methods beyond those of preceding examples as most of the code is taken from Room25's Driver (Figure 11-22). For instance, Manager's lines 111-138 (to create the template array and search the reservation array) are identical to corresponding lines 92-118 in Figure 11-22.

More About Collection Classes

Features of the Micro Focus Collection Classes

Preceding descriptions of the collection classes have alluded to the following properties of the sample classes.

Indexed—Some use indexing (Dictionary has an index element) and others do not (for instance, Bag).

Grow—The ability to increase the size. For some classes, the size is increased automatically when the capacity is exceeded; for others, the program must invoke a method to grow.

Duplicates—Some classes allow duplicate entries; others do not.

These properties are summarized for the nine Micro Focus collection classes in the table of Figure 10-28

Collection Classes

```cobol
       $set sourceformat "free"
 1 *>***********************************************
 2 *> Room Rental System
 3 *> W. Price   June 13, 2000            R26-MGR.CBL
 4 *>
 5 *> RoomManager controls access to room reservation
 6 *> data as requested by the user.
 7 *> Methods:
 8 *>   initialize-for-processing
 9 *>   process-room-request
10 *>   process-user-requests
11 *>***********************************************
12
13 Identification Division.
14     Class-ID.  RoomManager
15              inherits from BaseClass.
16
17 Environment Division.
18     Object Section.
19     Class-Control.
20         RoomManager        is class "r26-mgr"
21         DatabaseInterface  is class "r26-dbi"
22         BaseClass          is class "base"
23         CalendarClass      is class "r26-cal"
24         UserInterface      is class "r25-ui"
25         Array              is class "array"
26         CompX              is class "compx"
27         .
28 *>=================================================
29 FACTORY.
30
31 Procedure Division.
32     *>...............................................
33     Method-ID. process-user-requests.
34     *>...............................................
35     Data Division.
36         Working-Storage Section.
37         01 ws-room-number-request   pic X(03).
38         01 calendarArrayCollection
39                          object reference.
40
41     Procedure Division.
42         Invoke Self "initialize-for-processing"
43         Invoke UserInterface "announce-program"
44         Invoke UserInterface "accept-room-number"
45               Returning ws-room-number-request
46         Perform Until
47               ws-room-number-request = spaces
48            Invoke CalendarClass
49                  "get-room-calendar-object"
50                  Using ws-room-number-request
51                  Returning calendarArrayCollection
52            Evaluate calendarArrayCollection
53               When null
54                  Display "No such room number"
55               When Other
56                  Invoke Self "process-room-request"
57                     Using calendarArrayCollection
58            End-evaluate  *> ws-room-calendar-data
59            Invoke UserInterface "accept-room-number"
60                  Returning ws-room-number-request
61         End-Perform *> Until room-number = spaces
62         Invoke DatabaseInterface
63                  "disconnect-from-data"
64         .
65     End Method process-user-requests.
66     *>...............................................
67     Method-ID. initialize-for-processing. *>Private
68     *>...............................................
69     Data Division.
70         01 ws-room-calendar-table.
71            10 calendar-record
72                       occurs 10 times.
73               20 ws-room-number     pic X(03).
74               20 ws-customer-number pic X(04)
75                       occurs 31 times.
76     Procedure Division.
77         Invoke DatabaseInterface "connect-to-data"
78         Invoke DatabaseInterface
79                  "get-calendar-data"
80                  Returning ws-room-calendar-table
81         Invoke CalendarClass
82                  "create-calendar-dictionary"
83                  Using ws-room-calendar-table
84         Invoke UserInterface "announce-program"
85         .
86     End Method initialize-for-processing.
87
88     *>...............................................
89     Method-ID. process-room-request. *>Private
90     *>...............................................
91     Data Division.
92         Working-Storage Section.
93         01 ws-day-info.
94            10 ws-number-of-days pic s9(09) comp-5.
95            10 ws-from-index     pic s9(09) comp-5.
96         01 ws-day-index         pic s9(09) comp-5.
97         01 ws-emptyArrayTemplate
98                          object reference.
99         01 ws-display-2-byte-numeric  pic 9(02).
100        01 ws-empty-room-value       pic X(04)
101                          value "0000".
102    Linkage Section.
103        01 ls-calendarArrayCollection
104                          object reference.
105
106    Procedure Division
107            Using ls-calendarArrayCollection .
108        Invoke UserInterface
109                  "accept-day-request-info"
110                  Returning  ws-day-info
111   *>First create a subarray of the
112        Invoke ls-calendarArrayCollection
113                  "CopyEmptyWithSize"
114                  using ws-number-of-days
115                  returning ws-emptyArrayTemplate
116        Invoke ws-emptyArrayTemplate "AtAllPut"
117                  Using ws-empty-room-value
118   *>Now search calendar for subarray
119   *>Move day-number to start-index
120        Invoke ls-calendarArrayCollection
121                  "IndexOfSubcollection"
122                  Using ws-emptyArrayTemplate
123                        ws-from-index
124                  Returning ws-day-index
125        Evaluate ws-day-index
126           When 0
127              Display "Room not available"
128           When Other
129              Move ws-number-of-days
130                  to ws-display-2-byte-numeric
131              Display "Room available for "
132                  ws-display-2-byte-numeric
133                  with no advancing
134              Move ws-day-index
135                  to ws-display-2-byte-numeric
136              Display " days beginning day "
137                  ws-display-2-byte-numeric
138        End-evaluate *>ws-day-index
139        .
140    End Method process-room-request.
141 END FACTORY.
142 END CLASS RoomManager.
```

Figure 11-27. Room Manager—r26-mgr.

Class	Indexed	Grow	Duplicates
Bag	No	Automatic	Yes
Array	Yes	Manual	Yes
CharacterArray	Yes	Manual	Yes
OrderedCollection	By order of insertion	Automatic	Yes
SortedCollection	By sort order	Automatic	Yes
ValueSet	No	Automatic	No
Dictionary	By key values	Automatic	No
IdentityDictionary	By key object handles	Automatic	No
IdentitySet	No	Automatic	No

Figure 10-28 Properties of Micro Focus collection classes.

Some Other Typical Collection Class Instance Methods

As indicated earlier, each of the collection classes includes many instance methods. Following are a few of them that you might find useful in exploring the collection classes described in this chapter. The entry in parentheses adjacent to the method name indicates the collection class for which that method is available. The correspondence is: A—Array, D—Dictionary, and B—Bag. Each parameter is identified regarding its type. *Element size* means that the parameter must correspond in size and type to the data item as defined in the collection.

Instance methods	Parameters	Description
AddAll (AD)	using acollection (object reference)	Add all the elements of acollection to this collection.
At (AD)	using anindex (pic S9(9) comp-5) returning anelement (element size)	Return the element at index position anindex.
AtPut (AD)	using anindex (pic S9(9) comp-5) avalue (element size)	Store avalue at the index position anindex.
Capacity (ADB)	using thesize (pic S9(9) comp-5)	Return the total number of elements capable of being stored in this collection.
Concat (AD)	using anarray (object reference) returning newcoll (object reference)	Return a new collection (newcoll) containing the elements of this collection concatenated with the elements of anarray.
CopyEmpty (ADB)	returning newcoll (object reference)	Return the empty collection newcoll the same type and size as this collection.
CopyFromTo (A)	using fromindex (pic S9(9) comp-5) toindex (pic S9(9) comp-5) returning newarray (object reference)	Return newarray which is a subset of this array determined by the indexes fromindex and toindex.
CopyWithout (A)	using anelement (element size) returning newarray (object reference)	Return newarray that is identical to this array but with the elements equal to anelement.
DeepCopy (ADB)	returning newcoll (object reference)	Create newcoll which identical to this collection containing replicated elements.

Instance methods	Parameters	Description
DeepFinalize (ADB)		Destroy this collection and its contents.
DisplayKeysAndData (AD)		Display the keys (indexes) and value of every element in this collection. Note: element values are displayed by their ASCII values. This method is helpful in debugging.
GrowTo (A)	using newsize (pic S9(9) comp-5)	Change the capacity of this collection to the value of newsize.
Includes (AD)	using avalue (element size) returning truefalse (pic X comp-4)	If this collection contains avalue, return truefalse as true (value 1); else return false (value 0).
IsEmpty (ADB)	returning truefalse (pic X comp-4)	Return true (1) if this collection is empty; else return false (0).
Last (A)	returning anelement (element size)	Return the last element of this array.
LastIndexOf (A)	using anelement (element size) fromindex (pic S9(9) comp-5) toindex (pic S9(9) comp-5) returning anindex (pic S9(9) comp-5)	Return the index position of the last occurrence of anelement between the indexes fromindex and toindex. This method searches the array backwards.
OccurencesOf (AD)	using avalue (element size) returning anumber (pic S9(9) comp-5)	Return the number of times avalue occurs in this collection.
Remove (AB)	using avalue (element size)	Remove the designated entry from the collection.
RemoveAll (AD)	using acollection (object reference)	Remove from this collection, all the elements that are equal to the elements of acollection.
RemoveKey (D)	using akey (same as key element)	Remove the entry designated by akey.
ReplaceAll (A)	using avalue1 (element size) avalue2 (element size) fromindex (pic S9(9) comp-5) toindex (pic S9(9) comp-5)	Replace all the elements with a value equal avalue1 with avalue2 within the range of elements fromindex to toindex.

Summing Up

Project Summary

Room21 (Proj1101) illustrates basic principles of the bag collection class. It save user-selected room objects in a bag and illustrates bag methods to return the count of the number of objects in the bag, remove an object, and invoke a method on all members of the bag (iterate).

Room22 (Proj1102) illustrates creating a new bag whose contents meet a consist of objects from an existing bag that meet a method-specified condition.

Room23 (Proj1103) shows how to return data (through optional parameters) from a callback using the bag class of the preceding examples.

Room24 (Proj1104) uses the array collection class for storing and accessing a calendar object. The user enters a beginning date and an ending date request. The application searches the selected calendar object to determine the earliest date the room is available during the designated time period.

Room25 (Proj1105) is a variation of Room24 in which the user enters the desired number of days and the earliest acceptable day. The application searches the calendar object for the earliest date the room is available for the requested number of days.

Room26 (Proj1106) performs the same function as Room25 except it uses a dictionary collection object to hold the calendar for all rooms.

General Summary

This chapter has provided you a brief insight to the nature of collection classes by examining three Micro Focus classes: Bag, Array, and Dictionary.

Characteristics of the Bag collection class are: it is not indexed, its size grows automatically as needed, and it allows duplicates. This collection class can contain either intrinsic data or objects.

Characteristics of the Array collection class: it is indexed, its size must be increased by program action (it does not grow in size automatically), and duplicate entries are allowed. This collection class can contain either intrinsic data or objects.

Characteristics of the Dictionary collection class are: it is indexed, its size increases automatically as needed, and duplicate entries are not allowed. A dictionary consists of a key value and a data value. Both the key and the data can be instrinsic data or objects.

The Do iterator provides the ability to invoke a method on all elements of a collection (send a message to every element). Results can be returned using optional parameters. The Select iterator also invokes a method on every element of a collection. However, it applies a program-defined criterion for adding the element to a new collection.

Assignments

11-1

This assignment must use a Bag to store and retrieve dessert data. Within a loop, the user must be queried for a dessert ID (a blank entry terminates the loop). For each dessert request, the application must:

1. Calculate the inventory value. For Rope desserts use the product of the Roll length, Rolls on hand, and Per inch cost. For Delight desserts use the product of Quantity on hand and Price.

2. Generate a dessert object with Dessert ID, Dessert description, Dessert type, and Inventory value as object data.
3. Store the object in a bag.

Upon completion of the loop provide for the following

1. Display the count of the number of dessert objects in the bag.
2. Allow the user to request a display for either the Rope or the Delight data. For a Rope request, display the ID, Description and Inventory value for each object in the bag for which the Dessert type is rope. Do the same for Delight.

Modify code from earlier assignments in creating the needed classes for this assignment to minimize the amount of new code you must write. For instance, you can probably use the DBI of Chapter 4 with relatively little change.

11-2

Expand Assignment 11-1 to include a Select iterator that creates two bags, one containg Rope desserts and the other containing Delight desserts. Display the contents of each bag.

11-3

This assignment must use a Bag to store and retrieve event data. Within a loop, the user must be queried for a event ID (a blank entry terminates the loop). For each event request, the application must:

1. Calculate the Cost. For Ocean events use the product of the Duration and the Daily rate. For Space events use the sum of Accommodation charge and Launch fee.
2. Generate an event object with Event ID, Event description, Event type, and Cost as object data.
3. Store the object in a bag.

Upon completion of the loop provide for the following

1. Display the count of the number of event objects in the bag.
2. Allow the user to request a display for either the Ocean or the Space data. For a Ocean request, display the ID, Description and Cost for each object in the bag for which the Event type is ocean. Do the same for space.

Modify code from earlier assignments in creating the needed classes for this assignment to minimize the amount of new code you must write. For instance, you can probably use the DBI of Chapter 4 with relatively little change.

11-4

Expand Assignment 11-3 to include a Select iterator that creates two bags, one containg Ocean events and the other containing Space events. Display the contents of each bag.

The Examples CD

Appendix Contents

Loading the Examples CD 280
    Folder (Subdirectory) Contents 280
    Loading Files From the Examples CD 280
    Alternate Loading of CD 281
Conventions Used in this Book 281
    Example Applications Arranged by Project 281
    Folders for Examples and Assignments 281
    Program Naming Conventions 282

Appendix A

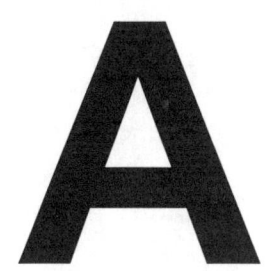

Introduction

This appendix explains how to load the CD accompanying this book and describes using its contents. From it you will learn about the following.
- The procedure for copying the CD contents to your hard disk and making them available for use.
- Arranging example applications and assignments by folder.
- A program naming convention.

Loading the Examples CD

Folder (Subdirectory) Contents

The Example Applications CD included with this book contains the folder **Eooc2** which itself contains the following folders.

Pertaining to the books examples
> **eProgs**: Contains Net Express project folders. Each of these folders includes components of a single Net Express example application.
> **eProgsPC**: Contains Personal COBOL project folders. Each of these folders includes components of a single Personal COBOL example application.
> **eData**: Contains indexed data files used by the books examples.

Pertaining to the books assignments
> **aProgs**: Contains class definitions for selected Net Express programming assignments.
> **aProgsPC**: Contains class definitions for selected Personal COBOL programming assignments.
> **aData**: Contains indexed data files required for programming assignments.

As you work with examples and prepare your own applications, you will probably need to look at data file listings. You will find them in Appendix D.

Loading Files From the Examples CD

Although you can load the Examples CD contents into any drive or folder, you will find life much easier if you load to drive C according to the following instructions.

1. Bring up Windows Explorer and display the CD directory. You will see the single folder Eooc2.
2. Copy this folder (not just its contents, but the entire folder) to your C: drive. Windows copies all of these files to your disk with the Read-only attribute on. Neither Net Express nor Personal COBOL can run them in this state.
3. Turn the Read-only attribute off. Do this from Windows Explorer by double-clicking on the file name FixAttr.bat stored in the Eooc2 folder.

Inspect any of the examples files to ensure that the ReadOnly attribute is off. For instance:
> Open the Eooc\eProgs\Proj0101 folder.
> Right-click the file r01-prog.cbl.
> Check the Read-only attribute.

If this attribute contains a check mark, the batch program did not function properly.

This book's file-accessing example programs look for the files in the folder C:\eooc2-files. Early copies of the CD do not create and load that folder. If after loading from the CD, you do not have the folder C:/eooc2-files, do the following.

1. Create the folder C:\eooc2-files.
2. Copy the contents of C:\eooc2\edata into the new folder.

Alternate Loading of CD

The Examples CD contains a number of programs, some used by the example applications and others that you will use in completing assignments. Those that access data files (database and file processor classes) include Select clauses identifying the file location as follows.

- C:\Eooc2-files for data files required by examples.
- C:\Eooc2\aData for data files required by assignments.

If you load onto a drive other than the root directory of drive C then you must change the above path entries (for Select statements) in the appropriate file processing programs stored in the folders aProgs and eProgs (Net Express) or aProgsPC and eProgsPC (Personal COBOL).

Also, be aware that copying the files from the CD brings the read-only attribute with them. The batch file of the preceding load Step 3 turns that attribute off. If you put the files in some other drive or folder, you will need to reset the Read-only attribute yourself. Inspect FixAttr.bat to see how to do this.

Conventions Used in this Book

Example Applications Arranged by Project

Examples of this book focus on various aspects of a room reservation system. In all, you will study 27 different example applications organized as projects, consistent with the Micro Focus technique for designating applications. A project is simply a grouping of programs needed for a given application (the project file itself is effectively a directory for the project). Except for the first two examples, each includes its defining project file in a ready-to-run form. The book's example projects are numbered consecutively beginning with one. Throughout the book you will see each application referred to by the word Room and the example (project) number. For instance, Chapter 7's second example is identified as Room12.

Folders for Examples and Assignments

In running either Net Express or Personal COBOL you can work from any folder (or from any drive, if you have multiple partitions or two hard drives). To provide the simplest possible working environment, each of this book's example applications is stored in a separate folder within the appropriate examples folder (**eProgs** for Net Express and **eProgsPC** for Personal COBOL). A naming convention is used to relate the folder to the book's chapter describing the application. For instance, the folder **Proj0301** pertains to Chapter 3's Example 1.

For your own assignments, I suggest you use the same technique. For instance, you might create the folder **My-Assg**. Then for each assignment, create a folder within **My-Assgns**, for instance, **Assg0301** for Chapter 3's Assignment 1 (3-1). This is a convenient means for keeping everything straight and for providing portability if you are using this book in a formal course and must hand in diskettes with completed assignments. Personal COBOL Note: You should limit all file names to eight characters as Personal COBOL truncates longer names making them difficult to recognize.

Program Naming Conventions

Both Net Express and Personal COBOL allow you to group programs of an application as a project. Beginning Chapter 3, each project consists of a conventional program, called a driver, and one or more class programs. A standard naming convention is used to make it easy for you to relate individual files. For instance, the folder Proj0702 (Chapter 7's 2nd example) includes the following three programs.

r12-drvr.cbl	A driver program, a conventional Cobol program to begin execution. Each application includes a driver.
r12-room.cbl	A class program (class definition) contains data and procedures defining the room class.
r12-dbi.cbl	A class program (class definition) that that describe characteristics of the database interface object.

Check comment lines at the beginning of the driver program; they contain a list of all class programs comprising the project. Program naming convention breaks down as follows (using r12-drvr.cbl as the example).

r	identifies this as pertaining to the Room application.
12	designates the twelfth example application of this book.
drvr	identifies this as the driver program. This portion of the name is the unique element that identifies for you the type of program or class.
cbl	is the required extension for a source program name.

As Personal COBOL was originally DOS based, it follows the 8-character file naming DOS convention. Consequently, I've used abbreviations for the filenames in order to stay within this limit. If you are using Net Express, do not so limit yourself. Use descriptive names and benefit from their documentation value.

Getting Started: Net Express

Appendix Contents

The Interactive Development Environment: First Look 286
    Net Express Projects 286
    A Sample Project 286
    Creating a New Project 286
    The Project Window 290
    The NetExpress Toolbar 290
    Compiling Programs of a Project 291
    The Animator—Running a Program 291
    Stopping the Animator 292
Handling Program Errors 292
    Correcting Compiler Errors 292
    Stepping Through a Program for Debugging 293
    Using Breakpoints for Debugging 295
Entering Programs 296
    Setting Edit Options 296
    Entering a New Program 296

Appendix B

Appendix Introduction

This appendix introduces you to the basic features of the Net Express Interactive Development Environment (IDE), a working environment that integrates all the tools you need for writing, editing, compiling, and running Cobol programs. From this appendix you will learn about the following

- The nature of IDE projects.
- Starting the IDE and accessing an application (project).
- Building a project (compiling the programs comprising the project).
- Running a project.
- Debugging programs using built-in assistance tools such as breakpoints and direct interaction with the program during execution.

The Interactive Development Environment: First Look

Net Express Projects

The Net Express Integrated Development Environment (IDE) is a working environment that integrates all the tools you need for writing, editing, compiling, and running Cobol programs. Typically, a Cobol application will consist of a main program and numerous subprograms; an object-oriented program will consist of a driver and numerous class definitions. One of the characteristics of the IDE is that it allows you to identify components of an application as belonging to a **project**. For each project you designate under the IDE, a special project file is created. (Its file extension is .APP, for **application file**.) This project file is somewhat of a directory to the programs comprising project. One advantage of the project concept is that it provides you simple means of keeping track of programs, subprograms, and classes that make up an application. Another very significant advantage is that the project file maintains information regarding whether or not changes have been made to any of the program components. At any time, you can request Net Express to rebuild a project and it will recompile all programs that have changed since the last rebuild.

A Sample Project

The best way to learn about the IDE and Net Express is to use them. So let's create an application consisting of the program and subprogram described in Chapter 2—Room02-prog.cbl and Room02-sub.cbl stored in the folder C:\Eooc2\eProgs\Proj0102. In this tutorial you will do the following.

- Start the Net Express.
- Create the project.
- Designate files belonging to that project (Room02-prog and Room02-sub).
- Rebuild the project (compile the programs of the project).
- Run the program.
- End the process.

> For this example, I'm using long filenames, the approach I recommend for Net Express users. All other example projects of this book adhere to the 8-character filename limitation for compatibility with Personal COBOL.

Before you begin the following sequence, check the contents of the Proj0102 folder and you will see that it contains only the above two Cobol source files.

Creating a New Project

You start Net Express by clicking on

        Windows Start/Programs/Micro Focus NetExpress/NetExpress

You will then see the Net Express window of Figure B-1. (You may see a different screen if you are using a version higher than 3.0. However, the basic OOCobol principles will not be affected.) If you or someone else has worked with Net Express,

Getting Started: Net Express

Figure B-1.
The Net Express opening screen.

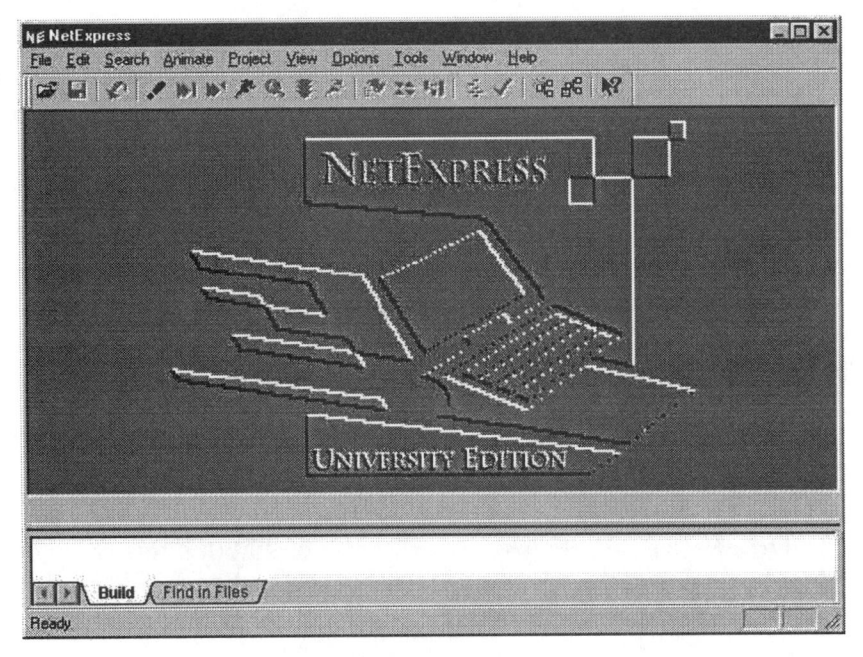

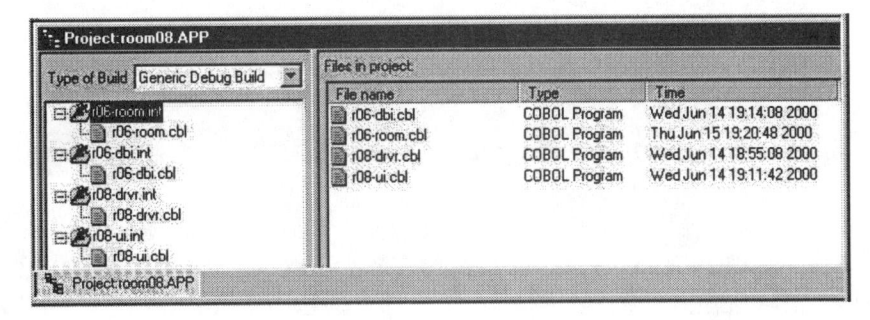

Figure B-2.
The Net Express project window.

your screen might include a window like Figure B-2 identifying the project that was open when Net Express was previously shut down. If so, then close it by clicking File/Close or by clicking on the close button of the sub-window title bar. (Be careful not to close the Net Express screen.) Proceed as follows to create a new project

1. From the Net Express main screen, click on File/New thus producing a window that looks like Figure B-3.
2. You want to create a new project, so double-click the Project entry and you will see the window of Figure B-4.
3. Notice four entries in this window. Highlight Project from an existing application as shown in Figure B-4 (your existing application consists of the program and subprogram you copied from the CD).

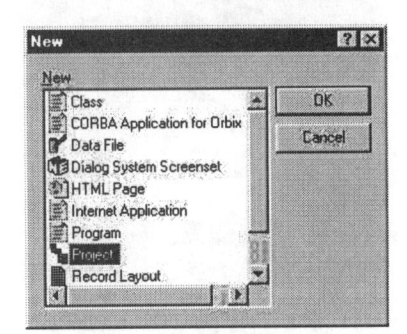

Figure B-3.
The New window.

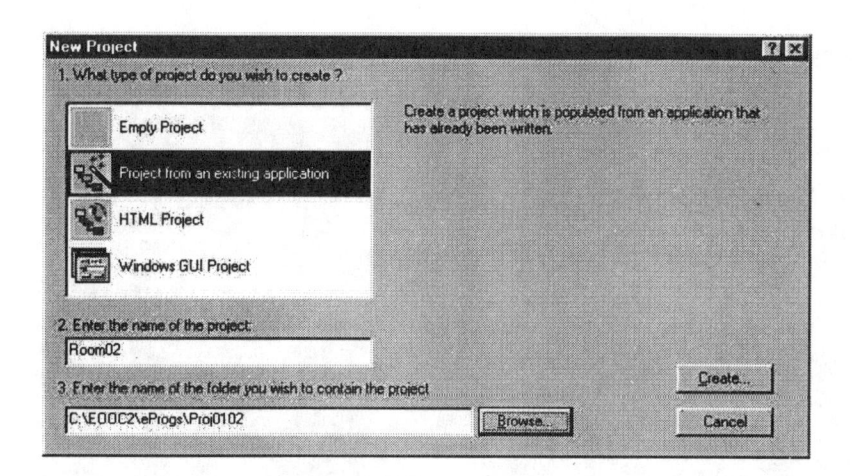

Figure B-4.
The New Project window.

4. Type Room02 for the project name. Note that this forms the basis for names of project components (that is, Room02-prog and Room02-sub).
5. Type the name of the folder containing the program and subprogram (or select it through the Browse feature). When you are finished, your display should look like Figure B-4.
6. When your entries are complete, click Create. The next window, Figure B-5, allows you to designate the files (Cobol program units) to be included in this project.
7. Click the Add files button and a list of all files in this folder will be displayed as in Figure B-6.
8. These are the two program units you want in the project so select both of them as in Figure B-6 and click Add. This window will disappear and the designated file names will be displayed in the Window of Figure B-5. Click Next and you will see the screen of Figure B-7.

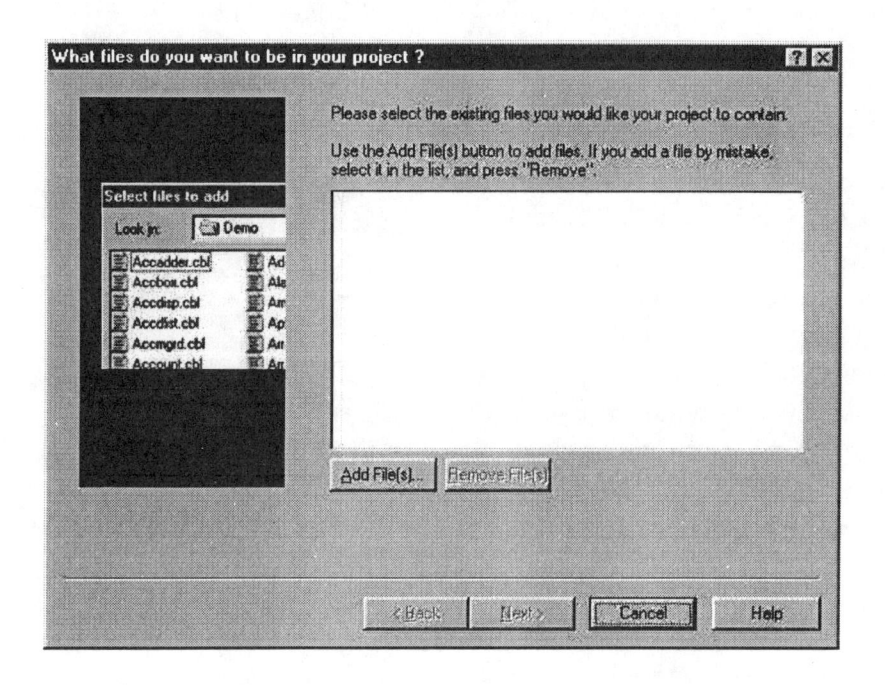

Figure B-5.
Adding files to the project.

Getting Started: Net Express

Figure B-6.
Selecting files for the project.

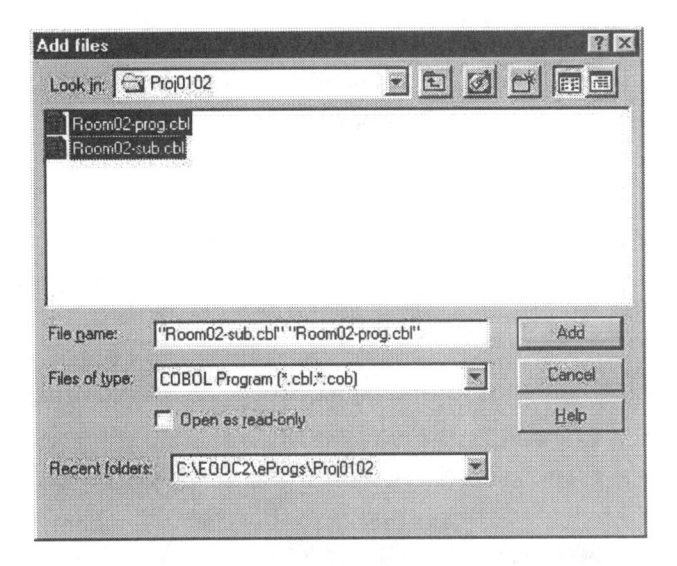

9. You must designate the program with which execution will begin (the main program of the project). In Figure B-7 you see Room02-prog. If yours shows Room02-sub, click the expand button to display the list of program files in the project. Then click Room02-prog.
10. Click Next. From the resulting window, click Finish. Net Express completes generation of this project and displays the window of Figure B-8.

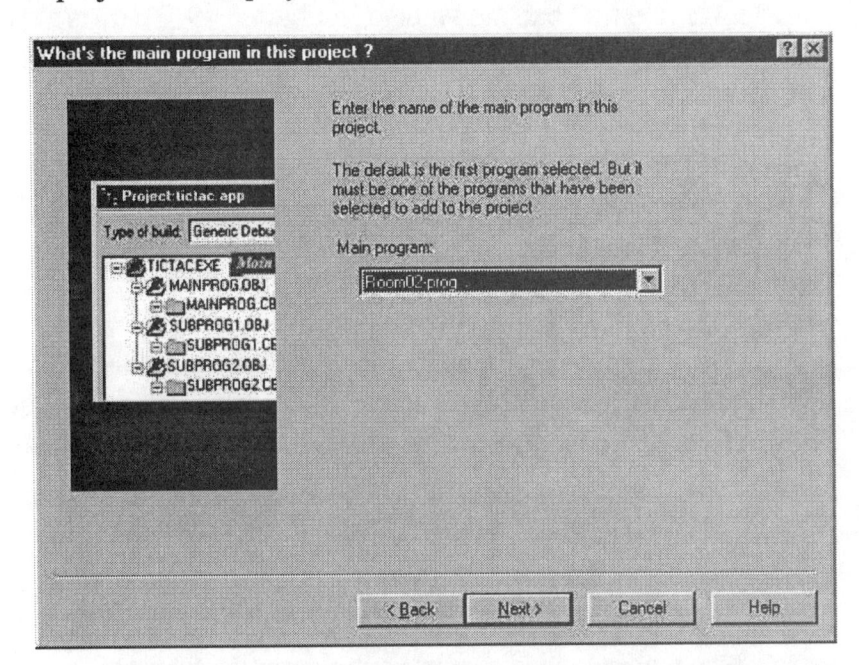

Figure B-7.
Designating the main program of the project.

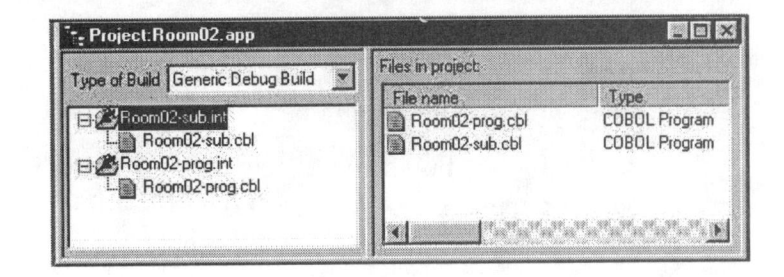

Figure B-8.
The project window.

Now check the contents of your Proj0102 folder using Windows Explorer and you will see that it contains another file: Room02.app. This is your **project file (application file)**—it contains data about this project including a list of all files comprising the project.

The Project Window

In the left pane of Figure B-8's project window you see a tree view indicating which files are created from which. The .cbl files are Cobol source code files; the .int files are the corresponding executable files in a special Micro Focus intermediate code. The .int files will be created when you compile the programs.

The right pane is a list of all files in the project—its contents are not limited to program files. (If you do not see all the details shown in Figure B-8, expand the right border.) Right click on this pane and you will see a popup menu. Ensure that the Show only source files selection box does not contain a check. If it does, click on it. Otherwise, this pane will list only program files (files that can be compiled).

Be aware that files need not exist to be listed in the project. This list merely serves as a guide to the IDE when you request that the program files be compiled through a rebuild operation.

The NetExpress Toolbar

Now look at the tool bar shown here in Figure B-9. There are five icons you will use during your first look at the IDE: Step, Run, Rebuild, Compile, and Context-sensitive Help.

Figure B-9. The Net Express toolbar.

The Context-sensitive Help icon exhibits the standard Windows features. That is, click on it and a question mark is attached to your mouse pointer. Then click on any element of your screen and a help pane is displayed.

The Rebuild icon causes Net Express to rebuild all parts of the current project that have changed, including files that are dependent upon changed files. This icon can be activated only when the color of the bricks is red; if grayed, it is inactive (standard Windows convention).

The Compile icon allows you to compile the single program that is displayed in a program window. It is only active when displayed in red.

The Run icon (solid-black icon on the left, not the grayed one on the right) allows you to run a program.

The Step icon allows you to step through a program, source statement by source statement. You will see how useful this is for debugging.

Getting Started: Net Express   291

Compiling Programs of a Project

Before you can run an application, you must direct Net Express to compile each of the programs comprising the project. You can accomplish this either of two ways: compile each program individually or direct Net Express to rebuild. Let's first look at the rebuild.

Move the mouse pointer to the Rebuild icon and hold it there for a moment—you will see the tool tip "Rebuild Project" displayed. Click on this icon to compile both programs. Alternately, you could click Project/Rebuild from the bar menu. As the compilation takes place, you will see the following lines in the lower pane of the Net Express screen.

```
Starting rebuild
Rebuilding         Room02-sub.cbl
Rebuilding         Room02-prog.cbl
Rebuild complete
```

Once again look at the project's folder using Windows Explorer and you will see that another folder (named Debug) was created by the rebuild operation. This folder contains intermediate code equivalents of you source programs, the result of the compilation process. It is ready to be run under control of the Animator, the topic of the next section.

You can also compile individual programs by opening the selected program (double-click on its file name) and clicking the Compile icon.

Net Express keeps track of whether or not you have changed a source program since the last compile. Anytime you click the Rebuild icon, Net Express recompiles each program that has been changed.

The Animator—Running a Program

To run a program, Net Express uses a **run-time system** called **Animator**. Animator is a software system that allows you to run your application with concurrent access to the source code of all programs comprising the application. As you will see in the next section, this capability is very useful in debugging.

1. You can now run the program so click on the Run icon (alternately, click Animate/Run from the bar menu). You will see the popup menu of Figure B-10; it identifies the particular program of this project at which execution is to begin (Room02-prog located in the DEBUG directory created by the original rebuild operation).

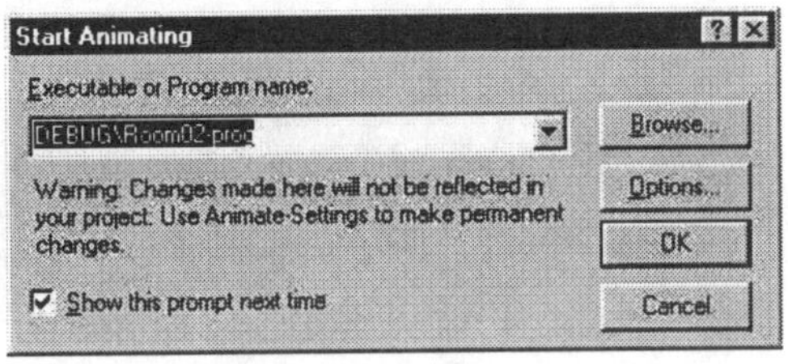

Figure B-10.
Starting program execution.

2. Click on OK and the program is run displaying the interaction screen of Figure B-11. Type either Y or N and press the Enter key. The program will display your results then terminate execution. [Note: You may need to enlarge the interactive pane at the bottom of your screen (it should be dark with white printing) and scroll to the top.]

Stopping the Animator

Execution of the runtime system Animator is terminated when your program run terminates by encountering a Stop Run statement. Sometimes you will end your activity but Animator is still running. To illustrate, try the following.

1. Click the Run icon to run your application.
2. *Without* entering a response to the request, close the resulting interaction screen (of Figure B-11).
3. Attempt to run again by clicking on the Run icon—nothing happens. Perhaps you noticed that the Run icon is not available as it is grayed out.
4. Click Animate on the menu bar and notice that the selection Start Animating is grayed out and that Stop Animating is available.
5. Click Stop Animating.

You have shut down the runtime system so your Run icon will now be available. Be aware that on some occasions I have seen the Run icon in solid black even though Animator was still running. However, clicking the icon did nothing.

Handling Program Errors

Correcting Compiler Errors

For an idea of how Net Express handles errors, let's introduce an error into Room02-prog then compile it.

1. From the right pane of the project window of Figure B-9, double-click the entry Room02-prog.cbl. This will display a source listing of the program.
2. Change the Working Storage entry

```
01  apply-discount-sw     pic X(01).
```

to

```
01  apply-discount-s      pic X(01).
```

Figure B-11. The program interaction screen.

Getting Started: Net Express 293

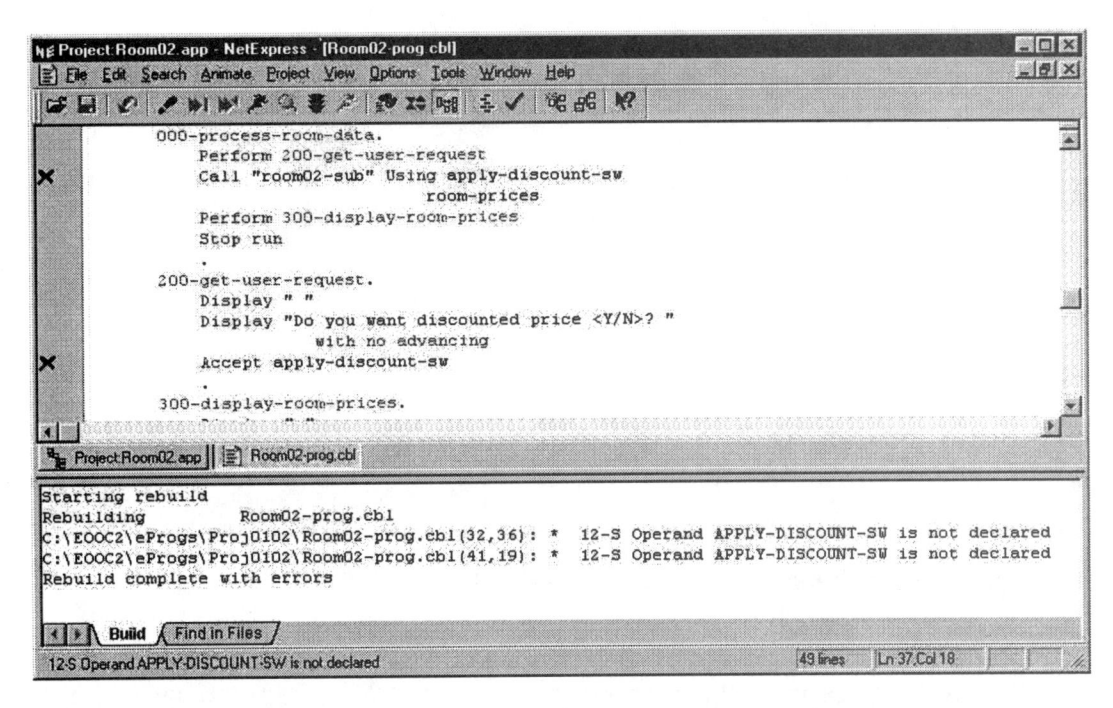

Figure B-12. Error messages.

3. Click the Rebuild Project icon on the tool bar; your Net Express screen will look like Figure B-12. Notice that statements the compiler finds in error are marked with a red X on the left.
4. If you double-click on the first diagnostic the entry apply-discount-sw is highlighted. This is the element Net Express ascertains to be in error.
5. Click View/Next/Syntax Error and the box indicator is moved to the next error—you may need to do this twice the first time.
6. For any of the errors, position the mouse pointer on the red X. After a few moments, you will see a brief message identifying the error. This is especially convenient if your program has a large number of errors and you do not see all the error messages in the pane at the bottom of the Net Express screen.
7. You know from Cobol that a "data-item not declared" message means you have an inconsistency between the definition in the Data Division and usage in the Procedure Division. So scroll up and correct the error you introduced in Step 2.
8. Rebuild the project. If your change was correct, you will see the message Rebuild complete with no error messages.
9. You can close the edit window and run the program.

Stepping Through a Program for Debugging

Occasionally you will encounter a program bug that simply defies all attempts to find it. The Animator component of the IDE gives you a graphical means to trace execution of your code and examine data values. If you've not already terminated the preceding run, do so now; then do the following.

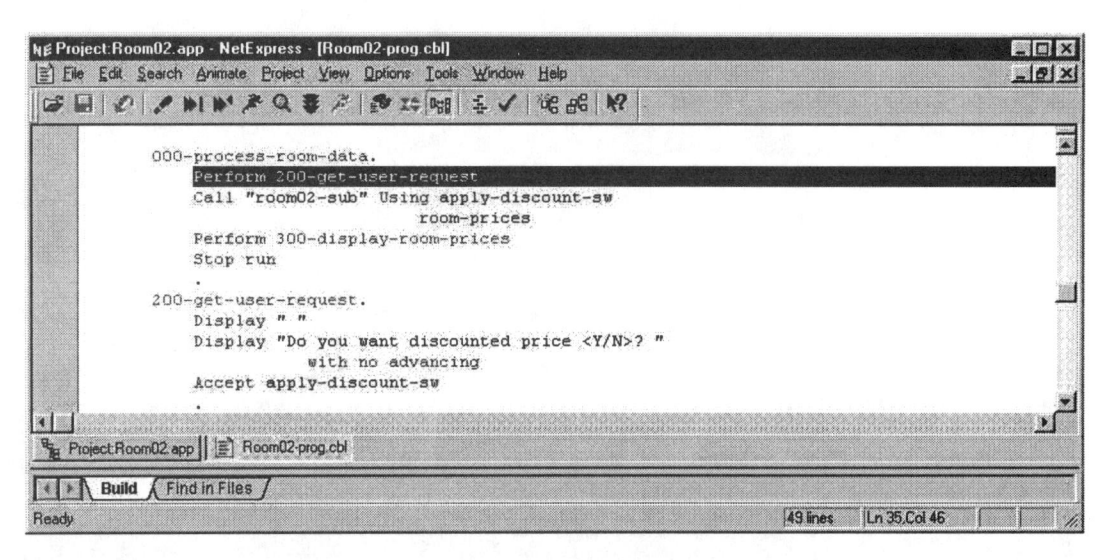

Figure B-13. Beginning execution in the Step mode.

1. Click on the Step icon (alternately, click Animate/Step from the bar menu).
2. Click OK from the popup (see Figure B-10). Your screen will look like Figure B-13.
3. The statement highlighted in red is the next program statement to be executed. Click on the Step icon again and you will see the highlight moved to the Display statement in the 200 paragraph. Click twice more and you will see the prompt displayed on the interaction screen. Expand or contract panes as needed.
4. Click the Step icon to execute the Accept statement. You will see the program statement highlight disappear and the interaction screen cursor appear.
5. Type either Y or N and press the Enter key. The highlight will return to the Call statement; the Accept statement has been executed thereby causing a value to be entered into the data item apply-discount-sw.
6. You can check the value stored in any data item by double-clicking on that data item. To illustrate, double-click anywhere in the name apply-discount-sw. The resulting popup window of Figure B-14 displays the selected data-name and its current value. To monitor it throughout the debug process, click the Monitor button and a small window showing only the data item will replace the window of Figure B-14.
7. If you reach a point where you no longer need to step through the program (presumably you've found the bug), you can switch to normal execution by clicking the Run icon. However, if you want to terminate execution immediately, click Animate/Stop Animating. Do so, then close all windows left open from this execution giving you the project window of Figure B-8.

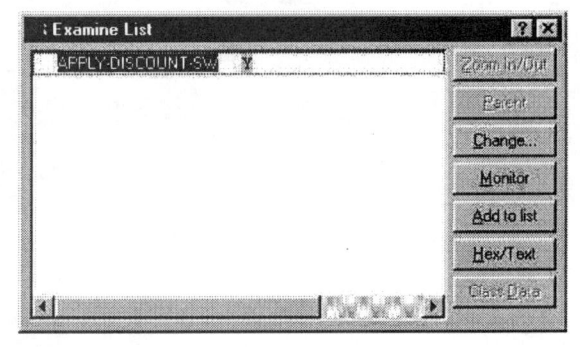

Figure B-14. Data item display.

Using Breakpoints for Debugging

With a large program, stepping through statements can be a very time consuming process. You can avoid that problem by using **breakpoints.** To illustrate, assume that the program does not return correct values for the discounted prices. So prior to calling the subprogram, you want program execution to stop so you can check the value in apply-discount-sw.

1. Double-click on the Room02-prog.cbl entry in the right pane of the project window (Figure B-8) to open a window listing the program source file.
2. Position the cursor in the gray area to the left of the following source line.

    Call "room02-sub" Using apply-discount-sw

3. Double-click and a Stop icon will be inserted to the left indicating this is a breakpoint (see Figure B-15). Double-click again and the breakpoint is removed. Alternately, you can position the cursor anywhere in the desired line and click the sequence Animate/Breakpoint/Set. You can both set and clear breakpoints from this menu.
4. With this breakpoint set, close the program window and run the application.
5. At the application prompt, type Y and press Enter. If you've set the breakpoint properly, execution stops on the Call statement.

You can now proceed to inspect the contents of apply-discount-sw (or of any other data items in the program).

6. Click the Run icon to resume execution.
7. When you are finished with a debugging session, you will usually want to clear all of your breakpoints. Do this by selecting Animate/Breakpoint/Clear all in program. If you have breakpoints in other programs of a project that you want cleared, then click Clear all in project.

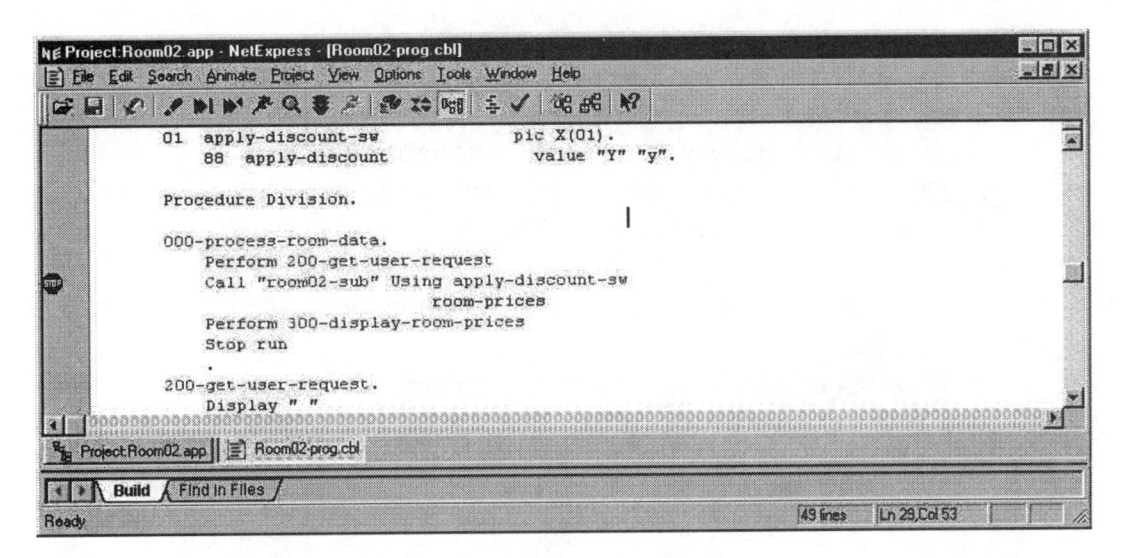

Figure B-15. Indication of a breakpoint.

Entering Programs

Setting Edit Options

Net Express allows you to modify your editing environment to suit your own needs. There are two modifications to the default that I found useful—you may find others.

Net Express's default margins are set to 7 and 72, consistent with fixed format. If you intend to use free format (described in Chapter 1) then I suggest you change these settings as follows.

1. Click Options/Edit.
2. Click the Profile tab if that tab is not already displayed.
3. Change the margin settings to: Left: 0 and Right: 100.

With default settings, if you drag the mouse on a line, that entire line is selected. As I prefer to be able to select a single word when editing, that mode is unacceptable to me. If you have the same preference, then change this as follows.

1. Click the Blocks/Clipboard tab.
2. Click the Select column blocks ... radio button.

Explore other options and set them to fit you style. When finished, click OK.

Entering a New Program

Being a heavy user of Microsoft Word, I create all of my programs and class definitions using Word then create a Net Express project as described earlier in this appendix. You can use Word or your favorite word processor but if you do, be certain to save in text mode as Net Express does not treat word processing codes kindly. You can also use the editor component of Net Express. Let's see how you would create a new project then enter the programs under Net Express. (If you are simply adding a new program to an existing project, then open that project and start at Step 4.)

1. Create a new project by clicking File/New/Project.
2. From the window of Figure B-4 select the Empty Project option.
3. Enter the name and folder of the project then click Create.
4. Create a new program by clicking File/New/Program.
5. Type your program. Notice that you have available the common editing functions (for instance, Edit and Search) through the toolbar at the top of the window.
6. When finished, click the Save icon: in the resulting popup type the program name, and click Save.
7. Close the program-edit window and you will see your program added to the lists of files in the project.

Your focus in this book will be on writing class definitions (class programs). If you look at Figure B-3 you will see that one of the options is Class. This selection brings up the Class Wizard which generates some basic code for you (in the usual wizard fashion). I do not use it as I prefer the flexibility I have when entering programs with Word where, as a rule, I create one class program using another as a starting point. I don't feel the Wizard is a good tool to use when learning OOCobol as it can mask over details that are critical to understanding object orientation.

Getting Started: Personal COBOL for Windows

Appendix Contents

Using the Class Browser 300
    The Browser Environment 300
    Creating a Project 300
Error Correction 303
Entering Programs 304
Animator.. 304
Breakpoints 306
Two Commonly Encountered Execution Errors 307

Appendix C

Appendix Introduction

The purpose of this appendix is to give you a brief introduction to working in the Personal COBOL for Windows environment. From this appendix, you will learn about the following.
- The Browser working environment.
- Creating a project and assigning files to it.
- Compiling programs.
- Error detection and correction.
- Using Animator, a debugging tool.

Using the Class Browser

The Browser Environment

The Personal COBOL **class browser** is an environment for editing, compiling, and running programs. Browser allows you to group files for a given application as a **project**. For instance, each topic of this book is introduced as a project: Room01, Room02, and so on. If you look at the CD directory, you will see a file for each project you create. Project files have an extension PRJ so, for instance, the project file Room04 has a full file name Room04.PRJ. This book uses a consistent naming convention thereby making it easy for you to relate program files to their projects. Program files of the Room04 project are r04-drvr.cbl (drvr for driver) and r04-room.cbl (room for the room class definition). Some projects include several class programs. (Note: In some cases, a project uses program files from another project. For instance, Room07 uses two of Room06's classes. This is perfectly legal.)

The best way to learn about the browser is to use it. So let's create an application consisting of the program and subprogram described in Chapter 2—r02-prog.cbl and r02-sub.cbl stored in the folder C:\Eooc2\eProgsPC\Proj0102. In this tutorial you will do the following.

- Start Personal COBOL.
- Create the project.
- Designate files belonging to that project (r02-prog and r02-sub).
- Rebuild the project (compile the programs of the project).
- Run the program.
- End the process.

Creating a Project

Because Personal COBOL operates from Windows, you must first be in Windows. Then do the following operations.

1. Click on the icon Personal COBOL and from the popup menu, click on *Object COBOL Browser*. Alternately, click Start/Programs/Personal COBOL/Personal COBOL Browser.
2. You then get the Browser screen shown in Figure C-1. Notice the three panes: Classes, Files, and Sections/Methods.
3. Click on the File option from the menu bar and you will see the drop-down menu of Figure C-2. The next-to-last option, Open/New Project is the one of interest now. You can either create a new project or open an existing one from this selection.
4. Click on Open/New Project. This gives you the popup menu of Figure C-3. Your screen should display the contents of the Personal COBOL tutorial folder (although your display might be different). This is a typical Windows screen for accessing files from a disk.

Getting Started: Personal COBOL for Windows

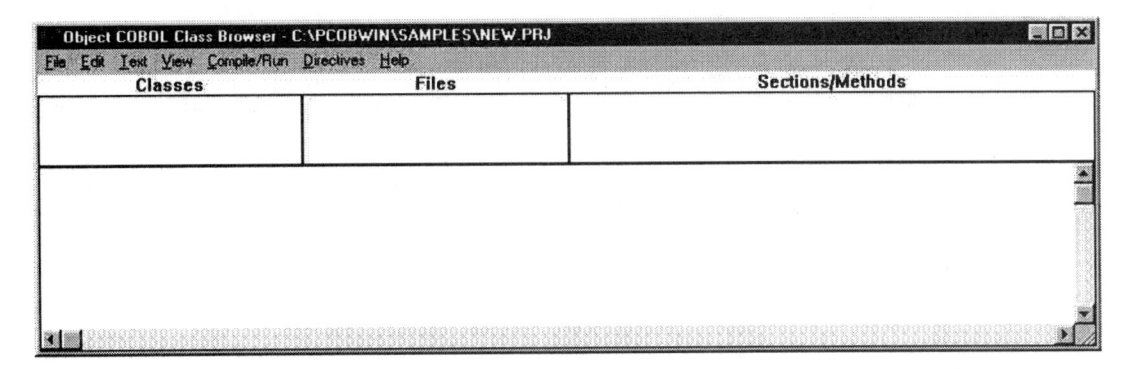

Figure C-1. The browser screen.

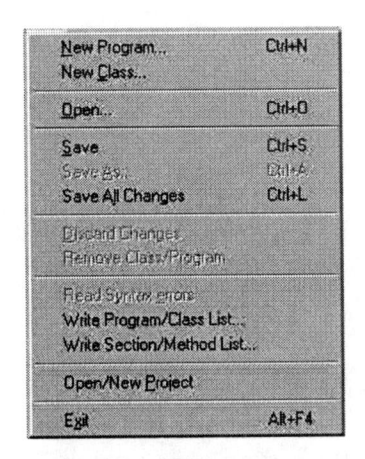

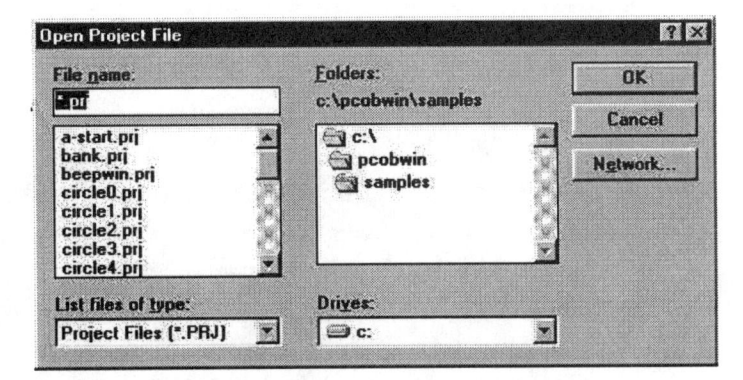

Figure C-2. File menu.

Figure C-3. The project open window.

5. Select the folder as shown in Figure C-4 and type Room02.prj as the File name.
6. Click OK. The menu disappears and the blank Browser screen of Figure C-1 reappears.
7. You must add two program files to this project: r02-prog.cbl and r02-sub.cbl. Do this by clicking File/Open (see Figure C-2).
8. If the box List files of type displays Project Files, change it to COBOL Files. Then all your Cobol program files will be displayed.

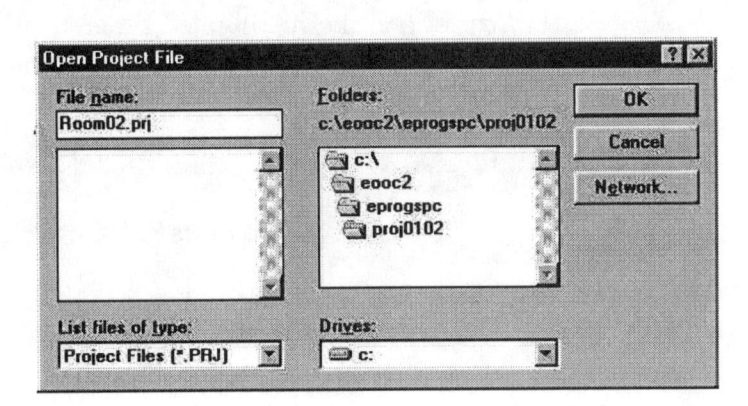

Figure C-4. Designating the project name and location.

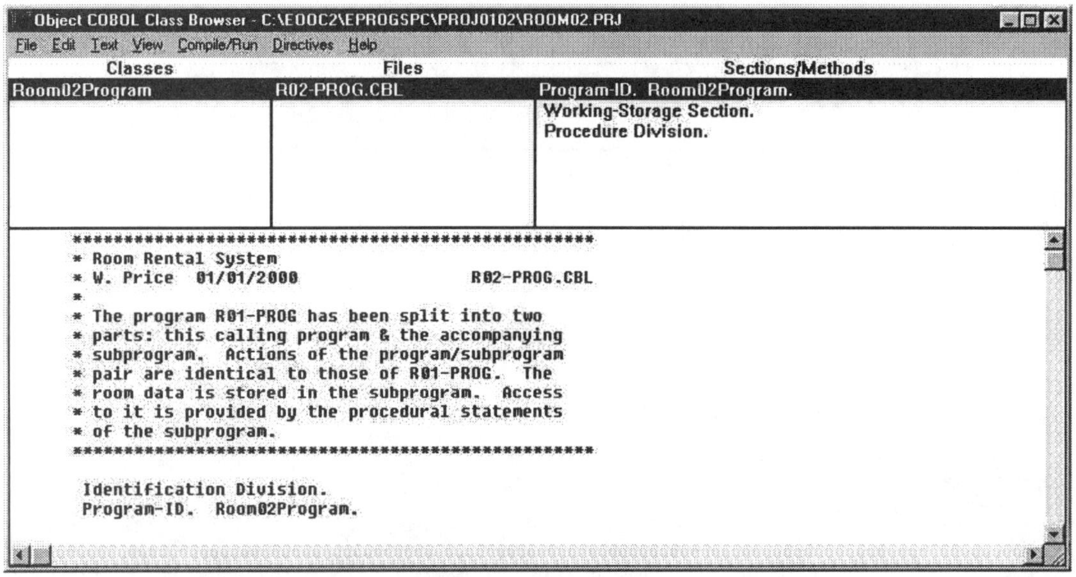

```
*****************************************************
* Room Rental System
* W. Price  01/01/2000              R02-PROG.CBL
*
* The program R01-PROG has been split into two
* parts: this calling program & the accompanying
* subprogram.  Actions of the program/subprogram
* pair are identical to those of R01-PROG.  The
* room data is stored in the subprogram.  Access
* to it is provided by the procedural statements
* of the subprogram.
*****************************************************

 Identification Division.
 Program-ID.  Room02Program.
```

Figure C-5. Limited view of a source file.

9. Select r02-prog.cbl, the calling program for this application. The browser screen of Figure C-5 does not display the complete program because the default view option is to display selected program sections or methods. Most of your programs will be relatively short, so you will probably find it convenient to display the entire program. Do this by changing the view.

10. Select View from the bar menu to get the popup of Figure C-6. From this, select File Only. The name of your program (R02-PROG.CBL) is displayed in the third column of the browser screen. Select it (highlight it with the mouse) and the entire program is displayed in the lower portion of the browser screen.

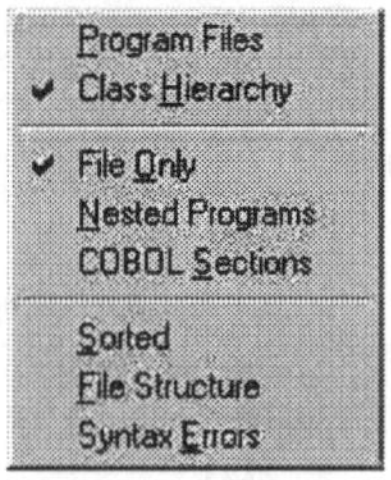

11. Repeat the preceding procedure of Steps 7-10 to add the subprogram r02-sub.cbl to this project. When you are finished, your screen should look like Figure C-7.

Figure C-6. View menu.

12. You can now compile the two programs of this project. From the main menu, select Compile/Run and you are presented with three options: Compile, Animate, and Run. Select Compile and the highlighted program is compiled (R02-SUB.CBL, in this case). Repeat the process for the driver program. Usually, the sequence in

Figure C-7. Program files of a project.

Getting Started: Personal COBOL for Windows

which you compile programs of a project makes no difference. However, Micro Focus recommends that they be compiled from the "bottom up." Do it that way to avoid an unexpected booby trap during execution.

13. After all programs of a project are compiled, you can run. First, make certain that the driver is highlighted. Then from the menu bar click Compile/Run; click the Run option from the resulting drop-down menu. Notice that for both compiling and running, you do not need to use the menu. Compile by selecting the desired file and pressing the F2 function key; run by selecting the driver program and pressing the F6 function key.

14. The action of this project is to display a set of room prices. When you run, you are asked if you want discounted prices. Upon completion, a popup menu appears with the message Program run complete. If the popup covers your screen display, drag it to one side.

Error Correction

Errors detected by the compiler are identified with appropriate error messages. For an idea of how Personal COBOL displays errors, let's introduce an error into the driver program.

1. Highlight the calling program Room02Program (see Figure C-7) to display the program.
2. Scroll down to the first Perform statement of the 000 paragraph. Change the word Perform so the statement reads as follows.

    Preform 200-get-user-request

3. Compile the program; Browser asks you to confirm saving your changed source file—do so. When the compiler is finished, an error message is displayed. Press enter to get the screen shown in Figure C-8.
4. All errors detected by the compiler are listed in the third column. Click on the error you want to investigate. If you changed only the single Perform statement, you will have only one error listed as in Figure C-8.
5. The source program is repositioned on the screen so that the statement in error is highlighted as shown in Figure C-9. Correct it and recompile.

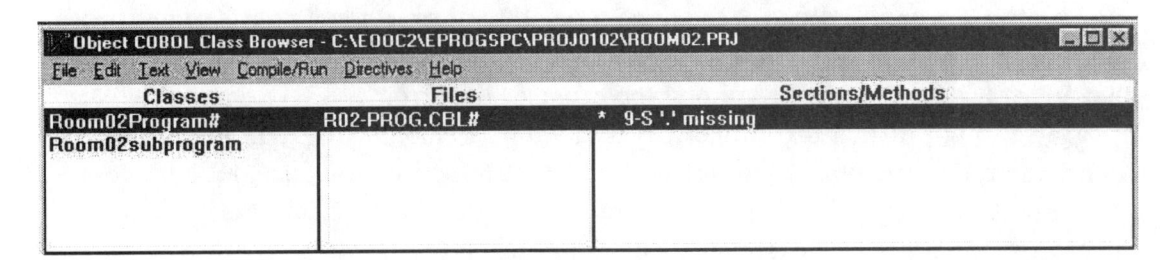

Figure C-8. Upper portion of compile screen.

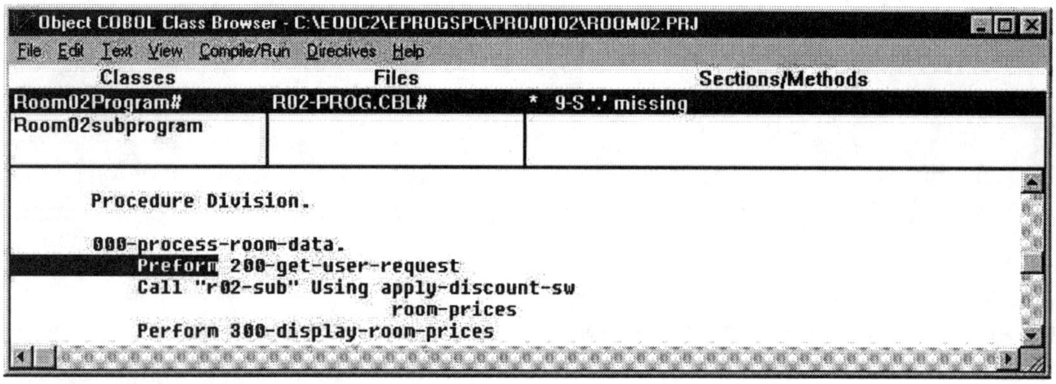

```
 Object COBOL Class Browser - C:\EOOC2\EPROGSPC\PROJ0102\ROOM02.PRJ
 File  Edit  Text  View  Compile/Run  Directives  Help
         Classes              Files                Sections/Methods
 Room02Program#           R02-PROG.CBL#        *  9-S '.' missing
 Room02subprogram


     Procedure Division.

     000-process-room-data.
         Perform 200-get-user-request
         Call "r02-sub" Using apply-discount-sw
                              room-prices
         Perform 300-display-room-prices
```

Figure C-9. Highlighting of a compiler detected error.

Entering Programs

As you have seen, you can edit your programs directly from Browser; it employs the conventional Windows look and feel. You can also enter a new program through the same screen by selecting New from the File menu. However, browser's editing capabilities are limited so you may want to use your word processor or some other editor with which you are familiar. If using a word processor, be certain to save your program as a text file. Browser does not react kindly to word processing formatted files. (Note: All example programs of this book were entered using Microsoft Word.)

Animator

As we all know, a clean compile does not necessarily mean a program will work properly; you may have logic errors. There are two types of logic errors that cause a program to malfunction. For instance, if you code a subtract operation rather than an add, your program output will be incorrect—most Cobol programmers are familiar with this type of problem. The other type directs the computer to do something it cannot accomplish. For instance, you direct it to open a file that does not exist. You will find that Personal COBOL introduces you to a whole host of "new and exciting" runtime errors. Because of the dynamic nature of object technology, your program might crash in one of the system's class libraries producing error messages that are of little value in determining the cause of the error.

Detection of difficult-to-find errors is aided by Personal COBOL's **Animator**: an interactive debugging environment. For an introduction to its use, let's try it on the current room project. However, before proceeding, correct the Perform statement from the preceding exercise, then recompile.

1. With Room02Program highlighted, click the Compile/Run menu bar option. From the resulting dropdown men, click Animate to produce the screen of Figure C-10.

Figure C-10.
The Animator screen.

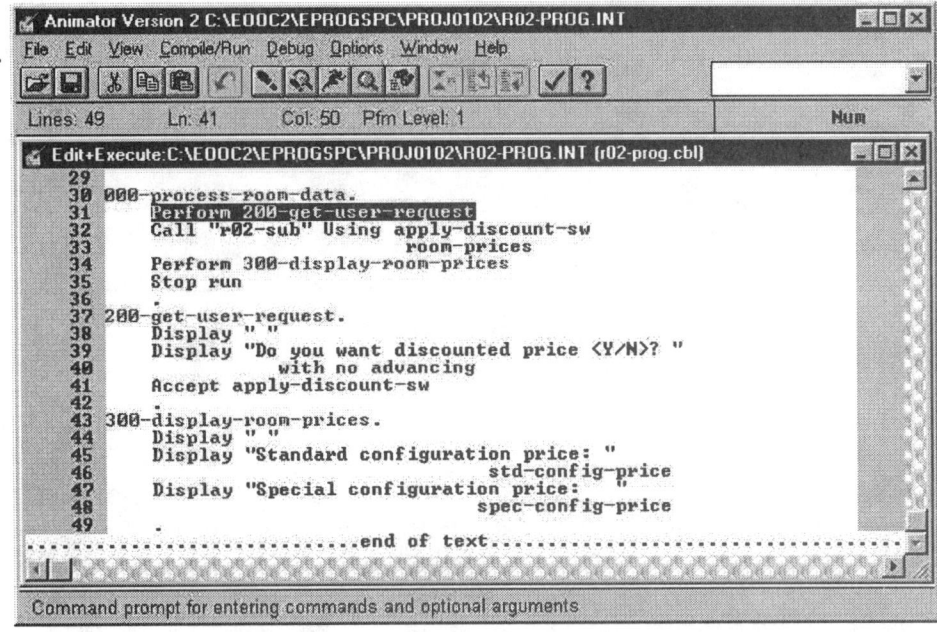

```
000-process-room-data.
    Perform 200-get-user-request
    Call "r02-sub" Using apply-discount-sw
                        room-prices
    Perform 300-display-room-prices
    Stop run
    .
200-get-user-request.
    Display " "
    Display "Do you want discounted price <Y/N>? "
            with no advancing
    Accept apply-discount-sw
    .
300-display-room-prices.
    Display " "
    Display "Standard configuration price: "
                        std-config-price
    Display "Special configuration price: "
                        spec-config-price
    .
```

The highlight is on the Perform statement, the first statement of the program. Animator is ready to execute this statement. If you click on the Run icon, Animator runs the program. If you click on the Step icon, Animator executes the currently highlighted statement; each click of the Step executes one statement.

2. Successively click on the Step icon until you reach the Accept statement. Clicking this statement causes control to be switched to the Animator COBOL Text Window (Figure C-11) with a blinking cursor following the prompt.

Figure C-11.
The Animator Text window.

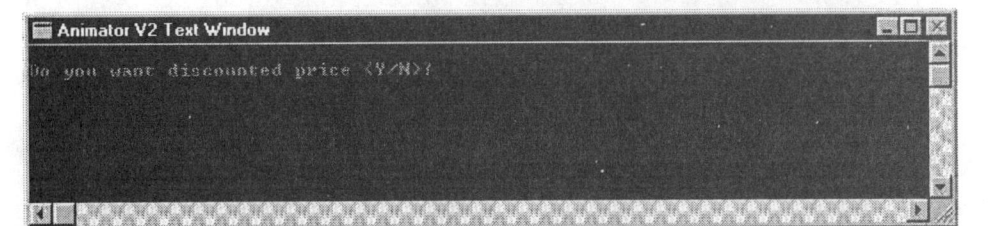

3. From the Text Window, type Y in response to the query, and press Enter. Control returns to the Browser window. Continue stepping until you reach the Multiply statement shown in Figure C-12.

```
100-return-data-set.
    Move rr-std-config-price to ls-std-config-price
    Move rr-spec-config-price to ls-spec-config-price
    If ls-apply-discount
        Subtract rr-room-discount from 1.0
                        giving price-factor
        Multiply price-factor
                        by ls-std-config-price
        Multiply price-factor
                        by ls-spec-config-price
    End-If
    Exit program
    .
```

Figure C-12.
At the Multiply statement.

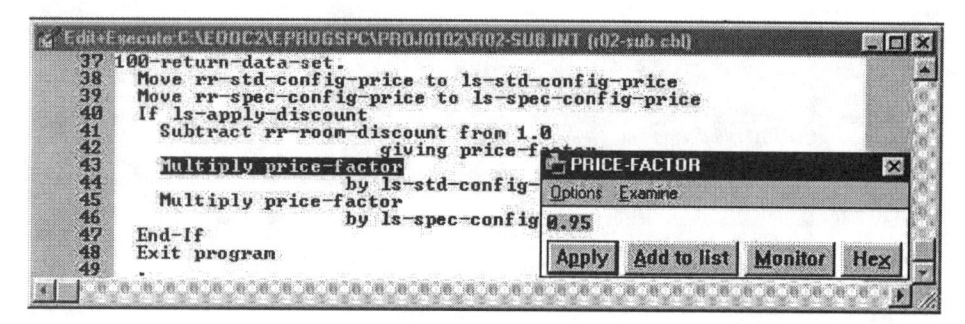

Figure C-13. Displaying a data-item's value.

4. Assume you suspect that the value stored in the data item price-factor is incorrect. Display it by double clicking on that data item name (preceding the Multiply statement) and you will see the popup shown in Figure C-13 displaying price-factor's value. Close the popup and you can proceed.

If the error for which you are searching caused execution to crash in one of the class library routines, the process of stepping through a program allows you to determine which Invoke of your program caused your problem.

Breakpoints

Animator allows you to set breakpoints: points in the program at which Animator halts execution when you select the run icon. This is useful if your program executes a large number of statements before encountering the statement of interest or if you want to stop at the same statement each time through a loop. You can set a breakpoint on any executable statement using either of three methods. Let's set a breakpoint at the second Multiply statement of Figure C-12.

1. Position the cursor anywhere in the gray area to the left of the Multiply statement (on the line number 45 will do).
2. Double-click (left-click). The breakpoint will be set as shown in Figure C-14. Double-click again and it is removed.
3. Alternately, right-click on the statement you desire to have the breakpoint. A popup menu appears.
4. Click Breakpoint to set the breakpoint.
5. Right-click again and you will see the Breakpoint option replaced by Unset (to clear the breakpoint).

You can also set and clear breakpoints from the Debug option of the menu bar. Click on Debug and check out all of its options.

```
   Edit+Execute C:\EOOC2\EPROGSPC\PROJ0102\R02-SUB.INT (r02-sub.cbl)
      40    If ls-apply-discount
      41       Subtract rr-room-discount from 1.0
      42                          giving price-factor
      43       Multiply price-factor
      44                     by ls-std-config-price
   BrkPt>     Multiply price-factor
      46                     by ls-spec-config-price
      47    End-If
```

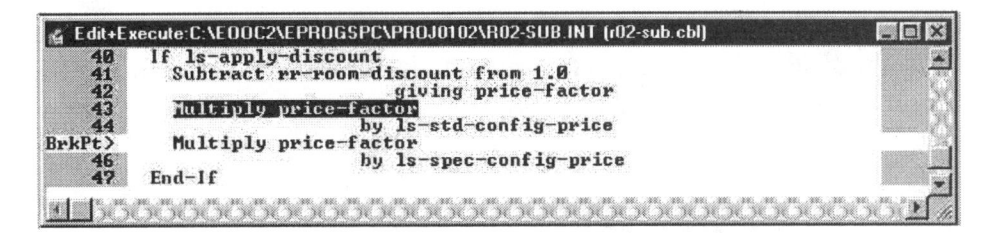

Figure C-14. A breakpoint.

Setting a breakpoint in a program module other than the one you see on your screen can be confusing at first. The key is to open the other program file in the execute mode. To illustrate, assume you want to set a breakpoint in r02-prog.

1. From the main bar menu, click File/Open for execution. If you click Open for edit you will be unable to set breakpoints.
2. From the popup menu, select r02-prog.int.
3. Set the desired breakpoints.
4. Close the file when you are finished.

You can now run the program under Animator and execution will halt when the breakpoint is encountered (a message is displayed). You can check data items then proceed by stepping or by running. Be aware that breakpoints are properties of Animator and have no effect when you are running with the browser.

Two Commonly Encountered Execution Errors

The last two examples of this appendix relate to class definitions and use Chapter 3's Room03 as an example. You may wish to wait until you reach that chapter and come back for this. Don't forget as this section describes a common error that is very baffling.

As any experienced programmer knows, there seems to be a never-ending supply of runtime errors you can encounter. In some cases, Personal COBOL displays diagnostics that are reasonably helpful. However, if your program fails in one of the system's class libraries, the resulting diagnostics are of little value at best, and very misleading at worst. Probably the most common error you will encounter results from errors in relating classes to their source programs. For an example, open Room03 (it is in the Proj0301 folder) from the browser. Then open the driver Room03Driver and look at the statement:

    RoomClass is class "r03-room".

Change this to the following (delete the m in room).

    RoomClass is class "r03-roo".

Compile and run the program and you will see the error popup of Figure C-15. This is an appropriate message: the system is telling you that it cannot find the source file r03-roo. Correct this line. Recompile, and run the program again to ensure that it is okay.

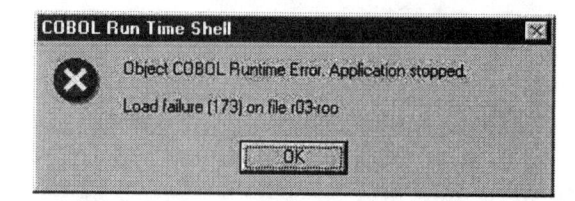

Figure C-15. Runtime error message.

Now open RoomClass and introduce the same error (change r03-room to r03-roo). Recompile, change the highlight back to the driver program, and run. The popup of Figure C-16 does not offer much of a clue regarding the source of the error. Improperly identifying classes is a common student error (I make it myself all the time). You probably will see it frequently. When you do, check all class assignments—the majority of the time, you will find incorrect assignments the cause of this error message.

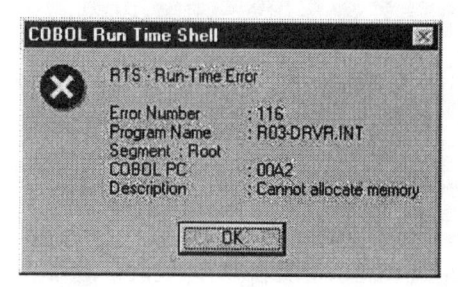

Figure C-16. Confusing runtime error message.

File Listings

Appendix Contents

Files in the Eooc2 Folder 312
Database Class Definitions 312
    Event DBI (Net Express) 312
    Dessert DBI (Net Express) 313
    Event DBI (Personal COBOL) 314
    Dessert DBI (Personal COBOL) 315
Data File Listings 316
  Data Files for Assignments 316
    Event record description 316
    Event file listing 316
    Dessert record description 316
    Dessert file listing 317
    Site record description 317
    Site file listing 317
    Box record description 317
    Box file listing 317
  Data Files for Examples 318
    Calendar record description 318
    Calendar file listing 318
    Company record description 318
    Company file listing 319
    Representative (Rep) description 319
    Representative (Rep) file listing 319
    Room record description 319
    Room file listing 319
    Tax record description 319
    Tax file listing 319

Appendix D

Files in the Eooc2 Folder

This appendix contains listings of the following files from the Examples CD.

Folder	Files
aProgs	DBI class definitions for Net Express required for Chapter 4's assignments
aProgsPC	DBI class definitions for Personal COBOL required for Chapter 4's assignments
aData	Data files required for assignments
eData	Data files used by examples

Assignment DBI Class Definitions

```
      $set sourceformat "free"
*>***********************************************
*> Event System
*> W. Price  July 10, 2000              F02-DBI.CBL
*>
*> This class definition is the database
*> interface for the EVENT system.  It reads a
*> requested record from the indexed file EVENT.DI
*> Object methods
*>    close-file
*>    open-file
*>    read-event-file
*>***********************************************
Identification Division.
       Class-ID.  EventDatabaseInterface
                  inherits from BaseClass.
Environment Division.
       Input-Output Section.
       File-Control.
          Select event-file
               assign to "c:\Eooc2\aData\event.di"
               organization is indexed
               access is random
               record key is er-event-id.
       Object Section.
          Class-control.
             EventDatabaseInterface is class "f02-dbi"
             BaseClass                is class "base"
             .
Data Division.
   File Section.
   FD Event-File.
   01 event-record.
          10  er-event-ID             pic X(04).
          10  er-event-description    pic X(20).
          10  er-event-type           pic X(01).
          10  er-facility             pic X(07).
          10  er-duration             pic 9(02).
          10  er-site-ID              pic X(02).
          10  er-daily-rate           pic 9(04).
          10  er-accommodation-charge pic 9(05).
          10  er-launch-fee           pic 9(04).

*>==================================================
FACTORY.
Procedure Division.
   *>_____
   Method-ID. close-file.
   *>_____
       Procedure Division.
          Close Event-File
          .
       End Method close-file.

   *>_____
   Method-ID. open-file.
   *>_____
       Procedure Division.
          Open input Event-File
          .
       End Method open-file.

   *>_____
   Method-ID. read-event-record.
   *>_____
       Data Division.
       Linkage Section.
          01  ls-event-id          pic x(04).
          01  ls-record-found-sw   pic X(01).
              88  ls-record-found       value "Y".
              88  ls-record-not-found   value "N".

       Procedure Division Using ls-event-id
                    Returning ls-record-found-sw.
          Move ls-event-id to er-event-id
          Read Event-File
             Invalid key
                Set ls-record-not-found to true
             Not invalid key
                Set ls-record-found to true
          End-Read *>Event-File
          .
       End Method read-event-record.
       *>_____
END FACTORY.
END CLASS EventDatabaseInterface.
```

Event DBI (Net Express)

```cobol
$set sourceformat "free"
*>***********************************************
*> Dessert System
*> W. Price   July 10, 2000           J02-DBI.CBL
*>
*> This class definition is the database
*> interface for the DESSERT system.  It reads a
*> requested record from the indexed file DESSERT.DI
*> Object methods
*>    close-file
*>    open-file
*>    read-dessert-file
*>***********************************************

Identification Division.
      Class-ID.  DessertDatabaseInterface
                 inherits from BaseClass.

Environment Division.
      Object Section.
        Class-control.
          DessertDatabaseInterface is class "j02-dbi"
          BaseClass                is class "base"
          .

*>==================================================
 FACTORY.

 Environment Division.
    Input-Output Section.
    File-Control.
       Select dessert-file
              assign to "c:\Eooc2\aData\dessert.di"
              organization is indexed
              access is random
              record key is dr-dessert-id.

 Data Division.
    File Section.
    FD  Dessert-File.
    01  dessert-record.
        10  dr-dessert-id              pic X(03).
        10  dr-flavor-description      pic X(10).
        10  dr-dessert-type            pic X(04).
        10  dr-roll-length             pic 9(02).
        10  dr-rolls-onhand            pic 9(03).
        10  dr-per-inch-cost           pic 9V99.
        10  dr-box-id                  pic X(02).
        10  dr-packages-onhand         pic 9(04).
        10  dr-unit-cost               pic 99V99.

 Procedure Division.
 *>_____
 Method-ID. close-file.
 *>_____
    Procedure Division.
       Close Dessert-File
       .
 End Method close-file.

 *>_____
 Method-ID. open-file.
 *>_____
    Procedure Division.
       Open input Dessert-File
       .
 End Method open-file.

 *>_____
 Method-ID. read-dessert-record.
 *>_____
    Data Division.
       Linkage Section.
       01  ls-dessert-id            pic x(03).
       01  ls-record-found-sw       pic X(01).
           88  ls-record-found           value "Y".
           88  ls-record-not-found       value "N".

    Procedure Division Using ls-dessert-id
                     Returning ls-record-found-sw.
       Move ls-dessert-id to dr-dessert-id
       Read Dessert-File
          Invalid key
              Set ls-record-not-found to true
          Not invalid key
              Set ls-record-found to true
       End-Read *>Dessert-File
       .
 End Method read-dessert-record.
 *>_____
 END FACTORY.
 END CLASS DessertDatabaseInterface.
```

Dessert DBI (Net Express)

```cobol
      $set sourceformat "free"
*>***************************************************
*> Event System
*> W. Price   July 10, 2000              F02-DBI.CBL
*>
*> This class definition is the database
*> interface for the EVENT system.  It reads a
*> requested record from the indexed file EVENT.DI
*> Object methods
*>    close-file
*>    open-file
*>    read-event-file
*>***************************************************
Identification Division.
       Class-ID.  EventDatabaseInterface
                    inherits from BaseClass.

Environment Division.
       Object Section.
          Class-control.
             EventDatabaseInterface is class "f02-dbi"
             BaseClass              is class "base"


*>================================================
 FACTORY.

    Environment Division.
       Input-Output Section.
       File-Control.
          Select event-file
                 assign to "c:\Eooc2\aData\event.di"
                 organization is indexed
                 access is random
                 record key is er-event-id.

    Data Division.
       File Section.
       FD  Event-File.
       01  event-record.
              10   er-event-ID              pic X(04).
              10   er-event-description     pic X(20).
              10   er-event-type            pic X(01).
              10   er-facility              pic X(07).
              10   er-duration              pic 9(02).
              10   er-site-ID               pic X(02).
              10   er-daily-rate            pic 9(04).
              10   er-accommodation-charge  pic 9(05).
              10   er-launch-fee            pic 9(04).

    Procedure Division.
*>_____
    Method-ID. close-file.
*>_____
       Procedure Division.
          Close Event-File
       .
    End Method close-file.

*>_____
    Method-ID. open-file.
*>_____
       Procedure Division.
          Open input Event-File
       .
    End Method open-file.

*>_____
    Method-ID. read-event-record.
*>_____
       Data Division.
          Linkage Section.
             01   ls-event-id              pic x(04).
             01   ls-record-found-sw       pic X(01).
                88  ls-record-found             value "Y".
                88  ls-record-not-found         value "N".

       Procedure Division Using ls-event-id
                         Returning ls-record-found-sw.
          Move ls-event-id to er-event-id
          Read Event-File
             Invalid key
                Set ls-record-not-found to true
             Not invalid key
                Set ls-record-found to true
          End-Read *>Event-File
       .
    End Method read-event-record.
*>_____
END FACTORY.
END CLASS EventDatabaseInterface.
```

Event DBI (Personal COBOL)

```cobol
       $set sourceformat "free"
*>****************************************************
*> Dessert System
*> W. Price   July 10, 2000              J02-DBI.CBL
*>
*> This class definition is the database
*> interface for the DESSERT system.  It reads a
*> requested record from the indexed file DESSERT.DI
*> Object methods
*>    close-file
*>    open-file
*>    read-dessert-file
*>****************************************************
Identification Division.
        Class-ID.  DessertDatabaseInterface
                   inherits from BaseClass.
Environment Division.
        Object Section.
          Class-control.
            DessertDatabaseInterface is class "j02-dbi"
            BaseClass                is class "base"

*>================================================
 FACTORY.

    Environment Division.
      Input-Output Section.
        File-Control.
          Select dessert-file
               assign to "c:\Eooc2\aData\dessert.di"
               organization is indexed
               access is random
               record key is dr-dessert-id.

    Data Division.
      File Section.
      FD  Dessert-File.
      01  dessert-record.
          10  dr-dessert-id            pic X(03).
          10  dr-flavor-description    pic X(10).
          10  dr-dessert-type          pic X(04).
          10  dr-roll-length           pic 9(02).
          10  dr-rolls-onhand          pic 9(03).
          10  dr-per-inch-cost         pic 9V99.
          10  dr-box-id                pic X(02).
          10  dr-packages-onhand       pic 9(04).
          10  dr-unit-cost             pic 99V99.

    Procedure Division.
    *>_____
    Method-ID. close-file.
    *>_____
        Procedure Division.
            Close Dessert-File
        .
    End Method close-file.

    *>_____
    Method-ID. open-file.
    *>_____
        Procedure Division.
            Open input Dessert-File
        .
    End Method open-file.

    *>_____
    Method-ID. read-dessert-record.
    *>_____
        Data Division.
         Linkage Section.
          01  ls-dessert-id            pic x(03).
          01  ls-record-found-sw       pic X(01).
              88  ls-record-found          value "Y".
              88  ls-record-not-found      value "N".

        Procedure Division Using ls-dessert-id
                           Returning ls-record-found-sw.
            Move ls-dessert-id to dr-dessert-id
            Read Dessert-File
              Invalid key
                Set ls-record-not-found to true
              Not invalid key
                Set ls-record-found to true
            End-Read *>Dessert-File
        .
    End Method read-dessert-record.
    *>_____
END FACTORY.
END CLASS DessertDatabaseInterface.
```

Dessert DBI (Personal COBOL)

Data File Listings

Data Files for Assignments

In all the following data file listings (except for that of Calendar) individual fields are separated by a space for the sake of easier reading.

Event record description

Field	Format	
Event ID	pic X(04)	
Event description	pic X(20)	
Event type	pic X(01)	
Facility	pic X(07)	
Duration	pic 9(02)	

Ignored for Space applications

Site ID	pic X(02)	A1, C7, E2, F9
Daily rate	pic 9(04)	

Used only for Space

Accommodation charge	pic 9(04)	
Launch fee	pic 9(04)	

Event file listing
```
1001 Basin Exploration   SMIR-3   07 A1 1800 18500 4200
1002 Dream Scape         OOCEAN11 10 E2 1600 00000 0000
1003 Sea Hunt            OLEEKIE3 14 F9 1350 00000 0000
1004 Brave New World     SSEE-LAB 12 C7 1500 31000 4500
1005 First Look          OOMEGA   21 A1 1300 00000 0000
1006 Aurora Borealis     SMIR-2   16 C7 1800 45500 4000
1007 El Nino             ODELTA-6 13 F9 1550 00000 0000
1008 Econo-Package       OLEEKIE1 05 E2 0999 00000 0000
1009 Hi Five             SORBIT-2 11 C7 1400 21000 4600
1010 Deep Probe          SMIR-3   28 A1 1250 61000 5200
```

Dessert record description

Field	Format	
Dessert ID	pic X(03)	
Flavor Description	pic X(10)	
Dessert type	pic X(04)	ROPE, DELI

Ignored for Delight applications

Roll length	pic 9(02)	
Rolls onhand	pic 9(03)	
Per inch cost	pic 9V99	

Used for aggregate structures

Box ID	pic X(02)	

Used only for Delight

Packages onhand	pic 9(04)	
Unit cost	pic 99V99 (less than $20)	

Dessert file listing
```
100 Mello Blue ROPE 36 100 075 25 0000 0000
101 X-Tacey    DELI 36 040 090 25 0360 1250
102 Strawberry ROPE 44 125 105 45 0000 0000
103 Elementary DELI 44 046 100 35 0440 0890
104 Stretch    ROPE 48 150 148 45 0000 0000
105 Vanilla    DELI 36 056 350 25 0481 1095
106 Superb     ROPE 60 161 097 35 0000 0000
107 Diet Plus  DELI 48 061 122 45 0441 1395
108 Super Rope ROPE 48 062 070 45 0000 0000
109 Dawn       DELI 60 165 205 35 0360 1149
```

Site record description

Field	Format
Site ID	pic X(02)
Site location	pic X(20)
Water depth	pic 9(03)
Site surcharge	pic 9V99

Site file listing
```
A1 Santa Barbara Coast  120 100
C7 Baja California      100 108
E2 Galapagos Islands    090 120
F9 Waimanalo Bay, Oahu  105 115
```

Box record description

Field	Format
Box id	pic X(02)
Box description	pic X(10)
Quantity on hand	pic 9(04)
Price	pic 99V99
Length	pic 9V9
Width	pic 9V9
Height	pic 9V9

Box file listing
```
25 Petite     0520 0750 40 40 20
35 Delectable 0212 0900 40 50 20
45 Big Yummy  0299 1005 40 65 18
```

Data Files for Examples

Calendar record description

Field	Format
Room-number	pic X(03)
Reservation-data occurs 31 times.	
Configuration-code	pic X(01)
Customer-number	pic X(04)

Calendar file listing

Notes: (1) Individual fields are not separated by a space.
           (2) Each pair of lines is data from one record

```
100A1004A1004A1004A1004A1004 0000 0000V1001V1001V1001A1002 0000 0000 0000B1004B1004
    B1004 0000 0000 0000 0000 0000A1002A1002A1002A1002A1002A1002 0000 0000A1010
101B1003B1003A1006A1006 0000B1007B1007B1007B1004A1004A1004A1004A1004 0000 0000 0000
    A1008A1008A1008 0000A1009A1009A1008A1005A1005A1005A1005A1005 0000 0000A1003
102 0000A1003A1003A1003B1004B1004 0000 0000A1003A1010A1010A1010A1010 0000 0000B1008
    B1008B1008B1008 0000 0000 0000 0000 0000A1007A1005 0000A1007A1007A1007A1005
103B1005B1005B1005B1005B1006A1006A1006A1001 0000 0000A1002A1002A1002 0000A1009A1009
    A1009A1009 0000A1006A1006A1006A1006 0000 0000 0000 0000 0000 0000 0000 0000
104A1004A1004A1004A1004 0000A1002A1002A1002A1002A1002A1002 0000 0000A1002A1002A1002
    0000A1004A1004A1004A1004A1004 0000 0000A1006A1006A1006A1006 0000 0000 0000
105A1001A1001A1009A1001A1001 0000 0000 0000 0000 0000A1009A1009A1009 0000 0000A1004A1004
    A1004A1001A1001A1001A1001A1003A1003A1003 0000 0000 0000A1010A1010A1010A1010
106 0000 0000 0000 0000 0000 0000 0000A1005A1005A1005A1005 0000A1004A1004A1004A1010
    A1010A1010A1010A1010 0000 0000 0000 0000 0000 0000 0000 0000A1001 0000 0000
107 0000 0000 0000 0000 0000 0000 0000 0000 0000A1008A1008A1008A1008A1004A1004A1004
    A1004 0000 0000A1006A1006A1006 0000A1010A1010A1010A1010A1010A1005 0000 0000
108A1005 0000 0000A1005A1005A1005A1005 0000 0000A1001A1001A1001 0000A1002A1002 0000
    0000 0000 0000 0000 0000 0000 0000 0000 0000 0000 0000 0000 0000 0000 0000
109 0000 0000 0000 0000 0000 0000 0000 0000 0000 0000 0000 0000 0000 0000 0000 0000
    0000 0000 0000 0000 0000 0000 0000 0000 0000 0000 0000 0000 0000 0000 0000
```

Company record description

Field	Format
Client-number	pic X(04)
Client-name	pic X(20)
Street-address	pic X(20)
City	pic X(12)
State	pic X(02)
Zip	pic X(10)
Unused	pic X(10)
Rep-id	pic X(05)

Company file listing

```
1001ABC Training          588 Quail Run Road   Winona       WY82780-0000   30045
1002Microhard, Inc        92A Sutter Road      Winona       WY82775-0000   30015
1003CompuSomething        1 Country Road       Rock Springs WY82901-0000   30040
1004Cobol Enterprises     P.O. Box 27          Winona       WY82775-0000   30015
1005Software Techniques   4310 Mesa Ave.       Winona       WY82775-0000   30005
1006Smith & Jones         2443 Pine Street     Split Rock   WY82293-0000   30045
1007Lattice, Inc          Route 1 Box 345      Bridger      WY82755-0000   30015
1008Media Z               1212 Jasper St.      Split Rock   WY82293-0000   30005
1009HyperFlex, Inc.       887 A St. Suite B    Rock Springs WY82901-0000   30045
1010Edu-Media             1 Dupont Circle      Bridger      WY82755-0000   30040
```

Representative (Rep) record description

Field	Format
Rep-id	pic X(05)
Assignment-code	pic X(01)
Rep	pic X(15)
Rep-phone-number	pic X(12)

Representative (Rep) file listing

```
30005 A Fern Aksent    307-555-0074
30015 B Sandy Eggo     307-555-9003
30040 A Jim Shorts     307-555-1232
30045 C Anita Hickey   307-555-1994
```

Room record description

Field	Format
Room number	pic X(03)
Accounting code	pic X(10)
Room type	pic X(03)
Standard configuration price	pic 9(03)
Special configuration price	pic 9(03)
Pricing code	pic 9(01)
Room discount	pic v9(02)
Room capacity	pic 9(02)
Room width	pic 9(02)
Room length	pic 9(02)
Work stations	pic 9(02)
Work station capacity	pic 9(01)

Room file listing

```
100 RC1199725   LAB 225 385 A 05 42 60 50 12 3
101 RC00344300  LEC 240 405 A 05 40 45 50 00 0
102 AQ00028899  LAB 255 425 C 05 40 65 50 12 3
103 AQ91102999  LEC 280 465 C 05 43 45 50 00 0
104 AQ11990288  LAB 305 505 B 05 30 60 55 15 2
105 RC39833300  LEC 340 565 A 05 47 50 50 00 0
106 RC32220983  LAB 350 610 C 07 35 65 55 16 2
107 RC399374    LEC 375 615 A 07 45 50 50 00 0
108 BC31928374  LAB 380 625 B 10 30 60 55 06 4
109 BC49937772  LEC 400 655 B 10 50 50 55 00 0
```

Tax record description

Field	Format
Room type	pic X(03)
County tax code	pic X(11)
Tax rate	pic V9(03)

Tax file listing

```
LAB ACQ133-6221 100
LEC ANN212-3459 085
```

Index

A

A-margin 21
Abstract class 175, 186
Abstract data type 32-34, 51
Abstraction 4, 29
Accumulator 257
Add method, Bag 250
Aggregate 124
Aggregate structure 124, 125, 192, 218
Algorithm 5
Analysis and design, object-oriented 112
Animate 304
Animator
   Net Express 291, 292
   Personal COBOL 304-306
ANS85 dialect 44
Application domain class 113
Application file 286, 290
Argument, table 266
Array 240, 274
   AtPut method 263
   collection class 243 260-266
   FirstIndexOf method 263
   OfValues method 261
As phrase, ISO2000 224
Association class 270
Association, NewClass method 270
At method, Dictionary 272
AtPut collection class method 263
   array 263
   dictionary 270
AtPutAll collection class method 265

B

B-margin 21
Back end 142
Bag 242, 246-260, 274
   Add method 250
   collection class 242
   creation of 250
   Remove method 250
   Size method 250
Base class 185
Box file listing 317
   record description 317
Breakpoint 295, 306
Breakpoint, Personal COBOL 306
Browser 300

Browser, Personal COBOL 300
By reference clause 256

C

Calendar array 260
Calendar class 208, 264-266
   Room18 212
Calendar file 207
   sequential read 216
Calendar file listing 318
   record description 318
Calendar search 264
Calendar table, searching 212-214
Call statement 16, 17, 19, 20, 47
Callback 251-260
   optional parameters 256
Calling program 17, 18
Camelback 244
Candidate class 119, 120, 121, 122
CD, Examples, contents 280
CharacterArray 274
CharacterArray collection class 243
Class 30
   CompX 261
Class, Application Domain 113
Class browser, Personal COBOL 300
Class builder 42
Class, Control 113
Class, Data Management 113
Class definition 32, 35, 48, 49, 57
   skeleton 49
Class diagram 118, 123, 124
   Room08 93
   Room09 99, 118
   Room17 194
   Room18 209
   Room21 247
   Room26 268
Class, Presentation 113
Class program 57
   r04-room 54, 55, 56
   r06-dbi 75, 76
   r06-room 77, 78
   r08-ui 94, 95
   r09-mgr 100, 101
   r10-dbi 103
   r10-mgr 105
   r11-dbi 142, 143
   r11-mgr 106, 140, 141
   r11-r-fp 143-146
   r12-mgr 152, 153
   r12-r-fp 154
   r12-room 148-151

Index

r13-dbi 157
r13-r-fp 158, 159
r13-room 155, 159
r13-t-fp 158, 159
r14-dbi 168
r14-lab 167
r14-lec 167
r14-mgr 169, 170
r15-lab 178, 179
r15-room 177-179
r16-lab 182
r16-lec 182
r16-room 181
r17-cl-f 204, 205
r17-clnt 198, 199
r17-comp 200
r17-dbi 206
r18-clnt 214
r18-mgr 210, 211
r19-cln 228
r19-mgr 231
r20-room 234
r21-room 248
r26-cal 269
r26-mgr 273
Class stereotype 113
Class user 42
Class visibility 123
Class-Control 59
Class-ID paragraph 35, 51
Class-Responsibility-Collaborator 113, 117, 118
Classification hierarchy 171, 186
Client record format 201
Cobol table 240, 241
Cohesion 11
Cohesive 38
Collaborate 28
Collaborator 116, 117
Collection 240, 241
Collection class
  array 243
  array 260-266
  bag 242, 243
  bag 246-260
  characterArray 243
  dictionary 266-272
  identityDictionary 244
  methods 245
  orderedCollection 243
  properties 242, 274
  sortedCollection 243
  types 242-244
Collection class
  method summary 274
  properties 272, 274
  types 245
Collection of references 244
Collection of values 244
Comment character 21, 22
Comp-5 data type 245, 246
Company file listing 319
  record description 318
Compile 302
Compiler directive 23
  Dialect 44
  repository update 235
Compiler errors 292
Compiling 291
Component reusability 98
CompX class 261
Constructor methods 244
Container 240
Control class 113
CopyEmptyWithSize collection class method 264
Coupling 10, 11, 12, 38, 123
CRC card 113, 117, 118, 121, 122, 123, 124

D

Data
  global 16, 19
  local 16, 19
Data abstraction 29
Data element, dictionary 267
Data file listings 316-319
Data flow diagram 6, 7, 12
Data item names 58
Data, local 16
Data management class 113
Data type 33, 80, 81
  comp-5 245, 246
Database class definitions, assignments 312-315
Database interface class 73-76, 120
Debug 293-295
  stepping a program 293, 294
Design tools, object-oriented 113
Dessert file listing 317
  record description 316
Dessert record description 188
Dialect
  Cobol 224
  comparison of 224
  compiler directive 44
  ISO2000 44, 224
Dictionary 274
  creating 268
  data element 267
  key 267

template 268
types of 267
Dictionary
  At method 272
  AtPut method 270
  collection class 243, 266-272
  IncludesKey method 271
  OfValues method 270
  template 270
Dictionary object
  accessing 271, 272
  loading 270, 271
Directive
  compiler 23
  dialect 44
Division header 23
Do iterator 252
Documentation 124, 125
Documentation for
  r06-dbi 128
  r06-room 127
  r08-ui 127
  r09-mgr 126
  r11-dbi 142
  r11-mgr 129
  r11-r-fp 145
  r12-mgr 149
  r14-dbi 165
  r14-lec 165
  r14-mgr 166
  r15-lab (subclass) 176
  r15-lec (subclass) 176
  r15-room (superclass) 177
  r17-cl-f 202
  r17-clnt 196
  r17-comp 197
  r17-dbi 203
  r17-mgr 195
  r19-cln 227
Documentation template 128-130
  setting up 131
Domain expert 114
Driver program 42, 45
Duplicates in collection class 242

E

Edit options, Net Express 296
Encapsulation 29
End marker 53
Error 307
  compiler detected 292, 293
  correction, Personal COBOL 303
  message 293, 303
  Personal COBOL 307

Event file listing 316
  record description 316
Event record description 189
Example Applications CD
  contents 280
  loading 280, 281
Execution error 307
Exit statement 19, 52

F

Factory definition 57, 68
Factory
  independence from object 106
  instantiating classes from 198
  object 48, 49, 51, 68, 185
  data 57
  object instantiation in 106
  paragraph 49
File names 58
  Personal COBOL 44
File naming convention 13
File naming format 44
File update application 146
File-processor class 138
Finalize method 86
FirstIndexOf collection class method 263
FirstIndexOf method, array 263
Folder, naming standards 281, 282
Four-byte binary 245
Four-byte comp-5 246
Free format 21, 22
Front end 142
Function, table 266
Functional cohesion 11
Functional component 5, 6
Functional decomposition 8, 10, 11, 29, 38
Functionally cohesive 11

G

garbage collection 86
Gen-spec hierarchy 171
Generalization-specialization hierarchy 171
Get method 236
Get method (property clause) 234
Global 19
Global data 16
Growable collection class 242

H

Has-a structure 192
Heuristic approach 5
Hierarchy chart 8, 10, 12
Hierarchy structure 123

Index

High-level design 122, 123

I

IDE 286
   toolbar 290
Identification Division header 49, 52
IdentityDictionary 274
IdentityDictionary collection class 244
IdentitySet 274
   Dictionary 243
IdentitySet collection class 243
Implicit invoke 236
IncludesKey collection class method 271
IncludesKey method, Dictionary 271
Indention standard 23
Indexed collection class 242
IndexOfSubCollection collection class method 266
Information hiding 29
Inherit 173
Inheritance 123, 124, 193
   in the Factory object 185
   scenarios 184, 185
Inline comment 22
Inline invoke 229, 230, 236
Instance 30, 31, 32, 35
   mulitple 81-83
   object 48, 49, 67, 68
Instantiate 30, 35, 67, 69
   multiple 84
   subclass/superclass 175
   Integrated Development Environment 286
Inter-program communication 18, 20
Interface definition 225-229
   general form 226
Interface-ID paragraph 227
Intrinsic class 254
Intrinsic data type 242, 243, 244, 254
Invoke statement 47, 48, 70
Is-a hierarchy 186
Is-a structure 171
ISO2000 53, 59
ISO2000 dialect 44, 45, 224
Iteration 112
Iterator 251-257
   Select 253
   Do 252

K

Key 267
Key, dictionary 267
Key value 271
Keyed table 267

L

Laboratory room 164
Lecture room 164
Life cycle 112
Linkage Section 18, 19, 20, 52
Local 19
Local data 16
Local-Storage Section 52, 56, 60
Logic error 304
Low-level design 124

M

memory leakage 84
Message communication 29
Method 35, 48, 51, 52-54, 56, 57
   Add (bag) 250
   AtPut (collection class) 263
   AtPutAll (collection class) 265
   collection class summary 274, 275
   CopyEmptyWithSize (collection class) 264
   FirstIndexOf (collection class) 263
   get 234, 236
   IncludesKey (collection class) 271
   IndexOfSubCollection (collection class) 266
   new 69, 197, 198
   NewClass (collection class) 270
   OfReferences 244
   OfValues 244
   OfValues (collection class) 270
   private 100
   public 100
   Remove (bag) 250
   Rewrite 154
   Set 234, 236
   Size (bag) 250
Method-ID paragraph 52
Methods
   collection class 245
Micro Focus Collection Classes 242
Micro Focus dialect 44
Monitor, a data item 294
Multiple file access 201

N

Names 58
Net Express 286-297
   dialect 224
New method 69, 185, 197, 198
NewClass collection class method 270
NewClass method, Association 270
Non-indexed collection class 242
Noun-identification 115

O

Object 30, 31, 68, 114
Object definition 68
Object handle 103, 240
   typed 233
Object handle 69, 81, 84
   subscripted 83
Object, independence from Factory 106
OBJECT paragraph 66
Object paragraph 49
Object reference 81
Object Section 224
Object think 114
Object think 113, 114
Object Training Center 13
Object-Ooiented design tools 113
Object-oriented analysis 112
Object-oriented analysis and design 112
Object-oriented design 112
Object-oriented development 119
Object-oriented methodology 37, 112
Object-Storage Section 57
Objectify 256
OfReferences 244
OfReferences constructor method 244
OfValues 244
OfValues collection class method 270
OfValues constructor method 244
OfValues method, Dictionary 270
OfValues method,array 261
OOA&D 112
Optional parameters, callback 256
Optional parameters, in callback 256-259
OrderedCollection 274
OrderedCollection collection class 243
OTC client example 193

P

Parameter 19, 20
Parameter 245, 246
Parameters 17, 52
Perform 16
Personal COBOL 44
   file definition limitations 145
   name restriction 282
Personal COBOL ~9 300-309
Pet selection example 171
Pic X class 254, 255
Polymorphism 29, 30
Polymorphism 82
Populate (object) 72
Presentation/Interface class 113

Private method 100, 225
Problem statement analysis 121
Procedure call tree 8
Procedure Division header 20
Progam
   r09-drvr 99
Program 21, 57
   naming standards 282
   r01-prog.cbl 14
   r01-prog 13-15
   r02-prog 17
   r02-room 50
   r02-sub 18
   r03-drvr 45-48
   r04-drvr 55
   r05-drvr 68
   r06-drv2 82
   r06-drv3 83
   r06-drvr 79, 80
   r07-drvr 84, 85
   r08-drvr 96, 97
   r10-drvr 104
   r20-drvr 232
   r21-drvr 248, 249
   r22-drvr 255
   r23-drvr 258
   r24-drvr 262
   r25-drvr 265
Program flowchart 8, 9
Program-ID paragraph 35
Proj0101 13
Proj0102 16
Proj0301 45
Proj0302 54
Proj0401 68, 87
Proj0402 74, 87
Proj0403 84, 87
Proj0501 94, 108
Proj0502 98, 108
Proj0503 100, 108
Proj0504 106, 108
Proj0701 140, 158
Proj0702 146, 158
Proj0703 155, 158
Proj0801 186
Proj0802 175, 186
Proj0803 178, 186
Proj0901 193, 218
Proj0902 207, 218
Proj1001 227, 236
Proj1002 232, 236
Proj1101 246, 275
Proj1102 252, 275
Proj1103 276

Index

Proj1103 257
Proj1104 260, 276
Proj1105 263, 276
Proj1106 267, 276
Project 286, 300
  creation of 286-290
  file 290
  naming standards 281
Property clause 232-236
Property phrase 233
Public method 100, 225

R

RDF file 235
Record description
  dessert record 188
  event 189
Record descriptions 316-319
Record format
  client 201
  rep 201
Redundancy 170
References, collection of 244
Remove method, Bag 250
Rep record format 201
Repository 47, 59, 233
Repository paragraph 224
Repository update compiler directive 235
Representative (Rep) file listing 319
  record description 319
Responsibility 28, 71, 116
Responsibility-driven design 115-117
Returning clause 52
Reusable code 38
Reusable component 28
Room class 43, 44
Room data file 164
Room file listing 319
  record description 319
Room manager class 113
Room record 164
Room rental system 13, 42
Room01 13
Room02 16, 286
Room03 45
Room04 54
Room05 68, 70, 87
Room06 74, 87
Room07 84, 87
Room08 94, 108
Room09 98, 108
Room10 100, 108

Room11 106, 108, 140, 158
Room12 146, 147, 158
Room13 155, 158
Room14 170, 186
Room15 175, 186
Room16 178, 186
Room17 193, 218
  class diagram 194
Room18 207, 218
  class diagram 209
Room19 227, 236
Room20 232, 236
Room21 246, 275
Room22 252, 275
Room23 257, 276
Room24 260, 276
Room25 263, 276
Room26 267, 276
Run-time system 291
Runtime error 307

S

Scenarios 122
Search 240
Search verb 267
Select iterator 252, 253
Self identifier 185
Set method 236
Set method (property clause) 234
Set statement 104
Side-effect 38
Site file listing 317
  record description 317
Size method, Bag 250
Smalltalk 12
SortedCollection 274
  ValueSet 243
SortedCollection collection class 243
Source program general format 57
Source unit 57
Sourceformat compiler directive 23
Specialization hierarchy 186
Spiral model. 37, 38
Standard form 23, 24
Statement, Cobol
  Call 16, 47
  Exit 19
  Invoke 47, 48
Step mode, debugging 294
Stereotype 113
Structure chart 8
Structured analysis 6
Structured decomposition 38

Structured design 6-8
Structured methodolgy 4, 9-13, 29
Structured programming 4, 8-15
Styles, programming 57, 58
Subcategory 173
Subclass 123, 174, 180
Subordinate file 155
Subprogram 15-21
Subprogram linkage 18
Subscript
   object handle 83
Super identifier 185
Super object identifier 178, 198, 200
Supercategory 173
Superclass 123, 174, 181
System flowchart 7, 12
Systematic 5

T

Table argument 266
Table, Cobol 240, 266
Table function 266
Tax file listing 319
   record description 319
Temporal cohesion 11
Toolbar 30
Toolbar, IDE 290
Typed object handle 233

U

UI. *See* User interface
UML 118
Unified Modeling Language 118
Update, file 146
Usage 245
Use case 114
Use scenario 119
Use-case
   analysis 114
   card 120
   scenario 113, 114, 119
User interface 92
User interface class 92-96, 120
Using 17, 20

V

Values, collection of 244
ValueSet
   IdentitySet 243
ValueSet collection class 243

W

Waterfall 12
Waterfall lifecycle 5-7
Whole-part hierarchy 192
Whole-part structure 218
Working-Storage Section 60